TENKILLER

By J. Richard Johnson

Copyright 2024

All rights reserved.

ISBN: 9781917238786

All rights reserved. No part of this publication may be reproduced, distributed, or transmitted in any form or by any means, including photocopying, recording, or other electronic or mechanical methods, without the author's prior written permission, except in the case of brief quotations embodied in critical reviews and certain other non-commercial uses permitted by copyright law. For permission requests, please get in touch with the author.

Contents

Dedication i
About the Author ii
Chapter 1: Broken Images 2
Chapter 2: Waiting 13
Chapter 3: First Light 33
Chapter 4: Execution 49
Chapter 5: Wohali's Hamlet 66
Chapter 6: Manumission 83
Chapter 7: The Road to Pittsburg 101
Chapter 8: The Wedding 114
Chapter 9: The Departure 128
Chapter 10: Cave-in-Rock 135
Chapter 11: Cahokia 149
Chapter 12: Fort Gibson 162
Chapter 13: Uncle Dutch's Ranch 169
Chapter 14: Ten 181
Chapter 15: Grandmother's Love 189
Chapter 16: Reunion 202
Chapter 17: The Walking Dead 210
Chapter 18: Ridge 216
Chapter 19: 1839 232
Chapter 20: The Colt Paterson 244
Chapter 21: Baker's Dozen 259
Chapter 22: Beloved Woman 267
Chapter 23: The Path 275
Chapter 24: The California Trail 284
Chapter 25: The Great Western Sea 307
Chapter 26: Cump 318
Chapter 27: Gold 331
Chapter 28: The Truckee River 342
Chapter 29: Home 350
Chapter 30: Tenkiller's Truth 370

Dedication

Tenkiller was inspired by the realistic, multidimensional portrayal of Native American warriors by the Cherokee actor Wes Studi.

This book is dedicated to him and his artistry.

About the Author

I developed a passionate interest in Native American history when I was ten years old and kept this interest throughout my life. This was partly due to my mom, a Cherokee mixed blood, who was born in a Chickasaw hospital in Tishomingo, Oklahoma. Her dad, who claimed to be half Cherokee and looked the part, had been working as a mechanic in Chickasaw territory at the time. She transmitted what little she knew of Cherokee culture to me, mostly unintentionally, as I grew up.

I earned a PhD in Sociology from the University of California, Los Angeles and for the next several decades worked as a management consultant, statistical engineer, general manager, and college professor, pretty much in that order. All the while, I dreamed of writing a book that would show a different picture of Native Americans from what I read about in high school textbooks or saw in cowboy-and-Indian movies made in the 'fifties and 'sixties, when I was growing up. I was outraged by most of them, since, thanks to my research, I knew better.

I dreamed about correcting this warped vision of our history, some way, somehow, someday. This book is the result of that dream.

<u>Additional note to the reader</u>: In the dialogues in this book, when the Cherokees are speaking in their own language, I use (relatively) good English to represent their speech, on the assumption that they were (and are) just as articulate in their own language as we native English-speakers are in ours. I chose to honor that in this book. When, on the other hand, they are *actually* speaking English—most likely in a Southern drawl—their speech is rendered that way. The quoted passages are usually presaged with parenthetical comments such as "speaking Cherokee" or "speaking English." I do not mean to imply that those of us who grew up speaking in a drawl are any less articulate than those who grew up speaking standard English. I didn't lose my accent until I was in the fourth grade and still have some remnants of it in my own everyday speech. I chose the approach just described to counter the way Native Americans were often depicted in the movies and TV shows I grew up with.

Concerning all acts of initiative and creation, there is one elementary truth…that the moment one definitely commits oneself, then providence moves too.

—*Johann Wolfgang Von Goethe*

Part 1: The Vendetta

Chapter 1: Broken Images

The full moon glowed above the western horizon two hours before sunrise on a crisp late September morning in eastern Tennessee, soon after the first frost had arrived, providing relief from the suffocating heat of summer. Sitting stoically among the trees on a low hill at the edge of a clearing was a tall, shirtless, muscular young man, his face, the shaven sides of his head, his shoulders, and chest smeared with red paint, the areas around both of his eyes painted black, the rest of his long black hair hanging to his shoulder blades, his blood as cold as the morning frost, his heart burning with the fires of vengeance. Next to him were his bow, a quiver with two dozen arrows, a war club, and a rope.

In the center of the clearing was a log cabin, the abode of three brothers, the Stricklin boys. For eight years, he had prepared for this moment, which would soon greet the rising sun. He intended that it would be the last sunrise they would ever see.

* * * * * * * * *

He reflected on his journey. Broken images of his childhood, near the ancient Indian warpath in a hamlet east of Knoxville. Memories of how he, who was a quarter Irish and three-quarters Cherokee, had been a good boy who went to church and studied at a school run by two Presbyterian missionaries. A civilized boy.

His father, a full-blooded Cherokee warrior, had fallen with Tecumseh at the Battle of the Thames River in 1813. He never met his father, having been born in March of 1814, a few months after his father died in battle. His mother, a dark-haired Irish-Cherokee beauty, ran off with a trader when he was six, leaving him with his grandparents, who owned a store near the eastern edge of the new town of Knoxville. He barely remembered her.

His grandmother was a full-blooded Cherokee. Her name was Ahyoka (in Cherokee, "she brings happiness"). She was tall, and though in her late forties or early fifties, she was still slender, with neatly coiffed, long black hair grizzled with grey, which made an attractive contrast with her smooth brown skin.

His grandfather, Will Sullivan, was an Irishman who, in search of beaver pelts, had braved the savage frontier to make his way in the New World. For him, it was either that or joining another generation of impoverished peasantry in his homeland on the far side of the great Eastern Sea. He was in his late fifties, his hair and beard white as snow. He was not very tall—perhaps five feet, nine inches—but was wiry and still strong, especially for someone his age. He was generally regarded as a good man. Being Irish, he understood what it was like to be "colonized", and he treated the Cherokee with respect. In response, when he converted his first harvest of beaver pelts into an inventory of cotton cloth, axes, needles, metal pots, gunpowder, guns, and lead, they didn't steal from him much, and when there were uprisings, he was spared the killing, scalping, and other forms of mutilation that often befell the white invaders. It helped that his wife—Johnny's grandmother—was full blood. By tribal law, Will became Cherokee when he took up with her.

Johnny recalled the time when he asked his grandfather, "Where is my father? What happened to him?" That was in the year 1821, when Johnny was seven.

Will replied, "Well, son, your pa is with the Great Spirit now."

"How did that happen?" Johnny had asked, his voice full of the innocent curiosity of a seven-year-old.

"Well, Johnny, there's a bit of a story behind it. The Cherokee had fought the white invaders for years, but it all came to an end in 1794, when the Americans burnt the town of Chickamauga—the center of their final resistance—along with their crops. It was a terrible thing for them. They were destitute, faced with starvation. They had no choice but to make peace. They had to give up a lot of land. That was part of the deal." Will paused, wondering how much of what he had just said had registered in the mind of his seven-year-old grandson.

"What happened after that?" Johnny asked.

Relieved that Johnny's question showed enough understanding for him to continue, Will replied, "After the fall of Chickamauga, some Cherokee warriors, who still had fight left in them, were inspired by the Shawano leader, Tecumseh. He was trying to build an Indian nation made up of a lot of the tribes. They wanted to keep the area west of the Allegheny mountains, where the Ohio River comes from. Now, the British king proclaimed in 1763 that there would be no further expansion of white settlements west of those mountains. So, when fighting broke out between the Americans and the British in 1812, it was reasonable for the Indians to take Britain's side. They believed that had the British won, they would have honored the proclamation of 1763, which the American colonists, hungry for land, had disrespected from the start."

"Did we win?" asked Johnny.

"No," Will answered. "The Indians lost….and their hope for an Indian nation died, along with Tecumseh and your pa, at the Battle of the Thames River in 1813, a few months before you were born."

For Johnny, the seven-year-old boy, the details were hard to understand, but he knew enough to feel depressed about what had happened to his people. He didn't ask any more questions. He cast his gaze downward, experiencing an indescribable emotion. A desire for vengeance, tempered by a sense of hopelessness. The suffocating realization that his people had been defeated.

Will, sensing this, added, "You should know, Johnny, that Tecumseh was one of the greatest men who ever lived—Indian or white. He was a man of vision and, as Indian warriors went, a gentleman. He discouraged his warriors from torturing prisoners and mutilating fallen enemies. That probably wasn't easy, and they probably still did these things, but perhaps not as much. The point is that Tecumseh tried. And consider this: He inspired fighters from a dozen tribes. Many of them had been mortal enemies from the beginning of time. And they spoke almost as many different languages. Yet he was able to unite them in common cause. Only a great leader of men could have done that. Remember that, Johnny. Tecumseh was an Indian. Like you."

* * * * * * * * *

Three years after Johnny's mother ran off, Will fell asleep one night and never woke up. Johnny was nine years old at the time. He mourned the loss of his grandfather. His grandparents were the pillars that held up his sky, and now, one of those pillars was gone, leaving an empty, dark space in the center of his being. He continued to live with his grandmother. She continued to run the store.

Johnny, whose Cherokee name was Onacona ("White Owl"), attended a small school run by a pair of Presbyterian missionaries. They taught their students about universal brotherhood and how to live according to the teachings of Jesus Christ. They believed that if the Cherokee people were to survive, they would need to learn to read, write, and work with numbers. And they believed that Cherokees had as much a right to education as the whites did. In this school, since Johnny White Owl had no surname, he took his grandfather's last name and went by "Johnny Sullivan". That is how the missionaries knew him. Indeed, that was how he knew himself. Johnny Sullivan.

In this school, he learned English grammar, history, and arithmetic. He was a diligent student. And when he was not in school or studying, he helped his grandmother in the store. Even at the age of nine, his mathematical competence was helpful to her. He kept records of transactions, both in cash and kind, when goods were bartered rather than sold for cash. He also kept track of the inventories of the various goods sold there.

When studying history from such books as the missionaries had available on that subject, he learned about places called "Egypt", "Greece", and "Rome". He found the descriptions at once strange and wondrous. However, he noticed that there was little information available about the people who lived in the land that became the United States of America before the Puritans landed in 1620. For that kind of information, he realized that the missionaries were not knowledgeable sources. So, he consulted tribal elders, who versed him in the oral history of the Cherokees and other peoples with whom they had dealings, including some that had been their traditional enemies. The elders had, during their narratives, taught him that his people had learned to work with metal—copper and gold, mostly—long before the whites came.

The missionaries told him that the Egyptians had learned to mix copper with tin to make bronze about 4,000 years before. The co-presence—for the Egyptians—of tin and copper made the change from the Stone Age to the Bronze Age possible. Johnny reflected on this. His ancestors did not seem to have access to tin, so they were stalled on the cusp of the Bronze Age. If this was so, he concluded, he concluded, the technology of the whites was about 4,000 years ahead of that of the Indians. This was where their great advantage had come from. He realized that, from the standpoint of tribal survival, the white man's "medicine" needed to be understood and mastered. It was partly about metals. Reflecting on this, he considered that he might become a blacksmith one day.

Occasionally, as he walked to school, he would be met with the derision of other Cherokee boys—who didn't go to school. Or rather, they were enrolled in a different sort of school. They were learning to hunt and to play the ball game.* The ballgame was a violent affair, sometimes resulting in severe injuries or even death, which was why some Indians called it "the little brother to war". It was an intermediate step to becoming a warrior. These boys all hoped to enter the world of the warrior. They would say things like, "Look at the white Indian. He thinks he's one of them!" Or "When are you going to start to become a real man, like us, White Owl?"

Johnny typically ignored them and would not be goaded into a fight. He did not resent the teasing. After all, some of these boys were related to him as first or second cousins. They were more curious than hostile. And he wanted to tell them things—things they were not yet ready to hear.

He wanted to tell them how hopeless their situations were going to be, and probably soon. With the little bit of knowledge that he had been given, by the time he was ten, he had realized how things were going to turn out for his people, the Cherokee, and for Indians generally. His people were already under intense pressure to move to an "Indian Territory" west of the Great River. That is why he wanted to learn as much of the white man's knowledge as he could. Even at the age of ten, he conceived a third path that straddled the options of physical extermination, on the one hand, and absorption, as second-class citizens, if that, into the alien culture of the whites. It would be a path where the Indian could survive, walk with his back straight and head up, and preserve the worthiest elements of his tribal

---

* The white men called it "Lacrosse".

heritage, whether it be that of the Cherokee, the Choctaw, the Chickasaw, the Muskogee, the Seminole, or whatever other nation he belonged to.

All around him was an admixture of hope and despair. Some of the high-status Cherokees had converted tribal lands into cotton plantations with African slaves. Some could read and write the white man's language. They had begun to build log cabins and wooden houses like their white neighbors. They raised livestock and used cattle and hogs for meat rather than hunting deer and other dwellers of the forests and foothills, though they still did that, too. Then again, there were those whose spirits had been broken by repeated defeats in the wars with the whites, who had them outnumbered and outgunned. They drank whiskey. They stopped practicing their warrior skills. They occasionally got beaten up by arrogant white men, who seemed to take pleasure in humiliating the pitiful remnants of the once proud and feared Cherokee warriors. Johnny hated those white men.

He recalled how he walked to and from the missionary school with his second cousin, Elias, who was fifteen, and Elias's girlfriend, Molly, who was fourteen. Elias was half-white. He was studious and disciplined. He planned to attend college. He treated everyone with respect, not just his elders but his juniors as well. Everyone, it seemed, liked and admired Elias. He was considering taking up the cloth one day and becoming a missionary and teacher.

Molly was also half-white. People thought that she and Elias would eventually marry. She, too, was a student at the missionary school. She, too, hoped to become a teacher. She was slender, graceful, and immaculate in all ways, from her well-groomed, coal-black hair to her clean, neatly filed fingernails. She could cross a room carrying a book on the crown of her head without it falling off. In Johnny's estimation, she didn't walk—it seemed as if she floated like an angel. He considered her beautiful. To him, everything about her was noble.

While he gazed upon the Stricklin's cabin under the tranquil moonlit night, he recollected the pivotal day that had altered his life profoundly eight years ago. He, Elias, and Molly were walking home from school. Three brothers, the Stricklin boys, encountered them on the country road from school to the settlement east of Knoxville where they lived. The

Stricklins were sitting next to a creek a little below the roadside, drinking whiskey. They had a bad reputation as local ruffians, which was saying something, given the comparison with the other rough frontier people who had settled in the land that had recently become the state of Tennessee. The eldest, Josh, was in his early twenties. The youngest, Joey, was about fourteen. The middle brother, Billy, was somewhere in between.

Elias, Molly, and Johnny were all smartly dressed in white men's clothing. Josh, mean when sober, was an even meaner drunk, and on this day, he was drunk on whiskey. He called out to them: "Look at them nice clothes! You decent church-goin' Indians pretending to be as good as us? You're still fuckin' Indians, nonetheless." He took a swig from his flask and passed it to Billy, who took a drink and smirked. They were looking for trouble.

Elias said under his breath, "Don't pay attention to them. Just walk on." He, Molly, and Johnny continued to walk without breaking stride.

Josh snorted, "You better listen good when a white man talks to you." He muttered something under his breath to his two brothers.

In an instant, the three brothers fell upon them. Josh, a big man hardened by farm work, grabbed Elias, and began to punch his face, knocking him to the ground. He continued to rain blows on him and seemed delighted when he knocked out one of Elias' front teeth. He crowed, "Now you'll have something to remember me by, Indian!"

At the same time, Johnny, who had learned what his Irish grandfather called "pugilistics", boxed the other two boys, but they were too much bigger than he was for his blows to have effect. Joey grabbed him from behind while Billy landed blows to his body and head, even as an enraged Molly jumped on Billy's back and tried to set a chokehold. Meanwhile, Johnny faded into blackness.

When he returned to consciousness, he viewed a scene that he would never forget. Elias, who had raised himself from the ground, sat up momentarily but helplessly, still in a daze from his beating, blood running down his chin, as these vermin took turns with Molly, who kicked and scratched to no avail. Elias tried to get to his feet, but Billy, who had just finished his "turn", ran over and kicked him in the head, putting him back on the ground semi-conscious. Joey was taking his turn when Johnny raised himself from the ground. Molly groaned as the little varmint, Joey, pounded her energetically. Billy said, "That's it, bitch. You love it, don't you?" After about one minute, Joey was finished. He stood up, leaving Molly sobbing on the ground as he cinched his belt.

Johnny found himself in the midst of a dark tunnel, his skin on fire with a rage far beyond anything he had ever felt. Then, suddenly, as if a wave had passed over him, he felt cold and hard as a stone. The fiery sensation abated, and he stood up. He realized that he could not win this one, not today. So, the eleven-year-old Johnny pointed his finger at the Stricklins. His green eyes glistening with rage, he declared in a Tennessee drawl, "One day, I'm gonna kill all three of you sonofabitches! And since you've made this about Indians"—his voice lowered as he glared icily at them—"I'm gonna kill y'all, Indian style."

The Stricklin boys just laughed as they walked away, whooping and hollering in self-congratulation. Josh was sarcastic: "Oh, boy, I'm scared shitless now! What're you gonna do, beat us to death with a bible?"

Joey interjected, "Well if you do, this would have been worth it. That squaw was a hell of fine frolic." As if that fourteen-year-old punk knew the difference...

For a second, Johnny stared at them coldly, envisioning what he was going to do to him one day when he was a grown warrior.

Then, he walked over to Molly, who was sitting up, crying silently as she tried to straighten out her torn clothes. Her sobs made Johnny's stomach turn upside down.

She was in a daze of her own, though not from blows to the head, such as had been endured by Johnny and Elias. Not just her dress, but her identity, her notion of who she was as a human being in this world, was in tatters, destroyed forever. He reached down, held her hand, and pulled her to her feet. As he did so, he assured her, "I promise you that this will be avenged."

With her eyes cast downward, she said listlessly, "It won't matter. My life is over." Elias, now standing, said nothing. How does one on the cusp of manhood respond to what had just happened? Was he fit to be a man in this world? He had failed to protect Molly. Was he worthy of being her husband? Would her love erode and degenerate, in time, into silent contempt? What was there for him to say? They walked in silence together to their little settlement.

They would have no recourse to the white man's law. Indian testimony in court, if the opportunity to give it even arose, would not be taken seriously. Even if it were heard, their words would not carry weight against those of white men, even mangy dogs like the Stricklins. They would have to live with humiliation, with no hope of legal remedy. And there was little chance of traditional vengeance. If some Cherokees had decided to punish them, they would be hunted down and summarily executed, or worse, an innocent surrogate for the white man's vengeance might pay the price.

As they walked to their settlement, tears of despair streamed down Johnny's face. Filled with bitterness, he reflected on the teachings of the missionaries, who taught that all men were brothers. He wondered how the white people, who received their religious instruction from that black book—mostly from pastors who could read it since most of them were barely literate—could be so goddam mean. And they never seemed satisfied with what they had. They always wanted more—land, mostly.

The eleven-year-old Johnny Sullivan gritted his teeth as he recalled his grandfather's narrative about Tecumseh and the father he would never know. At the end of it, Will had said, "The Indians lost." He hated that phrase, "The Indians lost." What he saw around him every day were the remnants of those failed struggles: bullying white men and drunken Indians who might have once upon a time been warriors, but now, their spirits and pride broken, drowned their despair in whiskey. Whiskey: the white man's ambrosia, the Indian's poison.

He felt a mighty force welling up within him, a force that was animated by fury so great that it defied expression in words. He seethed with rage as he wondered, "Where was the Great Spirit when we needed Him? Where was the white man's God, whose Son is called 'the Prince of Peace'? Was he sleeping? Did he give a shit?"

For the next few days, Elias, when he was seen at all, walked around as if only his body, but nothing else about him, lived in this world. He avoided Molly. He couldn't look her in the eye. His eyes seemed to focus on another world.

And then, about a week after the trauma, he went to that other world. He hung himself in the woods.

Molly, feeling hopelessly shamed, went away. Johnny heard she went to the Cherokee settlement in Arkansas.

Life as Johnny had known it was over, like Molly's. He resolved that, as soon as he was able, the Stricklins' lives would be over as well, whether it took ten years, or twenty, or fifty. His blood boiled with rage, and his heart rejoiced every time he thought of the vengeance he would one day exact.

Johnny's grandmother, Ahyoka, had been informed of the debacle. She saw Johnny's grief. He told her of his bold threat.

She said, speaking in Cherokee, "You're in no state to take revenge on those balls of pond scum. You're not a man yet. You have no warrior skills. You've been in a missionary school. I'm proud that you can 'read, write, and cipher' (she said these words in English) and that your teachers say you're an excellent student." She looked sad when she continued: "And those things might help you in the world that lies on the horizon for us, for our old ways will not last much more than another generation, if that.

"But getting back to those pieces of shit, you can't kill all three of them with your bare hands, not even when you grow up. You need to learn the use of weapons, including white men's weapons. And to use even those to good effect, you must learn the ways of the warrior."

She paused and looked intently at Johnny for a moment. Then she continued, measuring her words as she spoke as if to underscore a deeper meaning: "The warrior's way lies beyond the mere use of weapons. It is a matter of the spirit as much as of the body."

She paused again. As Elias' great-aunt, she, too, was full of rage and wanted vengeance. She had a foot in both worlds, but in her soul, she was still Cherokee. She believed in the vendetta as much as she believed in the changing of the seasons, as part of the natural and eternal order of things.

"Perhaps I was remiss in not finding an uncle to teach you the warrior's way. But the only child I had was your mother—no boys at all. That means you had no uncles on your mother's side—for that is how we have always done this—to teach you our warriors' ways. But I have a nephew, the son of my elder sister. He is your first cousin, once removed. He would be in his thirties by now. From what I have heard, he is a great warrior, hunter, and leader of men. I see from the resolve in your eyes that you, too, have the heart of a warrior. I believe your uncle will see it, too. And he is obliged to teach you, by our traditions.

"There is a place called Arkansas, far to the west of us, many days' journey. A group of our people, who wanted to preserve our ancient ways, moved there about thirty years ago. My nephew, Tahchee, lives there now. When you tell him you are my grandson, he will receive you and teach you the way of the warrior."

"I never heard a name like that, Grandmother. What does 'Tahchee' mean?" asked Johnny.

"It means 'Dutch'. That's how Cherokees say 'Dutch'."

Distracted for a moment, he asked, "How did his parents come up with a name like that?"

"I don't know. Only his parents knew. But that's his name. 'Dutch'."

Johnny's heart filled with hope and ambition. Beginning today, and with each passing day, he would be a day closer to punishing and killing the Stricklins. All three of them. Indian style. Whatever that might mean…

Chapter 2: Waiting

It was as dark as night can be when illuminated by the bright light of a full moon, which was sinking in the west. Johnny surmised that the Stricklins were still sleeping. He continued his remembrances as he waited through the night, perched on top of the low hill overlooking the abode of the Stricklins, gently running his fingers over the sharp tips of his arrows.

* * * * * * * *

When he was eleven, Johnny stopped going to school and became a blacksmith's apprentice. The master smith, James O'Brien, was an Irishman who had been a friend of Will, his grandfather. They had both come from the same county in Ireland—County Kerry, located in the peninsular southwest region of Ireland. Old Will used to say it was the greenest, most beautiful place on Earth despite being one of the poorer counties in Ireland.

James had worked his smithy in Knoxville since his arrival in Tennessee some years before. Johnny recalled how, at the end of his first day as James' apprentice, his forearms and hands hurt so much that he could barely pick up his food when it was time to eat. James understood the pain Johnny was experiencing and gave him two days off after his first day. He went back to work after that and applied himself with the same diligence that had impelled him to study with the missionaries. Within a few days, the pain he experienced had gone away. As he applied himself to the trade, his skills increased. And his hands and forearms became stronger and thicker.

He found making horseshoes and plowshares—an important part of the blacksmith's work and the bulk of the apprentice's job—to be dull, and he had complained about it once to James. "Is this all there is to it?" he had asked.

"Listen to me, Johnny," James replied, looking Johnny straight in the eye. "No matter how simple the work, there is an art to every job you'll ever do. You just have to discover it." He paused and smiled knowingly. "And from what I can see, you're still looking for it. But when you find it, the work won't be boring anymore. It will be a spiritual thing. At the end of each day, you'll feel good about what you've done."

James paused again, gathering his thoughts, for he knew he was teaching the boy about more than just blacksmithing. He concluded, "Always look for the art. And whatever you do, do it the best you can, or don't do it at all. To do otherwise is to waste your breath and your time."

James, like Will, was a pugilist. Johnny figured that it must be an Irish thing, their way of being warriors. Most afternoons, they wrapped their hands in leather and practiced. James directed Johnny to punch a burlap bag. Afterwards, they would spar with one another. James' teachings elevated Johnny's boxing ability. He learned to focus his rage. Every time he hit that bag, every time his knuckles bled, he thought of the Stricklin boys.

* * * * * * * * *

He worked with James for two years. Then, in 1827, when he was thirteen, he decided he was ready to go to the northwest corner of Arkansas Territory, where several hundred Cherokees had established the western band of their nation. Ten years before, the Turkeytown Treaty of 1817 opened the land along the north side of the Arkansas River to Cherokee settlers. But in fact, the Cherokees had begun to trickle into the area in the 1790s. Most of those who lived there were either the original immigrants or their children. Among those people was Dutch, who would teach him the warrior ways.

Before leaving, Johnny visited the missionary, Brother McLaurin, at the house that was at once a church, a school, and a residence for the two Presbyterian missionaries. Services were held in the largest room in the house. On one side of this room was a smaller one, where the missionaries taught school. Johnny, feeling guilty for having been absent for so long, diffidently approached the front door and knocked. When the door opened, Johnny recognized Brother McLaurin, one of his teachers, who also happened to be his favorite.

Brother McLaurin was a big, stocky man with brown hair, a short beard grizzled with grey. It took a moment for him to recognize his former student, whose long black hair now hung down to his shoulders, and who was several inches taller and more heavily muscled than the eleven-year-old boy he remembered. The green eyes gave away who he was. With a big smile on his face, he exclaimed, "Johnny Sullivan!" and gave a big hug to his former star student.

Then he led Johnny into the classroom where he had been taught for several years. On one of the walls was a blackboard. Next to another wall was a bookshelf with dozens of books, many of which Johnny had read while a student. He looked at the bookshelf with a twinge of regret. He missed those books, where he had learned of places and times far beyond his immediate experience in eastern Tennessee. He recalled the wonder and joy that he found in those books, back then.

They sat down at a long oak table where students sat to write their lessons. Johnny spoke first, in a voice tinged with shame. "I'm sorry that I stopped coming here, sir. And I owe you thanks for all your teachings, and for letting me read those books. But ever since those Stricklins beat us up and raped my cousin's girlfriend, all I can think about is getting revenge, some day." He burst into tears. Brother McLaurin embraced him again. He had heard about the incident and could feel the boy's sorrow as he embraced him.

"I know," Brother McLaurin said, as reassuringly as he could. "When I didn't see you here after that, I asked around and heard the ugly truth. I was saddened by it, Johnny, for I saw in you hope that the Cherokees could find their way in the world that was emerging, even as their old world was being swept away. I hoped that you could be shining light for others. And then, you disappeared from us. May I ask why?"

Johnny, knowing that what he was about to say wouldn't be something his teacher wanted to hear, chose to answer the question honestly. "I wanted to learn the white man's 'medicine', so I decided to learn about metals. I became a blacksmith's apprentice…"

Brother McLaurin interrupted Johnny. "Well, with the education you already have, learning a trade is a very good thing…"

Johnny interjected, "That's only part of the reason, Brother McLaurin. Blacksmithing is hard work, and it's made me much stronger. Physically, I mean. And in a few days, I'll be moving to Arkansas. I have an uncle there who'll teach me the warrior ways."

"And what do you plan to do when you learn those ways, Johnny?"

"I'm going to come back here and kill all three of them dogs who did that evil thing."

Knowing that the code of vengeance ran deep among the Cherokee, Brother McLaurin realized that reminding Johnny of his religious teachings would likely fall on deaf ears.

Hoping to do whatever he could to save Johnny from falling into a dark abyss, he said, "This world is full of evil men, Johnny. But consider this: A long time ago, there lived a Roman emperor named Marcus Aurelius. He is sometimes referred to by historians as the last 'good' Roman emperor. There is a reflection he had that might be of the most value to you. You may not understand it now because you haven't lived long enough, but here it is: *Beware of becoming what you hate.*"

Brother McLaurin was right. Johnny didn't get it. Surprised, he asked, "How could that happen to me?"

Brother McLaurin looked Johnny in the eyes and said, "You envision taking revenge on evil men. But what makes men 'evil'? Are you thinking of men who use their strength to oppress others? If you become a mighty man of valor, what will keep *you* from using your strength to oppress others? Because if you do that, you will become one of *them*. You will become what you hate. Do you understand this now, Mr. Sullivan?"

Tears ran down Johnny's cheeks. He hated the Stricklins with all his being. The thought of revenge was his only consolation, the only thing that made his life worth living. "Thank you, Brother McLaurin, I think I understand Marcus Aurelius better now." Whether or not he fully understood, the feeling he got from Brother McLaurin comforted him. But it didn't change anything about his intentions regarding the Stricklin boys.

As he stood up and looked around the schoolroom one last time, his attention alighted on the blackboard and the precious books he had loved so much during his childhood. His eyes met those of Brother McLaurin's one last time as he embraced him again, saying, "Thank you, sir, for giving this valuable knowledge to me. I know that I still have a lot to learn, and I'll think hard about what you said to me today."

Brother McLaurin, who had by this time run out of wise counsel for Johnny, just said, "Go with God, my son," his eyes glistening with unshed tears.

※ ※ ※ ※ ※ ※ ※ ※

In the late spring of 1827, Johnny left for Arkansas with some members of the western band. They had come east to visit their relatives, and to exchange beaver skins for lead for their rifles and other useful things. They traveled by horse. Ahyoka gave Johnny one of her horses for the journey.

Many days later, they reached the Mississippi. Johnny had never seen a river so wide. He reflected that it would have been very hard, probably impossible, to cross that river with horses back in the day when the only watercraft the Indians had were canoes.

This was no longer a problem. There was an island between the two banks of the Great River. A long, thick rope stretched from the shore to this island, and another connected the island to the far side. The horses, their burdens, and the men boarded a flat-bottomed wooden barge that was paddled and tugged to the island, where they disembarked.

They then boarded a similar craft, which took them to the other side. The owners of the ferry were Cherokee. They were well-armed, fierce-looking men. They still wore their hair in scalp locks. They ferried anyone who wished to cross this great river, Indians as well as white people, who had already begun to filter into the wild land west of the Mississippi. They did it for pay, of course. No doubt their apparent fierceness served them well. It was unlikely that these Cherokee would be bullied or taken advantage of by white, whiskey-drinking thugs.

They continued to travel westward across a land of forests, less dense than those of Tennessee, punctuated by expanses of grassy prairie. It was early fall when they completed their journey. The countryside was adorned with a riot of orange, red, and yellow autumn leaves. Johnny had seen the fiery display of fall colors before, but not in combination with these open expanses, these broad prairies. He marveled at them. Something about this combination of terrain made him feel free. A freeness he hadn't felt since his run-in with the Stricklins.

The leader of the expedition was a man in his forties named Enoli ("Black Fox"). He was tall and lean, his long hair streaked with strands of grey. He had come to this country when he was still in his teens and remembered what it was like back then. Speaking in Cherokee, he told Johnny, "We came out here to preserve our ancient ways. We wore moccasins and short leather leggings—like the ones I have on right now. But we also wore cotton shirts and trousers and turbans decorated with feathers. The moccasins, leggings, and feathers were 'Indian' enough, and the style of our cotton garments was different from those of the whites—I guess that made us 'Cherokee' at the time.

"We still play the ballgame. We still speak our language, though many of us also speak English. A few years ago, the great Sequoia taught us how to write our speech using our own way of writing. And we brought guns. This was a good thing because when we got here, we met the Osages."

He paused thoughtfully. "When we first came here, this land belonged to the Osages. These were—I should say, still are—a very impressive group of 'wild' Indians. They still lived as they had since ancient times. They were fierce, ruthless warriors, just like our ancestors were. Even up to today, they have refused to use cloth or anything else associated with the white men. Well, they have begun to use guns…but they still wear clothes made of animal skins. They paint their bodies and go shirtless in the warm months. On their scalp locks, they wear roaches[†] made of red horsehair and eagle feathers.

"When I first saw them, I felt a mixture of fear and admiration. They were looking down on us from a hilltop, mounted on their ponies, carrying their lances and bows. They are tall, some well over six feet. With those red roaches sticking up from their scalp locks, they looked like real giants. When I saw them mounted on their ponies, perched on a hill, all painted up, looking down on us with eyes full of murderous intent, I felt a sense of kinship with them, for they looked unconquered and proud, perched on that hill. Like we used to…

[†] Roach headdresses were made from deer hair, horsehair, porcupine quills, feathers and other materials. They were attached to the hair on the crown or back of the head. For examples, Google "Roach headdress". We're not talking about insects here.

"They didn't know it yet, but we had something in common. We were all 'Indians'. I think some of them are just now beginning to figure this out. But for most of them, anyone who is not an Osage is either an enemy, an ally, or else prey for their raiding parties, someone to kill, plunder, or enslave. It doesn't matter much to them whether their victims are white or Indian. In their world, there are only Osage and people who are not Osage."

Johnny asked, "Did we ever make friends with them?"

"Not yet," replied Enoli, who continued, "On the day of our first contact with them, they charged down that hill, screaming their war cries. We killed some of them with our Tennessee rifles. They killed some of us with their powerful bows, but they fell back after that. It's a good thing they did because those rifles of ours take time to reload.

"We knew this wouldn't be the end of it. We would have to fight them, for we were invaders of their land, as the white men had been invaders of ours. I should add that they have very strong bows made from a kind of orange wood that grows in these parts but not elsewhere. It's a good thing we had our guns because otherwise, with those bows of theirs, they would have kicked our asses all the way back to where we came from." Uncle Enoli laughed restrainedly as he said this. But it was an ironic laugh, not as one laughs at the absurdity implied by a joke.

"What's happened since then, Uncle?" asked Johnny.

"We have fought them for the last thirty years, an endless stream of raids, killings, and revenge, followed by more raids, killings, and revenge. Back-and-forth, back-and-forth. It could have gone on forever, as our back-and-forth with the Seneca and Mohawk did from the beginning of time.

"About ten years ago, the white man's government tried to arrange peace between the Osage and the Cherokee. They built a fort—Fort Gibson—in a place the white men call 'Indian Territory'. The bastards have plans for all of us, all the tribes. They plan to move all of us there. But even after this attempt to bring about peace, the fighting continued, just less often than before. Your uncle Dutch still fights with them. And you will probably fight them too—once we teach you how."

* * * * * * * *

When they arrived at Dutch's settlement on the Arkansas River in northwestern Arkansas, Johnny did not see a traditional Cherokee town filled with wood and wattle longhouses lashed together by root fiber. He saw cabins made of logs, topped by roofs, joined by metal nails. He wondered what there was about being Cherokee here, aside from their exotic modifications of cotton garments, as compared to the style of the whites, their moccasins, short leggings, and their feather-adorned cloth turbans. He reflected on what Enoli had told him. He thought, "They came here to be 'traditional', but…"

Enoli took him to a cabin in the center of town, if you could say this settlement had a center, for the cabins were irregularly situated rather than organized into straight lines, streets, and avenues. In this cabin lived Dutch, the nephew of Johnny's grandmother, Ahyoka.

It was late afternoon when the party arrived. The cabins emptied out, and folks hurried to greet them, as they had been gone for several months, since early spring. They were also curious about Johnny, who had already been identified by the first arrivals in Enoli's party as Dutch's nephew. They noticed that he was strangely dressed, like a white man, in dark grey cotton trousers, black boots, and a white cotton shirt.

Two boys, teenagers like Johnny, walked up smirking, probably at his strange clothes. The taller of the two said, in Cherokee, "Why did you come here?"

Johnny puffed up his chest and, in a deepened voice, said, "I came here to learn to be a warrior."

The boy replied, "You're a little late for that, it seems. You're practically grown. Do you really believe you can learn all of that before you're old enough to go into battle?" He looked down his nose at Johnny, sneering and bobbing his head contemptuously as if he were looking for a fight.

Johnny judged this boy, who was his age or a bit older, to be a mixed-blood Cherokee. He had brown eyes, and though his skin was darker than that of the whites, it was rather fair for an Indian. And his long hair was light, sandy brown. Having lodged his initial insult, the boy looked at his companion with a triumphant smirk on his face. The other boy looked down at the ground and chuckled.

"I can do just about anything I put my mind to," said Johnny.

The first boy, who hadn't bothered to identify himself, gave Johnny a withering stare and said in English, colored by a Southern drawl, "We'll see about that, white boy."

Johnny defiantly returned his glare, thinking, "I'm gonna knock you out one of these days." But he said nothing at the moment. He wondered if this young thug had ever looked at himself in a mirror.

They were—fortunately, no doubt—interrupted by Enoli and Dutch, who had been summoned from his cabin and came to greet his first cousin, once removed. The twenty-five-year age gap transformed this relationship into that of uncle-and-nephew. So, it would be proper for Johnny to address Dutch as his "uncle".

Enoli solemnly introduced Johnny to Dutch. "This is the grandson of Ahyoka, your aunt. She asks that you teach him the warrior ways. He went to missionary school and can read and write English. He can calculate with numbers. And he knows something about blacksmithing."

Dutch stood about six feet tall, his body spare of fat, with broad shoulders and lean, muscular, powerful-looking arms. He looked like a full blood, with his leathery brown skin. The irises of his eyes were so dark that they looked almost black, indistinguishable from his pupils. His head was shaved on the sides, but the rest of his long black hair hung down to the middle of his shoulder blades. The modern Cherokee did not shave off as much hair as they had in the past when the only hair left was a lock between the crown and the back of the head. Nevertheless, Johnny judged that he must have looked scary when painted for war. Dutch said nothing as he listened to Enoli's narrative. He just stood there in silence, stoically appraising this boy.

Enoli continued. "He doesn't know much about hunting, though. He knows how to fight like some of the white men do, using his fists," at which point Dutch nodded approvingly. "But he doesn't know about much else. He is eager to learn…Oh, and I should add, his Cherokee name is White Owl."

Finally, Dutch spoke. He said, in Cherokee, "Welcome, White Owl. You were wise to come here because it's going to be very bad for the Cherokee or any other Indians over there, east of the Mississippi. My parents saw this coming, and that is why we are right here, right now. And soon we will have to move again. We haven't decided where to go yet."

He paused for a moment, silently appraising Johnny, his thoughts inscrutable.

"You know a lot about the white man's ways. From those green eyes, I see you're part white. You might have been able to pass for white if you wanted to. Maybe it would have made the life that lies ahead easier for you."

The boy who had first approached Johnny exclaimed, "No way! He couldn't do that. He's obviously not white."

Johnny exclaimed, in his Tennessee drawl, "I thought you just called me 'white boy', asshole!"

Dutch looked over at the first boy and said, "Hold your peace, boy. If he wanted, he could convince some of those white people that he's 'black Irish'. He could just make up stories about how he came to be wherever he is and gets asked."

Johnny wasn't sure as to whether Dutch was joking or not. Deciding to take him seriously he declared, "I couldn't do that. I hate lying."

Dutch looked Johnny straight in the eye and, getting to the point, asked, "Why have you come here?"

Johnny told the story of the Stricklin boys. The people who had come to welcome the travelers were still present, and they listened intently. It was a story they could all relate to. Different names and places, same theme.

"So, you're going to go back there and kill them?" asked Dutch.

Johnny replied. "I'm not just going to kill them. That would be too kind." His breath shortened, his nostrils flared, and his eyes blazed with the fire of vengeance.

Dutch almost broke into a smile. He could feel the cold aura of Johnny's murderous spirit. He quickly concluded that this boy would be a devoted student and probably an asset to his new people, the western band of the Cherokee. And he was an impressive boy, a little above average in height for his age and heavily muscled. He clearly had discipline, having applied himself to learn to read the white man's language and how to do things with numbers. And though the Cherokee here in Arkansas had their own blacksmiths, this boy could help when needed. When he wasn't out hunting with his uncle. Or learning the skills of fighting and killing enemies.

To the small crowd that remained in front of his cabin, Dutch declared, raising his voice, "This is White Owl, my nephew. He is a Cherokee from the east. He will live in my cabin from now on. He will be one of us."

The people looked at Johnny, some smiling, some completely deadpan. Turning to Dutch, speaking Cherokee, he said, "Thank you, Uncle, for inviting me into your home. I will be worthy of your trust and your teaching."

* * * * * * * * *

On the morning of the next day, his uncle woke him before dawn. He asked him if he knew how to use a bow. Johnny said he did, though he was no expert. Dutch said, "Good. Today, we hunt."

In the course of the hunt, Johnny wounded a deer with an arrow. He was a bit embarrassed by what had turned out to be a messy kill. Dutch dispatched it and butchered it with some help from Johnny. They built a fire and dined on barbecued venison.

Johnny was feeling a bit uncomfortable, having botched his effort to kill the deer. A few minutes after they had begun to eat, Dutch said, "You are going to have to practice with the bow."

"I know, Uncle. I shot bow and arrow before when I was a boy in Tennessee. Not very much, though. And I never drew a bow as strong as today. I had to strain to draw it back. Was that one of those Osage orangewood bows?"

"Yes."

"Did you make it yourself?" asked Johnny.

"No," replied Dutch. "I killed an Osage warrior and took it."

"Oh," said Johnny.

"Would you like to keep it to practice with?" asked Dutch.

Johnny, feeling thrilled, exclaimed, "Yes, I would! I'll practice every day until I master it."

Dutch said, "Then, from now on, that bow will be yours. Take care of it. Always unstring it when you are not using it. Oil it from time to time. And one more thing…since you know a little bit about blacksmith work, you can make your own arrowheads. Then I'll show you how to make arrows."

Johnny was excited. He realized that it might be a few weeks before he was ready to practice with his new bow. He would have to make arrowheads first. Then, the arrows. Then, he could master the use of this very powerful bow.

Dutch must have been reading his mind. He said, "While you are busy making the arrows, you can start learning how to use our weapons. Not the rifle yet. First, wrestling. Then war clubs, lances, and knives."

The next morning, after they cleaned up their campsite, Dutch pulled out his knife and handed it to Johnny, who looked puzzled. Dutch said, "No, it's not another gift. I want you to try your best to stab me with it."

"Uncle, I would rather not."

Dutch raised his voice. "Do you think I would invite you to do this if I were not certain that you would fail? Now, come here and try to kill me, you little punk!" He repeated his demand, only now with a scream: "Come on!"

Johnny was a little more than half-hearted when he lunged at Dutch with his knife. Dutch grabbed Johnny's right hand with his left, pressing his thumb tightly in the middle of the back of Johnny's hand. It must have been a very special place because when Dutch twisted Johnny's wrist, he was powerless to stop it, even though his hands were very strong. He involuntarily dropped the knife as Dutch simultaneously placed his right leg behind Johnny's right leg and tripped him, still holding his right wrist in a powerful grip with his left hand. Johnny fell backwards, landing on his back. Meanwhile, a split second after grabbing Johnny's wrist and tripping him, Dutch, who had hidden another knife behind his back, drew it with his right hand and put the point of it against Johnny's throat. All of this happened in less than two seconds.

"You realize that you just died, don't you?" He released Johnny's right hand and withdrew his knife.

Johnny, who for a moment feared for his life but was now in wide-eyed admiration, jumped to his feet and exclaimed, "I want to learn how to do that!"

Dutch said, "You already know how to box, like those Irishmen taught you. Those skills might help you in a drunken brawl, but in a real battle, you will use weapons. Hand-to-hand weapons. And part of using them is knowing how to wrestle. So, this is what you should learn first. There is a lot to know. Moves that involve twisting joints and breaking bones. To do this, you will need a partner who will also teach you."

"Do you have someone in mind?" asked Johnny.

"Yes, I do. Tommy Smith."

"Have I met him?"

"Yes, as a matter of fact, you have. He's the one who called you 'white boy' when you arrived!" Dutch could not help himself. He laughed.

"Him?" Johnny asked incredulously.

"Don't take him lightly," said Dutch. "He is one of the toughest boys in our village. I expect he will be a fine warrior one day."

Johnny muttered under his breath in English: "I expect he'll be a perfect asshole."

Dutch, who understood English, looked at him quizzically.

Johnny, who realized that this hadn't been a good time to think out loud, just said, "Nothing."

* * * * * * * * *

The next morning, Johnny went to the blacksmith's cabin. Out in the back was a shed. A familiar setting around which Johnny felt comfortable. Kanuna ("Bullfrog"), the blacksmith, was shorter than most of the men but had a chest the size of a barrel and hands that looked like Johnny's, only bigger. His dark skin was permanently stained from years of smithing.

Kanuna didn't have any routine work for Johnny to do that day but was willing to show him how to make an arrowhead out of iron.

He made a cast out of sand and clay, poured some molten iron into it, and when it was solidified but still red hot, he pulled it out with a pair of tongs. Then he poured more molten iron into the cast, and while both halves were still red hot, he poured some liquid solder material on the edge of one of them. With his tongs, he placed the other half on top, making a whole arrowhead.

Johnny made two more arrowheads and filed them all, making them sharp. He touched the tip of one of the arrowheads with his finger, and it pierced his skin. Blood began to trickle from the cut. He couldn't help but think of the Stricklins as he held that arrowhead in his hand. He yearned to see their blood.

After making his first arrowheads, Johnny went home to Uncle Dutch's cabin. Standing by the front door was Tommy Smith, who smirked—Tommy seemed to do that a lot—and bobbed his head expectantly as if looking forward to kicking Johnny's ass. He gave Johnny a contemptuous look.

"You ready?" he asked in English.

"Sure." No sooner had this syllable slipped from Johnny's mouth than Tommy sprang upon him, spun around behind him, wound his elbow around Johnny's throat, and pulled him down to the ground, face up, his back on Tommy's chest. He applied pressure to Johnny's throat, and soon, Johnny started to faint.

"OK, that's enough," said Uncle Dutch in his deep voice as he looked down at the boys. "That's twice in two days that you've been a dead man." Meanwhile, Tommy still hadn't let go as Dutch had directed.

"Tommy, would you like to be my nineteenth scalp? Let him go, NOW!"

Tommy complied.

Directing his gaze at Tommy, Dutch said, "This is a good start. Now, teach White Owl the basics." Then he turned and walked away.

The boys got up from the ground. "So, your name is Tommy? Do you have a Cherokee name, too?" asked Johnny, speaking English.

"No, but I'm as Indian as any sonofabitch here," replied Tommy, in his own version of a Southern drawl.

"You can call me 'Johnny' if you want. That's the name I went by back where I came from."

"OK, 'Johnny'." He almost spat out Johnny's name as he spoke. "Let's get started."

He spent the next few hours with Tommy, learning some basic wrist holds, trips, and ways to block being taken down. Tommy wasn't as strong as Johnny, but he more than made up for it with experience. Johnny respected this about him.

The next day, after a bruised and battered Johnny made three more arrowheads, he once again found Tommy waiting at the door of Uncle Dutch's cabin. And again, without warning, he lunged at Johnny, trying to take him down, but Johnny was ready this time. He stepped to his right and cuffed Tommy with a right hook to his left jaw. Tommy lost his footing and fell, but he bounced back up in a split second and charged Johnny again. This time, however, he stayed upright just long enough for Johnny to land a straight left to his chin, making Tommy stagger backwards, his eyes momentarily glazed over.

The punch should have knocked Tommy senseless, and Johnny was a bit concerned that it hadn't. He considered that he might land more punches and maybe knock Tommy out, but he didn't want to do that, partly because if he failed and Tommy regained his senses, he might tie Johnny up in one of those human knots that wrestlers know how to execute. He might make him pay with a torn ligament or broken arm. Johnny preferred to avoid these risks.

"Are you OK?" Johnny asked as he lowered his fists.

"Fuck you," said Tommy. But then he added, smiling wryly, "I have to admit you made me see some stars."

Johnny, looking to make a friend, said in English, "I'm real grateful that you're teachin' me to fight the Cherokee way. If you want, and when you're ready, I can teach you to box. It would only be fair."

Tommy, secretly enraged at himself for being outdone for the moment, was moved by Johnny's apparent offer of friendship. He figured he knew more ways to kill Johnny if he wanted to than Johnny could count. Johnny, however, had a skill that he, Tommy, might need one day. Tommy said, "I'll let you know. Probably will."

And then, they continued to engage in the fundamentals.

Johnny and Tommy would wrestle several afternoons a week until winter set in. During the winter, when he and Tommy weren't wrestling, Johnny practiced with the bow and arrow when the weather allowed. But Arkansas winters were not particularly severe, so Johnny practiced most days. He did so under the direct guidance of Dutch, who was an expert marksman and archer. Johnny, for his part, was a "natural", a fact that was quickly spotted by Dutch. When Dutch noticed that Johnny was thinking too hard and calculating too much, he said, "Get your mind out of it. Shoot from your 'center'."

"What do you mean?" Johnny asked.

"Imagine that your mind is somewhere between your belly and your heart. Look at the target and relax your eyes. Don't squint. Stop thinking. Then shoot. In time, you will find that the arrow will go right to the target, like it just knows where to go, like it has its own mind." As Dutch spoke, Johnny recalled James O'Brien's words about finding the "art" in everything one does.

By March, after many hours of practice, Johnny could hit a swinging pendulum target about two-thirds of the time at a distance of sixty feet. Every time he hit the target, he expressed his silent gratitude to his uncle for having shown him this art and to the Irishman James O'Brien, who taught him to look for and appreciate the art in all things.

As spring gushed forth with carpets of colorful wildflowers, as the red growing tips on the trees and bushes turned into new leaves, as tadpoles appeared as if by magic in pools from the late winter rains, as the forked-tailed, shiny metallic-blue swallows returned from the south, and a thick, fresh, bright green grass carpet began to cover the hillsides and the prairies, Tommy and Johnny picked up where they had left off. Almost every day for the next several months, they practiced wrestling. Occasionally, Tommy would invite other boys to their practice, and Johnny would spar with them, too. Tommy had taught him well. Johnny usually prevailed in these sparring matches. He realized that the hand strength he had developed doing blacksmith work was an advantage in hand-to-hand combat.

In May, Johnny taught Tommy how to wrap his hands in leather and began to teach him boxing. Tommy, as it turned out, had lightning reflexes and was a ferocious adversary. He learned quickly.

Johnny recalled the day he decided not to try to knock Tommy out. He had wondered at the time whether Tommy had an iron chin. At that time, he wasn't willing to take the risk. "Good thing," he mused. "Tommy *did* have an iron chin." He laughed at himself. He was glad to have offered his friendship on that day.

Of course, he had no intention of sharing these reflections with Tommy.

Their sparring matches often resulted in bruises and black eyes. After one of them, Tommy declared, "Johnny, you got a black eye."

Johnny retorted, "If you get any more bruises on your face, you'll be darker than I am! Then you'll have the right to call *me* 'white boy'!" They laughed mirthfully.

During the summer, Johnny cut his practice with the bow back to about three days a week. He began to learn to fight with the knife and the tomahawk. His teacher was Uncle Enoli, who, though past his prime, was greatly skilled at the use of both weapons. Johnny quickly realized why training in wrestling was so important. The use of both weapons required that one attempt to tie up the arm of the opponent—the one holding his weapon—so that one could strike a significant, if not lethal, blow with one's own.

* * * * * * * *

By the time Johnny had been in Arkansas for a year, he and Tommy had become friends. They went hunting together. They talked. They shared their lives and their dreams. Johnny learned that Tommy's "white" looks were no accident: His father was half Cherokee, and his mother was only a quarter. Her connection to Cherokee culture was as diluted as her Cherokee blood, which was probably why Tommy did not have a Cherokee name. His father, seeing the writing on the wall in the East, knowing that forced removal was inevitable, had decided to move to Arkansas before being forced from his home at bayonet point. His foresight, as history would reveal, was accurate. When they left Georgia for Arkansas, Tommy was only nine years old. He had been in Arkansas for five years when Johnny had arrived. He was a year older than Johnny.

* * * * * * * * *

Two more years came and went. Uncle Dutch gave Johnny a Tennessee long rifle and taught him to use it. Dutch noted that when Johnny aimed the rifle, his hands were as motionless as stone. He reminded him to shoot from his "center". Soon, Johnny, who had a gift for this as he had for the bow, became an uncommonly accurate marksman.

Uncle Dutch also directed him to make up his own "death song", a chant that he could use to dissociate himself from the agonies of torture if he were ever captured by enemy tribesmen. All Indian warriors had death songs. It inured them to the physical torment sure to befall a prisoner of war and to the mockery they would endure if they lost control and began screaming in pain. The Cherokee, who had routinely tortured prisoners of war before they became "civilized" Indians, referred to this practice as "refining their manly spirits", as the torture would be the last thing a prisoner would experience before going to whatever afterlife the Great Spirit had in store for him.

Dutch, for his part, was not interested in capturing and torturing enemies. For him, fighting and killing enemies was a matter of practicality, though he did take scalps as evidence of his kills. He said he only did this after they were dead. "That was nice of him," thought Johnny, with a hint of sarcasm…

He recalled the first day of his and Tommy's wrestling "practice", when Tommy was about to choke him out but was directed by Uncle Dutch to let him go. Uncle Dutch had threatened to make Tommy his nineteenth scalp. One day, he asked his uncle, "That day when you told Tommy that he was about to become your nineteenth scalp, did that mean that you had taken eighteen scalps at the time?"

Dutch replied, "Yes."

Johnny's good manners stopped him from asking if Uncle Dutch had taken any since then.

* * * * * * * * *

Late one sweaty summer afternoon, as he and Tommy, who were on a hunting junket, sat by a creek that flowed into the Arkansas River, Tommy made a confession. He had feelings for a girl named Annabelle. Though she had a Cherokee name as well, Tommy referred to her by her English name.

"She's real pretty," Johnny observed. "Do you want her to be your wife one day?"

Tommy said, "I don't know about that yet. I only know that right now, every time I see her, I feel this power of somethin' risin' up in my chest." He paused for a moment, groping for words to express his deep feelings. "I feel like I'd go to the ends of the earth just to get her favorite flower, if that was what she wanted from me."

Johnny thought for a moment about Molly, who could balance a book on her head as she walked across a room. He realized that he had felt that way about her, too. He found out soon after arriving in Arkansas that she had drowned in the Mississippi River on her journey here. Folks said that she had jumped off the barge and just let herself die. His eyes began to tear at the thought.

Tommy noticed that Johnny's mood had turned blue. "What's wrong, Johnny? Aren't you happy for me?"

"I'm real happy for you, Tommy. Why wouldn't I be? You're my best friend."

Tommy paused, reflecting on the momentousness of Johnny's declaration, for neither of them had ever spoken of "friendship", though everyone in the settlement knew they had become close. And Cherokees preferred to express such matters—if they expressed them at all—indirectly. Tommy asked, "Then what's wrong?"

"Do you remember the story I told all of you in front of Uncle Dutch's cabin three years ago when I first came here?"

"I do."

"Well, I didn't say so at the time because I was embarrassed about it, but I loved the girl that those bastards raped. I mean, she wasn't my girl, she was my cousin's girl, and she was three years older than me, so there was no real chance of her bein' my girl anyways. After all, I was only eleven at the time." He paused, gathering his thoughts. "There was no lust in it for me. But when she smiled, it brightened the whole room. When she spoke directly to me and looked me in the eye, I felt like my feet were gonna leave the ground, like I was gonna float up to the sky!"

Tommy exclaimed, "That's how I feel about Annabelle, Johnny!" Then he asked, "Don't you have someone who's special to you, as Annabelle is to me?"

Johnny thought before he answered. Then he said, "Until I take revenge on the Stricklins, I don't feel I deserve to have a special girl or any girl at all. I've been puttin' my time and energy into learnin' how to hunt and fight. And when I'm not doing those things, I'm making horseshoes, plowshares, or arrowheads. Other than that, the only time I have left is for eatin' and sleepin'. Every hour of my day is taken up by these things. I ain't had no time, nor an inclination, for romance." Then, with a fleeting intuition that this might be a moment that would be engraved in their memories forever, he said, "Tommy, I wish that all good things will come to you and Annabelle. And if anyone ever tries to harm either of you, I'll kill 'em."

Continuing to speak English and seeming eager to lighten up their moods, Tommy declared, "Shit, Johnny, you ain't even made your first kill yet!"

They laughed.

Johnny retorted, "Neither have you, white boy!" They laughed again.

They made a fire.

The sun went down.

In silence, they admired the stars in the vast expanse of the clear summer sky.

And then they slept peacefully.

Chapter 3: First Light

First light glowed over the mountains in the east as Johnny waited for his targets to awaken and emerge from their cabin. He figured that the youngest would come out first to draw water from the well, made of rocks from the riverbed, which the Stricklins had dug just a few feet from the door of their cabin.

He had heard the elders say that when death is at hand, one's whole life speeds through the mind in an instant. He wondered if the memory of his life up to this point was a bad omen. Was his death at hand? Even "civilized" Indians believed in omens, Johnny being no exception.

He reflected on this for a moment as he focused his eyes, looking for any movement behind the dust-stained windows of the cabin. He concluded that if his plans were foiled by unexpected events, if he should die this morning, then he should honor such life as he had already lived by continuing to remember the people—the ones he hated as well as the ones he loved—and the events that had comprised it.

* * * * * * * * *

The Osages, on first meeting the Cherokee, were still "wild" Indians. They fought with the bow, the lance, and the war club, though they had begun to use rifles as well. But they were at a decided disadvantage, given that the Cherokees had adopted firearms a generation before and that most of their settlements now had their own gunsmiths.

Over twenty years had passed since the arrival of the Cherokees in this new land, including a decade of a US-brokered peace. The Osages still considered the Cherokees to be invaders, and they still raided Cherokee settlements. And, of course, some of the Cherokee—especially Dutch—reciprocated. Every act of violence and theft inflicted by each side on the other was, in their minds, retribution for past atrocities, an unending sequence of vendettas draped in blood and death. This back-and-forth persisted for a generation, even after the US Government's earnest efforts to establish peaceful coexistence between the two tribes.

They had plans for all these Indians. They were going to move them to an "Indian Territory", to a place that would one day be known as the state of Oklahoma, a place where the Indians could settle down, farm, and become "civilized".

In 1830, Dutch and his followers decided to leave Arkansas due to the increased influx of white settlers. Johnny had just turned sixteen when they traveled to the Red River valley in east Texas, which was, at this time, a part of Mexico. But it was also traditional Osage territory. It was common knowledge that the Osage would not welcome this migration any more than they had welcomed the Cherokee invasion of the Arkansas Territory. Worse yet, the Red River valley would put them in proximity to the Comanches, who had forged an empire on the southern plains, including central Texas.

It was in this valley, in 1832, when he was eighteen years old, that Johnny had his first experience as a warrior. One day, at first light, dogs began to bark as Osage warriors on horseback approached the corrals, intending to steal horses. The barking alerted the Cherokee, who were just beginning their daily routines, that something bad was about to happen. The Cherokee warriors dropped whatever else they were doing, seized their weapons, and ran outside their cabins to confront the enemy.

The Osages, some of whom had dismounted, opened the corral of the horses they planned to steal, believing that there were enough of them to repel the Cherokee defenders and get away with the horses. However, while facing the defenders, their desire for scalps changed their initial plans. A few scalps would give them something else to boast about when they returned home with their loot of stolen horses.

Johnny grabbed his knife and gun and ran from Dutch's cabin to join the fray. It was unlike anything he had ever experienced. No sport, not even the most violent ballgame, can compare to the overwhelming inner drama of a life-and-death, hand-to-hand struggle—one which, if lost, was likely to result in one's last moment on Earth. But before Johnny could shoot his rifle, a young Osage warrior attacked him from behind. Johnny dropped his rifle onto the dirt and drew his knife as they struggled, each trying to stab the other. There was a moment when Johnny had the advantage. His right hand, which held his knife, broke free from the grasp of the Osage's left hand. He now had an opportunity to strike. Could he cut the throat of his adversary and end it—his first kill? He was sure he could.

But he hesitated. In the midst of this struggle, he thought, "Why would I want to kill him? He's just doing what he was taught to do. I have nothing against him personally." During this split second of indecision, and seemingly out of nowhere, a giant Osage, about six and a half feet tall, entered the fray, grabbed Johnny's hair with a huge left hand, yanked him up from his adversary as if he weighed nothing and twisted Johnny's right wrist with his right hand, forcing him to drop his knife. Then he unsheathed his own knife and was about to take Johnny's scalp—while he was still alive—when a shot rang out.

A flood of relief swept over Johnny as the grip on his hair released. The big Osage fell forward, dead on the spot, with a bullet in his head. Johnny had never been so close to death, and he knew it.

The younger Osage sprang up from the ground, realizing that death had befallen his elder, and charged Johnny, knife in hand, hoping to stab him in the back. At the same time, running towards his friend, Tommy Smith grabbed the young Osage from behind, put him in a choke hold, and impaled his adversary's right forearm with his knife. The Osage warrior's knife, intended for Johnny, fell from his hand, and the chokehold soon rendered him unconscious. Tommy stood up, leaving the young warrior lying on his belly, unconscious. Then, in a smooth motion that seemed instinctual, he rolled him over and slit his throat.

As the young warrior's life bled out, Tommy grabbed him by the hair and scalped him. He jumped up, holding his bloody trophy in his left hand, and let out a loud whoop, quickly answered by the whoops of a dozen Cherokee warriors as the remaining Osages fled without their booty of stolen horses.

Johnny felt a mixture of embarrassment at himself and exaltation for his best friend. This was Tommy's first kill. In the process, he saved Johnny's life.

It was something Johnny would never forget.

Uncle Dutch was leaning on his long rifle, grinning at Johnny, with an eye on the western horizon, watchful in case the Osages changed their minds and returned. "He should have been your first kill. But you hesitated. Why?"

Enoli, still reloading his rifle as he walked, joined Johnny and Dutch.

Uncle Dutch continued, "If I hadn't shown up, you would be dead and bald right now. Or maybe the other way around: Bald now, dead later. I'd prefer it the first way if it were me." He and Enoli both laughed.

Johnny's eyes were cast down to the ground. His heart was still beating hard and fast in his chest from the raw emotion he was feeling. But his excitement was dampened by a feeling of utter failure.

Dutch said, "There are some lessons to be learned from this. First of all, that young Osage would have been happy to cut your throat, and he wouldn't have had the slightest regret about it. His intention was stronger than yours. Other things being equal, the power of intention wins.

"And that big warrior would have been more than a match for you on your best day. He's probably killed and scalped many warriors, some bigger and stronger than you. He was too big for you to defeat in hand-to-hand fighting. That's why I had to kill him…with my Tennessee carbine." He paused for a moment and then said, "So, the second lesson is, in war, there is no such thing as a fair fight. The goal is to kill the enemy and not to get killed yourself. If the enemy is too big for you to win in hand-to-hand combat, use a weapon that kills from a distance. A bow or a gun."

Enoli jumped into the conversation. "Whenever you run into somebody who is bigger, stronger, and more experienced than you are, always carry an 'equalizer'. And use it with conviction."

"What do you mean?" Johnny had asked.

Dutch, summarizing the "lessons" said, "Use weapons that make up for a disadvantage in size. And whenever you can, use weapons that can kill from a distance. Don't worry about what's 'fair', whatever that might mean." He repeated, "The objective is to kill the enemy. Forget that, die young. Do you think I would have taken on that Osage warrior hand-to-hand? Not if I could help it. That would be foolish. Big goons like him are the reason guns were invented and, before that, bows and arrows." Again, he and Enoli laughed.

Enoli, reflecting on Johnny's hesitation in killing when he had the advantage, said, "Son, you're not dealing with a deer or bear, who gives you meat and whom you ought to thank for it. That's why we pray to the animal's spirit to forgive us for taking its life. But in war, you're dealing with men who want to kill you, men with no remorse in their hearts. Theirs is the warrior's way. If you relax your vigilance, in a heartbeat, you will die, as you could have today. Unless you choose the warrior's way, one of these days you will die at the hands of one who has already become one with the warrior's path. And the way you're headed, that day may come soon."

Johnny, feeling more like a student now than the recipient of a scolding, said, "Thank you, Uncles, for your counsel. I will think hard about what you have told me. I will follow your guidance."

* * * * * * * * *

Enoli, whom Johnny addressed as "Uncle" out of respect, though he wasn't really his uncle by blood, made a traditional sling club for Johnny. It was like a sling, but the rock—a smooth chunk of granite bigger than a large goose egg—was permanently sewn into the buckskin pouch at the end of it. The pouch with the sewn-in rock was connected to a cord of twisted leather about two feet long. It could be rolled up and fitted into a large coat pocket or a saddle bag. Uncle Enoli told him it was a traditional weapon, though not in much use anymore. He did not know why it had been abandoned but averred its usefulness. It was a deadly weapon in the hands of an expert user.

Johnny practiced with it in his leisure time. After a while, his accuracy was such that he could kill flies with it.

* * * * * * * * *

Several months after the skirmish with the Osages, another of their war parties attacked the Cherokee settlement, seeking revenge for their last defeat. On this day, though, they didn't just get away with a few horses. They took two Cherokee girls. One of them was Annabelle, whom Tommy, by this time, had planned to take as his wife. They sped off to the north, heading deep into Indian Territory.

Dutch organized a war party. He said he needed about thirty warriors. Soon, thirty warriors volunteered. They didn't bother with war paint. They gathered up their weapons, mounted up, and took off in hot pursuit. Kanuna, the blacksmith, was also an expert tracker. He read the trail of the fleeing Osages, whom he judged to be only a few miles ahead of them by this time. He expected that the Osages would set up camp around sundown and that the Cherokees could catch up with them by then.

The Osages would surely be ready for a retaliatory party of Cherokees. Dutch didn't know how large the Osage party was, but he believed that there were probably about twenty warriors. Dutch had lived with the Osages for over a year in the past and could speak their language. He had hunted buffalo with them and had even gone with them on a raid against the Pawnee. He knew their practices well.

At sundown, the Cherokees arrived near the site where the Osage had set up camp. Before arriving, Dutch had directed the warriors to conceal themselves and be silent. He did not want the Osage to know the strength of his war party. Alone, Dutch approached the Osage camp but stayed just outside the effective firing range of the Osages' muskets, which were of inferior quality compared to the Tennessee long rifles the Cherokees had. He shouted out to them in their language: "Turn over the girls to us, and we'll let you take the horses home without a fight."

Dutch knew the leader of the Osage war party, whose name was Two Bears. He knew him from the days when he had lived among the Osage. He didn't like Two Bears, and neither did some of the Osages, for though he was a distinguished warrior, he was known to other Osages to be an overbearing bully.

Two Bears, true to form, replied to Dutch's offer by screaming a curse.

Johnny asked, "What did he say?"

Dutch laughed and replied in English: "Basically he said, 'Fuck you, Dutch!'" He chuckled and added, "I'm glad the sonofabitch remembers me."

Meanwhile, the Osages had picked up their arms and assumed battle positions behind the trees that rimmed the campsite. Dutch directed some of the Cherokee warriors—but not Johnny—to start firing their rifles.

Johnny and three other warriors, the best marksmen in the group, held their fire. After the first volley, the Osages fired back. Thinking that the Cherokee would need time to reload, they sprang from the shelter of the woods and charged with their war clubs and lances, looking to gain scalps and glory. Dutch said to Johnny, who was the best marksman in the Cherokee war party, "Now kill one of them." Johnny quickly took aim, concentrating on his target from his "center." He pulled the trigger, and one of the Osages fell, with a bullet in his chest. The other three marksmen also fired, taking down three more Osage warriors.

The Cherokees fell upon the Osages, and a bloody hand-to-hand battle began. At this point, the Cherokees had an almost two-to-one advantage. Johnny used his sling club to split the skull of an Osage warrior. Meanwhile, Two Bears, realizing that his party had misjudged the odds and were losing, defiantly slit Annabelle's throat, let her body drop, and fled on his horse, along with a few surviving Osage warriors, who took with them three of the five horses they had stolen. It wasn't a good day for them.

Tommy had killed two of them himself. But that no longer mattered to him. When the Osages fled, he ran over to Annabelle. She was still alive, though she was bleeding out. She looked at Tommy as life faded from her eyes and whispered, attempting a smile, "I will always love you, Tommy…I will see you in the next life…"

Tommy, crushed with grief, sat on the ground by her body. He beheld his first love as her life faded away. He recalled how he would have gone to the ends of the earth to get her favorite flower if that was what she wanted from him. He began to sing his death song.

Dutch, feeling the tragedy of the moment, said, "I know where Two Bears is going. He's going to Fort Gibson. He thinks the white soldiers will protect him there."

The administrator in charge of Indian Territory had recently put a large price on Dutch's head for his refusal to stop fighting the Osages. Five hundred dollars. Two years' income for a lot of folks on the frontier. Nonetheless, Dutch had considered this an insult.

Dutch said, "I'm going to go up there, and I'm going to kill and scalp that 'sonofabitch' (he said this word in English). Anyone who wants to can come along. I will go alone if need be."

"I will come," Johnny and Tommy, who interrupted his death song, said in unison. Then Tommy resumed his death song. Other warriors volunteered. Dutch thought for a moment and then said, "No, the three of us will do."

The exaltation Johnny might have felt at having made his first and second kills was extinguished by his deep sorrow for Annabelle and especially for his friend, Tommy. Though he was no stranger to grief, he knew he could not fathom the depth of Tommy's.

Dutch said to Johnny, "Today marks your transformation into a true warrior. I am proud of you."

Enoli asked in Cherokee, "Aren't you going to scalp them?"

"I can't," Johnny said as he wiped his tears away. He was crying for Annabelle and for his friend Tommy. He had failed to fulfill his promise to protect them.

And the truth was that he felt scalping humans to be a disgusting practice. Was it the residue of his Christian teachings? Was it because he didn't want to get lice from the grisly trophies? He didn't know. What he did know, however, was that Annabelle's relatives would find consolation in being presented with the scalps of some of the Osages who had wrought this tragedy.

So, he gritted his teeth and scalped them.

Dutch declared, "Now you know the Osages. I doubt you'll have any pity on them from now on, will you?" In Southern English, he added, "…now that you know what them heatherns are like."

Uncle Enoli chimed in, "And if you think the Osages are bad, farther out west are these people called 'Comanches'. Their little ones will eat your guts like candy if you're captured by them, and they'll do that while you're still alive. Will you feel sorry for them, too?"

Johnny said, "I really didn't want to kill Indians. Just white men."

Dutch said, "That's because you haven't met the Comanches yet!" In English, he added, "Talk about goddam heatherns!" He and Enoli, who had met the Comanches, both laughed, though they did so with an unmistakable air of uneasiness. Johnny surmised that those Comanches must be real heatherns, indeed.

"What about Two Bears? You feel sorry for him?" Dutch asked.

In English, Johnny said, "Well, he shouldn't have done what he did. The sonofabitch desperately needs killin'." He looked over at Tommy, who still sat cross-legged next to Annabelle's lifeless body, singing his death song. His heart ached for his friend.

Uncle Enoli asked, "So, do you have a vendetta against all white men?"

"Just the bad ones, the ones who need killin'," said Johnny, still speaking English, which seemed to him the most natural idiom for expressing himself at the moment.

Enoli mused, "You will never run out of work to do there, White Owl. But that is the problem. No matter how many you kill, there will always be more. You will never finish your work. More likely, it will finish you."

Dutch, a prolific killer for his part, in a rare moment of reflectiveness, for he was really a man of action more than of words, asked, "By what authority, White Owl, do you decide who needs killing and who does not? Who made you God?"

Johnny had never heard his uncle mention God before. He wondered if this was just a manner of speech or if Dutch really believed in a higher power. Then he replied, again in English, for at this moment, it seemed to be a better vehicle for his thoughts:

"If God existed, how could Elias and Molly have suffered at the hands of those Stricklin pieces of shit?" His voice amplified by rage, he continued, "When that happened, when Cousin Elias, a gentle soul if ever there was one, walked around like a dead man, with that missing front tooth and that far-off look in his eye..." Johnny paused to wipe away a tear of rage... "feelin' as if his manhood was destroyed beyond redemption and his spirit stolen from him...and when he hung himself, I felt that God, if He did exist, had forgotten us. I shook my fist at the sky and screamed obscene things that should have caused a bolt of lightnin' to strike me dead!" At this point, he began to scream: "But nothin' happened…Nothin'! Nobody was there!"

He lowered his voice, took a breath, and continued: "And then I wondered if anyone had ever listened to my prayers. So, if I now take license to do His work, who is there to complain?

"For the past eight years, my soul has thirsted for vengeance. If there were a God and He hadn't wanted those vermin exterminated, wouldn't He have told me by now?" Johnny's eyes glazed over with rage as he continued his rant. "And if He is so disposed, He needs to tell me so because I'm fixin' to kill all three of them sonofabitches! Indian style! Like I told 'em when I was still a boy!"

Dutch, feeling the power of Johnny's hatred, was impressed. But then he said, "You almost refused to take the scalps you earned this day. What makes you think you are able to kill these men, as you put it, 'Indian style'? Do you even know what that means?" Dutch looked knowingly at Enoli.

Johnny, calming himself, and after a short pause, responded matter-of-factly, "Maybe I'll just cut off their balls instead." Dutch, Enoli, and Johnny all broke out laughing. Then Johnny let out a war cry, quickly joined by Dutch and Enoli. They sounded like wild Indians. They were proud of that.

* * * * * * * * *

The next morning, at first light, Dutch and his war party left for home. Along with a dozen Osage scalps, they took the bodies of five of their fallen comrades and that of Annabelle. Traveling with them was the other girl the Osages had taken, who was unharmed, and the two horses the Osages had not gotten away with.

When they arrived at their village in the afternoon, they buried the dead. Everyone in the village helped. The next day, they had a scalp dance, another Cherokee custom they had preserved and one that surely differentiated them from the whites. Johnny and Tommy solemnly presented the four scalps they had taken to Annabelle's grieving family and swore an oath that more revenge would be taken. The other warriors presented eight more scalps to Annabelle's family. The Osages had had a very bad day, having lost more than half their war party.

The next day, Dutch, Johnny, and Tommy prepared for their journey to Fort Gibson, about three days' ride to the north. Dutch told them not to paint up. He was going to walk unobtrusively into the encampment, where he knew some people from his earlier sojourn with the Osages, go straight to Two Bears, kill him, scalp him, and then run before they would have figured out what had happened. Johnny and Tommy would be his rear guard if needed.

Just before they mounted up, Johnny noticed that Tommy, who was now nineteen years old, had grown to be about an inch taller than he was, a tall, rangy six feet two inches. His lean frame was covered with well-cut muscles. He said in English, for that was how he and his friend usually communicated, "Tommy, you got pretty big since we were kids, didn't you?"

Tommy replied, "But I think you're heavier than I am." He grinned wryly. He needed the distraction of this banal conversation.

"You callin' me 'fat', shithead?" asked Johnny, playing along with Tommy's deflection.

"You better be careful, Johnny, not to take up whiskey and become a drunkard, or you *will* be fat."

"No chance that will happen. I drank some of that shit once. I got sick and puked for a whole day after. I had a terrible headache, too. I don't understand what them Tennessee white men see in it. It's vile!"

The two young warriors laughed.

Dutch said, "I drink it once in a while. It's not bad if you have a little self-control, which you clearly do not, White Owl." He shook his head in mock exasperation and then declared, "Now, shut up, and let's ride."

As they rode, Johnny asked Tommy, "Now that you've killed three men, don't you want to change your name to 'Threekiller'?"

Tommy said, "I might consider it, but there's a couple of things...First of all, the name 'Threekiller' wasn't just a name for someone who had killed three people; back in the day, it was some kind of title or other. I don't even know what it stands for. The other thing is, why would I want to put limits on myself? Maybe I'll be a Tenkiller."

Johnny said, "Hey, Uncle Dutch, do they even have a name for someone who's killed as many men as you have? Is there such a thing as a Twentykiller?"

"At this point, it would be Twenty-five," Dutch replied in English, "and no, they don't bother to give names with numbers like that. Tommy was right when he said that those names were more like titles back in the days when we were 'wild' Indians. Like them heathern Osages."

When they arrived, they found an Osage encampment outside Fort Gibson. It was late afternoon. In the long shadows at the day's end, Dutch calmly walked into the camp. Johnny and Tommy waited with rifles ready to fire, as Dutch had directed. Tommy wanted to do the deed, but Dutch said that he could enter the camp, where people knew him, quickly kill Two Bears, and then run away with his scalp before folks could figure out what had happened. He saw no reason to sacrifice any more lives on either side. Revenge had already been exacted in the last battle, except for the vengeance due to Two Bears.

Dutch entered the camp unobtrusively, without war paint. Some Osages, the ones who had known him, looked at him warily, wondering why he had come. Dutch quickly found Two Bears. Before Two Bears knew what was happening, Dutch attacked and killed him with his tomahawk. Then he scalped him and, holding his rifle in one hand and Two Bears' scalp in the other, ran to a rise, brandished it at the fort, and let out a triumphant war cry. From the fort, a shot rang out, lightly grazing Dutch in the face—the only wound he would ever receive in battle. Other shots were fired, but in the confusion, it was impossible to tell whether they came from the fort or from the Osage encampment where Two Bears' dead body lay. Dutch declared, "Now let's get out of here, fast!"

And they did.

As they rode home, Dutch said, sardonically, "They thought that by putting a price on my head, I would stop fighting the Osages. That is almost laughable, as if I would care. Maybe I should just kill myself and collect those five hundred dollars." He laughed at his own absurdity.

Once they had put some distance between themselves and Fort Gibson, they stopped to rest their horses and made camp, because it was getting dark.

When Tommy dismounted, he fell to the ground. The back of his leather tunic was soaked with blood. Neither Johnny nor Dutch had noticed it before, as Tommy had brought up the rear of their tiny war party. Back at Fort Gibson, a bullet had found him as they began their flight. He had borne the wound in stoic silence for a couple of hours and nearly twenty miles of riding.

"Uncle Dutch, Tommy's been shot!" exclaimed Johnny. He helped Tommy stagger to a tree. Tommy sat down with his back against the trunk.

In English, he gasped, "I can't hardly breathe, Johnny."

Dutch carefully pressed Tommy's body forward to observe the damage. He gently straightened him up and leaned him back on the tree trunk. There was a bullet hole in the back of Tommy's shirt. The bullet had probably pierced his left lung. He gave Johnny a knowing look.

Johnny knelt in front of Tommy, who remained leaning against the tree trunk. He looked lovingly at his best friend. Tommy would have no doubt become a great warrior. He had killed three warriors already, and he was only nineteen.

Now, he would die a warrior's death.

As he knelt by Tommy, he recalled their joyful hunting jaunts and the secrets they had shared by the light of their campfires on hot summer nights. He remembered the bruises and cuts they had endured together. He smiled faintly as he remembered what an asshole Tommy had been at their first meeting.

Now that Tommy was about to die, Johnny felt as if a great hole was opening up inside him. How would he live without his friend's companionship, without his sharp wit, without his candor about matters of the heart, without his ferocity in battle? When Tommy made his first kill, he did so to save Johnny's life. How does one measure the value of that?

As the moments passed by, he felt more and more crushed by the thought of being in this world without his best friend. His eyes began to well up with tears. They began to stream down the sides of his face.

Tommy, still conscious enough to notice, looked at him admonishingly. He shook his head from side to side and wheezed, "Don't forget, Johnny…we're *warriors!*"

Johnny choked back his tears. He began to sing his death song. As he commenced, a faint smile crossed Tommy's face. He kept on singing it until after Tommy had exhaled his final breath, as the fullness of night fell upon them.

Meanwhile, Dutch made a fire.

Johnny slept fitfully that night.

The next morning, at first light, Dutch began to chop some branches and build a platform on which to lay Tommy's body. Johnny helped, but Dutch did most of the work, since he knew what he was doing, and Johnny didn't. The sun was well up in the sky when he finished.

The platform was the way in which some of the Indians of the West laid the bodies of their dead warriors to rest. Dutch figured that if some Osages came upon it, they would know that their vengeance—a life for a life—had been exacted. Tommy's head was still shaved on the sides, so Dutch and Johnny painted his face and the bare parts of his head red, as they did when they prepared for war. They blackened the areas around his eyes with paint made with ashes from their fire.

Thus did Johnny's best friend, the Cherokee warrior, Tommy Smith, painted for war, lay in state on a platform of branches, facing upward toward the western sky, having died in battle. A warrior's death.

* * * * * * * * *

Dutch and Johnny journeyed for two long days back to their settlement.

About a week later, an Osage from Fort Gibson showed up there under a white flag of truce. He summoned Dutch and told him that the white men had lifted the price on his head. Was he ready to make peace?

Dutch, who was sated with vengeance toward them, agreed to bury the tomahawk. He would never kill another Osage.

* * * * * * * * *

Johnny spent a lot of time, in between his hunts with Uncle Dutch, doing a bit of blacksmith work, practicing his archery and marksmanship, and pounding a burlap bag with his fists, going to the places where he and Tommy used to go, remembering his friend, recalling their talks, re-living their adventures, and mourning his loss. The winter of 1832-33 came and went.

It was during the mid-summer of 1833, when he was nineteen, that Johnny decided he was ready to exact vengeance on the Stricklins. Knowing he was ready, at last, to fulfill his purpose, he stood up one day, full of grim resolve, and declared, "I'm going back to Tennessee now."

Dutch understood. "You're going to need a horse, White Owl," he said. "That one my Aunt Ahyoka gave you to come here is no longer fit for the journey, nor for what will come after it. And I just happen to have one for you. I stole her from the Osages…before we made peace, I mean. She will make the trip back to Tennessee easier, and you can take more things with you. This will help you when you're on the run…which you will be if you accomplish your aim."

Johnny had already been planning his flight—assuming that he succeeded in his plans for the Stricklins. He wasn't sure he would need a horse. It might be better to do it the old-fashioned way, to go north on the ancient warpath, to the headwaters of the Ohio River in Pennsylvania, by foot, to live off the land, as the ancient warriors had done. From there, he would travel down the Ohio to the Mississippi and, from there, find his way to Indian Territory, where he hoped to reunite with his grandmother, Ahyoka. That is, if he could persuade her to move there before the whites forced her and her people to move there.

But his fantasy was short-lived. As he thought more about it, he realized that in the days of old, the Cherokee and Seneca warriors traveled the ancient warpath in the summer months, not in winter. And winter would be upon the land soon. Further, the route he would take to Pennsylvania was filling up with white settlers. Living off the land like his warrior ancestors had would likely make him visible, and not in a good way. He decided he would need the horse, after all.

Realizing that he was going to accept the gift horse, Johnny exclaimed, "Thanks, Uncle!" and walked away purposefully, already planning what to take with him.

Enoli, who was visiting Dutch at this moment, turned to him and mused, "I wonder where his path will lead him."

Dutch became pensive, gathering his thoughts, for he had grown to love the boy whom he had ushered into the Cherokee version of manhood. "I don't think even *he* knows where," said Dutch. "But he is on the warrior's path now. I have done what uncles have done since the beginning of time. My work is finished. Finding his truth, if it is something other than the warrior's path, is his work."

Enoli said, "You did well, old friend."

Dutch replied, "With a lot of help from you, my brother." A moment later, he added, "If I had had a son, I would have been proud of him if he had turned out like Johnny White Owl."

Chapter 4: Execution

The sun began to peek over the eastern horizon. Johnny felt a surge of excitement as he waited for the first signs of movement inside the weather-worn log cabin in the center of the clearing. His pulse rate increased, and his heart pounded strongly in his chest.

* * * * * * * *

He had ridden his horse from the Red River valley in Texas, over the hills of Arkansas, and ferried across the Mississippi River, eventually reaching his old home in Tennessee. His horse was a three-year-old bay mare with a black mane and tail, a fine figure of a horse. Her name was "Prairie Flower," though Johnny, translating the name into English, just called her "Flower." He didn't ride bareback like the wild Indians of the western plains and prairies. The Cherokees weren't originally a "horse" people, having travelled the eastern woodlands on foot or by canoe. So, when the Cherokees started using horses, they got them by trading with the whites, and along with the horses, they adopted the use of the saddle, bridle, and stirrups, like those used by the white men.

Not wishing to advertise his presence, he didn't stop in Knoxville. He travelled through it until he arrived at the house of Ahyoka, his grandmother. He didn't even stop to see James O'Brien, the blacksmith. He wanted to spare him any involvement in what he was planning to do.

He arrived just before sunset at Ahyoka's house, which was still fronted by her general store. He hadn't seen her for six years, and she didn't recognize him when he dismounted and walked to the front door. He had grown to a little over six feet in height and had put on a good deal of weight since he had left to live with his uncle. Ahyoka, after a moment of wondering who he was, realized she was looking at the man that Johnny had become—tall, broad-shouldered, and muscular, his long, dark hair slightly bleached by the sun of the western prairies, his hazel-green eyes glowing against the background of his dark, sunburned skin. The hazel-green eyes gave him away.

"Well, Johnny White Owl, you look like a warrior now." She smiled approvingly.

"It is so good to see you, Grandmother," he declared in Cherokee.

Then he smiled and gave her a big hug. They stood motionless, locked in an embrace. He felt her tears on his shoulder.

"I've missed you," said Johnny, speaking Cherokee. "You have always been the pillar that holds up the sky for me. And my heart is happy, being here with you."

Releasing Ayoka from his embrace, he continued. "I regret to say that I won't be staying long. I am about to do something that will cause me to disappear from this land, forever."

Ahyoka looked at him without speaking. She knew.

"Grandmother, do the Stricklins still live in the same cabin, the one at the foot of the ridge?"

Ahyoka answered, "They do."

"Does anyone live there with them? Is their mother still living there?"

"She died a couple of years ago."

"Is there anyone else living with them?"

"I heard they bought a girl from a Chickasaw slaveholder. She stayed for only a couple of months and ran away last spring. Poor thing, that slave girl. I have always wondered if she went to the North. I hope so. I heard there are good white people up there who shelter runaway slaves."

"*Good* white people? What kind of white people would they be?"

Ahyoka said, "They are called 'Quakers'."

Johnny knit his brows for a moment, then continued. "I wouldn't blame her…I hope she made it somewhere in the North, too. So," he went on, "they're living there, just the three of them, alone?"

Ahyoka replied, "As far as I know."

Johnny smiled darkly. All the conditions he had planned for were in place.

* * * * * * * * *

Ahyoka prepared dinner. As they dined, Johnny told her of some of the events that had happened during the six years he spent in Arkansas and Texas with his Uncle Dutch. He told her the sad tale of his friend, Tommy Smith.

Ayoka, who understood, looked at her grandson kindly, but said nothing. She changed the subject. "So, you have killed two men?" she asked.

"So far," Johnny replied as he took a bite of the hominy she had made. "Tomorrow, I might kill three more."

Then he changed the subject. "Grandmother, you should think about moving to the Indian Territory."

Ahyoka was aware of the impending forced removal of the Indians of the southeast, the so-called Five Civilized Tribes: The Cherokee, the Muskogee, the Choctaw, the Chickasaw, and the Seminole. The Muskogee and Choctaw were already being moved out. The Seminoles were holed up in the Florida swamps. She was not sure what she would do if the white soldiers forced the Cherokees to leave their homes. She wondered about that a lot.

Johnny, for his part, was revulsed by the hypocrisy of the whites. He said, "The white men said they wanted us to become 'civilized'. So, we learned their ways. We wear clothes made of cotton spun by our women. We know how to work with metal. We build log cabins. We developed our own written language. Many of us—like me—went to their missionary schools and learned to read and write their language, and some of us know how to cipher. We don't torture prisoners of war anymore. And some of our people own slaves…I guess that makes them 'civilized', too, though I think slavery is an awful thing."

He wanted to elaborate on this subject. He found the very concept of slavery to be repugnant. He knew that Indians had practiced it long before the whites came. Slavery was a common fate for prisoners of war, assuming they weren't tortured and killed. In the best of cases, they would be adopted into the tribes of their captors. In the worst of cases, they would be treated as mere tools or worse. The idea of slavery offended something deep down inside him. How could anyone do that to another human being?

But rather than digress from his main point, he continued: "None of that matters to them. Those greedy bastards in Georgia want us removed anyway. No matter how much land they have taken, they want more. And more. And more!" His nostrils began to flare with rage as he spoke. "I wish I could kill *all* of them!"

"Remember," said Ahyoka, "that your grandfather was white, too. You loved your grandfather, didn't you? You cannot hate all of them."

Johnny, realizing that she had made an irrefutable point, stopped his rant. He cried for days after the passing of Will Sullivan. When Will died, one of the pillars that held up the sky in Johnny's world had vanished.

* * * * * * * * *

Ahyoka loved this land, where her ancestors had lived since the beginning of time. The remains of her grandparents, their grandparents, and *their* grandparents, and so on forever, were interred in the soils of places now called Tennessee, North Carolina, Georgia, and Alabama. Before the white men had come, these had been Cherokee lands. She couldn't imagine leaving them and never coming back again. After a moment of silent reflection, she said, "I don't know, Johnny. Maybe the white men will change their minds."

"And if they don't, they will run you out of here with whatever you can snap up and carry. It has already happened with some of the Choctaws and Muskogee. Grandmother, the only thing you can trust them to do is to be greedy. That is predictable."

He continued, "I know you have white man's money hidden somewhere in this house. With that money, you can buy a covered wagon and store as much of your stuff, including the most valuable things in your store, as possible. You have three horses. Maybe you could even buy two covered wagons and another horse or two. You can wait until some people from the western band come to visit and trade next spring and travel back west with them. When you cross the Mississippi, you will need money to pay the ferrymen—who are our people—to transport your horses and your wagons across the river. Once you are there, you can inquire as to the whereabouts of Uncle Dutch. Everyone knows who he is. He is a chief. He would help you get settled. You could open a store again and live free with our people. And the land is rich and pretty, though there are more open spaces than we have here. You might have to get used to that. And it gets very hot in the summer, hotter than here. You might have to get used to that as well."

Then he changed the subject. "I will be gone for about a year until the white men who might hunt for me have given up and lost my trail. Then I will come and find you. And I will help you with your store if that is what you want me to do."

Ahyoka seemed lost in thought. She was in her fifties, her body spare of fat, and though her hair was now almost completely white, her skin was still firm and leathery brown, giving her an air of wisdom framed by a shadow of lingering beauty. At length, she said, "I will consider your words, Johnny. But do not feel as if you must change your life because of me. I gave life to the woman who gave you life. That does not mean you owe me anything. After all, you did not ask to be born."

"You gave me more than life, Grandmother. When I was hungry, you fed me. When I needed clothes to cover my body, you made them or bought them for me. When I needed schooling, you supported me. When I was alone and feeling lost, you gave me love. And when I lost my faith in God, I still had you."

"Be careful about the words you choose when you speak of God, Johnny. You might be skeptical of whether He exists, but you don't know that He doesn't exist. Best not to piss Him off."

"Sorry if that was offensive, Grandmother."

Ahyoka, who considered this topic worth pursuing further, continued: "So, you do not believe in a higher power than yourself? You think *you* have chosen your path?" The questions were purely rhetorical.

She continued, "It is true that you make plans. And when they turn out the way you thought, you humor yourself into believing that you created those results.

"But you do not see the whole picture. You do not and cannot control all the events that go along with your actions. Suppose that there were several more whites staying at the Stricklins' cabin. Were you prepared to deal with that when you came here, seeking vengeance? Did you bring enough arrows to go around? And if you had, could you have expected to accomplish your aim? And yet, right now, the conditions are perfect. Consider this.

"Did you make yourself six feet tall? Did you create the steady hands that make you a dead shot with a rifle, the ability to judge distances that made you a master archer? Did you create my nephew, Dutch, without whom you would not have had the life you have now? Did you create the horse he gave you to ride here? Did you 'plan' for any of those things?"

Ahyoka paused, gathering her thoughts. Johnny respectfully held his silence, knowing that he was receiving his grandmother's wisdom.

Then she continued. "You cannot control all the events that make things work in your favor. You cannot predict all the events that might come up and interrupt or ruin your plans. You will go through life as you have gone so far, and react to things as they occur, find the teachers you need when you need them—and hopefully, heed their counsel—and apply lessons you could not even imagine before you had received them. Besides working hard when opportunities come to you—you *can* control that—what control did you ever have? None!"

She paused for effect, and then concluded, "You do not choose your path, White Owl. *Your path chooses you.*

"Consider how you came to this moment in time. What might you have done, where might you be, and *who* might you be right now if not for the Stricklins? Can you even conceive of that? Where would the powerful purpose that guides you at this moment be without *them*? Consider this..."

Ahyoka paused again. "Understand now that I will not hold you to the generous promise you just made to me. If it turns out that I go to Indian Territory and you never arrive there, or that you do arrive and then feel yourself pulled elsewhere, I wish for you to follow your path without regret or remorse. I will not feel betrayed. My love for you is much greater than that."

"Well, Grandmother, it was my love for you that made me make that promise."

After a long, pregnant silence, he changed the subject: "Please do not wait for them to drive you from our homeland, Grandmother. If you go before that happens—and I am almost certain that it will happen—you will be better off. And right now, I hope to see you again in that new land. God willing…" He was surprised at himself for blurting out those last two words. He decided not to think about it right now.

Ahyoka and Johnny finished their meals in reflective silence. He helped her clean up. He noted that she had porcelain dishes, like the better-off whites.

Then he asked her to prepare his scalp lock. He gave her some specifications. "I don't need a traditional Cherokee scalp lock. I will be going to the North from here. I plan to follow the ancient warpath until I get to Virginia. Eventually, I want to arrive in Pittsburgh, hopefully in November or so. From there, I plan to go down the Ohio River to the Mississippi. So, I need to look 'civilized' by the time winter sets in. I just want you to shave the sides, back to a little past my ears—the way the Seneca wear theirs, nowadays. You can leave the rest of it long. When it grows out, I won't look like a wild Indian anymore." He grinned.

So, she shaved the sides of his head for him.

"I'll be needing some charcoal, Grandmother."

"I have some of that. What about the red paint?" she asked.

"I have some in my saddle bags," replied Johnny.

Ahyoka nodded her approval. She said, "In the days of old, our warriors took the ancient warpath north to harass our enemies, the Seneca and the Mohawk. They went on foot and only took the necessities—extra moccasins, a knife, an awl, a pouch with parched corn, and their weapons. With these, they lived off the land. But their forays took place in the summer, and winter will come soon. It's a good thing you have a horse. You can carry more things. You will want to take an extra blanket and a change of white man's clothes in case you need them so you can look 'civilized'."

As she finished shaving Johnny's temples, she said, "Since winter is coming, I'll give you a buckskin coat, too. And one more thing, Johnny White Owl. You are right that I have white man's money hidden here. Let me give you some. You might need it where you're going."

"Thank you, Grandmother. I will accept your gifts. See what I meant about that 'pillar' holding up the sky?"

Ahyoka responded in a manner that felt like a scolding, "Do you see what I was saying about the 'Path'?"

After finishing shaving Johnny's temples, she applied a light coat of red ochre to his face and upper body. She didn't want Johnny to spend half a day cleaning it off after he had finished his work with the Stricklins. Then she painted the areas around his eyes with the black paint.

She stood back and beheld her grandson, who now looked quite scary. She shuddered at the thought of being one of his victims. Was this painted killer the same grandson she had loved and protected as a boy? She found comfort in realizing that, for the Stricklins, he would be a nightmare come to life.

Next, Ahyoka gave him a blanket, a buckskin coat, some extra moccasins, some soap, some trousers and a cotton shirt, a pair of black boots, and some white man's money: gold and silver coins, about forty dollars' worth. Johnny judged that she must have accumulated a sizable cash hoard. He hoped so. He wondered how he was going to fit all of these into his saddle bags. Anticipating his concern, Ayoka gave him new saddle bags with more room for storage.

As they worked to squeeze Johnny's new possessions into the saddle bags, he said, "One last thing, Grandmother. Somebody will find the bodies. They won't be scalped, but the Indians might get the blame. So, I need a piece of parchment paper to write on. I am going to write and sign a confession and leave it for whoever discovers what's left of the Stricklins."

Ahyoka supplied the parchment and a pen and ink. Then she asked, "What is your purpose beyond just getting away with it? What do you hope to do after that?"

Johnny laughed. "I don't know. Maybe I'll just ask the 'Path'." He grinned.

Ahyoka just shook her head. Her dear Johnny White Owl was being a smart-ass.

After midnight, prepared for his journey and having taken a short nap, Johnny left for the Stricklin homestead. It was about three miles from Ahyoka's house. The way was lit by a full moon so bright he could see his own shadow. He had planned for this as well. As he rode, he thought, "But I had no control over the clear sky in which the moon shines this night, did I?"

He arrived at a creek that flowed southward, parallel to the ancient warpath. Just over a low hill on the eastern side of the creek was the Stricklin cabin. He tethered his horse to a tree in the gorge cut by the creek. He took his bow and quiver, his sling club, and forty feet of rope, with a noose tied at the end. A sheath with his knife hung from his belt. He walked silently up the hill. And waited.

* * * * * * * * *

The sun had just cleared the horizon when the door of the cabin opened and out came one of the Stricklins. Johnny hoped desperately that it wouldn't be Josh. He wanted to save him for last. But Josh had red hair; the young man who had come out to draw water had dark brown hair. He looked to be in his early twenties. It was probably Joey. Silently, Johnny picked up his bow.

Suddenly, he felt a deep sense of calm. The pounding in his chest abated. He felt darkness all around him, as if he were inside a black tunnel. When he had fought in the past, this always happened. He notched an arrow and drew the bowstring to the full length of the arrow. He let the arrow fly. It went through the throat of the young man at the well. He watched him collapse, choking, spitting blood, unable to scream. He recognized him. It was Joey. "Glad you enjoyed your frolic with that 'squaw', punk," muttered Johnny, speaking under his breath.

That left Billy and Josh.

Moments later, Billy, apparently sent out by Josh to see what was keeping Joey, emerged and, on seeing his brother, who had passed out and was lying bleeding next to the well, screamed, "Josh! Something's happened to Joey!" About the time he said "Joey," an arrow pierced his throat, too, for Johnny was a dead shot with a bow.

Josh came out with his rifle, looking for whoever was causing the trouble. Johnny shot an arrow into his left thigh. He didn't want Josh to die right away. He had a promise to keep…

Johnny let out a war cry and showed himself above the bushes. Josh fired but, distracted as he was by the arrow stuck in his thigh, missed widely.

As soon as he saw the puff of smoke from the rifle, Johnny ran toward Josh, whirling his sling club above his head with his right hand, and let out a screeching war-whoop. In his left hand, he carried his lariat. Josh was cussing, bent over, and grasping at the arrow lodged in his thigh, trying to pull it out. Johnny hit him on the right kneecap with his sling club. Josh collapsed, his face contorted, howling and cussing in pain. Johnny quickly slipped the noose of his rope around Josh's neck and dragged him to the nearest tree. Josh, who instinctively clutched at the rope around his neck, made this easier than it might otherwise have been, given that he probably weighed two hundred thirty pounds. When he had dragged Josh to the tree, Johnny tossed the rope over a thick branch and tugged at it, intending to hoist Josh up and place his back and torso against the trunk. He commanded Josh, "Sit up straight, you maggot! Do it, or I'll smash your shin bones next!"

Unthinkingly, distracted by his misery and thinking about what might come next, Josh complied. Johnny pulled the far end of the rope down from the branch and ran around the tree, trying to wrap the rope around the tree and Josh's upper body. Josh was flailing his arms in a vain attempt to prevent having them restrained by Johnny's rope.

"Be still, you sonofabitch!" demanded Johnny as he punched him in the jaw, knocking him momentarily senseless. Then he finished tying Josh's arms to his body and secured the rope. He had made sure to bring about forty feet of it, having long visualized what he planned to do that day.

Then he walked over to the two wounded brothers and, in turn, slit their throats with his knife, not to put them out of their misery but to make sure they were dead.

He walked back to the tree, where Josh, distracted by the agony of the arrow in his left thigh and the throbbing pain in his right knee, had become conscious and was feebly trying to free himself. "Sit still, you maggot, or I will start cutting off body parts. And I won't start with your balls." He sniggered as he toyed with his seven-inch knife blade. "I'll save them for last." All this with his Tennessee accent.

Josh looked at him with amazement, unable to find the words he wanted to say. Johnny thought he should help him out a bit.

"I know," he said, "You're wonderin' how it is that this wild savage Indian all painted up, wearin' a scalp lock, who just murdered your two little brothers with a bow and arrow, can talk the same kind of English as you do. *Ain't ye?*" Pleased at himself for his command of rural southern English, he smirked as he uttered the last phrase.

Josh, who had become somewhat numb to his pain, nodded his head. He asked, "Who are ye, and why are ye killin' us?"

Johnny smiled. "My name is Johnny Sullivan. Do you remember me? About eight years ago, you and that scum over yonder beat up my cousin and raped his girlfriend. I tried to help, but I was eleven, and your two brothers beat me up, too. Do you remember now?"

Josh looked a bit confused. Then, a glimmer of recognition crossed his face.

"So, it looks like you *do* remember. Do you remember what I said that day as you pieces of hog shit walked away from us?"

Josh looked blank.

"Let me refresh your memory. I said, 'One day, I'm gonna kill all three of you sonofabitches! And since you've made this about Indians, I'm gonna kill y'all Indian style.' Do you remember what *you* said next?"

Josh again looked blank.

Johnny continued, "Let me refresh your memory. You said, 'Oh, boy, I'm scared shitless now!' So how about it, Josh? You 'scared shitless' yet?"

Josh, in defiance, exclaimed, "Fuck you!"

Johnny, sighing, said, "Well, I guess I ain't been communicatin' effectively." He picked up his sling club and splintered Josh's right shin. Josh screeched in pain. Tears of agony streamed down his face.

"I guess that helped, didn't it?" Johnny drew his knife.

Josh, in between moans, asked, "What are you gonna do with that?"

"How will it feel to be butchered alive by a wild Indian, Josh?" Josh, knowing he was about to die but unsure as to how and terrified, began to weep.

"See, if you were like us—a real warrior and not a common bully—you'd be a-singin' your death song right now. You'd have mastery over the pain and sufferin' you're feelin'. You wouldn't be a-screamin' like a whipped little dog!" Johnny grinned and added in a lowered voice, "Oh yes, and the worst is yet to come."

He began to sing a Cherokee chant. He wasn't even sure what the syllables meant. To him, the chant was mostly "hey-yahs". But he did it with feeling as he shuffled around the tree to which Josh was tied, brandishing his blade as he did. At one point, he threatened Josh's private parts with his seven-inch blade. Josh lost control over his bowels. Johnny laughed. "Scared shitless now, I reckon." He resumed his singing and slowly shuffled around the tree one more time.

Then he stopped. He cut off Josh's left ear. "How'd you like that, boah?" he asked. Josh screamed as the blood flowed down the left side of his face. Johnny resumed his chanting and his victory dance.

After going around the tree another time, he stopped again.

He looked at Josh and observed, "I wish you could see yourself right now, Josh. You're a real fuckin' mess, *ain't ye?* And I ain't even done yet." He laughed.

Josh, knowing he would soon die but still unsure as to how, and having stopped his screaming and moaning, was losing consciousness. He just whimpered.

Johnny trotted over to the well, drew a bucket of water, and doused him, bringing him back to a conscious state. "Well," he said, "I ain't ready for you to pass out and die just yet. You're lucky I'm not gonna throw your ugly ass into that cabin over yonder and burn it down while you're still inside, alive. The only reason I ain't doin' that is 'cause I don't want to draw any attention. By the time anyone notices, you and your brothers will be half-eaten by buzzards."

Then Johnny grew pensive. He asked, "Josh, why did you guys do it?"

Josh, revived by the dousing Johnny had just given him, had stopped moaning and appeared fully aware. He thought for what seemed like a long time. At length, he said, "I don't know." And then, with a trace of derision, he added, "Because we wanted that good-lookin' squaw!"

Johnny drew out his knife again. "I was hopin' to hear somethin' a bit more enlightened from you, Josh. You're either braver or else stupider than I thought." He chuckled. "I think I'll go with 'stupider'."

With a single swift motion, he grabbed Josh's right hand and cut off his index finger. Josh screamed. Johnny rose and continued his chant as he shuffled around the tree for another couple of minutes, as Josh continued to moan with pain and bleed from his wounds.

Johnny stopped again and asked, "Did doin' that awful deed make y'all feel like 'somebody'? Answer me honestly, or I'll smash your other kneecap and cut off your manhood next."

Josh, freshly motivated, stopped wailing and thought about it. Then he answered, his voice quivering, "Maybe for a little while."

"Maybe for a little while..." commented Johnny. "Destroy two innocent lives and break their spirits so you could feel like 'somebody' for a little while." But then he said, "For your honesty, I'm gonna stop this Indian shit. Make peace with your Maker if you believe in one." Then he walked a few feet away from the whimpering Josh, turning his back on him.

At length, he turned around and asked, "You done yet?"

Josh nodded, his face soaked with tears.

"Oh," Johnny continued, "Since now you know who I am, I'll answer your second question. Why am I killin' y'all? Well, I'm killin' y'all because you and them two varmints lyin' over yonder desperately needed killin'. That's why." He walked over to Josh and squatted down in front of him. He demanded, "Look into my eyes, you piece of shit."

Josh complied. Johnny unsheathed his knife again and slowly cut Josh's throat from right to left. "This is for Molly," he said as he finished the first half of the task, Josh's blood spurting rhythmically from a severed artery. "And this is for Elias," he said as he slowly cut the rest of Josh's throat. Then he stood up and watched Josh convulse until his life finally bled out of him.

Johnny pulled his arrows out of Josh's thigh and from the throats of the other two. He had used his smithing skills to make the arrowheads especially for this moment. They were just as narrow as the arrow shafts and had no barbs, making their extraction possible without tearing the flesh and, more importantly, without damaging the arrows. He wiped the blood from them—using his victims' shirts for the task—and placed them back in his quiver. Now, he could use them again. He didn't take their scalps, though he had earned three more on this outing. But what would be the point? To whom would he boast of his accomplishments?

He trotted to the edge of the clearing where he had left a saddle bag in which he had carried his sling club and the lariat, which still bound the body of Josh to the tree in front of the cabin. In that saddle bag was the note he had written the previous night at Ahyoka's place. He took out a nail he had gotten from her store and used it to attach the paper to the door of the cabin. It read:

These men were not killed by any of the Eastern Cherokee. This was a personal vendetta, not done by authorization of any Cherokee chief. They needed killing for a vile deed they committed some years ago. I killed them by myself. I am glad I did.

I came here alone from Texas. Don't try to track me down, or I will do unto you as I have done unto them. And if I don't, the Comanches will.

Johnny Tenkiller

Johnny put the sling club back into the saddle bag and trotted down the hill past the road, on the other side of which he had tethered his bay mare. He cut a slender branch off one of the young trees in the gulch and used it to sweep away his moccasin tracks. Then he mounted up, rode uphill to the ancient warpath, and headed north.

Justice had been served.

Indian justice.

* * * * * * * * *

For hundreds of years, the ancient warpath stretched from the Southeast all the way to New York. The Seneca, Mohawk, and Cherokee had traveled every summer for centuries, going to one another's lands to create mayhem and trauma and collect scalps. Now, however, it was no longer used for this purpose. Now, it was just a country road used by pioneers in wagons, who trickled in from the north into Tennessee and North Carolina. Fortunately for Johnny, it was a lonely road. If he saw anyone coming in the distance, he would duck into the woods and wait quietly until they had passed by. Painted up as he was, he would surely draw attention, with possibly lethal consequences.

After he had put about ten miles between himself and the Stricklin cabin, he descended from the road to the creek below. There, he took out his soap and a brush from one of his saddle bags—more gifts from his grandmother, who had also put in a looking glass. He washed off his warpaint. He was glad he had the looking glass to help with the removal of the paint. It took about an hour. Then he put on his turban to cover the shaved parts of his head so that he wouldn't alarm any white passers-by that he might encounter on this road, and a cotton shirt. Now, he looked like a "civilized" Indian. When he resumed his trek, he didn't gallop his horse—that would make him too easy to track if some Tennessee lawmen, with the help of an Indian tracker, caught his trail.

He knew of a Cherokee hamlet up in the foothills, about two miles east of this road and about thirty miles northeast of Knoxville. The headman was an elder named Wohali ("Eagle"). He was a clan-brother of Ahyoka. They had grown up together. Johnny needed a safe place to grow his hair back so he wouldn't look like a "savage" Indian anymore, for the time being, at least. He expected—or more accurately, hoped—to be received in Wohali's hamlet.

He thought about how he had signed his "confession" with the surname "Tenkiller". Tommy would have laughed at his audacity. Johnny would have responded with something like, "Well, a lot of our names are aspirational, ain't they? We live into them, once given, don't we? And besides, I'm already halfway there, ain't I?" He laughed to himself, followed by a deep pang of grief for his best friend, the warrior, Tommy Smith. He wished Tommy were here to celebrate the completion of his vendetta with him. He would have happily shared every detail of the execution of the Stricklin boys.

* * * * * * * * *

It was a marvelous autumn day. The forest that rimmed the road was a collage of orange, yellow, red, and many shades of green. The sky was deep blue and cloudless, and he could feel the bite of the oncoming winter in the crisp morning air. As he settled into his journey, his senses absorbing the colors and smells of the woods, his spirit absorbing the majesty of the fall, he felt a deep sense of calm.

"What is this feeling I have?" he wondered. "It feels so real…"

Then he remembered that there were times when he was a boy, when he had felt this way. At those times, still in the innocence and wonder of childhood, his present moments undarkened by the uncertainty of an unfathomable future or by the long shadows of past regrets, he had felt the presence of "something" of great power and benevolence. Something of unimaginable vastness, of which he was a small part. Something that made him feel safe and secure. Was it the presence of God?

But in time, he stopped thinking about this, focusing instead on the immediate present and on the road before him, vigilant for the dangers it might hold, and feeling confident that he could deal with whatever might come his way.

Part 2: The Flight

Chapter 5: Wohali's Hamlet

It was a lonely road indeed. Johnny didn't see a soul for the next twenty miles. In the afternoon, he came upon a worn path on his right, leading from the ancient warpath up a hill. About two miles from this junction was a hamlet, the abode of Wohali, an old Cherokee warrior who was clan brother to his grandmother, Ahyoka. Johnny hoped that he could stay there for a while, perhaps even winter there, before continuing northward, reckoning that by that time, he would have regrown the hair on the sides of his head. That way, he wouldn't look like a "wild" Indian anymore and would be less likely to draw unwanted attention as he journeyed to the headwaters of the Ohio River. In exchange for the hospitality that he hoped to find there, he would hunt for Wohali and perform other services, if needed.

When he rode into Wohali's hamlet, there were a couple of men smoking venison over an open fire in the center of an irregular collection of log cabins. They saw Johnny ride in and wondered whether he was friend or foe. One of them went to Wohali's cabin to inform him, but Wohali had already emerged from the door.

Johnny dismounted. Other people had come out of their cabins or from wherever else they had been to see who this stranger was and to know his purpose. Wohali, a man in his early sixties, stood by his door and motioned for Johnny to approach him. There were a couple of chairs—many Cherokees used these by this time—in front of his cabin. Then Wohali said, in Cherokee, "Come over here and sit with me."

Johnny complied. Wohali nodded to the onlookers and waved his hand casually, wordlessly suggesting that they could go back to their business, knowing that he, Wohali, would find out whatever they might need to know about the handsome stranger who had just ridden into their midst. When the small crowd had dispersed, Wohali asked Johnny what his name was.

"Johnny White Owl Sullivan," he replied, speaking Cherokee.

Wohali was a big man who probably weighed two hundred forty pounds. He looked a bit older than Ahyoka, Johnny's grandmother, who said they had grown up in the same village. He had a long, deep scar on the left side of his face, stretching from his left jawbone, just above his chin, almost to his left ear. Johnny wondered what kind of weapon had made the scar. He wondered what the outcome for the bearer of that weapon had been, since Wohali was clearly still alive. He doubted that Wohali's assailant still was. His forearms bore the scars from ritual preparations for ballgames he had played in his youth. Johnny figured he probably had other scars, but these were covered by his buckskin tunic.

Looking intently at Johnny and smiling wryly, Wohali asked, in a Tennessee accent, "How came ye here?"

Johnny wondered how to answer this question, for Wohali wasn't asking him for the route he had taken. He wanted a narrative with reasons and events. When someone asked that question in that way, it was not necessarily a gesture of welcome. It was a not-so-subtle demand for an account.

As Johnny's mind fumbled for an explanation, and as he suffered the inner conflict of one who hates to lie but fears telling the truth, Wohali looked at him, or rather, seemed to look through him. Johnny was off to a good start, at least: He had disclosed his full real name. Unthinkingly, Johnny removed his turban. He really didn't like wearing them.

Wohali noticed some remnants of red war paint along the edges of Johnny's scalp lock but said nothing about it. Instead, he declared, this time in Cherokee, "You've been up to some kind of mischief, haven't you? And now you're on the run. Tell me the truth, and maybe I will invite you to stay here for a short while."

Johnny, still buying time to develop his story, said, "My grandmother, Ahyoka, said you and she grew up together."

"So, you're Ahyoka's grandson? That is worth something. But will it be worth the Hell that follows you?"

Johnny took a deep breath and then began, "All right, Uncle. I'll tell you the whole truth, but it will have to be our secret. And after telling you, I will do whatever you require."

"That is well," said Wohali, again in Cherokee. Then he leaned back in his chair expectantly.

Johnny said, "This will take a while to tell. We'll be sitting here until after the sun goes down."

Wohali, looking as if he wanted to grin—though he did not—said, "Time is no longer of much consequence to me. Let's hear your tale."

They sat there until well after dark. Johnny told him everything, the whole truth, beginning with his encounter with the Stricklins eight years before, when they raped Molly. He told of how, that very morning, he left the Stricklin's bodies in the yard in front of their cabin, of how he nailed the note with his confession to their front door, of how he brushed away his tracks before mounting his horse, and of how he avoided galloping her to indicate flight, the better to make his trail less visible to anyone who might track him.

As Johnny told his story, Wohali asked for details, partly from curiosity and partly to trip him up if he was fabricating anything. Now in his sixties, his warlike nature had been tempered by years of struggle, by having to learn to hold his head high, even in defeat, and the wisdom acquired therefrom. Wohali could see beneath the outer appearances of things. He saw things that the less knowledgeable, the less wise, could not see. Wohali ("Eagle") had not been given that name at birth. He had earned it during his adulthood because of his abilities as a strategist and because of his wisdom. He concluded that Johnny's narrative was plausible and very likely true.

Wohali shared some of his past with Johnny as well. He had fought in the Chickamauga War against the white men—the Cherokee had lost that one—and been part of the Cherokee contingent that aided Andrew Jackson at the Battle of Horseshoe Bend against the Red Sticks. The Red Sticks had lost, so at least the Cherokees had been on the winning side that time. Without the help of the Cherokee, Jackson would have won anyway, but at a greater cost of American lives. Now, he was President of the United States and aggressively advocating the removal of the Indians to a land west of the Mississippi.

Johnny, disgusted, asked Wohali, "What do you think of that?"

Wohali replied, "Jackson was a respectable warrior, a capable war chief…and a 'sonofabitch'," saying the last of those words in English.

He gave a faint, sardonic smile and added, "There is no purpose to be served by regret. We must do what we must. We're not leaving this land. Our ancestors' remains and spirits are here, where we have lived since the beginning of time. If it means living up in the mountains where it is harder to grow crops and having to spend more time collecting fruits and berries, digging roots, and hunting—we already do that anyway—then so be it. We will still make our young men play the ball game. We will still commune with our ancestors when we walk in the forest or climb a mountain. We will have to give up raiding other people, taking their lives, and looting them. But we have already given that up, for the most part. Otherwise, we will still be Cherokee."

Meanwhile, Wohali's niece, whom Johnny suspected of eavesdropping, prepared a meal for them. She lit a couple of oil lamps and announced that it was time to eat.

Wohali and Johnny brought in the two chairs and sat at the table. Wohali introduced his niece, who appeared to be in her late twenties. Though not young, she still had soft curves in all the right places. And she was very pretty, with thick, well-coiffured black hair, full lips, and large, almond-shaped eyes that seemed to turn upwards at their outer corners. When she smiled, the fine wrinkles in the outer corners of those dark brown eyes were like the frame of a picture, making it more beautiful. He noticed that her nails were filed evenly, as those of Molly had been. And she had the same name as Johnny's grandmother—Ahyoka ("she brings happiness"). He was comforted by these similarities to women he had respected and loved in the past. But he silently mused about what kind of "happiness" this woman brought, for there was something almost predatory about that smile of hers.

He was also comforted by the light rain he heard pattering on the roof of Wohali's cabin. He thought, "Now they won't even be able to track me with hounds." He smiled, recalling his last conversation with his grandmother. Had his "Path" made yet another decision for him?

As they finished their dinner, Wohali said, "You can stay here tonight. I haven't decided whether to let you stay any longer than that. I will have to sleep on it."

"That is well," said Johnny. "I have my own blankets. Let me unsaddle Flower and get my things."

"Unsaddle who?" asked Ahyoka.

"My uncle Dutch gave her a name that means the same as 'Prairie Flower' in English. When he gave me the horse, I just called her 'Flower' for short. It took a while, but now she answers to that name."

Having spent two days with almost no sleep, Johnny quickly faded into oblivion as soon as he lay down on his blanket, which Ahyoka had spread on a raised platform—a Cherokee bed—next to one of the cabin walls.

As Johnny fell into a deep sleep, Wohali told his niece, "Don't fool with him. He has the fires of Hell on his tail." He knew his niece. He knew that her wanton look was more than skin deep.

* * * * * * * *

Earlier that day, a man on his way to Knoxville passed by the farm where the Stricklins lived. He saw circling vultures and wondered what dead thing had attracted them. He didn't stop; he went on his way without further investigation.

Two days later, a merchant in Knoxville, who had bought corn from the Stricklins for years, noticed that he had not seen them around, much less having brought their harvest to him. He mentioned this to the local constable.

A day after that, the constable went up to the Stricklins' cabin and discovered the grisly results of Johnny's work, along with the written confession. He realized that the perpetrator of this butchery must have been long gone. If he were really going back to Texas, he would have a hundred-mile head start. The road west was well-traveled enough that even an Indian tracker would not know how to identify the hoofprints of the killer's horse if, indeed, he had a horse. And how would he identify him even if he gave chase and somehow found him, whatever that might mean? He didn't even know for whom he was looking or what he looked like. He thought about the situation for a moment. If the whites living in the area thought the deed was done by local Cherokees, there would be violence and death on both sides. The constable, who felt that the Cherokees had already suffered enough, preferred to avoid this. Besides, if the killer really was of the western band and had returned to Texas, which was part of Mexico at this time, and assuming his identity was verifiable, could he even be arrested?

With these considerations in mind, he decided to take the confessional note at its face value. He would explain it to the local judge and townsmen in a way that would prevent violence. He would go through the motions of recruiting a posse to head westward. But there were no clues for them to follow; winter would soon be upon them, and it was unlikely that there would be any volunteers. Besides, the Stricklins had a bad reputation as drunkards and brawlers, especially Josh. Who would really mourn for them?

When the constable went back to town, he filed a report to this effect and notified the local undertaker that there were three bodies that required disposal out at the Stricklin place.

* * * * * * * * *

Three days before the constable filed his report, Johnny awakened from his first night at Wohali's hamlet. He looked for Wohali, wanting to find out what decision he may have made after "sleeping on it". But Wohali was still sleeping as first light waxed on the eastern horizon. Johnny got his bow and arrows and headed east into the mountains to hunt. In the middle of the afternoon that day, he returned with the body of a young buck, which he had already bled and gutted.

He and Wohali skinned and butchered it together. Ahyoka busied herself, scraping the skin clean with an awl. Wohali hung some of the meat on the smoking frame in the center of the hamlet. One of his neighbors lit a fire under it. He and Johnny took the choice cuts and roasted them on a spit over a fire. Then, they invited the neighbors for the feast.

After dinner, when he and Johnny were alone, Wohali spoke. "At the edge of this village is a small cabin. It's not much bigger than a lean-to. You can clean it up and stay there for a while. But if there is even a chance that some Tennessee lawmen come here looking for you, I expect you to take your horse and your things east, up in the mountains, and hide out for a while. I will tell them that a stranger from the west came here looking for a place to hide and that we sent him on his way. I will tell them that you took the ancient warpath and headed north. I will tell our people that they are not to say anything at all unless it accords with this. If any of them does, I will kill them."

Though Wohali was aging, Johnny took him seriously. A man who had survived two wars, fought in countless skirmishes, and carried Wohali's bulk was still capable, even in his old age, of backing up a threat like that.

Comforted by Wohali's words, Johnny said, "Thank you, Uncle. I don't know how long I should stay here, but I was thinking of trying to get to Pennsylvania before winter sets in."

"Why would you go to Pennsylvania? It gets cold up there," declared Wohali, who knew that the winters in Tennessee were milder than those in Pennsylvania.

"I want to go to the headwaters of the Ohio River, which I heard are in Pennsylvania, and when winter gives way to spring, ride a flatboat down to the Mississippi. From there, I will travel to the Indian Territory, where I hope to find my grandmother. That is, if she listened to my advice and went there before the whites kick our people out of this land."

Wohali asked, "Why would you use such a roundabout way of getting from here to the Indian Territory?"

Johnny replied, "Because the whites who might come after me would not expect it. They would expect me to run to Texas."

Wohali thought about this for a moment and then pursued his inquiry. "You would be safe if you ran to Texas because they don't know who 'Johnny Tenkiller' is. They would have no way of identifying you as the one who laid waste to the Stricklins. The only mischief that might come from this would be that they thought one of us—the Cherokees who still live here—did it."

Johnny said, "Very well, Uncle…I have another reason for wanting to travel down the Ohio River. A long time ago, there were cities—built by people like us, maybe even our ancestors—along the Ohio River. Cities with thousands of people. Then, there was a great dying from some disease or other, and those cities were deserted. But their ruins remain, as do the ones our ancestors built hereabouts. I heard that some of them are pretty large. I want to see them. I want to understand how our people got to the threshold of 'civilization', and then things fell apart."

"You probably won't find the answer, White Owl," said Wohali.

"Maybe not…probably not. But I just want to see them. What else is there for me to do right now?"

"Did you ever wonder how that little cabin you will be living in became empty? Our people already know what awaits us. Some of us do not want to move to Indian Territory. Some of the people who used to live here have already gone way up into the Smokey Mountains. The rest of us will soon follow. This hamlet will become a town of ghosts." He thought for a moment, then asked, "Do you wish to come with us?"

"Thank you for asking, Uncle. But no, I want to find my grandmother, your clan sister, and serve her by working in her store and protecting her from brigands and thieves."

Wohali nodded thoughtfully. Then he said, "That is worthy."

"One of these days," said Wohali, "I'll tell you a story that might give you insights about our ancestors back in the days when, as you put it, we were on the threshold of 'civilization'. My grandfather told it to me, as his grandfather had told it to him. It might be of use to you as you seek to know where we came from and who we were before the white man came with his guns and sicknesses."

"One day, I hope to hear that story, Uncle," said Johnny.

Then Wohali said, "We have a sweat lodge at the edge of this village. You need to go and cleanse yourself and avoid talking to people, unless it is absolutely necessary, for seven days. They taught you that out in Arkansas, didn't they?"

"Yes, Uncle," replied Johnny. Among the Cherokee, it was required that warriors returning home from a battle or after a raid would do this to bury their violent spirits before resuming normal lives. "I will begin the cleansing tomorrow."

* * * * * * * *

A week passed. Johnny brought home two more deer. One afternoon—a day on which he came back from the hunt empty-handed, he went to his cabin and found it swept clean and decorated with hard red and orange berries and some strands of beads. The berries weren't edible. They were strictly decorative. There was a mint plant in a clay pot filled with fresh soil. Its scent filled the air. And a small, rough wooden table, a foot-and-a-half high, had appeared, from where he had no idea. A woman's touch...

Not long after he had put his weapons away, he heard a voice behind him. A soothing woman's voice.

"How do you like your home now, White Owl?"

Johnny turned around and saw Ahyoka, wearing a colorful cotton shift, smiling at him.

"I do like it. You must have been the one who decorated it."

"I was," replied Ahyoka. "Why don't you rest for a while? And soon, I will bring you some dinner from Uncle Wohali's cabin."

"I would be grateful," Johnny responded.

It was fall, and the days grew shorter. Within an hour of her visit, Ahyoka returned with bowls of food. She even brought a pink tablecloth with which to cover the wooden table. Since it was already twilight, Johnny lit one of the oil lamps. Then they sat cross-legged on the floor and dined in silence, the pink tablecloth and oil lamp adding a touch of elegance to their dinner in the single room of that small, rustic cabin.

When they were finished, Ahyoka folded the tablecloth, picked up the bowls, and placed them outside the cabin door. She came back inside and closed the door behind her. She looked at him with an inviting gleam in her dark eyes. She walked up to him, clasped his hips with her hands, and pressed her abdomen against him.

Johnny began to quiver with anticipation, for he had never had carnal knowledge of a woman, even at the relatively advanced age of nineteen. He did not know what to do or what to say.

Ahyoka fondled him. For Johnny, it was over as soon as it began. Ahyoka sniggered and said, "Now that that is over with, I am going to teach you some things..."

She pulled her cotton shift over her head and dropped it on the floor. Johnny marveled at the beauty of her full, well-formed breasts. "Now take off your clothes, White Owl."

Nervously but without hesitation, he complied, still quivering with anticipation. He almost tripped and fell as he hastily removed his trousers.

"Now lie down on that bed," she commanded, her voice just above a whisper.

* * * * * * * *

Back in Knoxville, a week after Johnny had delivered his Indian justice to the Stricklins, a Cherokee in his forties named Tayanita ("Beaver") came to the store of Johnny's grandmother, Ahyoka. He had come to buy some lead for his gun. He asked, "Did you hear about the Stricklins?"

Ahyoka, worried about what had happened to her grandson, was powerfully curious but maintained her stoic composure. She replied, feigning disinterest, "No, what about them?"

Beaver said, "They found all three of them dead in the yard in front of their cabin. The oldest one, Josh, was tied to a tree. It looked like he was tortured before whoever did it cut his throat."

Inwardly, Ahyoka rejoiced. The vendetta had been completed. But again, she kept her cool, detached composure. She asked, "Do they know who did it?"

Beaver replied, "Whoever did it left a letter. He confessed to the killings. He said he was from Texas and told them not to follow him, or he would do unto them as he had done unto the Stricklins. And he wrote his name, too."

"What was his name?" asked Ahyoka.

"Johnny Tenkiller," replied Beaver. Then he gave Ahyoka a penetrating look. "You have a grandson named 'Johnny', don't you? He used to work here with you in this store when he was just a boy."

Beaver knew of the Stricklins' gang rape of Molly. Like the other Cherokees in the area, he hated them for it. And he knew that Johnny

White Owl Sullivan was blood to Elias. He wondered if Johnny had grown up and exacted revenge.

Ahyoka, proud of her grandson but unwilling, given the circumstances and the risks, to own it, said, "Johnny went west to Arkansas about six years ago. I haven't seen him since. Hardly a day goes by when I do not think about and miss my grandson."

With a suspicious twinkle in his eye, Beaver asked, "You have not seen him since then?"

Ahyoka replied quickly. "No."

Beaver, still suspicious, ceased his inquiry and bought the lead balls. He gave Ahyoka another of his penetrating looks and said, "Well, if he was my son—or grandson—I would be proud of him right now." Then he walked out the door, leaving Ahyoka alone with her thoughts.

* * * * * * * *

For several days after his first night with the "other" Ahyoka, Johnny found himself distracted from the hunt by visions of the pleasures he expected to find upon returning to his little cabin. A couple of deer had successfully evaded his arrows, distracted as he was by his anticipation of another evening with her. He couldn't wait to get back home, where she would be awaiting him, probably with a tasty meal, followed by the pleasures of the night, such as he had never known before he came here.

And indeed, she came to Johnny's cabin almost every night. On one of these nights, four weeks after their first tryst, she asked him how he had kept his chastity for so long. He told her.

She declared, "For a moment there, I thought maybe you preferred boys to girls."

Johnny, offended, said, "Please show yourself to the door."

She looked at him incredulously. "I was only teasing you."

Johnny regained his composure, realizing that he had reacted too severely to what was meant as a lighthearted joke. Trying to minimize the situation that his momentary burst of anger had created, he took a deep breath and then smiled benignly at Ahyoka.

He said, "I'm sorry for getting angry. Maybe I was just looking for a reason…"

"A reason for what?" she asked.

Johnny mustered his thoughts for a moment. Then he said in Cherokee—he usually spoke in Cherokee when talking with her— "I do not know what your life's path has been, Ahyoka, and it is just as well that I do not know. I just want to think about here and now." He paused thoughtfully. Then he continued, "I have never known such pleasures as I have had with you, how you warmed this little shack with your presence, your smile, your cooking…and the rest. But the folks here know what we are up to, and some, from the sideways looks I'm getting lately, from their hesitation to return my greetings or just looking the other way when they see me coming, do not approve. I think it is time for me to leave."

Ahyoka looked hurt.

Johnny, feeling her pain, said, "I think you knew from the beginning that there was no future in this. I do not know where my path leads me. But I must follow it alone."

Ahyoka said, with a hint of resignation in her voice, "I did. I am not a fool."

She paused for a moment, searching for her next words. "I have never known someone like you, White Owl. I know I am too old for you. But those moments, those moments that you helped me steal back from my lost youth, made me remember what it felt like to be respected and loved by someone worth loving in return. I will grieve your departure, but I will not try to stop you. I know you must follow your path wherever it may lead. And unlike you, I do pray, even though I am seen by some as a fallen woman. The Great Spirit loves all of us…He even loves me. And I will pray for you, Johnny Tenkiller."

He smiled, her use of "Tenkiller" confirming that she had been eavesdropping that first night at this place when he explained to Wohali whence he had come. He decided to hug her one last time, warmly, without lust. "Just in case He is listening, I welcome your prayers. Thank you, beautiful Ahyoka." They stood there, locked in an embrace, for a long moment.

It was Ahyoka who broke the embrace. She stepped back, struggling to hold her tears, and regained her composure. She said, "One day when you are older, remember who taught you the pleasures of the night."

Johnny said, "I never will forget that, or the way you made this little shack into a home with your decorations, your good cooking, that pink tablecloth…and you. And if I ever pray again, I will ask the Creator to guide and keep you, to bring you happiness, as you have brought me happiness."

Ahyoka said nothing more. Her eyes growing misty, she turned and walked briskly to Wohali's cabin on the far side of the hamlet. Johnny stood by his door and watched her until she arrived safely. He thought he saw her wipe her eyes as she walked and felt a deep, sinking, empty sensation in his breast. His eyes moistened with tears that he would not let flow.

He knew there was no place for her on the journey that he felt compelled, by a force within him, to take. There was nothing that he could do to make this situation any better other than to give up this journey. But for what? His next conjecture was that if he stayed, if he and Ahyoka became a couple, they might be objects of derision. He might have to kill someone—another Cherokee—aiming to preserve her honor, and then there would be a vendetta. He surmised that their life together would bring more sorrow, more complications, than happiness. And though his grandmother had declined to accept his promise to help her in the new land out west, he had every intention of fulfilling it. All things considered, it was best to leave these stolen moments here, in Wohali's hamlet, and move on. And so, they parted.

Johnny realized that this was as good a time as any to move on. So, before he went to sleep, he packed his things and put them into his saddle bags. He planned to stop by Wohali's cabin on his way out the next morning. He planned to thank him for his hospitality—and to offer an apology, if necessary, for the scandal that his affair with Ahyoka might have caused.

He rubbed his fingers on his temples. The hair had grown about half an inch. In another few weeks, he wouldn't look so "wild" anymore. It was the right time for him to leave.

* * * * * * * * *

The next morning, just before daybreak, Johnny fetched Flower and saddled up. He led her by the halter to Wohali's cabin. Wohali was already awake and sitting in a chair on the front porch. He seemed to know that Johnny was leaving.

Johnny approached him respectfully, lowered his head, and said, "Thank you, Uncle, for your hospitality. And if I have caused you any inconvenience or brought shame, I am sorry."

Wohali said, "You more than paid for any inconvenience you might have caused with all those deer you brought us. And anyone who was ever young—and can still remember it—would understand your part in that little scandal." For the first time in the month since they had met, he saw Wohali openly smile when he added, "It will be forgotten a week after you have gone. They will be all over somebody else for whatever reasons they can find. That is just the way of villages."

Johnny said, "The truth is, I came to love her. And I will always love her, as I will always treasure the memory of my time in Wohali's village. And I will always revere you, Uncle." Wohali merely nodded.

After a long, pregnant silence, Johnny changed the subject: "Remember that ancient tale you were going to tell me about our ancestors? The one your grandfather told you, the same one his grandfather told him. Will you tell me that tale before I go away from here?"

Wohali said, "I will. Tie up Flower and let me bring you another chair."

Johnny tethered Flower to a post in front of Wohali's cabin. Wohali brought out the chair. Then he began to speak:

"A long time ago, there was a clan among our people called the Ani Kutani. They say that they're the ones who built those big ancient mounds that you can still find all over these parts. They used to build townhouses on top of them. They had ceremonies there, and the Ani Kutani lived in those houses. The rest of the people lived on the lower ground, below them.

"The Ani Kutani had very powerful medicine. They could make the moon turn fire-red, and sometimes, they could even make the sun go dark. They could heal the sick with their magic and put curses on people who displeased them, curses that could kill. For these reasons, they were respected and feared. The other clans had to serve them. Their warriors did not hunt because they needed the meat; they did it for amusement and to practice with their bows and lances. The other clans provided the Ani Kutani with corn, meat, and other food."

"Do you mean that they didn't have to work to get their own food?" Johnny asked.

"It does not seem that they had to. I always figured that their warriors spent all their time practicing the arts of war. They were probably feared for this reason as well. And they were very tall, taller than the rest of the people."

Johnny had seen many of the mounds, some of which were very large and would have taken tens of thousands, perhaps millions of baskets of earth to build. And there must have been many people—possibly thousands—involved in their construction. Would mere religion get that many people to do all that work just to bury some chief? He doubted it. He surmised that force, possibly due to a prior conquest, must have been involved. After this moment of pondering, he said, "It seems that those warriors, along with their witches, were part of the reason for their power."

"Perhaps," replied Wohali. Then he continued. "Anyway, the Ani Kutani became arrogant and helped themselves to whatever they wanted, including the wives of men from other clans, when they found them attractive.

"I should add that they did nothing to earn their status. All one had to do to have the privileges of the Ani Kutani was to be born into that clan. Not like us...Among us, even if one is the son of a chief, he must earn the status of being a chief by his own deeds. He cannot just inherit it."

"The Ani Kutani remind me of wealthy white men," mused Johnny.

"Indeed," continued Wohali, nodding thoughtfully. "Anyway, a long, long time ago, something happened that caused our ancestors to abandon those mounds and the towns that surrounded them. It was a pestilence of some kind. No one these days remembers what it was. But even after this happened, the Ani Kutani continued their arrogant ways, including helping themselves to the women of other clans whenever they took a fancy to them. They did not care whether those women were already married. They just took them."

"I would kill the bastards for that!" declared Johnny, his nostrils flaring.

"Well, you are getting ahead of my story, young man," said Wohali with the faintest shadow of a smile. "Mind you, a generation or two after the pestilence, long after the days when the Ani Kutani led the ceremonies from the tops of those mounds, they were still feared for their magic and persisted in their arrogant ways. A young warrior who had a beautiful wife was off on the hunt one day when some Ani Kutani abducted her and took advantage. When he returned, he was enraged. He organized others who had suffered similar abuses at the hands of the Ani Kutani. They rose up under his leadership and massacred the whole clan—men, women, and children."

"So, there was no need to worry about anyone inheriting the Ani Kutani status," Johnny surmised.

"That is right. The Cherokees do not tolerate hereditary privileges anymore," concluded Wohali. "The son of a chief may have an advantage if he desires to be a chief, but he still has to earn it through his own deeds."

"Thank you for giving me this knowledge, Uncle. I will reflect on it."

"You are welcome, my nephew." Realizing that this was a moment of farewell, Wohali declared, "May your journey be fruitful. Go in peace."

As Johnny rose to leave, Wohali suddenly asked him to wait and went inside his cabin. He appeared with a buckskin shirt with fringes on the front and back panels and sleeves. It was a very attractive, carefully stitched shirt. He presented it to Johnny, saying, "This fine shirt came from that deer you killed your first day here. Ahyoka worked hard to make it for you. She asked me to give it to you before you left."

Johnny accepted the gift. "Please give my thanks to the beautiful Ahyoka. And my love, too."

For a moment, Wohali and Johnny stood on the porch of the cabin in a silence that stood on behalf of a thousand words. Words that could not be spoken. Johnny simply said, "Goodbye, Uncle."

Wohali responded, "Farewell, Tenkiller. And good hunting."

Chapter 6: Manumission

Johnny rode down the hill to the ancient warpath, made a right turn, and proceeded northward. As if to honor the memory of Wohali's hamlet and the woman he had briefly loved, he wore the new buckskin shirt she had made for him.

The ground was covered with light frost, and the chill of the oncoming winter was in the morning air, though the sun was shining that day. He wondered how he would get to the headwaters of the Ohio, near a place called "Pittsburg." He only knew that he would have to leave the ancient warpath and head due north after about a hundred miles. He didn't worry much, because he was well-equipped for the hunt, and with his blankets, his buckskin shirts, and other supplies, he could keep himself warm as the weather grew colder. He figured he could make it to Pittsburg in about a month, and that was without making the trip in haste. Once there, he would try to find work in a smithy to make ends meet until the spring. When spring came, he would ride a flat-bottomed boat down the Ohio to the Mississippi.

As he rode, he realized that as star-crossed and devoid of a livable future he and Ahyoka may have been, and whatever she may have been before he knew her, he had loved her. When her image arose in his mind, he felt a lingering pang of longing. It felt as if there was a deep, dark hole in the center of his body. In the past, whenever he'd had this feeling, he focused on what he planned to do next. It had always worked before, when punishing the Stricklins was the primary goal in his life. But now he realized that he had no specific plan—other than finding Pittsburg—on which to focus his attention, no powerful, compelling purpose that could distract him from his sorrow. He felt unmoored. And lost. In his longing for Ahyoka, he grieved.

He had traveled for two hours and covered about fifteen miles when he saw a creek on the left side of the road, swollen with water from a recent rain. Thirsty or perhaps needing distraction, he decided to stop for a drink of the fresh, cold water. He looked for a way to leave the road that would not be too steep for Flower to manage. Soon, he saw such a way, dismounted, and led Flower down to the creek bed. He dropped to his knees and cupped his hands to catch a drink. It was cold, clear water, suffused with the clean, stony flavor of eroded minerals from the rocky terrain above. He took several gulps.

Satisfied, he sat down, leaned against a pine tree, and tried to relax. He looked upstream and downstream to see what he could see.

Then he was startled. He saw what looked like the body of a man fifty feet downstream to his left. Whether the body was dead or alive, he couldn't tell. Cautiously, he approached it. When he was about twenty feet away, a man suddenly sat up with a look of panic on his face. He was a Black man. Johnny guessed him to be in his middle twenties.

"Don't be afraid; I mean you no harm," Johnny assured him, facing his right palm in the man's direction. He sat down cross-legged on a flat rock about six feet away from this stranger. After a moment's pause, he asked, "How came ye here?"

The man said, "My master freed me—I have my manumission papers here in my bag. His oldest son, though, wanted to keep me working at the plantation. When his father passes, he'll inherit the land and everything on it, including the slaves. And he wants to keep me there because of my skills. So, I'm on the run."

Johnny wondered what kind of skills those might be. He figured he would learn of this in due course. He said, "My name is Johnny, Johnny Sullivan," and then asked, "What's your name?" extending his right hand.

"Isaac MacDermott," replied the man. He and Johnny shook hands, white man style.

"Where are you headed?" Johnny asked.

"Pittsburg," replied Isaac.

"Well, I'm goin' there too," Johnny said. "Do you know how to get there?"

"Yes, I do," replied Isaac. "I have a map."

"That is good to hear," Johnny said, "because I wasn't sure how *I* was gonna get there."

Johnny noticed that one of Isaac's boots had been removed and that the foot it had covered, Isaac's right foot, was black, blue, and swollen. He asked Isaac, "What happened to your foot?"

"I got on this here path down in Georgia—the 'ancient Indian warpath,' I've heard it called—where my master's plantation is. I've been traveling by foot for two days. This is my third day on the road. Anyway, as you can see, I'm carryin' a pretty heavy load. Earlier today, my foot got caught in a hole I didn't see comin', and I twisted my ankle real bad. I kept on walkin', though, until I couldn't stand the pain no more. I saw this creek bed and came down to get a drink and take off that boot. It felt like my foot was gettin' crushed in it 'cause of the swellin'." Isaac smiled and added, "I just thought I'd lay down for a few minutes and rest that foot, and then along comes this big Indian…"

"Well, I'm actually black Irish," protested Johnny, who at this moment in time preferred not to claim an Indian identity due to his concern about legal exposure.

Isaac grinned and, with a twinkle in his eye, declared, "Yeah, you *black* all right! And I'm black Scottish!"

They both laughed.

Johnny noticed that Isaac was carrying two bags. One apparently had food in it—it looked like bread and other foodstuffs—and the other appeared to have soft goods—probably clothes and other personal effects. The two bags together looked to weigh forty or fifty pounds.

"So, how came ye here?" Johnny asked again, more insistently this time.

Isaac knew that Johnny was asking for more backstory. He replied, "My master was old and in failin' health. He was bedridden, somethin' about his heart.

"Now, he'd been very good to me all my life. Arranged for me to learn to read and write. And taught me how to make cabinets and other furniture. He had a workshop on the plantation and made a lot of money selling these kinds of things to other white folks. Probably made more from that than from his cotton, though he grew that, too. He had several other slaves makin' furniture, but he liked my work the best. Said he believed the wood spoke to me, that I knew just how to make it cooperate when I was splittin' logs, shapin' 'em into wood slats or whatever, cuttin' 'em, puttin' 'em together to make a cabinet or a chair or a dinner table, and finishin' it. He approved of me so much that he let me read books in his library. That library had a lot of books. I even built some of the shelves for them books. Then, about a year ago, he had my freedom papers drawn up by a lawyer. As of my twenty-sixth birthday, which just passed, I'm legally free. Anyways, I figured the least I could do was stay by his side and keep him company until he went to the Promised Land.

"Now, a couple of weeks ago, his son, David, went to Alabama to court some country princess whose family owned a plantation down there. As I think about it, he probably got home yesterday. Not wantin' David to spoil his plans for me and knowin' he might not last much longer, he ordered me to leave as soon as possible. He was afraid of what would happen to me if he died, and David was around. Told me not to worry about him, that I'd see him again one day, in the Promised Land.

"So, I packed for the journey to the north. A lot of Black people go to Pittsburg because there ain't no slavery up there. And there are some folks—good white folks known as Quakers—who receive and shelter runaway slaves."

"But I thought you weren't a runaway slave," said Johnny.

"Until I get to the north, I might as well be a runaway. With those papers, I'm legally a free man. But if some slavecatchers find me and destroy the papers, they can re-sell me to someone else or return me to David for a reward if he's offerin' one. But the real reason I'm going to Pittsburg is because my Lizzie is there. And she *is* a runaway."

Johnny wondered who "Lizzie" was. The obvious interpretation was that she was probably romantically involved with Isaac. Now he understood why Isaac wanted to go to Pittsburg.

"Why would this David want to come after you or have somebody else do it?" asked Johnny.

Isaac explained, "Like I said before, the furniture shop is profitable. My skills are a valuable part of the operation. David is greedy. 'Nuf said?"

"Do you know for sure that someone's after you?" Johnny asked.

"I don't know," replied Isaac. "But Mr. MacDermott didn't trust his son. He told me that the most important thing right then was for me to head out and go to Pittsburg, where Lizzie was supposed to be. I apologized to him for leavin'. I felt bad about that, after all the things he had done for me. But he insisted, told me I had no reason to regret leavin', but that I would sho' regret stayin'. He also put some money in a bank up there in Pittsburg. I have a piece of paper from him that gives me the right to take it out as I need it. It's for me and Lizzie to start a new life together. That would make him real happy, he said.

"Anyways, once I packed my bags, I got out of there fast to put as much distance between me and them as I could. If they planned to hunt me down, they would probably have horses and hounds. Since I was on foot, I figured that the best I could do was to get a good head start and hope that they either lose my trail or else give up after a while.

"So, the first thing I did was go to the next plantation over, where a lady named Ruth is a slave. She is the one who helped Lizzie escape. Did you ever hear of the Underground Railroad? Well, Ruth is part of it. I had a short meeting with her in the woods and asked where I could find someone who was in it. She told me about a house forty miles or so north of the plantation, half a mile west of the ancient warpath. She told me the landmarks so I could find it.

"I took off in that direction. Two days later, I found the path that led from this road to a house—they call them houses 'depots'. When I got to the house, I found that it had been burned down to the ground.

"For a moment, I just stood there, lookin' at the ruins. I felt so beaten. How was I gonna get to Pittsburg? To Lizzie? I just didn't see a way. The food I brought wouldn't last more than a couple more days. I've never hunted or had to forage in the woods. I had a terrible sense that I'd never see Lizzie again. I thought I might starve to death. I even thought about headin' back to the MacDermott plantation. At least I'd still be alive, and there'd still be some hope that I would get to see Lizzie again…Someday."

Isaac paused pensively for a moment, then continued: "I spent the night in the woods. I prayed for the Lord's guidance. I tried to sleep, but I couldn't. Then, I decided to just head north and put the rest in God's hands.

So, early this mornin', I headed north. I didn't know how I was goin' to get there, and I didn't know how long it was gonna take me. I didn't know what I was gonna eat. I was ready to give up on this life. I wondered if I might see Lizzie in the next one. And then I stepped into a hole..."

Johnny observed, "Your foot looks pretty tore up. It must be painful to walk on it. Is it broke?"

"I don't think so," said Isaac. "Probably a bad sprain."

"Let's hope so," Johnny said.

"But no matter what, I'll do what I have to do to get to Pittsburg," declared Isaac.

Johnny thought about what he had just heard. How was Isaac planning to get to Pittsburg with a few days' food supply, no gun, no way to hunt along the way? He could easily starve to death. Johnny said, "Isaac, there is no way you could make this trip with what you have on you, even without that messed up ankle of yours. How the hell were you gonna get all the way up there? Anyway," Johnny continued, "This is your lucky day. Since I'm goin' to Pittsburg, too, we'll travel together."

Isaac said, "Johnny, did you know that when you're talking to a Christian man, it's better to say 'blessed' than 'lucky'? What common heathens call 'luck' is actually God's blessin's, because He is in control of all." Upon uttering these words, Isaac smiled benignly.

Johnny marveled at the faith of this man, who likely would never have reached Pittsburgh but for his fortuitous meeting with Johnny. And perhaps not even then. Only time would tell. Pittsburg was a long way off.

Johnny asked, "Do you mind if I look at those papers? Don't worry, I'll give 'em back to you. I'm just curious to see how the white man's law handles things like makin' a human being 'free'." There was a tinge of sarcasm in Johnny's voice when he uttered the word, "free".

Isaac opened his backpack. Johnny noted that, besides some extra clothing and a blanket, there were a couple of books in it. Isaac reached down deep and pulled out an unsealed envelope. In that envelope was a paper document. He handed it to Johnny, who inspected the document. There was some verbiage identifying the officer of the county court who certified that Isaac was a free man. He had been given his freedom by his owner, Stuart MacDermott, who also gave him permission to use "MacDermott" as his surname. This was followed by a general description of his appearance, height, and moderately dark skin tone. "Thank you," said Johnny, handing the document back to Isaac. "So, that's how your last name came to be MacDermott?"

Isaac said, "Truth be known, that man was my natural father."

"Well," quipped Johnny, "that explains how you're 'black Scottish'." He looked again at Isaac's foot and asked, "Can you set a horse?"

"What horse?" asked Isaac.

"There's only one here."

"I can. But why would you offer up your horse?"

Johnny thought for a moment. Then he blurted out, "Because I owe it to someone."

Isaac wondered what he meant by that.

Then Johnny said, "Now, let's get you up and get moving. I'll carry your bags and my rifle. You can carry my bow and quiver on your back. You ride the horse. I'll let you ride the horse until we get off this path and cut over through Virginia."

Isaac, still boggling over Johnny's generous offer, asked, "So, you're gonna let me ride while you walk?"

Johnny laughed. "Ain't you heard Indians can cover twenty-five miles a day on foot and hardly bat an eye about it? If you ride and rest your foot for a few days, it'll get better. When it's better, we'll both walk and let Flower carry our belongings. She won't mind that at all, I suspect."

Isaac looked in wonder at this big Indian, whom he was sure God had sent his way.

Johnny cut a branch off a sapling and used it to wipe away their footprints all the way up to the road. All that was left for the slavecatchers—if there were any—and their dogs to track were Flower's faint hoofprints and Johnny's moccasin tracks. If they guessed correctly that there was a connection between Flower's hoofprints, the moccasin prints, and the missing Isaac, they would be likely to continue their search. He figured that they might figure it out quickly, or just as likely, that they might fumble around for hours before deciphering what had happened. He hoped for the latter but would not count on it.

Johnny was secretly hoping that the slavecatchers would catch up with them so he could kill them and stop worrying about being pursued. Then again, a lot would depend on how many there were. Contemplating this for a moment, he put himself in their shoes. If there were a bounty, or if they planned to re-sell their captive, they would have to split the money more ways, depending on how many there were. Likely, there would be just enough of them to safely do the job—in this case, to capture a single, probably unarmed Black man. They would bring this minimum number to maximize each one's share. Johnny figured that this meant three to four slavecatchers, plus an extra horse for Isaac…if they caught him.

* * * * * * * *

It was mid-morning when Johnny, Isaac, and Flower resumed their northward trek. Though winter was coming, Fall was still in her glory. Johnny thought again about Ahyoka…

They traveled until it was almost dark and stopped to camp for the night. They left the road and climbed up into the foothills for about a quarter mile until they found a clearing. The bushes and trees around the clearing would block anyone on that road from seeing them. Johnny waited until it was almost dark to make a fire.

There was a creek flowing down from the mountains that ran about fifty feet from their campsite. Johnny had a pot in one of his saddle bags. He trotted over to the creek, filled it with water, brought it back, and held the pot over the fire until the water started to steam. He asked Isaac if he had anything made of cloth, other than his spare clothing, in one of his bags. Isaac opened one, grabbed a small towel—he believed that cleanliness was next to Godliness—and handed it to Johnny. Johnny poured the hot water on the towel, wrung it out, and gave it to Isaac to apply to his sprained ankle.

"I hope that helps reduce the swellin'," said Johnny.

"I'm pretty sure it will. Thanks, Johnny. You shoulda been a doctor," smiled Isaac.

"You need some meat, too," suggested Johnny. "It'll help you heal. I have some smoked dried venison in one of my bags. Want some?"

Isaac, again flabbergasted by Johnny's generosity, said, "My debts to you just' keep pilin' up. I don't want you to sacrifice your own health for mine."

Johnny said, "When we've put more distance between us and the places we're runnin' from, I'll go huntin' and get us some fresh meat. For right now, I've got provisions, and it looks like you do, too. By the way, I see you have some of the kind of bread that white folks eat. You can share a little of that, and I'll share my venison. How about that?"

"That sounds good," replied Isaac. He pulled out a half-eaten loaf from one of his bags. It was partially molded. He peeled off the molded part and handed half of what remained to Johnny.

They dined on smoked venison and bread. The bread was dry and crunchy. The venison had only recently been butchered and smoked, so it was still a little moist and quite tasty. As they ate in silence, Isaac reflected that it was, given the circumstances, the best meal he had ever eaten.

Then Isaac commented, "You mentioned a while ago somethin' about the places we're runnin' from. Are you on the run, too?"

Johnny wondered if there was any point in sharing his past with Isaac at this moment. He decided not to. He just said, "We all got our stories."

* * * * * * * * *

They awoke before first light. Johnny scattered the ashes from the fire. They packed their things, Isaac mounted Flower, and they went downhill to the road.

"We'll put a few miles behind us and stop to rest for a little while around noon," Johnny said. He asked, "How's your foot today, Isaac?"

"The swellin's gone down enough to where I could put my boot back on, so that's a good sign," Isaac replied.

"Good," said Johnny.

"When are you gonna tell me what you're runnin' from?" asked Isaac.

"Well, it's hard for me to trot alongside Flower, carryin' these bags and this gun, and talk at the same time. It's a long story. I'll tell you the first part tonight when we stop to set up camp. But since I'm walkin' and you're a-ridin', breathin' while you talk shouldn't be all that hard. So, if I ain't bein' too nosey, I've been meanin' to ask you about this special person in your life, this 'Lizzy'. Will you tell me about her?"

Isaac paused for a moment to gather his thoughts. Then he said, "There was a church where us Black folks went on Sundays, Black folks from our plantation and the one next to it. Lizzy was a slave on that other one. Ever since I was young, my mother and me went to that church. We heard sermons and sang the praises of God and His Son, Jesus.

"Lizzy is four years younger than me, and I remember watching her turn from a girl into a young woman. She has light skin, kind o' like coffee with a teaspoon of cream in it. A beautiful young woman." He gave Johnny a knowing look and added, "That's not necessarily a blessin' for a slave if you know what I mean…"

Johnny nodded. He understood.

"Anyway," Isaac continued, "we used to stay after church while the older folks socialized, and we'd talk to each other. I don't remember how it started, but it got to be a pretty regular thing. How I treasured those few minutes every week when I saw her after church! And you should have heard her sing when we was in church! An angel walkin' on earth among us mortals, and when she sang, it felt like God was speakin' to us through her voice." Isaac paused again.

Johnny asked, "How did she get to Pittsburg? You said she was a runaway."

"The Underground Railroad," Isaac replied.

"I see," said Johnny. "And you believe she's waitin' there for you?"

"I know she is," said Isaac.

"How do you know?" Johnny asked.

"We write letters to each other," replied Isaac. "The lady I spoke of when I told you 'bout the Underground Railroad—Ruth—would take mine and somehow get them to Lizzy, and every so often, she would slip me a letter from her. We've been doin' this for three years now.

"Lizzie left four years ago when she was eighteen. So, there was a whole year when we didn't communicate. I can't tell you how much that first letter from Lizzie meant to me, knowin' she was safe…and free."

"How will you find her when we get to Pittsburg?" Johnny queried.

"I have directions to the place where she's stayin'."

"What does she do up there?" asked Johnny.

"She been working as a housekeeper for some white folks. And she's been improvin' her readin' and writin'. She hopes to become a teacher so she can teach Black children to read and write."

"That's worthy," said Johnny. "And what will you do up there? Will you start makin' furniture?"

"That's my plan. And God willin', that's what I'll do. I don't know exactly how much money Mr. MacDermott set aside for me and Lizzy, but I'm sure it's enough to buy some tools and rent a place to work."

Johnny, recalling how he had wished good things for his friend Tommy and his wife-to-be, Annabelle, was hesitant, though inclined, to wish the same for Isaac and Lizzy. But being superstitious, he feared putting a jinx on them. Instead, he said, "That sounds like a good plan, Isaac."

That night, they set up camp again, heated some water, and applied Isaac's towel to his ankle. They ate bread and dried venison again.

Isaac reminded Johnny that he was supposed to tell him what he was running from.

Johnny said, "I'll have to tell this tale in parts. I'll tell you the first part now." Then he told him the part of the story that ended when the eleven-year-old Johnny stretched his hand out at the Stricklins and told them, "One day, I'm gonna kill all three of you sonofabitches! And since you've made this an Indian thing, I'm gonna kill y'all, Indian style."

Isaac asked, "So, did you?"

Johnny smiled. "I guess you'll have to wait for the next part next time we camp."

* * * * * * * *

The next morning, as they packed their things, Johnny asked, "How is your ankle today?"

Isaac said, "It's a lot better. Thanks."

Johnny looked at the ankle and noted that the swelling had gone down a bit. The black and blue was beginning to fade. "I'll let you ride Flower until the healin' has really set in." Johnny noted that Isaac, who was lean and wiry, was about five feet nine inches tall and weighed around one hundred seventy pounds. He said, "You probably weigh twenty or thirty pounds less than I do, Isaac. Flower ain't gonna mind you ridin' her instead of me anyways. She'll be happy about it."

Isaac commented, "That's why I referred to you as that 'big Indian' the other day," laughing as he said this.

"I told you I was black Irish, asshole."

Isaac laughed again, saying, "Oh, you *black* all right!"

Johnny, knowing he was dark—compared to a white man, anyhow—laughed with him.

They crossed the Virginia state line in the afternoon of this, their third day together.

* * * * * * * * *

Three days after Isaac had left the MacDermott plantation, a party of three mounted men, two bluetick hounds, and a spare horse took off in pursuit, enticed by the $300 reward offered by David MacDermott for the capture and return— "in one piece"—of Isaac, the master woodworker. His father, Stuart MacDermott, lay in a coma, soon to depart this earth, and was unaware of this plan. In any case, he was powerless to stop it. Stuart MacDermott would pass away a couple of days later.

The men asked for and received a sample of clothing that Isaac had not packed for his journey—he couldn't take everything—and let the hounds familiarize themselves with his scent. The party took off, and on the second day of their pursuit, the dogs led them to the burned-down "depot" and then to the place next to the creek where Isaac had met Johnny. When the dogs ran back up to the road, they lost the scent since Isaac had ridden Flower and no longer touched the ground with his boots. They milled around, barking in frustration.

The leader of the slavecatchers, Buck Dinsmore, puzzled over this development and decided that somehow, Isaac had obtained a horse and was now riding it northward. He compared the hoofprints leaving that site with those that had led up to it and surmised that someone with a horse had come along and let Isaac ride it. He surveyed the road, both on the south side and the north side of the way down to the creek. He noticed some moccasin tracks that appeared along with the hoofprints at precisely the place where Isaac's scent had disappeared. The moccasin tracks had not appeared before. He scratched his head, wondering what could have happened. Were the moccasin tracks those of the owner of the horse? Why would he walk and let a Black man ride? Was he just trying to fool the hounds for a while by taking Isaac's footprints and the scent of his boots off the road? Was he involved in the so-called Underground Railroad? Buck concluded that some Indian had probably come along and let Isaac ride his horse while he walked or ran alongside. Maybe this Indian *was* involved in the Underground Railroad.

Three hundred dollars was a lot of money in those days, especially if it could be gotten from a few days' work. Each of these men could net $100, minus a few dollars for their travel expenses—three- or four-months' income. There was a risk, of course, that his judgment was in error and that they would come back empty-handed. But the upside was worth pursuing at this point, as they had been on the road for only two days.

He shared his thinking with his companions. "Let's track that horse and see where it leads us. The tracks look to be only a couple of days old, and the horse don't appear to be a-runnin'," he said. "Are y'all up for continuing the chase?"

His companions said they were. So, Buck led the hounds to the moccasin tracks and held their noses to it. "Go get 'em!" he ordered, and the dogs were off on the chase. At the end of that day, the slavecatchers found the campsite where Johnny and Isaac had spent their first night. Buck figured that they would catch up with them soon, maybe in one or two days.

* * * * * * * *

The shadows lengthened on the afternoon of the third day that Johnny and Isaac traveled together. It was almost November, and the days were growing shorter. The night would soon fall. They would soon be at the place, according to Isaac's map, at which they would get off the ancient warpath and head due north, towards Pittsburg. They would reach this junction by tomorrow, he figured.

For some reason, Johnny felt a sense of unease. He had done the calculations. If a party of slavecatchers had left two or three days after Isaac had, and if they were well-mounted, they would be catching up with them any time. The next campsites would have to be chosen not just for visibility barriers but for defensive purposes in case there was a fight.

He searched the east side of the road, where the ground was higher, for a suitable place for camping that would be defensible in case of an attack. Before long, he saw a promising place. It was an ancient mound—it looked like a mere hill—that had been unused for so long that there were oak trees growing on its sides, though they were hardly a forest, being spaced apart by intervals of thirty or forty feet. He knew that some of these mounds still had battlements around the flat area at their tops, battlements that at one time had been earthen walls but were now rounded off by centuries of changing seasons and erosion.

"Isaac, we're going to set up camp early, right up there on top of that ancient mound."

Isaac said, "It looks like a hill to me."

Johnny said, "My ancestors built it hundreds of years ago. It looks like a hill, but it was made by men."

"Really?" asked Isaac. "It does look like a pyramid, kind of. I thought that only the ancient Egyptians built pyramids."

"They built them in ancient Mexico, too. Only there, they are said to have used stone instead of earth. But whatever they use to build such things, it seems like every time mankind tries to cross the borderline between 'savagery' and 'civilization', there are some folks who just think they're better than the rest and need to make that obvious by finding ways to place themselves physically higher. In ancient Mesopotamia, they built these things called 'ziggurats.'"

"I read about ziggurats, too, Johnny. Mister MacDermott had books about ancient history in his library."

Johnny, impressed with Isaac's knowledge, continued. "They would address those below from the tops of 'em and probably conduct ceremonies, too. These mounds were used for the same kinds of things. We know that we, too, had 'priest-kings'. These mounds are all over these parts. Hundreds, maybe thousands of 'em."

Johnny led Flower off the road. About fifty yards away on the righthand side of the road was that "hill" that Isaac and Johnny had been discussing. Johnny and Flower, with Isaac still riding her, climbed up the side of it. Sure enough, when they got to the top, they saw a ridge—remnants of ancient battlements—rimming the flat top of what was once an earthen pyramid. Isaac dismounted, and Johnny carefully led Flower over the top of this eroded, ancient wall. It was fortunate that it had been worn down by centuries of weather, or Flower might not have been able to safely climb over it.

Then, Johnny held his breath. Off in the distance, they could hear the baying of hounds. "Oh, shit!" he exclaimed under his breath.

Once on the other side, in what used to be a plaza, Johnny lay down, watching the south side of the road to see who was coming. He strung his bow. He gave Isaac his hatchet. He said, "I'm gonna sneak down to the left side of the clearing that leads up here, where I'll have cover. If those goddam dogs come runnin' up here, kill 'em with this tomahawk."

Isaac, with some trepidation in his voice, said, "I never killed anything in my life."

Johnny said, "It's easy to do when your life is at stake. Don't think about it. Just kill the fuckin' dog that comes first. The other one will turn tail and run. If he don't, whack him, too."

"What about those men?" asked Isaac.

"I intend to kill 'em," responded Johnny.

"What if you don't?" asked Isaac.

"I will. I figure there's no more than three or four of 'em. I assure you that at least three of 'em will die. If anything happens to me, get on Flower and run like hell. You'll have at least a chance that way."

"I don't like it," said Isaac.

"Think of your choices," said Johnny. "Now, when they come, keep 'em occupied while I sneak up on 'em. You heard that Indians are good at sneaking up, ain't ye?" Johnny smiled wryly. "Talk with 'em. Argue with 'em." Then he took his bow, quiver, and rifle and silently slipped away, taking cover in the thicket on the south side of the mound. He disappeared into the thicket and was so silent that soon, Isaac had no idea where he had gone.

The baying hounds stopped at the point at which Johnny, Isaac, and Flower had left the road. Soon, three mounted riders, with a fourth horse in tow, stopped there. Buck, the leader, hollered out in a baritone voice with a Southern accent, "Isaac! If yer up there, yer need to come on down, nice and peaceable like."

Isaac replied, "I'm a free man! I got the papers to prove it!"

One of the men with Buck shouted out, with derision in his voice, "Well, boah, why don't you jis' come on down and show us them freedom papers?" His comrades sniggered.

Buck shouted, "Look, Mr. MacDermott's orders are to bring yer home in one piece. He didn't say nothin' about yer havin' yer balls when we brought yer back!"

The same man who had beckoned Isaac to bring his papers down added, "Yeah, they don't plan to use yer fer breedin' stock, no-how."

"Shut up, Dipshit," Buck said. "I'm tryin' ter nergotiate." Redirecting his attention to Isaac, he demanded, "Where's that Injun that's with you?"

"There ain't no Injun here," said Isaac, who was speaking truthfully as it happened. Johnny was downhill, in the trees and bushes behind the slavecatchers. About the time Isaac answered Buck's question, an arrow pierced Buck's back and buried itself deeply inside his torso. A second later, the one he called "Dipshit" had an arrow in his back as well. The arrow was blocked from entering Dipshit's body by bone, and Johnny, noting this, quickly fired a second arrow into Dipshit's back. This one penetrated more deeply. The third member of the party, disoriented, wanted to shoot but had no idea where to aim his rifle. While he was thinking about it, a rifle shot rang out. A lead ball from Johnny's carbine pierced his chest, and he fell off his horse. The horse ran back down the road in panic, dragging the rider, one of whose feet was trapped in a stirrup. The dogs didn't know what to do. Johnny shewed them away. They ran down the road, back in the direction from which they had come, and then sat down and waited, though they didn't know what for.

Buck, lying on the ground, moaned in a wheezy voice barely above a whisper, "I cain't breathe...I cain't breathe." The arrow had pierced one of his lungs. Johnny ran over to Buck and cut his throat. He did the same to Dipshit, who was lying on the ground cursing at the "goddam arrows" in his back. He trotted a few yards down the road and verified that the third man was dead. Then he looked up at the top of the mound and yelled, "Isaac, come on down. These sonofabitches are all dead now. I need help disposin' of 'em. Oh, and wasn't it nice of 'em to bring you a horse?"

The afternoon was waning. In another two hours, it would be dark. Isaac and Johnny dragged the three dead bodies into the same thicket in which Johnny had hidden when he ambushed them. Though Isaac still limped, he was very strong, probably from wrestling with wood most of his life, and was up to the task. Johnny uncinched the saddles of each of the three horses and carried them to the same thicket, placing them next to the bodies of the dead slavecatchers. Then he went through their pockets and saddle bags, looking for papers that might make it easy to identify these men and their purposes, which might include the capture of Isaac. He found some in Buck's saddle bag. He didn't bother to read them. Whatever they were, he planned to use them for kindling for the campfire.

He removed the arrows from the bodies of Buck and Dipshit. He had to break all three of them because he'd used arrows with barbed heads. He trotted up the low mountainside, dug a hole, and buried their remnants. The only possessions he took from his victims were a powder horn and some lead balls. Next, he took the saddles farther up in the hills, spread them out in separate places, and covered them with brush. Then he swatted the horses to encourage them to run free—that is, except for the fourth horse, which was now Isaac's horse. When tomorrow's light came, they would inspect it for a brand. If it had no proprietary markings, perhaps Isaac could keep it. They could think about that later. At some point, they might have to dispose of it. There was nothing to be gained from having Isaac branded as a horse thief or as an accomplice to a triple murder.

"The moon is on the wane right now, so it won't come up for a couple of hours," observed Johnny. "But when it does, it'll be bright enough to light our path even before first light. And then we'll need to get the hell out of here, fast." He added, "This place is so isolated that it'll be a day or so before circling buzzards draw attention 'cause you can't see the bodies from the road. So, by the time a posse is organized—if one ever *is* organized—we'll be far away, maybe even in Pennsylvania. But after we get to Pittsburg, we'll have to part company. You won't have to admit that you even know who did this or that anything like this ever happened where you were, for it was clearly the work of a wild Indian." Johnny smiled.

"Hey, I thought you was black Irish," Isaac quipped, trying to put some levity into a situation that he had found terrifying.

Johnny laughed, though a bit nervously, for he was shaken by the risks he had just taken, by the immense adrenaline rush he was experiencing, and was only now thinking about the possible alternative outcomes that might have occurred.

Then, he added, "If anyone ever asks, just tell 'em you was brought there by the Underground Railroad."

He led the fourth horse, a bay gelding, up to the top of the mound. It had a passable saddle on it. The saddle bags were empty. Some of Isaac's burden could be placed in them. "Congratulations, Isaac. Here's your new horse. When the moon rises, we should get away from here. And it should rise in a couple of hours. It's a good thing there ain't no clouds tonight…"

Johnny made a small fire. He used the papers he had stripped from the slavecatchers, along with some twigs, for kindling. He burned them to ashes.

Neither Johnny nor Isaac could so much as take a nap, though they probably needed one. They lay wrapped in their blankets, eyes wide open, in silence. About three hours after sundown, when the waning moon had ascended in the broken sky, they mounted their horses and headed towards the road that would lead them to Pennsylvania, to Pittsburgh, to Isaac's new life with Lizzie.

Chapter 7: The Road to Pittsburg

When Johnny and Isaac left, they let the moon, which was still more than half full, light their way. They didn't rush their horses. Johnny wanted to stay on the safe side.

As they rode, Isaac asked Johnny, "Are you ready to tell me the next chapter of your story? The part that came after you tellin' them Stricklin boys that you were fixin' to kill 'em Indian style?"

"Sure, it'll help us pass the time," replied Johnny. So, over the next two hours, he shared with Isaac the journey to Arkansas and his meeting with his uncle Dutch. He told the story of the rough beginning of his friendship with Tommy Smith. He told of his failed first attempt at killing, of how he had inner constraints to taking the life of another human being.

At that point of the story, Isaac interrupted him, declaring, "You didn't seem to have no trouble at all takin' the lives of them slavecatchers."

To which Johnny replied, "That was because the sonofabitches desperately needed killin'. I don't have no problem with that at all." He didn't smile when he said this. His voice quivered with rage. He seemed like a different person as the words slipped from his mouth, the dark aura of his inner warrior spewing into the space that he and Isaac shared as they rode in the moonlight. It gave Isaac the creeps. He didn't ask any more questions.

After a silence that lasted about half an hour, Johnny continued his narrative. He told how Uncle Dutch and Tommy had saved his life when he made his first failed attempt to kill. He told how he learned to sing his death song, to inure himself to the pains of physical torture. He told of his first two kills. He related the sad story of losing his best friend, Tommy Smith, and of how he had used his death song, not to inure himself to the agony of physical torture but to prevent himself from shedding tears at the moment of the death of the warrior, Tommy Smith, the best friend he had ever had. On remembering this, Johnny felt a deep pang of grief and began to sing his death song. Isaac noticed that Johnny's eyes glistened with tears in the moonlight. Isaac didn't interrupt or ask him what he was doing. He understood.

A few minutes later, his moment of grief assuaged by his death song, he asked Isaac, "Do you remember what I said on the day we met when you asked me why I was willin' to walk and let you ride my horse? When I said, 'Because I owe it to someone'?"

Isaac, who had been listening intently, answered, "You owed Tommy Smith, didn't you?"

"Yes," said Johnny. "More than you know. I promised to protect him and Annabelle. And I failed. They're both dead now. Could I have done any different?" he mused. "I don't see how, but I still feel like I broke a sacred promise. Meetin' you gave me a chance to fulfill it, somehow."

On hearing this, Isaac fell into a state of deep reflection about the mysterious designs of the Creator, followed by an intense feeling of gratitude. At length, he said, "Well, Johnny, it looks like now I'm the one who owes."

Johnny said, "You might want to wait until we're safe in Pittsburg before you mark this up as a debt. And if you do, you'll owe someone else, not me."

* * * * * * * * *

The rising sun glowed in the east. Isaac, viewing his map, said, "We're about to get to the road that leads to Pennsylvania."

"Good," Johnny commented. "I suspect that it'll be days, maybe weeks, before folks wonder where them horses came from or find them bodies. We'd be in Pennsylvania by that time."

After another hour, as the morning sun shined brightly in the deep blue of the early winter sky, Isaac saw the place where they would turn due northward, the road that would eventually take them to Pittsburg. "Here it is," he said. And so, they left the ancient warpath to take Isaac to freedom.

After a few miles, they stopped to rest their horses and drink from a creek. Isaac, contemplating Johnny's tale, asked him, "So when did you set things aright with them Stricklins?"

"A few weeks ago, I fulfilled my promise to them."

"Did you kill 'em 'Indian style'?" asked Isaac.

"If arrows are part of what you mean by 'Indian style', yes, I did, but with the third one, the ringleader, I did a little more than that." Johnny smiled darkly. "I'm not sayin' I did the kind of shit that real heatherns, like them Comanches in Texas, do, but I'm sure that Josh Stricklin wouldn't have known the difference." Then Johnny related the details.

Isaac listened, once again, feeling the creeps. Then, recalling the efficiency with which Johnny had dispatched the slavecatchers, he asked, "How did you folks lose to the white men? I mean, you slaughtered those men with a primitive weapon, except for the last one. You shot him with your rifle. It seemed no harder than slaughterin' pigs. You made it look easy."

Johnny replied, "Those bastards needed killin'."

Then, having reflected on this matter himself, Johnny continued, "To answer your question…First of all, I had the advantage of stealth and surprise. Second, these men were not trained soldiers. They were just common thugs, and so it wasn't like attackin' a bunch of soldiers who were prepared for war. That's why it was kind of easy to kill 'em. Why did we lose? Well, the whites are far more numerous than we are, as numerous as the leaves on the trees. Second, they have more guns and ammunition than we do and the means to make more of both, which we don't have. Finally, they know where we live and can burn our crops and villages. The white soldiers live all over, and so we can't exact revenge on them in the same way. We'd have to burn the whole United States of America to have the same effect as they had when they burned Chickamauga. It comes down to numbers, weapons, and vulnerability. They have huge advantages in all those ways. We might as well try to sweep back the Tennessee River with a straw broom during the spring floods. It would be easier to do that than to stop 'em from takin' our lands. Basically, life as we've known it is over. Now, havin' said that, I do get satisfaction from killin' the ones that need it."

"How many have you killed, Johnny?"

"So far, I've killed eight men: two Osage warriors and six white men," Johnny replied.

"How old did you say you were?" Isaac asked.

"Nineteen."

"I'd say you're off to a great start if your goal in life is killin' folks. Is that your goal?" Isaac asked.

"I don't have a goal. The only goal I have is the path I'm on. I guess you could say that my goal is to stay on the warrior's path."

Isaac knit his brows thoughtfully, searching for words. At length, he said, "You're gonna die young if you stay on this path of yours. Have you talked with God lately?"

Johnny might have said a thousand words…words about how his faith had been shattered by the events of his childhood, doubts about whether anyone had ever heard his prayers, doubts about whether there was an afterlife or any life at all apart from what he could perceive through his five senses. Yet, he recalled his grandmother's admonition to be careful not to "piss off God" in case He did exist. Guided by these thoughts, he wondered how he should answer Isaac's question. At length, he merely said, "I'm startin' to think about it."

* * * * * * * * *

Johnny and Isaac inspected the horse taken from the slavecatchers—the one that would take Isaac to his freedom or that would have taken him back to the life of a slave had the slavecatchers been successful in their mission. They were relieved to find that it had no markings that would identify it as someone's property. He was a bay gelding, probably seven or eight years old. He would blend easily and unobtrusively with other horses. Johnny was glad he wasn't a pinto, a buckskin, or a roan, which would stand out from the other horses, even if viewed from a distance. He decided that there would be no need to get rid of it before reaching Pittsburg.

The gelding wasn't in his prime, but he was up to the job of carrying Isaac and his belongings. Johnny figured they could cover about thirty miles a day. In a week, he surmised, they would be at the Pennsylvania state line. Meanwhile, they would be going through the mountains of western Virginia. They would stop and make shelter if it rained, which might slow their journey. It was now almost November, and that could happen.

As they journeyed northward, they occasionally passed by farms—not plantations, but small farms run by white settlers and Indian/white mixed-bloods who claimed to be white. Some of them, Johnny had heard, had Cherokee blood. They rode along as unobtrusively as possible. They didn't make eye contact unless they were acknowledged by the folks they passed. When they were so acknowledged, Johnny put on a friendly face, raised an open right hand in a peace gesture, and then looked straight ahead, keeping his eyes on the road. Isaac avoided making eye contact at all. At one point, a white farmer, who was gathering wood not far from the road, asked, "What are you boys doin' in these here parts?"

Johnny, again putting on his friendly face, answered, "We're on our way to Pennsylvania, sir."

The farmer nodded, suspiciously it seemed, but turned away, looking briefly at his rifle, which was leaning on a tree a few feet away from him, and then went about his business. Johnny, who had noted this, secretly hoped that this farmer wouldn't be Number Nine.

One day, as they traveled through an area that appeared to be very sparsely settled—if, indeed, there were any people there at all—the sky to the northeast of them filled with dark, menacing clouds. It looked like rain was coming. They decided to stop at midday and make a lean-to. They found some high ground under a grove of evergreens and cut some wood, an activity at which Johnny was competent but at which Isaac was expert. Isaac just said, "Let me borrow your hatchet, Johnny."

Johnny gave Isaac his hatchet and said, "Since you're better at this than me, how 'bout if I go hunt us some fresh meat while you're fixin' us a place to stay when the rain comes?"

Isaac responded, "I can handle the rest of this. Good huntin', Johnny!"

Johnny just said, "Well, I hope for good huntin'." Then he took his bow and quiver and set off to find a deer or anything else he might find to feed them.

About two hours later, he came back with a yearling buck. Isaac had finished the lean-to and placed their saddles and bags safely within it. Johnny made a fire, cleaned the deer, cut the choicest parts, and, to his pleasure, found that Isaac had already made some sharpened sticks with which to impale the meat so that it could be roasted over the open fire.

"It was nice of you to make them cookin' sticks, Isaac," declared Johnny. "But s'pose I'd come back empty-handed."

Isaac groused, quoting from the New Testament, "Oh, ye of little faith!"

Johnny said, "I read that one, too. When I was in the missionary school. I didn't really understand it at the time."

"Well, Johnny, it might be a good thing for you to contemplate what it means. The apostle Paul wrote somewhere that faith is the substance of things hoped for, the evidence of things unseen. If you think about the tale—the tale of 'Johnny Tenkiller' that you have told me so far—you would see that your faith has carried you this far, in spite of things that could have destroyed your plans or taken your life. Have you thought about this?"

He hadn't. But he marveled at the ease with which Isaac's speech had transformed from the vernacular of everyday life into what seemed to be the words of an educated scholar. Having read a few books himself, he recognized the difference. He said, "My grandmother asked me some questions like that the night before I ridded the world of the Stricklins. Now, Isaac, why would your Christian God help me so? By my people's values, I am a warrior who has made righteous kills. But by the white man's law, by the laws of Christianity, ain't I a ruthless killer, a murderer?"

Isaac replied, "First of all, Johnny, He isn't just 'my' God or the white man's god. He is the one and only God. That means He is your God, too. And if you were a 'ruthless' killer, you would kill people for any reason—money, for example—not just for reasons that you feel in your heart to be just." Isaac paused for effect. Then he asked. "Since it's pretty clear to me that you've read the Bible, may I assume that you read the Ten Commandments?"

"Yes," admitted Johnny.

"So, one of those Commandments said, 'Thou shalt not kill.' Well, if you kept on reading the book after that, you would see that after they received those Commandments and got loose from Egypt, the Israelites invaded the land of Canaan—which they claimed to have been given to them by God—and killed tens of thousands of Canaanites: men, women, and children. They even killed their goats and cattle. So, notice that the Ten Commandments only applied to *them*—the Israelites—not to the heathens who lived in Canaan at the time. In their minds, God had given permission to kill all those folks and take their land. Think about that."

Johnny reflected for a moment. Then, his hunger overcame his desire to wade into the depths of philosophy. He decided to come back to this matter another day. He remarked, "'Member how you said I shoulda been a doctor? Well, you shoulda been a preacher, Isaac."

Then they barbecued some cuts from the deer. It had been almost two weeks since either of them had eaten fresh meat of any kind. As they ate, the rain came. Involuntarily and without a conscious thought, Johnny thanked God for this lean-to.

As they finished their meal, Johnny asked Isaac, "What do you plan to do once we get where we're goin'?"

Isaac replied, "God willin', I'll buy some tools and find someone who needs some kind of furniture. When I do, I'll do my best to make it so it serves its purpose, be it a table, or some chairs, or a hutch, or a bed frame…whatever. And I'll make it beautiful. If it's a table, I'll make it so shiny that folks can see their faces in it, like a mirror."

"It seems like you'd be puttin' in a lot of unnecessary effort to do that, Isaac," Johnny reflected. "After all, it's just somethin' for people to use to eat on or put things on."

"That depends on what you mean by 'unnecessary'," replied Isaac. "Remember when you told me about that lady who decorated that little cabin for you, up in the mountains, where you stayed before you met me? How did it make you feel when you came back from the hunt and saw that it was decorated. How 'bout that pink tablecloth she put on that rough wooden table?"

Johnny had shared that story with Isaac by this time, the story of the beautiful Ahyoka in Wohali's hamlet. He said, "I remember that cabin. And I'll never forget that pink tablecloth."

"So, there's an example of what I'm talkin' 'bout," said Isaac, descending momentarily from his elevated eloquence to their everyday vernacular. "Y'all took dinner on that table, which served its natural function, but you'll never forget the touch of beauty and your experience of that meal, thanks to that simple pink tablecloth, will you?" Then he added, "What you consumed that day goes far beyond the food that Ahyoka set on that table for you."

Johnny understood. He had been filled to satiety, and not just by the food or by what came after…Something about the soft touch of that pink tablecloth and the small room dimly lit by an oil lamp felt nourishing, somehow.

Isaac went on: "I want folks who buy my furniture to feel that way when they put it in their homes when they use it for whatever. And when they ain't usin' it, it'll add beauty to their lives, like hangin' a picture on the wall. It'll make 'em feel happy—like Ahyoka's pink tablecloth on that rough wooden table made you happy."

"What if you have trouble getting business?" asked Johnny.

"That won't matter. As long as I can make enough for Lizzie and me to live, I'll be happy to work as hard as it takes to make people happy to have the things I make. And if I do that, they'll tell other folks, and I'll get more business. If I make a lot of money, that'll be good, but for me, it ain't just about money. It's about making things that make folks happy—and makin' a decent livin', of course. In that way, I can make the world a little bit better place. I won't just be here to waste the air I'm breathin'. I'll be giving to the world more than I take from it. It's my way of showing my love for my fellow human beings and, beyond that, my love of God. And besides, working in wood, whether for money or not, gives me joy."

Isaac paused. Then he added, "You're on the warrior path. Did you ever get paid for doin' 'warrior' things? Did you even think about pay? Well, I'm a craftsman. That's my path."

Johnny reflected deeply on Isaac's words, which seemed to come from an old soul, not a young man in his mid-twenties.

Isaac, seemingly feeling as if a concluding statement were needed, said, "And I thank God for the blessings He's given me, for His guidance, for havin' a good-hearted master like Stuart MacDermott...and for that big Indian who saved my life." He grinned as he uttered the last words.

Johnny recalled the wisdom he had received from James O'Brien, the Irish blacksmith who taught him that there was art in all things. He realized that Isaac had found his art. He didn't protest when Isaac referred to him as "that big Indian." He just smiled with a distant look in his eyes.

In the silence that followed, he realized that this man, Isaac MacDermott, would probably be successful in this world, the world of white men and white men's business. He hoped that good things would come to Isaac and Lizzie. He hesitated to say so, though, because he still felt as if he had jinxed Tommy and Annabelle when he wished that "all good things" would come to them, one sweaty summer night on the Arkansas River three years before. It seemed to Johnny like a lot more than three years had passed since then.

They finished their meal. Sated, they wrapped themselves in their blankets and slept soundly, sheltered from the rain by the lean-to Isaac had built.

They awoke the next morning at first light. The sky was partially cloudy. Would it rain more? Should they travel onward, and risk having to stop and build another lean-to? Johnny figured that since this rain had not been heavy enough to seriously muddy up the road, they should make haste to reach the border of Pennsylvania.

He shared his reasoning with Isaac, who agreed. He couldn't wait to get to Pittsburg, where Lizzy awaited.

They saddled up and headed northward at sunrise.

Two days later, they arrived at the border of Pennsylvania. Mercifully, it had not rained again. But it was getting cold by this time, with winter looming in these northerly climes. Johnny gave Isaac the buckskin coat that his grandmother, Ahyoka, had given him.

Three days later, they arrived at the town of Pittsburg. On the east end of this town was a large house owned by a Quaker, where former slaves who had completed their arduous and dangerous flights from the South could find respite. Johnny and Isaac arrived just before sunset.

Johnny said, "If anyone asks where you got that horse, tell 'em you bought it from a farmer here in Pennsylvania. You can tell Lizzie the truth if you want, and after I'm gone from here, you can tell whoever you like. It would be a good example of the power of your faith. Just don't use my real name." Johnny smiled as he said these words.

Isaac chuckled, "Well, what *is* your real name, anyway?"

* * * * * * * * *

They walked to the front door of a large, whitewashed wooden house. Isaac knocked. The door was opened by a tall white man who looked to be in his forties. He smiled warmly and said, "Welcome, friends. Come in."

Isaac, followed by Johnny, entered the house.

The man asked their names and whence they had come. Isaac said, "My name is Isaac, Isaac MacDermott. I'm a manumitted slave from Georgia. And this is my friend, Johnny Sullivan. He didn't know it, but he was a 'conductor'."

The white man, whose name was William Johnson, owned this big white house. He said, "You are both quite welcome here. But may I ask why you have chosen to come to this place?"

Isaac said, "I've come here to find Lizzie—maybe you know her as Elisabeth. She wasn't set free. She's a runaway and came here by way of the 'Underground Railroad'. It won't be hard to identify her. She sings like an angel."

William said, "You're right. She is here. Did you know it's Sunday? They're out in the back having an evening service. She is singing right now. Would you like to join them?"

Isaac replied, "Mr. Johnson, I would like nothing in the world more than that."

"Well, then, let's go out back and join them."

He led them to the backyard. There were a dozen Black men and women out there, singing the gospel. They had no musical instruments other than their voices and the clapping of their hands. Their three-part harmonies warmed the chilly air.

Not wanting to interrupt, Isaac and Johnny stood in the lengthening shadows of the afternoon and listened. As the chorus chanted refrains to a gospel song, holding rhythm with their clapping hands, a charismatic woman in her early twenties sang the lead line with a powerful voice of mid-range. She appeared to be in a trance as she repeated the phrase, "Jesus, show us the way!" changing the melody a bit every time she sang it out. Her voice was as beautiful as she was, coming forth from her diaphragm in a powerful, resonant, rich vibrato.

Johnny was transfixed by her singing. Something about her voice and the emotion behind it caused a strange vibration in his solar plexus and made his hair feel like it was standing up. For reasons he could not fathom, his eyes grew misty with tears, not tears of sadness, not tears of happiness, but of something else…something he could not name. He tried to figure it out but having no baseline experience with which to compare it, he realized that he should just honor this moment by giving it his full attention.

He asked Isaac, "Is that your Lizzie there?" furtively wiping away a tear that had escaped from the corner of one of his eyes.

Isaac just nodded. He made no effort to stop the flow of the tears that streamed down the sides of his face. His were tears of happiness.

Johnny reflected aloud, "I'm glad we risked our lives to get here, just to be in her presence."

When the singing had ended, William diffidently approached the group and said, "We have two new friends who just arrived here."

Before he could give an introduction, Lizzie saw Isaac. As she ran to him, all she could do was yell, in a voice full of indescribable joy, "Isaac! Isaac! God brought you back to me!"

They embraced joyfully. The other singers clapped their hands in applause as Lizzie and Isaac embraced one another.

Then Isaac introduced Lizzie to his "conductor", Johnny Sullivan. All he said after introducing him was, "When I tell you the whole story, you will know what a friend he's been to me…to us."

Johnny, who knew something about white man's manners, gently took her right hand in his and said, "Pleased to meet you, ma'am," tipping his head forward in a slight, courtly bow as he did so.

Isaac and Johnny, soiled from their journey, asked if they could bathe before turning in for the night. William obliged them—he intended to offer that anyway but was pleased that they had asked first. When they had cleaned up, he showed them to their sleeping quarters, a room in another structure behind the big white house. Each had his own bed—a real bed with clean linen.

As Johnny lay down, waiting for his body to descend into a much-needed deep sleep, he thought to himself, "If this were my last day on earth, bringing Isaac here would have been the finest thing I ever did." Then, no longer under the surveillance of other men, Johnny let his tears flow freely, silently, as he lay on his back on this warm, comfortable bed, safe at last.

Part 3: Down the Ohio

Chapter 8: The Wedding

The next morning, Johnny and Isaac went into town to file Isaac's freedom papers. On their way back to the Quaker house, Isaac said, "Johnny, I want to marry Lizzie as soon as possible. When I do, will you be my best man?"

"I'd be honored, Isaac. But won't I have to wear a suit?"

"Of course. But don't worry about buying one. I'll buy yours and mine," Isaac said.

"It seems like a waste to do that," said Johnny, "since I doubt I'll have much use for it afterwards."

"You never know," said Isaac. "You might have a use for it, and besides, with a suit like that and a white man's haircut, you might even be able to persuade folks that you really are 'black Irish'." Isaac and Johnny both laughed. Isaac added, "Don't worry how you're gonna carry it around with you. You have two horses, now."

"I was gonna give that old gelding to you, Isaac."

"I won't be needin' it," Isaac replied. "And if I need a horse, I can buy one with the money I'll earn from my woodwork or from the money that Mr. MacDermott put in the bank for me."

"So, you think I should get a white man's haircut?" asked Johnny.

"It would make you less conspicuous," replied Isaac. "And besides, you're educated enough—probably more educated than the average white man—to make folks want to believe your story if bein' black Irish is the story you wanna tell."

Johnny paused, then said, "I'm gonna consider that. I'll accept the suit, then, with much gratitude. So, when do you s'pose this weddin's gonna happen?"

"I'm gonna talk to Mr. Johnson about that when we get back to the big house."

"I shoulda asked this before: Have you asked Lizzie about this yet?" Johnny inquired.

"Not yet. But do you think she's gonna say 'no'?"

Johnny realized that his question was absurd. "I just thought I'd ask."

Isaac said, "I'll talk to Mr. Johnson first. Then I'll ask Lizzie."

Johnny asked, "When y'all get married, is there gonna be some kind of written public record? Will my name be on it?"

Isaac said, "The purpose of a best man is to be a legal witness to the ceremony. He is supposed to sign his name somewhere, on some document. The preacher will know."

Johnny asked, "Remember yesterday when you asked me, 'What *is* your real name, anyway?'"

Isaac nodded.

Johnny continued, "Well, I'm not going to use my real name at your weddin' or on any documents I sign. If you're all right with it, I'd like to be 'Tommy Smith' on that day, at that ceremony."

Isaac said, "No one understands why that should be so better than I do. So, 'Tommy Smith', you will honor me by being the best man at our wedding?"

* * * * * * * * *

Isaac spoke to William Johnson later that day when they returned to the Quaker house. He gave his blessing, of course. He and Emma, his wife, began making plans for the ceremony, which would be held in the courtyard behind the house, where Johnny and Isaac had heard the people singing hymns the day they arrived. Since winter was approaching, there weren't any suitable decorative flowers available. But Emma Johnson and some of the Black ladies would hang brightly colored ribbons on the eaves of the big house over the back porch, where Lizzie and Isaac would exchange their vows. And they would make Lizzie a white cotton gown for the occasion.

William solicited a member of his congregation, who was a justice of the peace, to preside over the ceremony. The Quakers didn't have specialized priests or pastors. Theirs was as democratic a religion as ever existed. Everyone was a pastor of sorts or at least endeavored to be. A Quaker justice of the peace would do just fine.

The date was set for November 30, 1833.

That gave Johnny and Isaac two weeks to get their suits ready. The next day, they went into town to find a tailor. But not just any tailor. Though Pittsburg was a center for abolitionists, not all the white folks there were sympathetic to the cause, and indeed, there were many who harbored prejudice against Black people, whether they were "free" or not. However, it was common for some freemen to have acquired skills while in servitude, as had Isaac, for instance, who was a master woodworker.

The tailor they engaged was a Black man named Elijah Smith. He was so good at it that a lot of white folks engaged him as well, overlooking the fact that he was a Black man. He had a little shop at the edge of town, the town that would one day become the great city of Pittsburg.

Isaac and Johnny walked into his shop. Elijah was busy at his cutting table. He was a big, very dark man in his fifties with grizzled hair and a short, neatly trimmed beard. He looked up, stopped working, and greeted them. Isaac told him they needed two black suits for his upcoming wedding. Elijah offered his congratulations. Then he took Isaac's measurements, and after that, Johnny's. Elijah said he would have the suits ready by November 28, but that Isaac would have to pay for half now and the rest later. Isaac, who had already gone to the bank, had the necessary cash and handed it to Elijah. They shook hands.

Before they left, Isaac asked Elijah, "Is there someone around here who cuts hair? This here wild Indian wants to get a white man's haircut." He grinned.

Elijah told him about a young man named Caleb who had a little shop not far from there. He did odd jobs, repairing things that were broken. Elijah said, "Caleb can fix jus' about anything. And he cuts hair, too. He'll do right by you."

"Thank you, Elijah," said Johnny.

As they walked out the door, Johnny said to Isaac, "And by the way, I'll pay for my own haircut."

The prospect of cutting his long hair bothered Johnny, though he didn't know exactly why. Maybe it was because he had read the story of Samson and Delilah when he was in the missionary school. But upon reflection, he realized it would grow back, and in the meantime, as Isaac had suggested, he would be less conspicuous. He didn't plan to wear his turban anymore, not, at least, until he arrived in Indian Territory, if even then.

Sure enough, there was a Black man named Caleb, not far from Elijah's tailor shop, who cut hair. Caleb's name, like Elijah's, came from the Old Testament of the Holy Bible. Isaac and Johnny walked in and greeted him. He was about thirty, an inch taller than Johnny, slim but heavy-boned. Johnny couldn't put his finger on it, but there was something about Caleb that didn't seem too "biblical".

Isaac introduced himself and Johnny, and said, "This here big Indian is gonna be the best man at my wedding. He says he wants the kind of haircut that white men have—so he won't look like a 'wild' Indian, right Johnny?"

"That's right, Isaac." Looking at the barber, Johnny said, "I saw a likeness of Andrew Jackson in a newspaper. I want a haircut like him if you can do that kind."

Caleb swelled his chest up and declared, "I can give you any kind of haircut you want. As long as it don't involve scalpin'." He laughed.

Johnny wondered whether he should take offense, not so much because of what Caleb had just said, but because of something about the way he delivered it. He decided to accept the reference to scalping as a way of being "familiar", a token of what might have turned out to be a friendship. He said to Caleb, "You definitely wouldn't wanna do that. Scalpin' is a nasty business."

Caleb wondered, silently, how much this Johnny actually knew about "scalpin'".

Before this conversational theme could develop further and possibly give Caleb the creeps, Isaac changed the subject. "If you're available to cut hair right now, we'd be right grateful."

"Sure, I am," responded Caleb. He pulled out a tall chair. "Have a seat right here, and I'll make you look just like Andrew Jackson."

"That old sonofabitch," Johnny muttered under his breath as he lowered himself into the chair.

Caleb cut Johnny's hair and then handed him a mirror. Johnny was startled when he beheld his countenance. The man he saw in the mirror looked strange to him. With his new haircut, he looked like a dark-skinned, hazel-eyed white man. Maybe he really could pass for "black Irish".

Isaac, who seemed to be reading Johnny's mind, said, with a mirthful glint in his eye, "Yeah, but you still *black*!" They both laughed.

Caleb, however, did not seem to get the joke. He said, "He ain't black. He's Indian."

Johnny said, "To be specific, Caleb, I'm Cherokee—a Cherokee warrior." He went on, "But it won't serve me well to look like one—not in these parts."

Caleb said, "Well, you folks lost your wars already, so I don't know what difference being a Cherokee warrior would make at this point, anyway."

A shadow passed over Johnny's face. Caleb was starting to piss him off.

Isaac, who was growing concerned, said, "Caleb, don't mess with Johnny unless you wanna be next in line for one of *his* haircuts."

They laughed uneasily.

Johnny, satisfied with Caleb's artistry, stood up and gave him six bits.

Caleb protested: "It's four bits for the haircut."

Johnny replied, "The extra two bits are for your artistry. Thanks for givin' me this white man's haircut. And it was nice to meet you." It wasn't nice, really, other than the fine haircut. As he spoke these polite words, he glared briefly at Caleb, who was absent-mindedly fingering the straight razor he had used to finish Johnny's haircut. He wondered if Caleb had other uses for it…

****

The next day, Johnny approached William Johnson and asked if he knew where he might find some blacksmith work. William looked at him and marveled at the transformation wrought by Johnny's new "white man's" haircut. He declared, "Why, Johnny, you're starting to look like one of us!"

Johnny responded, "Do you think it'll help me find a job to keep me busy until spring?"

William said, "It might help you get a job, but of course, keeping a job is another matter."

"I wondered if you knew someone who needed some labor. If you're concerned that I won't be a reliable, hard worker, you needn't be. I'll never be late, and I'll earn my wages every day from the time I start 'til the time I go home."

William, who was middle-aged, had learned to be skeptical about the relationship between people's words and their actions. They did not always match. Thus, though he was a generous soul, he was not quick to bestow trust. Johnny had said the right things, but would his actions match his words? After a brief, thoughtful pause, he asked, "What kind of work can you do?"

Johnny replied, "I've done blacksmith work. I'm not a master smith, but I'm good at routine things like makin' horseshoes, plowshares, axe heads…things like that."

"How did you come to take up blacksmith work," asked William.

"I realized, when I was about ten years old, that in order for us—the Indians—to survive in the world that was sweepin' ours away, we'd have to learn the white man's 'medicine'. I figured that it was partly about understandin' the secrets of metal. So, becomin' a blacksmith seemed to be a logical thing for me to do at the time. I apprenticed with an Irishman named James O'Brian. He taught me a lot. Not just blacksmithin', but about life, about how there's an art in every activity we do if only we look for it."

William fingered his chin thoughtfully. Then he said, "I might know someone who needs your skills. Let me look into it, and I'll let you know. Meanwhile, you're welcome to continue to stay here. After all, you brought Lizzie her husband-to-be, braving who knows what dangers…"

Johnny said, "I don't wanna be a burden. I can pay for my keep. I have some money, and once I start working, I can pay and still save money for my journey."

William was intrigued by Johnny's talk of a "journey". He was inclined to inquire about it, but for the present, he simply asked, "When do you plan to embark on this journey of yours?"

Johnny responded, "When spring comes."

"Where will you go? That is if you don't mind my prying into your business…"

"No sir, I don't mind," said Johnny. "I plan to go down the Ohio River all the way to the Mississippi. From there, I'll go to Indian Territory to help my grandmother with her store."

That was what he hoped for, anyway. He wondered about his grandmother. Would she leave before she was forced to go? He hoped so.

* * * * * * * * *

Two days later, right after sunrise, William showed up at the door of Isaac and Johnny's quarters. He had a big smile on his face. "I have good news for both of you," he declared. "Isaac, a family in our congregation needs a dining table and six chairs to go with it. They are giving it to a young couple for Christmas. They are well-to-do and willing to buy the wood. And they will pay you fifty dollars for your labor. Can you do this and get it done before Christmas?"

Isaac, excited, said, "I'll have to buy some tools. But I have the funds."

William said, "That's nice, Isaac, but your client has most of what you'll need, and you can do your work at their farm, so you won't have to rent a space, at least not for this project."

Ecstatic, Isaac asked, "When can I start?"

William replied, "I'll take you there this afternoon to meet them. You can work out the details at that time."

He turned to Johnny. "I have an opportunity for you, too. There is a blacksmith who is getting so much work from people moving into this town that he needs a helper. I told him about you, and he's willing to take you on."

"Did you tell him I'd be leavin' come spring?" asked Johnny.

"Yes, I did, and though that concerned him, he needs help right now."

"Did you tell him that I am an Indian?"

William smiled and said, "I told him you were a 'civilized' Indian."

"Does that mean I can start right away?" Johnny asked.

"Yes," confirmed William. "He has a smithy near here, on the east end of town. I'll take you down to meet him first thing in the morning."

"Thank you, Mister Johnson," said Johnny, bowing his head slightly as he expressed his heartfelt gratitude.

After William left, Isaac and Johnny were jubilant. "We are so damned lucky!" exclaimed Johnny.

Isaac said, "Johnny, ain't I already told you there's no such thing as 'luck'? It's called 'blessin's'. When are you gonna stop thinkin' like a heathen and recognize God's grace?"

* * * * * * * * *

The next morning, William Johnson and Johnny went to meet Robert Franklin, the master smith for whom Johnny would work through the winter. When they arrived at the smithy, William and Robert shook hands cordially, followed by William's introduction of Johnny to Robert.

"Pleased to meet you, sir," said Johnny as he and Robert shook hands.

Robert Franklin had been a blacksmith since his youth and was now in his forties. It showed. He wasn't very tall—perhaps five feet, nine inches—but was stoutly built, with the massive forearms and hands that come from plying this trade for over twenty years. He was balding and had a short, neat beard. His brown hair and beard were both grizzled with grey. He had an aura of calm confidence. He got down to business at once, asking Johnny what he knew about the trade.

Johnny was appropriately deferential and modest. He said, "I apprenticed with an Irishman named James O'Brien from the time I was eleven 'til I was thirteen. Then, I went to Arkansas and worked part-time as a blacksmith there. I made horseshoes, plow shares, axe heads, and arrowheads…"

"Arrowheads?" queried Robert.

"Yes, sir."

"Why arrowheads?" persisted Robert.

Johnny looked furtively at William as if to ask, "How much of my past should I reveal?" But William just nodded to encourage him to go on.

Johnny replied, "In Arkansas, we hunted game and fought Osages with guns and also with bows and arrows. Bows and arrows are efficient, especially when the arrows have iron tips."

Robert looked at Johnny intensely. He asked, "Did you ever kill anyone in those fights with the Osages?"

Johnny answered truthfully. "Yes, sir. I did."

Robert wondered if he could trust this tall, strapping young man who had already taken at least one life, maybe more, in his own short life. At the same time, he found something admirable about his forthrightness and his calm candor in answering a question as invasive as the one he had just asked. He was curious about Johnny's green eyes. He asked, "You're part white, too, aren't you?"

Johnny answered, "Yes, I am. My grandfather was Irish, from the County Kerry in Ireland. My grandmother is a Cherokee. They ran a store a little east of Knoxville, Tennessee. I think Mister Johnson might have already told you that we were 'civilized' Indians…" He looked at William, who smiled and nodded for him to continue. "…and I went to a Presbyterian missionary school and learned to read, write, and cipher. I helped my grandmother run her store after my grandpa died. I did the bookwork to keep track of the inventory and sales."

"Tell me about how you go about doing your work," Robert asked.

"I'm always at work on time. I don't waste time while I'm at work. I have never stolen a paycheck in my life, and I don't ever plan to. My smithing master, James O'Brien, taught me that there is an art to everything human beings do if only one can find it. So, I always try to find it." He paused and then added—a bit sheepishly—"That doesn't mean I always succeed in findin' it. But I try."

Robert, impressed, continued to question Johnny. "Have you found art in blacksmithing?"

Johnny, again being truthful, replied, "I got real good at makin' plowshares and axe heads. I'm pretty good at horseshoes, too. When I am doin' jobs that are real repetitive, I focus on how many I can get done in a day. At the end of the day, when I see how much I got done, it makes me feel sort of satisfied. But when it comes to the finer parts of the blacksmith's craft, I must confess that I've not yet found the 'art' in those."

Robert knew he was going to hire Johnny. He didn't need a top craftsman for his business. He wanted someone who would be perfectly happy making plowshares, axe heads, horseshoes, and other things of use to farmers. He wanted someone with the requisite skills to make these things, someone who knew how to work and wanted to work, someone who respected his elders. Johnny seemed to fit the bill in all these respects.

Robert said, "Let me tell you how I run this business, Johnny. I've been here in Pittsburg for going on ten years. I started off with a little shop next to a stable and made a lot of horseshoes…Lots and lots of horseshoes." He smiled sardonically and looked knowingly at William.

William said, "I remember."

"Then I started getting more and more business making plowshares and other things as well. I focused on finding the 'art'—as your Mr. O'Brien called it—in all things blacksmithing. But I found another 'art' as well. I kept records of how many horseshoes, plowshares, and the rest that I sold each month. I've been keeping those records for nearly ten years." He paused, then asked, "Do you know what the word 'average' means, Johnny?"

Johnny replied, "The word 'average' can mean a lot of things. But if you're talkin' mathematical averages, it means addin' up a bunch o' numbers and then dividin' by the number of the numbers that are in the sum. So, if you add eight numbers and want to know the average value, you divide the sum by eight."

Robert, who was quite familiar with the abysmal lack of even this level of mathematical competence in the general population, was impressed. He continued, "Good, Johnny. So, with those averages, I can predict with pretty good—not perfect—but pretty good accuracy how many plowshares, shovel heads, and so on I will sell in March, April, and May.

"I only make the best quality in each of these kinds of things. I've got a name because of it. So, I work hard all winter making them, according to how many of each product I'll probably sell. And when spring comes, I sell most or all of them. If I see that the sales in March are higher than I predicted, I work my a—..." He stopped himself, not wanting to offend the Quaker gentleman, William Johnson, who was still present, with even a mild display of profanity. He cleared his throat and continued, "I work very hard to make sure that I'll have enough inventory for April. If I make too much...well, iron and steel don't spoil, so to speak. I can always sell 'em later.

"The advantage I have over other blacksmiths—not all, but most—is that customers don't have to wait to get what they need. And I always sell for about the same price. I don't gouge people when things are scarce. For these reasons, my customers speak well of me to other people, and that draws more business. So, the business has grown, and for the past two years, I've hardly had a day off. That's why I need help nowadays."

Robert didn't mention it, though Johnny would find out in due course, but he had no sons. He had two daughters, who were both married to men who were already situated in life and had neither the interest nor the need to work as a blacksmith's assistant. He had a nephew who had worked for him until recently, but he was unreliable, not interested in the job—or perhaps in working at all—and so, after much frustration and disappointment, Robert had let him go. Johnny would eventually learn that he was this nephew's replacement.

Robert concluded his soliloquy by making Johnny an offer. "If you come to work here, here's the deal. You can stay here—I have a small room attached to this shop—and you can take your meals with me and my wife, Jennie. I'll take ten cents for each meal you have with us. I won't charge rent for the room, but I'll expect you to keep it tidy and clean. In addition to that, I'll pay you two bits an hour for your work. You'll work about eight hours a day, Monday through Friday. So, I'll pay you ten dollars a week. I'll pay you half of what you make until the end of winter, and I'll clear the rest of my debt to you when you leave—I understand you'll be leaving us—in the spring. Is that acceptable to you?"

Johnny did the math in his head: Four weeks in a month is twenty days, twenty-five cents an hour times eight hours is $2 a day, $10 a week, and about $40 a month. He would spend about $8 a month on meals from the Franklins. Stable fees for his two horses would come to about $12 a month. By the time he was ready to leave, he would have made about $80 net—$20 a month times four, all of which would be payable at the time of his departure. He still had almost all the $40 given to him by his grandmother. He planned to buy a pack saddle for the gelding, which would cost him less than $5. He could resume his journey with about $100 in his pockets. More than enough, he reckoned, to get him to Indian Territory or to wherever Uncle Dutch might be by that time.

Johnny thought to himself, "That's pretty damned good money!" Upon concluding this, Johnny exclaimed, "That is more than acceptable to me, sir! When can we start?"

Robert replied, "How about tomorrow morning?"

"What time shall I be here?" Johnny asked.

"Can you be here by sunrise?"

"I'll be here," Johnny replied. Then he said, "I am going to be the best man for my friend's wedding on November 30. I have to pick up a suit on November 28, which would be, I think, a Thursday. Is it all right if I take the last half of that day off? I'll make it up to you."

"Thanks for letting me know. Marriage is a sacred thing. Of course, you can."

Johnny showed up at Robert Franklin's smithy at sunrise the next day.

* * * * * * * * *

On November 28, Johnny and Isaac went to Elijah's tailor shop and picked up their suits, shirts, and neckties. Johnny had some black boots that he had brought from his grandmother's store. They were brand new. Isaac had to buy some boots to match his suit. He was able to afford them without raiding his bank account because of the earnings from his project, which was almost complete. He expected to finish well before Christmas.

Two days later, Isaac and Lizzie were wed on the back porch of the Quaker house. In attendance were the Black folks who were staying in the quarters behind the big house, half a dozen members of the Quaker congregation, and, of course, Emma and William Johnson. After the vows were taken, Lizzie sang a song, accompanied by the free men and women who lived there. As she sang, Johnny felt the same mysterious feeling, somewhere between his heart and his stomach, that he had experienced the night he and Isaac had arrived a month before. Something about Lizzie's voice, its vibrato, and the passion that drove it moved him to the verge of tears. Not tears of sorrow, not tears of joy…something deeper. He could not understand what it was, but whatever it was, it was tangible, powerful, majestic.

Afterwards, the justice of the peace asked Johnny to sign his name as a witness to the wedding. He signed it "Tommy Smith". The justice of the peace knit his brows, looked up at Johnny, and remarked, "I thought your name was 'Johnny'."

Johnny said, "It's actually 'John Thomas'. So sometimes I go by 'Johnny', and sometimes I go by 'Tommy'. I'd tell you more, but it's a long, kinda complicated story." Johnny smiled.

The justice of the peace seemed satisfied. Then he signed his name to the document, folded it up, placed it in his coat pocket, and said, "That's fine."

After the wedding, there was a banquet—courtesy of William Johnson—in a large room in the big house. The Quakers and the free men and women sat at different tables. At the Quaker table, one of the ladies looked admiringly at Johnny and asked Emma, William's wife, "Who is that dark, handsome young man standing up for Isaac and Lizzie?"

Emma answered, "He is rather mysterious. We don't know much about him at all, except that he is a diligent worker and that he has befriended the groom. They say he is a Cherokee. But he's part Irish, too. Isaac and Lizzie have said that without him, Isaac would not have made it here alive."

The justice of the peace silently agreed that Johnny, or Tommy, or whatever his name was, was mysterious, indeed. Not wanting to make an issue of it or contribute to idle gossip, he kept his silence. In the privacy of his thoughts, he surmised that "Tommy Smith" was on the run from something. But whatever it was, he had served a higher purpose in bringing Isaac safely here and making this day of joy possible. He didn't waste any more time considering who this young man was or what, if anything, he might be running from.

He changed the focus of the conversation: "Mrs. Johnson, will you pass the gravy, please?"

Chapter 9: The Departure

Lizzie moved into the quarters that had been shared by Isaac and Johnny. Johnny's new residence was just a few minutes' ride from the Quaker house. He visited Isaac and Lizzie on weekends. By Christmas, Lizzie knew everything that Isaac knew about the biography of Johnny White Owl Sullivan.

* * * * * * * * *

Down in Georgia, on the day that Isaac and Lizzie were wed, David MacDermott sat down in a big chair in his smoking salon, wondering what the hell had happened to Buck Dinsmore and his little crew of slavecatchers. They had been gone for two months, and he hadn't heard a word from them. He did not know whether their mission had been a success or a failure. The good news was that they hadn't come back to claim their $300. The bad news was that the gelding he had provided—the one that would have brought Isaac back to the plantation—was gone as well.

Had they caught Isaac and turned around and sold him for a higher price? Or had something bad happened to them? He didn't really care. They were just riffraff to him, instruments he needed to carry out his purpose at the time.

As he sat there, puffing on his briar pipe, he had a fleeting moment in which he acknowledged that Isaac, whatever else he may have been, was his half-brother. Somewhere in that cold, self-absorbed heart of his was a spark of compassion. He decided that he could afford the loss of a gelding that was over ten years of age. For a few seconds, he hoped that if Isaac had made his way to the North, he would be fine. And then he decided to let go of the matter.

He knocked the ashes out of his pipe and walked out to the workshop where Isaac had learned to work his magic with wood. There were three young men refinishing a maple dining table. The most able one was named Joseph. David asked him to step outside the workshop for a private conversation. Then he asked him, "How much did Isaac teach you about this business, Joseph?"

Joseph said, "I can do almost anything Isaac could do. I'm not as fast as him, but I can learn to be."

David said, "Well, Joseph, that would be a good thing. And if you attain Isaac's mastery, maybe we can arrange for you to buy your freedom someday."

Joseph, filled with hope, said, "I'd be very grateful, Massa David."

When David left the workshop, Joseph thought, "I hope he's more honest about this deal than he was about the one his pa made with Isaac."

And then he sent up a solemn, silent prayer that Isaac had made his way to freedom.

* * * * * * * *

Winter came and went. Johnny bought a pack saddle for his gelding, which he would use as a pack horse while he rode Flower. He buried the gelding's original saddle in the woods.

The snow began to melt in March. Johnny, who had just turned twenty, gave notice to Robert Franklin and thanked him for the opportunity he had been given.

The day before he planned to leave, he went to the Quaker house to have dinner with Isaac and Lizzie. When he entered their humble but clean and well-organized quarters, he couldn't help but notice that there were three chairs. And a table covered with a pink tablecloth. Upon seeing it, his heart jumped into his throat. Then he looked lovingly at Lizzie and said, "Isaac told you about my first love, didn't he?"

Lizzie smiled benignly. "Have a seat, Mr. Tenkiller."

"You know you can't tell anyone else about that, don't you, ma'am?"

"Of course. Now, try some of my chicken!" demanded Lizzie.

As they dined, Isaac spoke words of hope for his business and for the child that would be born in the late summer or early fall of that year, for Lizzie was now pregnant, though it didn't show yet. Johnny asked, "What will you name the child?"

Isaac said, "If it's a boy, we're gonna name him Johnny."

Johnny blushed. "And if it's a girl?"

"If it's a girl, we're gonna name her Ahyoka," interjected Lizzie.

Johnny struggled to keep his composure. Then he said, "I'm deeply honored, Mr. and Mrs. MacDermott. If it is a girl, I hope she lives into her name, for in Cherokee, it means something like 'She brought happiness'. And if it's a boy, I hope he has a different life from mine."

"Why would you say that, Johnny?" asked Isaac.

Johnny thought for a moment. He didn't even know why he had blurted these words. Then he admitted, "I don't know why I said that. But as I think on it, I feel like I'm on a canoe that's bein' carried on its way by a strong river current, a current that I didn't create and that I can't control. It's takin' me somewhere, but I don't know where. I don't know what I'm supposed to do when I get to wherever that is."

He stopped speaking, gathering his thoughts. "When I had a clear purpose—like the one I had with the Stricklin boys—I didn't think about anything but preparin' for that. Killin' those two Osage warriors was just part of that journey. And to be honest, I never really felt good about killin' 'em. But after I dealt with the Stricklins, when I was on my way to Wohali's Hamlet, I'd never felt more complete in my whole life. Then, when I left Wohali and Ahyoka, I felt empty. Like a hollow gourd. My life had no meanin' until I found you by that creek, Isaac." He paused again, and added, "You gave me a reason to go on livin'…"

Lizzie interrupted Johnny. "Well, we're glad you *did* go on livin'. And a child will one day bear your name or the name of your two Ahyokas. Wherever you go, whatever you do, you'll have left a legacy behind you."

Johnny, feeling a bit embarrassed and wanting to change the subject, declared, "If I was a drinkin' man, I'd toast to your future right now: To the MacDermotts of Pittsburg!" he shouted, holding an invisible glass and raising it in salutation. Isaac and Lizzie, pretending to have their own glasses, feigned their rejoinders to Johnny's toast as Isaac declared, "Hear! Hear!"

Johnny stayed the night in a spare room in the Quaker house. The next morning, as he made final preparations for his journey, William Johnson emerged from the front door of the big house, wearing his characteristic benign, calm smile. "I don't know where you're going, Johnny—or Tommy or whatever your name really is—but I wanted to say a prayer for you before you left. I won't speak it aloud but come and join hands with me, if you will."

Johnny complied. They stood in silence for what seemed like several minutes. Johnny experienced something like a glow of white light passing through his body. It made him feel a comfort he hadn't felt since he headed north to Wohali's hamlet after having fulfilled his purpose with the Stricklins. When William released his hands, Johnny felt as if he were in a trance. He asked, "Sir, may I ask what you prayed for?"

William said, "I prayed that you would find your truth and, through that, attain a state of permanent grace."

"May I ask what you meant by finding my 'truth'?" asked Johnny.

William answered Johnny's question with one of his own: "What would you say your truth is right now?"

Johnny, overcome with a need to disclose his current "truth," said, "Mr. Johnson, other than my grandpa, the Presbyterian missionaries, and the Irishman who taught me blacksmithing, and until I met you and these good Quaker folks, I thought that my 'truth' was to kill white men. Not good ones like you. Just the bad ones that needed killin'. Now I've come to a different point of view. You Quakers call yourselves the 'Society of Friends'. And you really are that—friends. I wish the whole human race was like you folks."

"Johnny," William said, "if everyone treated everyone they met as if they were an old friend, there would be no more wars. And most of the world's problems would go away. Remember that. And if you can, imagine it to be so."

Johnny smiled and replied, "If I approached the Comanches in Texas that way, they'd carve me up and eat my liver." But then, realizing that his effort at humor had been poorly placed, he added, "But, I do hope that someday, we can all be that way." The words came tumbling out of his mouth, seemingly involuntarily. At that moment, he meant them.

William commented, "The words you just spoke, and the feeling behind them, came from the voice of the soul that abides within you. When you're alone, when all is quiet, have conversations with that voice. It's a faint voice, easily drowned out by the noise of the world we live in. But if you heed it, it will teach you. In time, through it, you will find your truth...whatever that may turn out to be."

Johnny, his mind overloaded with the wisdom William had just shared, and his heart overcome with gratitude, said, "Mr. Johnson, thank you for everything you've done for me, for Isaac, and for Lizzie. And thank you for the wise words you just spoke. It may take me a long time to figure out their meaning. But I won't forget 'em. May God bless you and your family richly, sir."

William replied, "And may He bless you too, Johnny."

Johnny went to Isaac's and Lizzie's quarters to say goodbye. Lizzie, whose eyes were wet with tears, came outside to silently hug Johnny goodbye, then went back inside, leaving the two young men alone to say their farewells.

Isaac said, "Since we can both read and write, I was hoping we could stay in correspondence when you get to wherever you're going. You can send your letters to this house, care of Mr. Johnson. I have no idea where to send letters to you, but when you have some place I can send a letter to, you can inform me. And I hope you will. I don't want us to lose touch. You're forever woven into the fabric of our lives."

"Did I ever tell you how I much liked it when you talk like a scholar, Isaac?" asked Johnny in a vain attempt to defuse the powerful emotions that pervaded the moment...the last moment they would likely ever see one another. Then he asked, "Do you think you'll have a good life here? Will the white folks even let you have a good life? I'm sorry if I sound like someone without faith, but other than those Quakers, the two Irishmen in my youth, the Presbyterians, and Mr. Franklin, I don't trust white men much."

"Seems like the list of white men you *don't* want to kill is gettin' longer, Johnny," said Isaac, with a subtle, knowing smile. "Now, listen here. I'm gonna tell you what I really think, and I won't bury too much of it under bible talk. When a man has been a slave, once he is free, nothin'—nothin'!—is better than that. Rich or poor, bein' free is wealth unto itself. All those things I have said in the past about faith and its great power were things that I meant. And havin' you come along when you did just confirms my feelin's about faith. I'd have surely died and never made it here if you had not shown up when you did. Or I would have been caught by those men you killed and taken back to Georgia. God only knows if I would have ever gotten away from there...I would not be here right now. That's for sure.

"Now, to address the realities of the moment, I don't expect to be treated with the same regard by white men—most of them—as they treat each other. And I expect to deal with things that aren't very...pretty. But I'll always do the best I can at whatever I do. I'll be generous in my dealings with other human beings, be they Black, white, or Indian. If things fall apart, I'll just pray and put them back together the best I can. I'll do my best to educate my children. I'll teach them the virtues of hard work, respect, and knowing when to keep their mouths shut, even if they have a burnin' desire to show their anger. The present state of the world is the result of laws that God created, though we can't always see the 'justice' in those results from where we stand. But with grace, we can accept what the world brings our way, the bad along with the good, and hope that one day, things will be better and that there will be more justice, more kindness, and more love in this world.

"For my part, even if I do prosper, I'll live simply and avoid drawin' attention to myself. I'll save my money and invest it if I have enough left over to do that. I'll buy Lizzie new dresses and shoes from time to time. My children will be dressed in good but simple clothes. They'll go to church on Sundays. God willin', they'll always have enough good food to eat. And I will thank God every day for His blessin's." He paused and looked Johnny in the eye. "How can I go wrong with that philosophy?"

Johnny had nothing to say. He wanted to say that Isaac had found his "truth" but didn't feel as if he had sufficient wisdom to say something like that and mean it. But at some level, in his heart, he knew that Isaac had indeed found his truth. And he was happy for him.

The two young men stood in silence, facing one another but looking at the ground, not knowing what else to say, not wanting to say "Farewell". Though they had known each other for only half a year, it seemed to have been much longer than that, like half a lifetime.

Suddenly, Isaac said, "Hang on, Johnny, I'll be right back," and went inside. In a short moment, he came out with a neatly folded pink cloth. "Lizzie wanted me to give you this before you left. When you wind up somewhere you might call 'home' and use this, you can remember us—and your Ahyoka. It will add a little softness, a little beauty to your life. And perhaps this tablecloth will bring you happiness, as your two Ahyokas brought you happiness, and as you've brought us happiness."

Johnny couldn't bring himself to say "Goodbye". Instead, he put the gift in one of the saddlebags on the old gelding. He turned and said, "I promise to write you when I get to wherever it is that I'm gonna go."

Then the two friends stood in silence, each of them looking at the ground again, another one of those silences that stand on behalf of a thousand unspoken words.

Johnny climbed into his saddle, briefly looked at his friend with kindness in his eyes, turned towards the road, and silently waved his hand as he, Flower, and the gelding rode away towards the confluence of the two rivers that flowed into the Ohio.

Chapter 10: Cave-in-Rock

Johnny had worked through the winter for the blacksmith Robert Franklin. Robert was not related, as far as he knew, to Benjamin Franklin. But like the other Franklin, Robert was eminently practical. Knowing he would make his money back in the spring, he bought iron and other materials in sufficient quantities to produce inventories for sale. He made a deal with the proprietor who owned the building containing Robert's shop to catch up with the rent for the months of December through March when April came around. Of course, Robert had to pay a nominal interest rate on the forbearance of his rent.

During those months, Robert and Johnny produced an inventory of the essential things that farmers would need when spring came. Robert had made a deal with Johnny, giving him a room through the winter, with the expectation that he would pay him his back wages when spring came. Johnny would pay for his board and the stable fees for his horses as he went, since Robert paid him half of his wages every week during the winter months. In late February of 1834, Robert's business began to pick up dramatically. The fact that he was one of the few smiths in town who even built up an inventory gave him an advantage, and he prospered. When he realized that he would be able to easily catch up on his rent by April, he paid Johnny his back wages: One hundred dollars.

Johnny, who had already been paid $80—half of his total earnings—was surprised. He remarked, "Mr. Franklin, you only owe me eighty dollars." He would not accept the money.

Robert replied, "The first three days after I put our products out for sale, I made enough to pay you your back wages, plus part of my back rent, plus some profit for me. Besides, your housing didn't cost me anything extra, and you did damned good work. So, just take the money. You earned it. And just as I pay interest to the landlord for deferring my rent, I'm paying a little interest to you, too, Johnny."

Johnny, finally taking the money, couldn't help but make a comment. He said, "That's a lot of interest, Mr. Franklin. You didn't have to."

"I know I didn't have to," replied Robert. "But you worked hard for it, it is the right thing to do, and I can afford it. Wouldn't you do the same if you were in my place?"

Johnny, who had never been in Robert Franklin's place, said, "I think I would, come to think of it."

Then he changed the subject. "You know, Johnny, you could just stay here if you wanted. I'm in my forties right now and wouldn't be able to do all this work without help. I have two daughters and no sons. I would never have expected the girls to do this kind of work anyway. They married well, and their husbands already have trades. I have no one to help run the business when I get old—and that's just around the corner. And the kind of help you provide is rare. We could be partners someday. We could share in the profits of this business. You could stay here and be close to your friend, Isaac. You could have a life, Johnny. A life!"

Johnny stood for a moment in silence. He wondered if Robert meant by "a life" the same thing as finding his "truth". He reflected on Robert's words and, more importantly, on Robert's actions throughout the time they had known each other, including his present display of generosity. This was a good man...a good *white* man. He thought about his grandfather, about James O'Brien, about the Presbyterian missionaries who had educated him, about William Johnson, and now, about the decent man standing before him. His general distrust of white men was melting away like the remnants of the snow when winter gives way to spring. He even wondered if he could remain committed to the idea of killing the ones who needed it.

"Mister Franklin," he began, "I'm real moved by your kindness, sir. I'd like to think that if I ever needed to come back here, I could at least count you as a friend. But it's not likely that I ever will. I have a journey that leads elsewhere. And though I wonder if I'll ever regret this decision, I must, with great respect and gratitude, decline your generous offer. All I can do is offer my sincere thanks to you for the way you treated me while I was here and for the generous offer you just made as I was leavin'. May you prosper greatly, sir." He extended his hand to shake with Robert. Robert reciprocated, shaking his head sadly as he did so. He believed that

Johnny might live to regret having passed up this opportunity. Silently, Johnny wondered the same thing.

* * * * * * * * *

Pittsburg sat at the confluence of three rivers: the Ohio and its tributaries, the Monongahela and the Alleghany. Its existence began with the construction of Fort Pitt in 1758, during the French and Indian War. A town had quickly grown up around it. One of the industries in Pittsburg, beginning in the late 1700s, was the building and launching of flatboats. These vessels, which varied from sixteen feet to twenty feet in width and from twenty to one hundred feet in length, were built of wood, usually maple or pine, had flat bottoms, and carried both trade goods and settlers from the East to the expanding western regions of the new country known as the United States of America.

Building the flatboats was typically financed by the farmers or merchants who either planned to move to the virgin (and cheaply gotten) lands of the west or who wanted to transport their agricultural products down to the Mississippi, some going as far as New Orleans with their cargo. In addition to the expenses of getting the lumber and the labor to build their boats, these entrepreneurs would pay a crew of boatmen—typically, four to seven in number—and a pilot to navigate them down the Ohio River. Johnny hoped to travel on one of these flatboats down the Ohio to the Mississippi.

He arrived at the confluence of the rivers in the early afternoon of the day he left the Quaker house. There were a couple of finished flatboats and several under construction, in various stages of completion. There was one that looked large enough to accommodate a couple of covered wagons and several horses. It looked like it was finished.

Johnny approached the man who appeared to be in charge of the work on this boat. He asked him, "Do y'all have room for another passenger with a couple of horses?"

The boss, a big, burly bearded man in his forties, asked, "Who wants to know?"

Johnny replied, "I do. And I can pay my way. I know about how much it costs to build one of these things and am willing to pay for a third of that—that is if you're goin' all the way to the Mississippi. Are you?"

"That's where we're going," said the burly white man. "So, you have about thirty dollars to spend?" he asked.

"I thought it would be more like twenty-five," replied Johnny. "I'll throw in another twenty-five for food for me 'n' my horses and for part of the crew's wages. And besides, I can help with steering and poling the boat, if necessary. And I can help protect the passengers from pirates if that turns out to be necessary."

"Ever since those scoundrels at Cave-in-Rock were cleared out, there isn't too much of that left," said the burly white man.

"Not too much?" asked Johnny. "So, that means there may still be some left, doesn't it?"

The burly white man, whose name turned out to be "Jones," thought for a moment, looked at the long rifle on Flower's saddle, and asked, "Do you know how to use that thing?"

Johnny said, "I know how to 'use' lots of things, including my Tennessee carbine. Please don't call her a 'thing', or her feelin's might get hurt." Johnny looked Jones straight in the eye unflinchingly and quickly broke a smile so that Jones would recognize the attitude of congeniality behind his comment. "So, will you take a payin' passenger along?"

"Show me the money," demanded Jones.

Johnny pulled out twenty-five dollars and showed it to Jones.

Jones said, "I said thirty dollars."

Johnny said, "I'll give you twenty-seven fifty and twenty-five for the rest. And if that ain't enough, I'll work off the difference and then some."

Jones, who was the principal financier of this flatboat, said, "All right. Twenty-seven fifty it is." He was happy, no doubt, to recover part of his investment in advance.

Johnny handed Jones twenty-five dollars. Jones looked at him quizzically. Johnny said, "I'll give the rest of the money before we leave tomorrow. I don't have two dollars and fifty cents on me right now. When are y'all embarkin'?"

"Tomorrow, first thing in the morning," said Jones.

Jones, feeling a bit annoyed at something about this young man that he couldn't quite identify, said, "We'll pack at sun-up. That'll take a couple of hours. You should come at sun-up, too. Don't be late."

Johnny went to a hotel and checked into a room. He paid extra to stable his two horses.

The next morning, he awoke at first light, as always. He saddled Flower and the gelding and went down to the embarking site, where he found Jones and paid him the rest of the money. It took a couple of hours to load the boat. There was a covered wagon, two horses, and two cows in addition to Johnny's two horses. Jones planned to buy another covered wagon and a couple of horses in St. Louis.

The boat was half covered by a rectangular wooden structure—it resembled a log cabin—where the passengers and boatmen could sleep and store their personal effects. The structure had no windows, but it had slits in the walls large enough to accommodate rifle barrels in the event they were attacked by Indians or pirates. It was like a floating fort.

The passengers included Jones, his wife, two sons in their late teens, two nephews in their early twenties, one of whom was married with a five-year-old daughter, three boatmen, and a pilot. It was expected that the young men would help with steering the unwieldy craft. It was ninety feet long and about twenty feet wide. Jones and his two nephews had pooled their resources to finance the construction of the flatboat. Jones, who paid for two-thirds of the boat, had gotten half of his money back from Johnny's fare, so the truth was that he was happy to take Johnny and his horses along.

There would be thirteen people on this voyage, including Johnny.

They left mid-morning, riding the spring melt down the Ohio River. Johnny, who had not done this kind of work before, was instructed by one of the experienced boatmen as to how to use a long pole to steer the boat, typically to avoid running aground on the accumulated debris that washed down the river during the spring, or else to maximize the alignment between the boat and the current that propelled it down the river. For the first week, he was quite sore in muscles he didn't even know he had. But eventually, he became accustomed to the brutish efforts needed from the boatmen.

* * * * * * * * *

The Jones party stopped in Cincinnati and changed crews. The original crew would have to walk back to Pittsburg. Jones replenished some of their supplies there, and they all walked around to enjoy the solidity of dry ground. After a day, Jones recruited a new crew, and his party resumed its journey.

Their next stop was a place called Shawneetown in southern Illinois. Once again, they replenished some of their supplies. Since the crew members had to walk back to Cincinnati, where they had been the replacements for the original crew from Pittsburg, they also disembarked in Shawneetown. Jones would once again have to hire a new crew before resuming the journey.

Johnny, who had heard of a place called Cave-In-Rock, about half a day's journey downriver from Shawneetown, suggested that, since he, Jones' two nephews, and his boys had learned the basics of navigating a flatboat by now, maybe when they replaced the crew, they should hire at least one who could double as a gunman. Jones asked why.

Johnny said, "As long as there's even a chance of pirates down there, shouldn't we just be on the safe side?" Cave-in-Rock had long been the abode of pirates and other criminals. Though the piracy problem had apparently been "mostly" resolved, Johnny didn't like "mostly". All it would take was one group of criminals to see what appeared to be some pilgrims on their way to the promised land, families who were more apt to farm than to fight. Easy prey.

But Jones didn't feel the need to bring on a gunman. So, they just replaced the crew, this time with only two crew and one pilot, and moved on. By this time, Johnny and the other young men had learned enough to effectively control the flatboat under the supervision of the two more experienced crew members and the pilot.

Up to this point, Johnny had avoided all conversation except for greetings in the morning. Not that he had much choice. These folks were all either blood or related by marriage and were rather clannish. Johnny didn't care. He was learning to do boatman work, which was as much a matter of brute strength and endurance as skill. He could feel the strength building in the muscles he didn't know he had before he took this trip. And he had much time to think—that is, when his mind wasn't numbed by the strenuous work of managing the boat's path downriver. But something about this region gave him the creeps. Johnny had heard stories from Robert Franklin about the heyday of Cave-in-Rock, and none of them was pretty.

It was mid-afternoon when they passed the old pirates' lair. The pilot had directed the crew to steer the boat to the middle of the river before passing this den of ill repute. Off to their right, they could see several very rough-looking men at the mouth of the cave, which opened out at the river's edge. They were burning a fire and drinking. Most likely, they were drinking whiskey because they were talking loudly. A couple of them were engaged in a fight, wrestling on the ground in front of a group of excited, grubby ruffians. Some of them looked menacingly at the Jones flatboat as it passed.

About an hour later, a keelboat appeared a few hundred yards behind. Jones had a spy glass and observed them. "How many?" asked Johnny.

"Looks like twelve," replied Jones, who seemed to be checking his count to be sure. "Yep, there's twelve of 'em."

"Is it possible that we can turn the boat so that the cabin faces them? This will protect our animals in case there's shootin'," suggested Johnny.

"Is that what you're expecting?" Jones asked.

"That is the worst thing I'd expect, other than them actually boardin' this craft," Johnny answered. "We need to be ready to kill them sons o' bitches. They bear us ill will. I can feel it."

Jones, surprised but not put off by Johnny's insistence, directed the pilot and his crew, which now included his two nephews and sons, to turn the boat so that the fortified section would face the oncoming keelboat, which was steadily approaching.

"Are you fellas good shots?" asked Johnny.

"We're all passable, except for my nephew, Josiah. He's real good," replied Jones. Josiah was the brother of the married nephew, whose wife and little girl were onboard.

"Well, I fear that today he'll have to use his talent. Them comin' yonder are pure scum." Johnny paused menacingly. He was entering his black tunnel. He stared at the oncoming keelboat, his green eyes icy with murderous intent. He said, in a deep voice that seemed to emanate from the depths of Hell, "Them sonofabitches need killin'."

He checked his rifle to ensure that it was ready for battle. The powder was dry, and it was ready. He also strung his bow.

"Where did you get that bow, anyway?" asked Jones, who had obviously seen it before but had not made so much as a comment about it.

"It was a gift from an old Indian out in Texas," said Johnny. "I use it to hunt deer."

Jones, knitting his brows and showing more expression than Johnny had ever seen in him, asked, "Is that where you're from? What were you doing in Pittsburg?"

"Yes, Mr. Jones, I'm from Texas. As to why I was in Pittsburg, well…that's a long story. Right now, though, I am headin' back to Texas. My grandmother is there, and I want to help her run her store."

Johnny hoped his grandmother was there. He actually had no idea. He wasn't even sure where she would be if she did move to the west. It would likely be somewhere in Indian Territory, not Texas. But Jones didn't need to know that…

Jones wanted to ask more questions. Was this Johnny an Indian? He looked Indian, but he had light eyes and was well-groomed, wearing white man's clothes and sporting a white man's haircut.

Before he could launch this line of inquiry, Johnny said, "Let's get our weapons ready and get the ladies and young ones inside. I suggest we get Josiah ready for a skirmish. And I suggest that the boys and your other nephew load their rifles and stand by in case things get real bad and these varmints get in a position to board this boat."

Jones called his nephew Josiah to come over to speak with them. When Josiah arrived, Jones said, "Get your rifle and make sure it's ready to use. Johnny here thinks these fellows in the keelboat have evil intentions. I agree. I don't like the looks of 'em."

Josiah got his rifle and checked its readiness. He could feel his heart pounding with a mixture of fear and anticipation. Meanwhile, the pilot and crew had turned the boat halfway around. Because of its flat bottom, turning it did not dampen its speed by much. After a few minutes, the front of the flatboat faced the oncoming keelboat, which had come to within less than fifty yards of them. It was coming fast. Jones hollered out to them, "Turn around and go back where you came from!"

One of the men on the boat hollered back, "Why don't you just pull that boat of yours over to the side of the river? There's a beach about a quarter mile downstream! We don't mean you no harm!" Some of the men on the keelboat sniggered. Meanwhile, the distance between the keelboat and Jones's flatboat was closing fast.

Johnny got involved. He shouted, "Do we look that goddamned stupid? Come closer, assholes! I need some target practice!"

"Everybody should go inside now," suggested Johnny. He got no argument from Jones, who quickly ushered his family inside the structure.

"Josiah, how about if you and I take our positions inside?" suggested Johnny. "As soon as they cut about half the distance between us and where they are now, it'll be time to start shootin' those mangy dogs."

Josiah and Johnny went inside and placed the heads of their rifle barrels through the holes that had been designed for just this purpose. The keelboat drew nearer.

"Josiah, see the fella at the back of the boat with the steering oar?" asked Johnny.

"Yes," replied Josiah.

"Will you shoot him, please?" asked Johnny.

Josiah's face turned pale. He said, "I've never shot a man in my life."

"Let me help you out here, Josiah. If those balls of pond scum board this craft, they'll kill us, have their ways with the ladies here, and maybe even your little niece. If that happens—and it is likely—you would curse the day of your birth. That is, if you were still alive, which is unlikely."

Without saying another word, Josiah aimed at the steersman through the gunhole. He fired his gun. The steersman was hit in the shoulder. Most likely, he would suffer from that wound and remember it vividly in his old age, especially in the winter, but the shot did not kill him. Meanwhile, another man had to take his place to keep the keelboat on course.

Johnny took aim at one of the men in the front of the keelboat. He pulled the trigger. He hit the man in the head. "Number Nine," muttered Johnny, sure that he had ended that man's life.

"What does 'Number Nine' mean?" asked Josiah.

"Nothing," replied Johnny. "It's just a private joke between me and my best friend in Texas," Johnny said as he reloaded his rifle.

Half the remaining men in the keelboat fired on the Jones craft. Their bullets lodged in the wooden walls of the structure, near enough to the gun slots to indicate that they were fair shots. The keelboat was now about fifty feet away. Two of the men lifted Johnny's victim, who was clearly dead, and threw his body into the river. The others were hastily reloading their rifles. Johnny said to Josiah, "Just aim to hit, not necessarily to kill, though you should do that, too, if you get a clear shot." He paused and aimed his rifle. "See that idiot with his hand over the rail of the keelboat?" he asked.

"Yes," responded Josiah.

"Well, he's fixin' to lose a couple of fingers. Watch!" Then Johnny fired. The man whose hand had been over the rail screamed in pain as he drew his mutilated hand to his chest. "Good, that's three that have been taken out of action," averred Johnny. "I hope they're thinkin' twice about comin' any closer. But then again, they're pretty stupid, ain't they? I want 'em to come closer so we can kill or maim a couple more of 'em. That'd lower their number to about seven active fighters, if that. Plus, if they have some wounded ones, they'll be distracted by dealin' with 'em, and that'll reduce their will to go on fightin'. Plus, they ain't yet inflicted any casualties on us. They gotta be thinkin' about that. I know they're stupid, but they can't be that stupid. What do you think?"

"It sounds like you've done this sort of thing before, Johnny," commented Josiah.

Johnny said nothing. He had already loaded his rifle, getting ready to take his next shot. "Josiah, why don't you kill the fella who replaced the steersman you just shot? Stop hesitatin'. This is serious business. The bastard desperately needs killin'. Now do it!"

Josiah fired. This time, the consequences were lethal. The steersman fell backwards into the waters of Ohio, the front of his shirt soaking with the blood that gushed from his heart as he fell.

"That's four," said Johnny. "Congratulations, Josiah. You're a warrior now."

The keelboat stopped pursuing them. As it turned to go back to the cave, Johnny shot another of the pirates in the buttocks. He screamed out in pain. While not immediately lethal, it would be disabling enough to reduce the effective crew to seven, with three wounded on board, and two dead ones floating in the river.

They would have to struggle to get back upstream to their cave. Meanwhile, the Jones party would need to get to the junction of Ohio and Mississippi as soon as they could because there would be more settlements around and more visibility, which would likely mean more risk to the pirates if they chose to pursue a course of vengeance. Johnny suggested that they continue through the night, as there would be a half-moon lighting the broken spring sky. Given what had just happened, no one on the flatboat felt much like sleeping.

* * * * * * * *

That day, right at sundown, the keelboat with the remnants of its crew straggled back into Cave-in-Rock. Jed, a big man with a beard, long hair, and bushy eyebrows, glowered at them as they disembarked from the blood-stained boat. He greeted them with derision: "Looks like yer got yer asses kicked. Where's Pete?"

"He's floatin' down the Ohio, Jed. Those pilgrims kilt 'im."

Jed noted that another member of the crew was missing. He asked, "Who else got killed?"

"Jimmy," one of the survivors replied.

Jed growled, "Yer dumb asses should have known better than ter try to pull off a raid when yer fucked up on whiskey. Serves yer right!"

"Ain't we gonna get revenge?" asked the boss of the keelboat.

"For what purpose?" asked Jed. "For one thing, from the looks of yer sorry-ass bunch of would-be pirates, it looks like they got a couple of good shooters on board. And what would we get for our trouble? A covered wagon, some farm tools, probably, a couple of milk cows, maybe some pussy, and probably a couple more dead guys." He paused and added, "Any of you scamps into milkin' cows?"

He looked at the remnants of the rag-tag group of buccaneers for a moment. No one said anything. Then he continued, "I didn't think so. Anyways, it ain't worth the risk. I hope yer dumb shits learnt somethin' today. Now, first thing in the mornin', clean up that fuckin' boat."

Jed turned around, grabbed a jug of corn whiskey, and downed a slosh of it as he walked away in disgust.

* * * * * * * * *

The Jones party kept its vigil until they reached the Mississippi River a few days later. No pirates showed up, to everyone's relief.

There were, by this time, steamboats appearing on the great rivers of the West. Jones planned to hitch a tow with one of them and go upstream on the Mississippi to St. Louis. Steamboats occasionally made extra revenue by providing this service. Once in Saint Louis, Jones planned to scrap the boat, sell the wood, buy another covered wagon and a pair of horses, replenish the family's provisions, and stock up on gunpowder and shot. From there, they would travel to a large tract of land he had acquired in western Missouri, near the border of Kansas Territory. Johnny wanted to tell them that it was not yet safe out there, as there were still hostiles—especially the Pawnee—living in that part of the country. But he assumed that they understood the risks, and in any case, after going through all that they had gone through to get here, what would be the point of saying discouraging words?

Jones asked Johnny, "Where are you headed from here?"

"St. Louis," Johnny replied.

"We're going there too. I'm going to wait for a steamboat and try to make a deal for a tow. You wanna come with?"

"I've been told that it's over a hundred miles to St. Louis. It would take me three or four days to get there by horse. How long will it take to get there by steamboat?"

Jones said, "Two or three days. And it'll be a lot easier on you and your horses."

Johnny considered this. He asked, "How much would it cost?"

Jones said, "It costs me the same whether you come along or not. You can just come. It won't cost you anything. After Cave-in-Rock, I feel I owe you at least that."

The day after the Jones party had arrived at a town with no name at the confluence of the two great rivers, a steamboat came by. Jones made his deal. The steamboat was a side-wheeler, which made it easier than it might have otherwise been to tether the flatboat to its stern. Three days later, in the middle of the afternoon, they arrived in St. Louis.

Johnny and the Jones family said their farewells. After the farewell rituals were done, Josiah approached Johnny. He said, "I'm not sure what to say to you, Johnny. I feel like you've initiated me into a different life. The life of a warrior." He sounded excited.

Johnny responded, "You killed someone who needed killin', Josiah. It was him or you. That's what warriors do. And when y'all get where you're going, you might need to kill again. There are some real heathens out there on the plains, and some of 'em ain't even Indians. They're white men who've gone wild. So, may you all be well. But be careful out there."

"Johnny, we might not even be here talking to each other if you hadn't come along with us. We owe you," said Josiah.

Johnny said nothing. He extended his hand to Josiah, who quickly responded with his own. They exchanged strong, lingering handshakes before turning and walking away, each heading out on his own separate journey. Josiah thought to himself, as he walked away, who among the Jones party would ever forget Cave-in-Rock? Or the young man they knew only as 'Johnny'?

Johnny took his two horses to a ferry on the west bank of the Mississippi. The ruins of the ancient city of Cahokia were a few miles east of the Great River…the next stop on the trail of Johnny Tenkiller.

Chapter 11: Cahokia

Johnny and his two horses rode a ferry to the east bank of the Mississippi, arriving in late afternoon as the shadows grew long. Johnny figured he would camp there this evening, look at the stars, and wonder about the history and ultimate demise of this place.

As he rode eastward, Johnny soon saw what looked like hills jutting up from the prairie, looming in the distance to the east. They were covered with a thick carpet of winter grass that glowed an unearthly, pale green aura in the afternoon sun. The beauty of the aura made him feel as if they were magical. He suspected that they were not really hills but the ancient man-made structures of which the elders had told him.

But there was something eerie about them. They were relics of an age gone by when the original people of this land had first arrived at the threshold of civilization. Then something had happened. The people left. Where did they go? Were their descendants still around, as the Cherokee, Choctaw, and Muskogee descendants of the mound builders of the Southeast were still around?

Was this mysterious place the site of the birth of what might have been—or become—a great civilization? Was it also the site of a great tragedy?

As Johnny and his horses approached those mounds, he found himself astounded at the scale of the site. There were more than a dozen big, flat-topped earthen pyramids placed in some kind of order, though Johnny couldn't fathom what the principle of order might have been. He knew that in the days of old, there were wise men who, like the ancient Greek geometers, knew about shapes and measures. They could read the stars. They could plan big projects that resulted in the imposing structures he was looking at. "I wonder how they got people—there must have been thousands involved—to build these things," Johnny wondered as he rode into the complex. "Did they use slaves?"

The size of the whole complex was far greater than any other remnants of a by-gone age that he had ever seen. The largest of them had two tiers, and the top tier appeared to be at least a hundred feet above the base. To his surprise, he saw a house at the top. It was clearly a house built by whites. He wondered what the view from the top of that pyramid would look like. He wondered what kind of white man owned that house. Not really wanting to know, he rode onward.

He soon saw another mound, lower than the great terraced one he had just passed but still of impressive size. Sitting on the flattened top of this one, he saw a man, apparently an Indian. He sensed that this man might know something.

He dismounted, tethered his horses to a tree at the bottom of the mound, and noted a horse, a pinto, tethered to another tree a few yards away. He surmised that the horse belonged to the man at the top. As he made his ascent, the man noticed him. Johnny raised his right hand, palm out, in a gesture of peace. The man at the top of the mound did not move or make any further effort to communicate other than to turn his head in Johnny's direction and reciprocate the peace gesture. When Johnny was almost at the top, he saw that the man was quite old, with long white hair. He was definitely Indian.

Not sure if the man spoke English, Johnny greeted him: "Good day, sir. May I join you?"

"Suit yourself," replied the old man.

Johnny sat cross-legged a few feet away, relieved that they had a common language in which to communicate.

The old man said, in a matter-of-fact tone, "You look like an Indian. What tribe are you from?"

Johnny saw no reason to perpetuate a "black Irish" narrative. "I'm Cherokee," replied Johnny.

The old man nodded and grunted. Then he asked, "What brought you here, to this ancient place?"

"I wanted to know more about our ancestors," said Johnny.

"They weren't *your* ancestors," declared the old man. "Long ago, your ancestors lived up the river—the one the whites call 'the Ohio.' The people who lived here were *my* ancestors."

"What tribe are you?" Johnny inquired.

"I am Pawnee."

"I thought your people lived on the other side of the Mississippi," commented Johnny.

"Our people lived along the rivers that flow into the Great River, on both sides of it, long before the white man came. We once ruled this part of the earth. We were as numerous as the leaves on the trees." He waved his hand expansively as he spoke. Then he continued. "The other tribes feared us. We raided them and took slaves and victims to sacrifice to the gods."

Then the old man asked, "What did you come here to find? Now that you know that the builders of this place were not your ancestors."

"I see something here that our peoples had in common," Johnny began. "We built mounds in the old days, though they weren't as big as these," said Johnny. "We were at the threshold of something when we built these places. If we had gotten past it, we might have been better able to push the white men back to the East. Or maybe not. But it gives me pride to know that the difference between us and the whites has nothin' to do with our blood or our brains. It has everything to do with their four-thousand-year head start."

"How do you know it was four thousand years?" asked the old man.

Johnny shared the reasoning behind his estimate. He concluded, "Where the white man's civilization came from, they had a metal called 'tin' to mix with copper. From these things, they made bronze, which is much harder than copper and better for weapons and armor. They figured it out about four thousand years ago. We didn't have much tin or easy access to it, anyway. That was the difference. From this beginning, they improved their knowledge. Then, they learned to make iron weapons and armor. Then, they learned to make steel weapons and armor. And so on."

"They have brought us havoc with their metals and the things that can be made with them," said the old man.

"That they did," Johnny remarked. "May I ask your name, sir?"

The old man said something in his native language. Johnny tried to pronounce it, but the syllables were too alien to his tongue and palate to easily get them out. Seeing Johnny struggle, he said, "That is the way it is said in the Pawnee language. In English, it means 'Black Wolf'. You can call me that. I even have an English name—Joseph."

"So, your name is Joseph Black Wolf?" asked Johnny.

"That is how the white man knows me," said the old Pawnee.

"My name is Johnny White Owl," said Johnny. You can just call me 'Johnny'. Everyone else does."

"Then you can call me 'Joe'," said the old man.

"Pleased to meet you, Joe," said Johnny.

Joe nodded stoically.

They sat in silence for half an hour. Then Joe grabbed a leather pouch—his medicine bag, as it turned out—and began to pinch a powdery substance from it and load it into a long-stemmed pipe.

"Want to smoke with me?" asked Joe.

"What would we be smokin'?" asked Johnny.

"In the old times, when people lived here, there was a flower that had seeds with magic in them, magic that caused powerful visions. Our priests used it to commune with the 'other side', to figure out the will of the gods," said Joe.

"Is that what's in your pipe?" asked Johnny.

"No. There is something even better out on the prairie. Underneath the buffalo droppings grows a mushroom. When those mushrooms are dried and ground into powder, we put that powder in these pipes and smoke that," replied Joe.

"What does it do to you?" asked Johnny.

"It will give you a new way of seeing the world."

"Drinking the white man's whiskey—I think it's poisonous, myself—will do that for you, won't it?" Johnny asked.

"It is nothing like that. When you get drunk on whiskey, all you get is sick, and when you're over it, all you remember is a bitter journey of evil dreams," answered Joe. "When you smoke this, you will have visions, insights that will stay with you long after the effects go away."

"Will it make me sick?" asked Johnny. "Whiskey did. That's why I never touched it again after the first time."

"It might make your stomach feel funny for a while. You might even puke. But then again, you might not. Either way, you will not be sick afterwards. And while your journey into the spirit world lasts, you will feel great joy. Hard to describe in words."

Johnny thought about it for a moment. Then he said, "I'll try."

Joe made a small fire, ignited a twig, and lit the pipe as he took a long draw. Then he handed the pipe to Johnny. Johnny took a long draw. He coughed and choked as he exhaled a cloud of smoke. Joe laughed. "Give me that pipe, Johnny," he demanded. Joe took another long draw but added, "You need to wait a while before you smoke anymore. You are new to this."

Johnny, who had just recovered his composure after his coughing and choking spell, did not argue. He would soon realize that coughing and choking is Nature's way of telling a person that he's had enough of whatever it was he was smoking.

They sat quietly for another half an hour. The sun was sinking in the west. From the north, a light breeze, still carrying the bite of winter, blew across the remnants of the ancient city. It made Johnny glad he had worn the buckskin tunic that Ahyoka had made for him while he abided in Wohali's hamlet. It seemed like a lifetime since he last saw her, though only two seasons had passed since then. Two seasons and four more killings...

Joe said, "Beneath where we are sitting are many bodies. The bodies of warriors, slaves, prisoners, and chiefs. Some were tortured to death; some were sacrificed. And warriors, especially chiefs, are laid out in dignity, buried with some of their possessions, things that came from as far away as you can imagine." He paused for a moment and then continued, "Some of their spirits are restless and come out at night...Does that frighten you?"

"I mean no disrespect, Joe, but I don't believe in spirits anymore," said Johnny.

"When the morning sun rises," said Joe, "you may have changed your mind."

"Assuming there are ghosts here and that they are real…"

"*They are real*," interrupted Joe.

"Assuming they are real," persisted Johnny, "Can they harm us?"

Joe replied, "They might be able to, but they have no reason to do that." He looked up at the big mound with the white man's house on top. "I can't say whether they bother him, though. He really doesn't belong here. I have not spoken to him, so I do not know if they bother him. He is still walking around, so they haven't killed him. That should make you feel safe."

Johnny, comforted by Joe's words, asked, "Will they communicate with us? Will they tell us things about the far past?"

"They might," replied Joe. "Especially if you have a curious heart."

* * * * * * * * *

Not long afterwards, Johnny noticed that the colors of nature began to take on a bright glow, even though it was growing dark. Green turned to orange, red to grey, and blue to pink. The colors danced back and forth between their phases. When he heard sounds, he saw colors. When he saw colors, they seemed to sing to him. He and Joe began exchanging stories, stories he could not remember the next day but stories that seemed riotously funny at the time of their telling. They laughed until their sides hurt.

During that night, Johnny saw an apparition. It must have been more than a mere appearance because Joe saw it too and, indeed, claimed to have seen it in the past. As he and Joe sat in the dark silence of the night, a night brightened by the waxing moon, a figure slowly materialized a few feet away from them. He stood at least six and a half feet tall but looked even taller because of the stiffened hair of his scalp lock, which jutted another four inches above the crown of his otherwise shaven head. His face, head, upper body, arms, and legs were painted red, but one could see the tattoos that ringed his arms and thighs through the lightly smeared red ochre. A linear pattern of black paint covered the bridge of his nose and his eyes and extended back to his ears. The Pawnee, Johnny reflected, still painted their faces in this way. He was wearing a fawn kilt of some kind of woven fiber—was it cotton?—and embroidered moccasins. He had a copper nose ring and a luminous disc hung from the lobe of each ear. They looked as if they were made of seashells.

"Do you see what I'm seeing?" Johnny asked.

"Yes. His name was Oya Tse," replied Joe.

Oya Tse slowly raised his right hand in greeting.

"Can he speak with us?" asked Johnny.

"He can speak through images that might appear in your mind, and sometimes he can make sounds. That is why I know his name is Oya Tse," responded Joe.

Johnny recalled the giant Osage who had almost killed him in his first battle. Oya Tse was even bigger than him. He was glad he was a ghost. He noted the cloth kilt, the copper ornaments, and the shells, which must have come from the eastern sea. Whoever these people were, their trading network must have been vast. Johnny was fascinated with the cloth. "Did these people grow cotton?" he asked.

"I do not know," said Joe. "They knew how to weave some kind of fiber. And they knew how to read the stars. They knew when the blood moons would appear and when the sun would go dark in the middle of the day. They had profound knowledge. We Pawnee still have priests who know those things."

Johnny remarked, "You said something about sacrificing people to their gods. How do you know that?"

Joe looked at Johnny: "Human sacrifice? The Pawnees were still doing this up to about fifteen years ago. At that time, a captive Comanche girl was hung from a scaffold and about to be shot with arrows by some of our warriors. Her blood would feed the earth. It's called the ceremony of the Morning Star. The priests say it is necessary to sacrifice a young maiden in this way to guarantee a good harvest. But a young warrior named Petalasharo cut her from the scaffold and took her back to her tribe. He was not punished for it, and many thought he had done a good thing. I did. Sacrificing young girls, even though they were captured from other peoples, bothered me. It bothered a lot of other men, too, even warriors hardened by battle. I do not believe that this practice continued after that."

"I see," remarked Johnny. "Are you a priest, Joe? You seem to know a lot."

"No," Joe replied.

"Then, are you what might be called a 'holy man' of some kind?" asked Johnny.

"Some see me that way," replied Joe.

They fell into silence again. Johnny looked for Oya Tse, but he had faded away. He wanted to rest his mind, but he could not. He knew that in the ancient world on the far side of the great eastern sea, the first civilizations were also ruled by "priest-kings" who either claimed descent from the gods, were regarded as gods themselves, or had special access to the gods. That was how they must have gotten all those other people to serve them, how they made their rule legitimate. If the gods appointed them, who could argue with that? As his reflections continued, he reasoned: With the people at the bottom of their society doing the work of raising crops and hunting, the people at the top, who were freed from the toil of producing the means of life, had the leisure to design these great structures, coordinate their construction, practice the arts of war, read the stars, and develop crafts, including weaving, pottery, and such metallurgy as they were able to handle, given the resources they had at their disposal.

This, he concluded, is what made them "civilized": the existence of an elite group of people supported by others, who had to work to produce enough for both them and these overlords. He recalled the Ani Kutani clan of his own tribe, about whom Wohali had told him.

In the ancient world, on the far side of the eastern sea, the rulers and their servants developed written language, mathematics, laws, and science. The Indians, given another few hundred years, probably would have done the same. But he wondered: Would they have been any kinder, any more just, or less greedy than the white men? He saw no reason, at this point, to think they would have been.

* * * * * * * *

At first light, Johnny realized that though he wanted to rest, he would be unable to sleep. He reflected on the visions he had seen during the night. The fact that both he and Joe had seen the ghost, Oya Tse, was convincing evidence that there existed another order of things in this world—things that were real, even though they were not flesh and blood.

As he reflected on this, he asked Joe, "Do you believe that Oya Tse was real?"

"You saw him, too, didn't you?" responded Joe. "If we both saw him, he could not just be something you imagined, could he?"

"I reckon not," said Johnny. "I was thinking that if Oya Tse exists, then all the rest of it might be true, too."

"All the rest of what?" queried Joe.

"You know, gods, spirits…a world of things that is different from, but touches on the world we live in, when we're wide awake, walking around, seeing and touching things that are…real," reflected Johnny.

Joe looked at Johnny quizzically and declared, with a dismissive tone of voice, "Of course."

Johnny's mind was overloaded. He knew that something of great and lasting value had taken place during the night. He would puzzle over it, probably for a long time. But there was something liberating about the experience, something he could not yet characterize in words. At length, he said, "Uncle Black Wolf, I thank you for opening this door for me. I'll consider what we have seen this night—maybe for the rest of my life."

"That is well," said Joseph Black Wolf, the Pawnee holy man.

* * * * * * * * *

Johnny stood up, not an easy task, given that he had sat cross-legged for many hours without moving. Though he was a young man of twenty, his knees and hips popped as he raised himself from the ground. He simply nodded farewell to Joe and stumbled down the ancient mound to his horses. When he got to the bottom, he realized that they had stood all night with their saddles still strapped onto them. He led them to the Mississippi River, which was a couple of miles away, removed their saddles, and let them drink. At this moment, he was getting sleepy. After all, he had not slept all night.

He waited a couple of hours for the ferry, his back against a tree, dozing off periodically. As he sat there, he had a recurring thought:

God exists. He hears the prayers of our hearts but doesn't pay much attention to the prattling of our minds.

Every time he dozed off, he had this thought. Was it the faint voice of the shy soul of which William Johnson had spoken?

A bit before midday, the ferry arrived. He was half asleep but heard the activity and roused himself. He re-saddled his horses. He paid the ferrymen. They boarded and returned to St. Louis.

Once there, he searched for a hotel. He stabled his horses. He paid for a bath, put on his suit—the one he had worn at Isaac's and Lizzie's wedding—got a haircut, went to a nearby restaurant, and ate a steak dinner. The server looked at him curiously, wondering who this dark-skinned, elegantly dressed young gentleman might be. When he finished, he went up to his room and fell asleep just as the sun was setting. He slept deeply, with a multitude of thoughts whirling in his mind.

He would have plenty of time to sort them out. Uncle Dutch's new ranch, a destination to which he would begin a journey the next day, was hundreds of miles away.

* * * * * * * * *

Johnny awoke well before dawn the next morning, well-rested and fresh. Before leaving Pittsburg, he had bought some writing paper, a pen and ink, and some envelopes to fulfill his promise to Isaac that he would write when he arrived at a place that had a post office. St. Louis had at least one.

He lit an oil lamp in his hotel room and sat at a small table next to an eastward-facing window. While it was still dark, he opened the curtain and the window behind it, sat down, and began writing. By the time he finished his letter to the MacDermotts, the rays of the sun were peeking over the eastern horizon. He addressed the envelope and blew out the lamp. He packed, went downstairs to the hotel lobby, checked out, and asked where he could drop the letter. The desk clerk informed him that the general store down the street was also a postal service.

Johnny went to this general store, sealed and paid for the letter, and bought an iron frying pan, a spatula, some corn meal, a small pot, a bedroll, and a jar of maple syrup. This would supplement his diet of wild game, roots, fruits, and nuts as he trekked to the Indian Territory, a journey that he expected would take about a month to complete.

He also bought plenty of powder and shot. He expected that game would be plentiful, for the frontier remained relatively untouched by white settlers. He still had his bow and twenty arrows, along with his rifle, so he did not expect to go hungry. His main concern was with whatever Indians he might meet along the way.

Johnny and his horses began their journey in the middle of this bright spring morning. As they left St. Louis behind, he thought about the letter he had just mailed to the MacDermotts of Pittsburg. He smiled to himself as he recalled its contents. It read:

April 27, 1834

Dear Isaac and Lizzie,

I have arrived safely in St. Louis. I will soon travel west and south from here to the Canadian River in Indian Territory. I hope to find my Uncle Dutch there.

It will be a long journey. I also hope to find my grandmother. I hope she has responded to my pleas and left Tennessee.

The journey down the Ohio was mostly quiet, except for a run-in we had with some pirates. There was a young man with us who was a pretty good shot, and we repelled their attack. I found my Number Nine that day...

I don't have enough paper to write down how it happened, but my belief in our Creator has been restored.

Know, therefore, that I will pray for the well-being of you both and for the children you will have.

When I get to the next place I land, and if there is a postal service, I will write you another letter. I don't know from where or when I will write, but I promise to write to you again.

Your friend,

Johnny

As he rode away from St. Louis, he remembered the strange night he had spent in Cahokia. As he did so, a deep sense of calm overcame him, as a voice inside his mind said:

We are all the same.

Was it once again the voice of the shy soul of which Mr. Johnson had spoken? Wherever it came from, the statement had the unmistakable feeling of wisdom, and Johnny felt in his heart that it was true.

The world being as it was and the American frontier being what it was, he believed that he would probably kill again. But his grudge against white men was over. How could he hold onto it, with people like the Presbyterian missionaries, the Quakers, Will Sullivan, James O'Brien, William Johnson, and Robert Franklin in the world? In letting go of this long-standing vendetta, he felt a powerful sense of being free from an old burden.

Part 4: Indian Territory

Chapter 12: Fort Gibson

Johnny traveled westward from St. Louis, following the Osage River upstream. It flowed northeastward from the low, rolling Ozark mountains and emptied into the Missouri River, which, in turn, poured into the Mississippi River, north of St. Louis.

Spring was in its prime as Johnny made his way, traversing hills and prairies covered with lush greenery and wildflowers. For the first two weeks, his journey was uneventful. He saw no one for days, though he passed a deserted village that had been built by Indians. Had they left to hunt buffalo on the plains? Or were they dead, victims of one of the white man's diseases? He didn't stop to investigate.

He had no aim other than just getting to Uncle Dutch, who had planned to move from the Red River Valley to a place deeper in Indian Territory, near the confluence of the Canadian and Arkansas Rivers. Johnny figured that Dutch and his people had made that move by now.

Meanwhile, game was plentiful on this journey. Johnny was not worried about going hungry, and he was in no hurry.

One morning, he noticed dark clouds looming in the distance on the northern horizon. They boded the possibility of rain. He decided to stop and build a lean-to in a meadow overlooking the river. He spent the bigger part of the day finding and cutting the right branches for the job. In the afternoon, he made a fire and boiled some river water to make it safe to drink. He tethered Flower and the gelding under some trees and stored their saddles under the lean-to. He speared—or rather, shot with an arrow—a large brook trout and cleaned it. He mixed some of his cornmeal in a bowl with a blend of wild herbs, as he had learned to do from Ahyoka back at Wohali's hamlet. He fried the pancake and dipped it in maple syrup as an hors d'oeuvre. Then he roasted the trout on a spit and took the rest of his dinner in the peace of the late afternoon.

As he dined, his thoughts returned to Wohali's hamlet and the beautiful Ahyoka. He thought of the pink tablecloth in the saddle bag and, for a moment, was overcome by longing, followed by a deep pang of loss, as he considered the likelihood that he would never see her again. He wondered if he would ever have an occasion to use that tablecloth. Would he ever share it with someone other than Ahyoka?

He dreamed of having a home somewhere, someday. But he could not fathom where it might be, or when he might find it. He hoped to see his grandmother again, safely in the Cherokee lands of the West. And in his heart, he wished to see his Ahyoka again, though he couldn't imagine how that could ever happen. She would probably evade the Removal by going up into the mountains of North Carolina, along with other Cherokees with the same goal. All he would have left of her would be the precious memories of those stolen moments in Wohali's hamlet and the pink tablecloth that, for him, symbolized them. Then he thought of Lizzie, who had given him that pink tablecloth, and offered up a silent prayer for the well-being of her, Isaac, and the child they would bear later in the year.

In the stillness of the lonely moments he was feeling, as the afternoon faded to dusk under the broken sky, he looked out at the river, its blue waters gleaming silver in the light of the waning sun. Not another soul was present other than the animals and birds who lived there.

In the distance, he heard the rumbling of thunder. He was glad he had made the lean-to, though it wasn't as sound as the one Isaac had made on their journey to Pittsburg the previous fall. He thought about Isaac and smiled to himself as he hoped it wouldn't leak much. He unfurled his bedroll beneath the lean-to and spread it out. He let his fire burn, sat beneath his modest shelter, and waited for the rain to come.

****

Few things inspire more gratitude than even the crudest shelter when it rains. As the clouds darkened the sky, spilled their contents on the earth, and extinguished Johnny's fire, he sat in relative dryness under his lean-to. He liked the smell of the dirt when it rained. In the quiet of the evening, punctuated only by the pattering of the raindrops, he felt an immense "something" all around him.

In a short while, his mind became quiet. He just thought about the pattering of the raindrops. Soon, his feelings of sorrow, regret, and loneliness dissipated like the smoke of the remnants of his fire. He felt a deep sense of calm, like the one he had felt that glorious autumn day just six months before, riding north on the ancient warpath towards Wohali's hamlet.

As he drifted off to sleep, he noticed that the lean-to was not leaking. He must have done a decent job on it, after all. Warmed by his blanket and sheltered from the rain, a faint smile crossed his face as he thanked the Great Spirit for the bounty of his table, shelter from the storm, and the warmth of his blanket. And unconsciously, he longed for Ahyoka.

* * * * * * * * *

When Johnny left the Red River valley the previous fall, Uncle Dutch and his people were already planning to move northward to an area by the Canadian River, deep in Indian Territory, near its confluence with the Arkansas. Dutch's vision was to create a ranch there. Johnny's tracks had barely cooled when the whole group pulled up stakes and moved. They took their horses, cattle, hogs, seeds for the spring planting, their tools, and their weapons. It took them a bit more than a week to make the trek. By late September, they would have been, Johnny surmised, splitting logs and building the first cabins in their new abode.

They would have to share cabin spaces for the next year until they could build more, but it would be worth the price: Things were becoming tense between the American settlers in Texas and the government of Mexico, which still, at that time, owned Texas. Dutch and other elders in the Red River settlement thought it would be best to put some distance between their people and the chaos that was likely to ensue, and probably soon.

And then again, there were those pesky Comanches. To the west and south of the Red River settlement was a region that had been named the "Comancheria" by the Spaniards. The Comanches had originally lived farther north, where the northern great plains met the Rocky Mountains, but had moved to the southern plains before 1700. There, they found and learned to ride horses that were descended from those that had been loosed after the 1680 Pueblo Indian rebellion against the Spanish colonists in the Southwest. They had taken to the horse admirably, becoming among the first and the greatest native horsemen on the continent.

Buffalo were much easier to hunt and kill from horseback. The Comanches, newly wealthy in horses and the buffalo that horses enabled them to harvest in greater quantities than ever before, prospered and multiplied. They had so many horses that even their three-year-olds had their own mounts. Some said that the Comanches spent so much of their lives on horseback that they were a bit clumsy when on foot. Though they did not have saddles, they could sling their bodies over the side of a running horse, held only by a heel over the horse's backbone and a hand grasping its mane, a leather thong bridle, and a bow with one hand, notching arrows, and drawing a bowstring with the other, shooting the arrows from under the horse's neck as the horse ran. Meanwhile, the horse was, in effect, a shield from the projectiles—arrows and bullets—of their enemies.

No European power, not even the armored Spanish butchers, could penetrate the Comancheria, partly because the Comanches were fully nomadic and could set up or tear down their encampments in a matter of a couple of hours. Compared to the sedentary peoples of Mexico, the Comanches were a moving target, with fewer vulnerabilities for the Spaniards to exploit. Further, single-shot, ball-and-powder firearms were inferior, in battle, to the mounted Comanche warrior, who could shoot eight arrows in the amount of time it took to reload a musket or carbine.

These advantages were put to effective use by the Comanches, who were among the most brutal people in North America. As Dutch and Enoli had said, they were energetic and sadistic butchers of prisoners of war. And their propensities for torture were legendary, even among other Indians, among whom the torture of captured enemies had been practiced from the beginning of time. They stole women and children between three and ten years of age to use or sell as slaves. Sometimes, these victims were adopted by their captors and became members of the tribe. Otherwise, they remained in servitude until they found a way to escape. The Comanches killed everyone else they encountered in a successful raid—men, children under three, even babies. Captured men might be killed slowly, say, by being roasted alive. Or worse, sometimes they would be buried up to their chins with their eyelids cut off to increase their misery as they slowly died of thirst in the hot summer sun.

The Comanches used their military advantages and their reign of terror—mostly stemming from their mastery of horse warfare—to conquer and depopulate the southern plains. They drove the Apache, who were formidable warriors in their own right, from the west Texas plains into New Mexico, where they hoped to get protection from the Spanish colonial government. Native tribes that didn't leave or die were reduced to a state of vassalage.

Trading in horses and slaves, they established a wide empire that stretched from the Southwest to Kansas, to the lands of the Osage and Cherokee in Indian Territory, down through west and central Texas, and into northern Mexico. Though they had little to recommend themselves other than organized violence and predation, they were masterful at these things. Such artifacts as they had, other than things that could be made from the hides, bones, and horns of the buffalo, were acquired through trade or through theft and plunder. Johnny had learned these things from Dutch and Enoli, who, in turn, had found them out through talks with the elders of some of the other tribes or from Mexican informants they had met while trading in Texas.

Johnny had not yet had the pleasure of meeting these lords of the southern plains. But he knew enough about them to understand the rationale for moving further north, deeper into Indian Territory. Finding Uncle Dutch's ranch would pose a minor challenge, but the good news was that it would shorten his journey from St. Louis by about a hundred miles. The better news was that it would put another hundred miles between his people and those heathern Comanches.

* * * * * * * * *

Johnny followed the Osage River until it began to fragment into smaller streams that flowed from the low mountains from which they sprang. He turned southward to find the Neosho River, which would take him to Fort Gibson. He did not tarry on this part of his journey. There were still wild Indians out there. He didn't know exactly which tribes and didn't want to, really. He just wanted to get to Fort Gibson as quickly and as unobtrusively as he could.

In three days, he found the Neosho River. It meandered through the hills but flowed in a generally southward direction. On May 26, he arrived at Fort Gibson.

Almost as soon as he had arrived, Johnny saw Dutch come out through the gates of the fort. He couldn't believe his eyes. "Uncle Dutch!" he shouted.

Dutch, on seeing Johnny, smiled as they approached each other. They shook hands and gave one another a brief ritual hug. Speaking Cherokee, Dutch declared, "It's good to see that you have made it back here alive. I wondered if you would…"

"It seems like a long time, Uncle, though it has only been a few moons since I left. A lot has happened since then," replied Johnny.

Dutch said, "You can tell me about your travels on the way back to our new ranch. Where did you get that gelding?" he asked.

"That is part of the story," Johnny replied.

Dutch simply nodded. He said, "We will head south as soon as Enoli and I get some things from the store. As you can see, there is a store here now."

"It's starting to look quite 'civilized' here," mused Johnny.

"This is the beginning of the new world that we are entering," said Dutch. He went into the store and started gathering the things he wished to buy. Having made a bit of money from prior service to the US Army as a hunter and scout, he had cash to make his purchases.

Johnny was surprised to find that a new military unit—the United States First Dragoon Regiment—had assembled there in preparation for an expedition to meet and establish relations—hopefully, positive relations—with the wild tribes of the west. Dutch had gone to the fort to close a deal for himself and seven other Cherokees, who would scout and hunt for this regiment on its expedition. They were scheduled to leave in a couple of weeks.

It was late in the day when they loaded their wagons and prepared for the trip back to the ranch on the Canadian River. Dutch planned to leave the next morning. Though they could have made the trip in two days by horseback, it would take three or four days with those wagons. There would be plenty of time for them to catch up on Johnny's doings.

Johnny looked around at the sprawling settlement that was growing up around the fort. There were Cherokees, Osages, Seneca, and Lenape (the whites called them "Delawares"), all living together in peace. Members of each of these tribes would join the Dragoon expedition.

In the past, the Cherokee had fought every one of these tribes. They had fought the Seneca for hundreds of years. The Osage had fought all of them as well since what was now Indian Territory had once belonged to them, among other tribes, but mostly to them. The Lenape and the Haudenosaunee‡—the "Six Nations" or "Iroquois", as the whites knew them—had fought each other for hundreds of years. The emergence of the new nation—the United States—with its modern industry, gunpowder, and teeming millions of European immigrants, had provided common ground for these hereditary enemies. Outnumbered, outgunned, decimated by European disease, and compelled to move to this place by forces beyond their control, they were all just "Indians" now.

---

‡ The Seneca were one of the Six Nations.

Chapter 13: Uncle Dutch's Ranch

The next morning, Dutch and the other Cherokees headed southward towards the ranch on the Canadian River. Dutch, Enoli, and Johnny rode ahead of the rest of the party. Both of his uncles were eager to hear of his adventures during the nine months since he had left them in August of 1833.

Dutch declared, "We have a few days' journey ahead. That should give you plenty of time to tell your tale, White Owl."

"I know it does not seem to be a long time since I went away. But so many things happened that I have to think about how to tell you that tale." He would be happy to share the details of killing the Stricklins, the slavecatchers, and shooting the brigands at Cave-in-Rock. As to his romance with Ahyoka and the pink tablecloth...not so much. He would surely tell them about the conversation he had with his grandmother about coming west.

He gathered his thoughts for a few minutes. Then he began. He shared how he had entreated his grandmother to leave Knoxville and join the western band of Cherokees. He hoped that she would arrive this coming summer or fall but was not sure she would. Then he told how he had executed the Stricklin boys. Every last detail. Uncle Dutch and Enoli smiled approvingly and even laughed when Johnny described how and why he had cut off Josh's index finger just before he slowly cut his throat and let him bleed out.

At this point, Dutch said, "I remember that talk we had before you left about whether you even knew what killing someone 'Indian style' meant." He paused for a second and added, "It looks like you figured it out." Turning to Enoli, he asked, "What do you think?"

Enoli said, "Yes, I believe White Owl figured it out." Then, he and Dutch both laughed. Enoli added, "He did well for a beginner." Both he and Dutch laughed from their bellies at that comment.

Johnny responded, "To tell the whole truth, I do not think I would ever want to be an expert at that kind of thing. I could not just do it to anyone, like the heatherns do. But as for Josh Stricklin...he needed it." Then, in

English, he added, "If I'd had more time, I would have burned their fuckin' house down, too…with him in it, and still alive."

"What did you do next?" asked Dutch.

Johnny told of his journey to Wohali's hamlet and his stay there, earning his keep as a hunter. He tried to slide past that little cabin he inhabited so as not to divulge much about his initiation into the pleasures of the night, courtesy of the beautiful Ahyoka.

Dutch, suppressing a smile, asked, "What did you say was the name of Wohali's niece?"

"Ahyoka," replied Johnny.

Enoli, sensing that Johnny was hiding something, asked, "How old was she?"

Johnny replied, "Her late twenties or maybe thirty, I think."

Dutch, no longer suppressing a smile, queried, "So what kind of 'happiness' did she bring, White Owl?" Dutch and Enoli began to laugh. They were sure that Johnny had been a virgin…until he met Ahyoka…

Johnny blushed, wordlessly confessing to what his uncles had implied. Wishing to change the subject, he told of leaving Wohali's hamlet, of his journey to Pittsburg, of meeting Isaac MacDermott, and of killing the three slavecatchers.

At that point, Dutch interrupted him. "So, how many men had you killed at that point?"

Johnny answered, "Eight."

"Not bad for a nineteen-year-old," commented Enoli.

Dutch observed, "It will not be long before you have fulfilled that boast you made…the one you made in the letter you left on the door of the Stricklin's cabin. So, you're an 'eight-killer' now, are you?"

Johnny replied, "No, I am a 'nine-killer'."

Dutch wanted details. "Where did you get the ninth one?"

Johnny told the story of the trip down the Ohio River and the incident at Cave-in-Rock. Enoli laughed at the point at which Johnny had yelled at the would-be pirates, "Come closer, assholes, I need some target practice!"

Johnny added, "But by that time, I was twenty."

"That's my boy," affirmed Dutch. Then he remarked, "The one you shot in the ass might have died later. That would make ten."

"But I cannot confirm that," said Johnny. "So, I can only claim nine."

Dutch, nodding approvingly, declared, "That is why we used to take scalps. They were our proof. Since you didn't, I'll just have to take your word for it. As for the one you shot in the ass, who cares anyway?" Dutch and Enoli both laughed. Johnny laughed along with them.

* * * * * * * * *

After Johnny had settled into Dutch's new cabin, his uncle asked him if he wanted to go with the Cherokee scouts who would be traveling west with the First Dragoons. Johnny wanted to go, but he was worried that if his grandmother arrived that fall, she might not find anyone she knew and would be at a loss as to where to go after arriving in Indian Territory. He had already advised her to look for Dutch, but what if she arrived while he was out in the western wilderness?

"The money is good," said Dutch, trying to convince Johnny to go along with the expedition.

"I cannot take the chance that my grandmother will arrive here while we're gone," protested Johnny.

Dutch thought about it for a moment and said, "That is well, White Owl. But what if she does not come here this year?"

"I would rather not take that chance," repeated Johnny.

"I understand," said Dutch. He would not mention the possibility again. "Then stay here and help build this ranch. Your Uncle Enoli will be in charge while we are gone. Do what he tells you."

"I will, Uncle." Then he added, "May the Great Spirit guide and keep all of you."

Dutch seemed perplexed. He asked, "White Owl, did you just speak of the Great Spirit? I thought you had lost your faith."

Johnny told him of his experience with the Pawnee shaman at Cahokia. He had not mentioned it when telling his narrative to Dutch and Enoli on the way home from Fort Gibson.

Dutch laughed. He confessed, "I smoked that stuff, too, when I was out on the plains with the Osages—back when we were friends, the first time around."

"Do you believe those experiences were real, Uncle Dutch?"

Dutch asked, "Are you asking me if what you saw and felt were real?" But before Johnny could answer, Dutch provided an answer of his own: "Since you and Black Wolf—that was the old Pawnee's name, wasn't it?—both saw the same thing, that confirms that it was real, does it not? I would see it that way. But what really matters is whether it was real to *you*."

Johnny said, "I asked Black Wolf the same question, and he said the same thing you just did. And then I asked him if Oya Tse exists, then is all the rest of it true? And he asked, 'All the rest of what?' I said, 'You know, gods, spirits…a world of things different from, but touches the world we live in when we're wide awake, walking around seeing and touching things that are…real.' Black Wolf looked at me like I was a fool and said, 'Of course!'"

Seeing an opening to teach, Dutch continued, "If you look at an apple and see that it is red, do you need someone to prove that what you see is red? Or is it enough that you have no doubt that you are looking at a red apple? Feeling the presence of the Great Spirit is like that. It is there, always has been there, and always will be there, whether or not someone can see or feel it. At one time, when you were an angry boy, you *chose* not to see it. And now that you have grown up, perhaps you have come to see that it was always there and always will be. If you thought about it deeply, you would realize that the Great Spirit has been with you, protecting you, showing you the way, all along, even when you thought you were doing things, making things happen, all by yourself."

Johnny did not speak right away. He recalled that his grandmother had told him essentially the same thing. He struggled to understand. Frustrated with his fragmentary understanding, he admitted, "Well, the things I saw with Black Wolf were real…to me. And what you have said about the providence of the Great Spirit feels real to me as well."

"That is what matters, White Owl," declared Uncle Dutch. "Hold onto that belief. I always have."

* * * * * * * *

Three weeks later, Dutch and seven other Cherokees left with the First Dragoon Regiment on its mission to contact the wild tribes of the west: Comanches, Kiowas, and Pawnees. What they would not yet know was that the Comanches, while they recognized one another as "Comanche" and spoke closely related dialects of a common language, did not have a central government. The ones in Texas operated independently of those who lived west of the Indian Territory, north of Texas, and thus, could not have been expected to respect an agreement made by the other bands with the US government, or any other government, for that matter.

The Dragoon Regiment would be gone from the end of June until the end of August or thereabouts. While they were gone, many of them would become sick from heat prostration and the effects of drinking bad water. Dutch was one of them. Fortunately, he would come back alive.

And while Dutch was gone, Johnny would meet the Comanches.

* * * * * * * *

It was a hot, sweltering day in the middle of July. The cattle, about seventy head, had been brought in close to the settlement and corralled by some young Cherokee cowboys. As the sun set, a huge yellow moon arose on the eastern horizon. It was a perfect night for a raid. Enoli, knowing this, advised everyone to be vigilant. There were seventy-five Cherokees living at this ranch. Thirty of them were warriors. But they were eight shy of a full force that night since Dutch and seven others had gone with the First Dragoons.

As the moon rose in the sky, Enoli said, "We cannot leave the work of raising an alarm to our dogs. Some of us must stay up and watch for trouble. They call this a 'Comanche moon' for good reason. Keep your weapons nearby and prepare for battle. Now, who will volunteer to be the watchers?"

Several young warriors, including Johnny, volunteered.

Enoli chose Johnny and two others for the duty. The people took their dinners, viewing not just the southern horizon but all the horizons, for no one knew from what direction the Comanches might come. Just looking southward towards Texas alone would not be helpful. The Comanches would expect that the Cherokees might expect them to come from the obvious direction—south. They didn't create their empire by being stupid.

The night passed without incident.

The next day, Enoli spoke to the people. He said, "The moon will be full again tonight. We must make the same preparations."

* * * * * * * * *

Just before dawn, they came. About twenty of them. One of them opened the corral and began to shew the cattle out the gate. The others waited on their mounts for the Cherokees' inevitable reaction. When the Cherokees appeared from their cabins, armed with their rifles and bows, the Comanches, with black-painted faces, charged, showering them with arrows fired from the backs of swiftly running horses, creating cover for some of their party to make off with the cattle.

Enoli shouted to his warriors, "Shoot the horses."

Johnny protested: "The horses are not at fault. Why should we kill them? We aren't going to eat them, are we?"

Enoli gave him a look of contempt. "White Owl, the horse and the Comanche riding him are not two separate beings. When those bastards are mounted, the horse and the man are one, as you can see if you open your eyes. When the warrior is on foot, he is far less of a problem. Easier to kill. Now, shoot the damn horses!"

While this exchange was going on, three Cherokee defenders were wounded by the arrows of mounted, sharp-shooting Comanche archers. An arrow had missed Johnny by a hair's breadth.

Following Enoli's direction, the Cherokees fired a volley of rifle shots, knocking down three horses. They shot the unhorsed Comanches with arrows. But arrows rarely kill immediately. No sooner had these warriors been shot than some of their comrades sped by on their horses, scooped them up with dazzling grace and speed, and took them to safety behind the enemy lines, beyond the effective range of the Cherokee rifles. Meanwhile, a particularly bold Comanche warrior, wearing a horned buffalo headdress and carrying a large white buffalo skin shield and lance, charged the defenders. Uncle Kanuna was reloading his rifle when the Comanche ran him through with his lance, quickly backed up his horse, yanking the lance out of Kanuna's torso as he whirled around and sped away, with fragments of Kanuna's internal organs still dangling from the head of the lance. He let loose a blood-curdling war cry as he retreated. He was answered by the other Comanches, who whooped their approvals. He must have figured that he would come back later for the scalp. A true bad ass.

Realizing that there were enough armed Cherokees to make taking captives or scalps more expensive than it would be worth, the Comanches turned and rode away, daring the Cherokees to try to reclaim the two-dozen head of cattle that they had stolen. The bad ass with the lance must have figured that the witnessing of his bold deed by his comrades could stand on behalf of the scalp he had foregone. Perhaps he planned to come back and take a scalp or two later.

Those cattle represented about a third of the Cherokees' herd.

Enoli knew that, with those cattle, the Comanches would not be traveling very quickly. He would have to hold counsel with his people to decide whether to give pursuit and, if so, how to reclaim the cattle.

* * * * * * * *

While the Cherokee wounded were being treated, Enoli held a meeting. The issues were those of whether they should try to reclaim the stolen cattle, if so, how to do it, and whether revenge should be taken for Kanuna, who had been run through by the Comanche warrior's lance.

Some of the younger warriors, youths still in their teens and early twenties, wanted to give chase. Enoli warned them that they would not be dealing with common outlaws. Did they not see how skilled and deadly those Comanches were?

Johnny decided to speak up. He asked permission to speak from Uncle Enoli. It was granted.

Speaking in Cherokee, he declared, "I am as outraged by all of this as anyone here. I loved Uncle Kanuna like he was my own blood. And I wish I could kill all those bastards. But let us be honest. We just got our asses kicked. Even the whites, with their firearms, short of using their cannon, would be lucky to win a match with those Comanches. Someday, when the time and conditions are right, I want to exact vengeance. But for now, I suggest we accept our losses and prepare for the next time those dogs come back."

Billy Starr, one of the Cherokee mixed bloods, spoke next. He was about Johnny's age, six feet tall, with long black hair, slate grey eyes, and a fair complexion. He almost looked white, like Tommy Smith. He asked, "What do you suggest we do to get ready?"

Johnny looked at Enoli as if to ask for further permission to speak. Enoli nodded.

"We need to build battlements to shield us from their arrows. We can shoot them from behind those battlements, and if we shoot enough of their horses, they will not be able to rescue their fallen. Then, once they're off their horses, we'll kill them with our guns, arrows, and war clubs. We will make it so costly for them to steal again that they will think twice about it."

Enoli fingered his chin thoughtfully as this brief dialogue took place. He said, "Let us reflect on the matter for a couple of hours and come back to talk about it some more."

After the group broke up, Billy Starr approached Johnny. Speaking in English, for he was half white, he asked, "Hey Johnny, why don't we get some warriors together and go after those goddam Comanches and get our cattle back?"

Johnny, speaking English, answered, "There are about twenty of 'em. Even if all three of their wounded died, there would still be seventeen. We had twenty or so warriors here, and now three of them are wounded, and one is dead. How many do you think it would take to deal with that many fuckin' Comanches? They're unbeatable on horseback. They might kill half of our war party. And then what would happen if another Comanche war party attacked us? Our ability to defend would be compromised, wouldn't it?"

Billy, whom Johnny judged to be more brave than smart, looked confused. He said nothing. He looked dejected.

Johnny said, "I see you're a fightin' man. One of these days, Billy, we will set things right with them goddam heatherns. Right now, we need to make it hard for 'em to repeat what happened tonight. Don't you agree?"

Billy, who turned out to not be as dumb as Johnny had suspected, looked him in the eye and said, "If you promise to go with me one of these days and lay waste to those bastards, I won't stir nothin' up right now. Uncle Kanuna really *was* my blood."

"I don't know what the future holds, Billy, but I can tell you this: I *want* to do that."

Enoli called a second meeting that day. Johnny asked for permission to speak and shared his conversation with Billy. Billy confirmed the content of their agreement. There were no objections.

Enoli said, "In the old days, when our people lived in the East, everyone built stockades around their villages. That would be a huge task, and we would have to use a lot of timber—more than we should since the forests are not as thick or as plentiful out here. But we might be able to use less timber and place it correctly to accomplish the same thing. We could have two lines: One could be placed so that the corral is between it and our cabins. We could make it high enough so that their horses couldn't safely jump it, and we could leave a couple of openings with just enough room for them to ride through. The second line would be a clear arrow shot back behind it. Maybe fifty feet. Then, we could concentrate our fire and shoot them as they came through the openings in the first line of barricades. There would only be enough room for them to come through at most two abreast, and they couldn't turn their mounts sideways and shoot at us, using their horses as shields until they got all the way through. To make this work, we will need more shooters—and more guns. We can teach our women to load and shoot as well. Some of them already know how."

At this point, several women raised their fists and shouted, "Yes, we can!"

Enoli said, "We have twenty-five rifles here already. If we bought a dozen more, we could have nearly forty. One bullet for each Comanche horse, and one for each Comanche." He smiled.

"I propose to go to Fort Gibson with a few cattle and some money to buy those rifles and plenty of powder and shot. Our women will need a lot of powder and shot to practice with." He smiled again.

One of the young women, whose name was Sarah Studeville, shouted out, "Yes, we can kill them, too! Just get us guns and teach us to use them!" Some of the other women let out war cries, like wild Indians.

Johnny said, "I have some money. I will gladly give some of it for this."

Others offered up cash as well.

Enoli asked who wanted to go with him to Fort Gibson. He planned to take a wagon to bring back the guns, powder, and lead and six cattle to sell at the fort.

The trip, the negotiations at the Fort, and the return would take no more than seven or eight days. Enoli asked for two volunteers to go with him. Johnny volunteered, but Enoli believed it would be better to leave him at the ranch in case there were more hostilities. He saw that Johnny, though still young, could lead. Though he hoped that nothing would occur in the next week, he preferred to trust Johnny with a leadership role in case there was an attack. Two older men volunteered to go with him. He accepted their offer.

That afternoon, some of the elders assessed the area and decided where to place the battlements. The younger men immediately began cutting trees for the project.

* * * * * * * * *

Enoli, his two companions, a wagon drawn by two horses and six cattle left for Fort Gibson the next day. All the other men and boys were busy cutting down trees, trimming off branches, splitting logs, and shaping them with awls.

When Enoli's party returned, the outer perimeter was almost completed. It consisted of fences made of sharpened wooden poles arranged in "X" patterns, about five feet high. They were placed in segments, with two openings of six to eight feet in width between them. Fortunately, one side of the settlement was rimmed by a deep creek bed with a steep incline up to where the cabins were built. Dutch and Enoli had obviously chosen the site for this reason. This left only three sides needing battlements since the cabins at the top of the steep bank of the creek had windows from which guns could be fired if anyone tried to enter the settlement from that direction. Furthermore, it would be impossible to ride a horse up the steep bank.

The partially constructed inner perimeter looked more like a wooden fence. It was about three feet high, with thick, overlapping slats and holes large enough to slide a rifle barrel through by a prone marksman. An archer could position himself on a bended knee behind it and shoot accurately. It was completed two weeks later.

From the time Enoli returned with fifteen rifles and plenty of powder and shot, the women learned to shoot, load, and care for their new weapons. Some of them seemed to have a gift for shooting.

Johnny, remembering what Uncle Enoli had said to him four years earlier, saw in guns the greatest "equalizer" of all. A small woman with good shooting skills could kill a giant. If those Comanches came back, they would be in for a foul surprise…

* * * * * * * *

August passed uneventfully. At the end of the month, Dutch and his Cherokee scouts returned from the First Dragoon expedition to the west. As he approached the settlement, he noticed that almost half of the cattle had disappeared. He noticed the fortifications around the corral and the cabins and figured out that some kind of disaster had occurred in his absence. He and his men dismounted and corralled their horses. As they did so, Enoli and Johnny approached them.

"It looks like some shit happened in our absence," remarked Dutch.

Enoli narrated the events and their aftermath. One of the three Cherokees who were wounded had succumbed to his infections and died, but the other two had survived. He told him of the fate of Kanuna. Dutch, who had been Kanuna's friend for over half his life, was saddened by the news.

"So, these fortifications are the result of this raid? Good thinking, Enoli. What other provisions have been made?"

Enoli replied, "It was Johnny's idea originally. Anyway, we took six cattle and some money that was donated by the folks here to Fort Gibson and bought fifteen more rifles and a lot of powder and shot. We taught the women who did not already know how to shoot how to use them. And they have been practicing."

Johnny interjected, "Some of them are getting good. Sarah Studeville is a better shot than I was at her age!"

Dutch laughed. He needed to. He was much aggrieved over Kanuna. "Good," he said. "I hope she kills plenty of them if they come back. And they will. From what you told me, they probably think we're going to be easy pickings. But they will wait until they have eaten all those two dozen cattle they stole from us. That means they could be back in another month."

"If they do come back," declared Enoli, "they will be sorry." He gave an expansive look at the work that had been done. In the distance, they could hear the gunfire of the women and girls who were having target practice. They had these practice sessions two to three times a week.

Dutch turned to his men. "When we go to Fort Gibson to collect our pay, we will buy some more powder and shot. And then we can go down to Texas and buy a few cattle to cover our losses."

Chapter 14: Ten

The next day, Dutch left for Fort Gibson.

Johnny went to the north side of the settlement, where the women and girls practiced with their new rifles. He saw Sarah Studeville taking aim at a target that her friend had swung from a tree branch. He stood back, not wanting to distract her. Her hands were as steady as stone. The target was about forty feet away. She fired. She hit the target—a flat piece of board scrap that was left over from the fence construction—squarely in the middle. She quickly reloaded the gun, not noticing that she was being watched. She turned around to take a few paces further from the target and saw Johnny.

"Hi, Johnny! You watchin' me?" speaking English in a southern drawl.

"I hope you don't mind," said Johnny.

"Of course not. But you might make me a little nervous. I heard about you. You're a legend around here," she declared.

"Why?" asked Johnny. He wondered if someone had repeated the information he had given to Uncle Dutch and Enoli.

"I heard you already killed nine men."

"What else did you hear?" asked Johnny.

"I heard you killed most of 'em two or three at a time," replied Sarah.

"Did whoever said this say anything else?" asked Johnny, wondering if he should worry about legal exposure.

"No, except that the sonofabitches all needed killin'," said Sarah.

Sarah amused johnny. Though she talked tough, her voice lilted like that of a Southern belle when she spoke. Quite feminine for a future killer of men, he thought. Keeping his thoughts private, he said, "Well, Sarah, I felt a little bad about those two Osages I killed two years ago. They weren't sonofabitches. They were just enemies. It was kill or be killed. Nothin' personal. But you're right about the otherns. They were sonofabitches. And they desperately needed killin'." Johnny's eyes flashed with an ever-so-brief glaze of rage as he uttered the last sentence. Then, he quickly broke into a smile. "The way you shoot, you'll probably be a tenkiller before me."

Then he changed the subject. "Excuse me for askin', Sarah, but from the way you cuss, it don't seem like you ever been to church, have you?"

"I don't go to church. But that don't mean I don't believe in God."

"That's good to know," said Johnny, who almost laughed.

"Now, if you don't mind, I'm practicin' my shootin'. If you'll just stand back, I'm fixin' to shoot that target over yonder." Having moved back three or four paces, her target was now about fifty feet away. She yelled out to her friend, "OK, Adsila, swing that target!" Adsila complied. Sarah shot. Hit it almost dead center. Watching this, Johnny whispered to himself, "Shit!" She was scary.

Johnny stood back while she reloaded. One would never have thought of Sarah as a warrior. She was sixteen years old. She was about five feet, five inches tall. Her hair was sandy brown, like her eyes. Her skin was the color of coffee with two teaspoons of cream. She was slender, her movements controlled and graceful. If one looked at her for more than a few seconds, no flaws of any kind were visible, though her beauty was not of the sort that just jumped out at a person…like that of Ahyoka. It was the kind of simple beauty that grew on the onlooker. Then, for a split second, Johnny felt that just looking at Sarah was an unfaithful act. Indeed, he couldn't take his eyes off her. In a private act of contrition, he resolved never to share that pink tablecloth with her. That made him feel better.

And then he wondered why he was being faithful to Ahyoka, whom he would never see again.

* * * * * * * * *

Dutch came back from Fort Gibson ten days later, laden with powder and shot, and four of the six cattle that Enoli had taken to the fort to exchange for rifles. He bought them back from the fort's quartermaster. He planned to go to Texas in October to buy a dozen more cattle.

It was the third week in September—time for another full moon. It had been two months since the last Comanche raid. Dutch and Enoli had reason to believe that there could be another one at any time. Since the pickings had been so easy last time, the predatory Comanche would surely be back for more.

As it turned out, the expectations of Dutch and Enoli would not be disappointed.

* * * * * * * * *

It was past midnight but well before sunrise when they came. Unbeknownst to the Comanche war party, they would face twice the number of guns on this venture as they had the last time around. The mounted warriors were surprised to find those wooden stake battlements on the perimeter of the corral but noticed the two openings, just large enough to shew the cattle through. The bulk of the war party stayed well back while two daring young warriors crept through one of the openings to the corral and quietly opened the gate.

Johnny and Sarah were keeping watch that night, laying low behind the wooden slat fence, the second line of fortification. They had heard the pounding of the Comanche horse hooves off in the distance. Sarah had alerted Dutch, who had dispatched messengers to the other cabins to wake them up. Their weapons were already loaded.

When the two Comanches got to the corral, two shots rang out: One from Johnny's rifle, one from Sarah's. Both warriors dropped with mortal wounds.

The war chief—the one with the buffalo-horned headdress—signaled his warriors to attack. The mounted Comanches began to charge through the opening. By this time, Dutch, Enoli, and several other warriors had joined Johnny and Sarah, who were reloading their rifles. As the Comanches charged through the opening, they all fired their rifles. Two Comanche horses fell, sending their riders to the ground. The two warriors were hit, though not mortally, by Cherokee gunfire. Two others, unable to turn their mounts sideways, were shot off the backs of their mounts. Meanwhile, several of the women had come up behind Dutch and his warriors with their loaded rifles. As more Comanche warriors tried to charge through, a volley of rifle fire disabled their horses and sent three more warriors to the ground. Rather than give themselves up to more slaughter at that opening, a dozen Comanche horsemen galloped past the other opening, trying to flank the defenders by going all the way to the back of the settlement and rushing them from that direction.

This did not work out well for them. There were twenty more guns, held by an equal number of young men and women, waiting for them there. As they sped through the opening in the back fortification, they met a volley of a dozen rifle shots. Six of them were killed or wounded. The others scooped their comrades off the ground and retreated without the war horses ridden by their wounded and dead comrades.

The war chief with the buffalo horns was the bad ass who had boldly charged the Cherokee in the last raid and impaled Uncle Kanuna with his lance. Realizing that half of his force of two dozen warriors were now dead or wounded and that he had ridden into a much more lethal resistance than he had encountered the last time, he paused for a moment. He realized that this venture was going to fail. He wouldn't steal any cattle or horses, and his war party had suffered significant losses. He would be dishonored despite his past successes: his many scalps, his many captives, and his many successful acts of plunder. He believed he would lose face.

He reflected on these things for a moment.

Then he made his decision.

He told his warriors to stay back as he charged solo towards the defenders. He hoped he might kill one more enemy before meeting certain death. He let out a blood-curdling war cry and charged, his white buffalo skin shield shining in the bright moonlight. The Cherokee remembered who he was, though they did not know his name. When he rode through the opening in the outer perimeter, Billy Starr exclaimed, "That's the sonofabitch that killed Uncle Kanuna! He's mine!" He aimed his rifle and fired. The bullet pierced the Comanche's shield and wounded him in his left arm, but he continued to hold his shield and had almost reached the second fortification when another shot rang out.

It was Sarah Studeville's bullet that ended the life of the great warrior. She hit him right between the eyes. He fell off his horse as it jumped the wooden slat fence. There he lay, face up, his lifeless eyes staring vacantly at the bright sky, illuminated by the full autumn moon, the blood from his forehead spilling out on the left side of his face and skull. The remnants of his war party, deprived of their leader, realizing that they might all die if they persisted in this failed venture, turned around, intending to head back to Texas.

Billy Starr took out his knife and wanted to scalp the buffalo horn-clad Comanche warrior. Dutch told him not to do that. Billy protested, but Dutch told him that this man wasn't even his kill, though he had wounded him. It was legitimately Sarah's kill. Billy, angered at being denied the scalp and credit for the kill, stalked away.

Dutch summoned one of the Cherokees who had gone on the expedition with the First Dragoons. He spoke passable Spanish. He directed him to call out to the Comanches in Spanish and ask if any of them spoke that language. He did so. One of the Comanche warriors replied, "*Yo!*"

"Tell him that we will give them the body of this great chief, who died in honor, and that we will give them two cattle to take home as a sign of our desire for friendship. And ask them the name of this great warrior."

The interpreter did his best. He shouted out the question, "*Como se llama ese guerrero?*"

The Comanche who spoke Spanish shouted back, "*Diez Osos!*" Ten Bears.

Some Cherokee warriors dragged the lifeless body of Ten Bears to the opening in the outer perimeter through which he had made his final, heroic charge. Two Comanche warriors lifted his body onto the back of one of their spare horses. Comanches always took plenty of these spares wherever they went. Meanwhile, two Cherokee cowboys led two young steers out of the corral and solemnly presented them to the remnants of the war party.

The closest thing to a "Thank you" proffered by the Comanches was a simple nod, given by the apparent leader of what was left of their war party, as they turned and rode away with their dead, their wounded, the two cattle that they had been given, and those of their horses that had not been shot by the Cherokee defenders. No scalps were taken by the Cherokee, though a dozen had been earned that night.

When they had been gone for a safe while, the Cherokee gathered in the center of their settlement. There were multiple animated conversations going on. Everyone was excited at their victory over the notorious Comanche. Some were claiming credit for their kills. Some were narrating the events as they had seen them from their individual perspectives. Not a single Cherokee had even been wounded this time. It was, for them, a victory worth celebrating.

It wasn't much of a celebration for Billy Starr, though. He was bitter at having been upstaged by Sarah Studeville. He was talking loudly about how Dutch had shown the Comanches weakness by allowing them to take those two cattle.

Dutch, who was beginning to grow impatient with Billy, spoke up. He said, "The Comanches are not used to losing like this. This war party underestimated our willingness and ability to fight them, and they made a bad error in judgment. We were prepared. We understood their vulnerability. We had them quite outgunned. They must have been surprised that our women could shoot as well as they did. Altogether, we killed or wounded at least a dozen of them. It was a serious defeat. Ten Bears lost over half of his war party.

"We did not have to give them any cattle. Because we chose to, they are likely to see it as a gift, not as tribute. And because we gave their war chief an honorable death, gave his body to them to take home, and did not mutilate him, we showed our respect for a great warrior. When they get back to wherever they came from—probably down in Texas—they will speak of the honorable death of their war chief and of our respect. In both cases, they will claim honor. Ten Bears was clearly a great warrior. Now, he will be remembered that way.

"They lost, but they will go home knowing that we respect the Comanche people. They will see our gift of two steers as a token of that. They may contemplate vengeance, and we need to continue to be ready for them if they decide to launch another raid. But I think that they might also realize that stealing from us is costly, that the cost in Comanche lives is not worth a few head of cattle. If, on the other hand, we had scalped that chief and mutilated his body, and if we had used our superior numbers to chase and kill more of them, it would have increased their appetite for revenge, and then we would have a long war on our hands—one that we could lose. I was trying to make it less efficient for them to wage war against us.

"I might turn out to be wrong. But this was my thinking," concluded Dutch. "Does anyone else wish to speak?"

No one had anything to add. Not even Billy.

Dutch spoke again. He said, "Many of you are too young to remember this, but not too long ago, we were like those Comanches. Ten Bears would have been a hero among our people back then. He was fearless and bold. He chose certain death over dishonor. He made the last sacrifice that a man who is one with the warrior's path can make. He valued his honor more than he valued taking another breath. He died a true warrior's death. Consider this…

"In showing him respect, we also respected ourselves, for what we once were, and for what we may yet continue to be: A nation of brave warriors!" The people responded with a chorus of war cries.

Then, he looked at Sarah, who had just killed two of the fearsome Comanche warriors. He said, "And our women have shown themselves to be worthy warriors, too. I am proud of you, and we are all grateful for your courage and skill."

At that point, these "civilized" Indians broke out in a massive din of war whoops. Whoops of victory. Someone picked up a drum and began to beat it rhythmically. Two dozen older Cherokees formed a dancing circle and began singing an ancient chant.

As they danced, others, exalted with the thrill of victory, continued to recount the details of the battle until the sun rose. After about an hour, they retired to their cabins to prepare breakfast.

Dutch, in whose cabin Johnny was staying, approached him after the crowd had broken up. He asked him, "How many Comanches did you kill today?"

Johnny replied, "One for sure, and maybe another, but I cannot prove that one."

"Well, son, to look on the bright side of things, you are a tenkiller now, aren't you?"

"Yes, Uncle. I am," replied Johnny, his chest swelling with pride, having fulfilled the boast he made in the note he left on the door of the Stricklin's cabin a full year before this moment. "But when I took a close look at Number Ten, I saw that he was little more than a boy. I wondered if I should even count him."

Dutch said, "He would not have minded counting you if you were the dead one."

Johnny recalled the conversation he had with Dutch and Enoli when he botched his first kill. After a brief reflection, he acknowledged to Dutch, "All right, I am a tenkiller now." Then he changed the topic. "That Sarah Studeville is a great shot. Maybe better than me. In her first battle, she killed two Comanche warriors. I am impressed."

"As am I," said Dutch. "She's pretty, too," he added, looking at Johnny from the corner of his eye, wearing a knowing smile.

Johnny did not comment. He was still missing Ahyoka.

Chapter 15: Grandmother's Love

One afternoon in the middle of October 1834, some Cherokees from Uncle Dutch's ranch returned from Fort Gibson. They had news for Johnny. His grandmother, Ahyoka, had arrived with two wagons from the east.

When Johnny asked with whom she had traveled that distance, they said that some other people from Tennessee had formed a wagon train, that one of her two wagons had been driven by her and the other by a man named Tayanita, whom people also called "Beaver." ("Beaver" was a loose English translation of his Cherokee name.) The last part of the journey had been on a flatboat pulled up the Arkansas River by a steamer.

This was the same Beaver who had dropped into Grandmother Ahyoka's store, back in Tennessee, a year earlier to report the murders of the Stricklin boys. The same Beaver who had interrogated her about her grandson, "Johnny." The same Beaver who had declared, as he walked out of the store, that if the perpetrator had been *his* son or grandson, he would have been proud.

Johnny felt relief, followed by great excitement at hearing this news. His grandmother was safe here in Indian Territory. He couldn't wait to greet her. He planned to take Flower and a pack horse to Fort Gibson. Not the old gelding, though. Having served him faithfully, the old horse was, so to speak, on his last legs.

He left at daybreak the next day. The pack horse carried saddle bags with his modest possessions, extra powder and shot, soap, and other things he still had from his stop in St. Louis. He arrived at Fort Gibson at sunset two days later. He quickly found the Cherokee area outside the fort and saw his grandmother before she saw him coming. She, Beaver, and another woman were tending a fire. Suspended above the fire, hanging from a tripod, was a kettle, probably filled with some kind of stew.

As he got closer to them, he looked closely at the other woman.

She smiled at him. As she did, his heart leaped into his throat. It was the younger Ahyoka.

He dismounted and approached his grandmother, his knees shaking as he walked towards the campfire, trying not to look at his other Ahyoka. He did not want to disrespect his grandmother. In the Cherokee language, he said, "Hello, Grandmother." Ahyoka quickly arose, and they joined in a warm embrace.

"This is Beaver, White Owl." Beaver arose, and they shook hands.

Johnny said, "Pleased to meet you, Beaver. You can call me 'Johnny'."

"And I believe you know who this is," gesturing towards the other Ahyoka. He gazed straight at Ahyoka, who was as beautiful as the last time he had seen her. He walked over to her as she stood to greet him, and they joined in a warm, lingering embrace. They did not kiss, both of them seeming to understand that it might look rude. But that was fine with Johnny. He had been sure he would never see her again, and yet, here she was, standing before him in the flesh, his heart pounding so strongly that he thought he might faint, his knees still shaking.

Grandmother said, "I know you must be surprised. From the looks of you, it is a pleasant surprise." She smiled broadly.

"To be truthful, I was afraid that you would not come here. And I had accepted that I would never see Ahyoka again." He remembered the night he spent in the lean-to he had built on his journey from St. Louis to Fort Gibson, on that spring afternoon when the dark clouds rolled in and poured rain, when he felt a powerful longing to see Ahyoka again. Then, he recalled the insight he had when he left Cahokia: *God hears the prayers of our hearts but doesn't pay much attention to the prattling of our minds.* Concluding that his prayers had been answered, he declared, "Seeing both of you here is a great gift. A gift from the Great Spirit."

His grandmother remarked, "It seems you have changed your way of thinking since last we spoke. Something must have awakened you, White Owl."

At a loss for words, Johnny tried to respond. He remembered his grandmother's admonishments about the "Path" and her suggestion that he "best not piss off God, just in case He does exist." The best he could do now was to reply, "Your words were part of it. The rest is a long story. I am not even sure I can tell it and make any sense. It's better that I do not try, right now. But yes, Grandmother, I realize that I am but a tiny thread in the Great Spirit's tapestry."

"I assume you plan to stay here, don't you?" asked Grandmother Ahyoka.

"All the way here, I thought only about seeing you. I brought the things that are most important to me because I thought it likely that I would stay a while. Better that I should ask, what are your plans?"

"I have two wagon loads of things here," said Grandmother. "Most of the things I brought are for a store I was hoping to set up. Some of them are personal things. The question is where to go from here, where to put down new roots."

"Have you any ideas about those matters?" asked Johnny.

"I have been told by some of the Old Settlers that there is a place east of here where those of us who have come from the east are welcome. It's called 'Tahlequah'. I brought some seed for corn, and I have heard that there are wild plum trees and oak trees with plenty of acorns. I thought about buying some hogs and raising them. First, though, we would have to plant corn. We could feed the hogs with that, wild acorns, fruits, and whatever we throw away from our dinner table. Hopefully, we will have enough food to do that."

"I could buy an anvil and other tools to set up a smithy there," said Johnny. "Folks will need horseshoes, plow shares, ax heads, and the like."

"Does Dutch know that you will be moving up here with us?" asked Grandmother.

"All I told him was that I did not know when I would be back. He understood." Changing topics, he said, "Shouldn't we be going to this Tahlequah as soon as possible so we can build a cabin before winter comes?"

* * * * * * * *

They left the next day. They spent a night on the trail and arrived in Tahlequah at noon the day after. Johnny and Beaver found the elders and asked permission to settle there. They also asked where they could set up their living quarters and store. Johnny identified himself as Dutch's nephew and let them know that Grandmother Ahyoka was Dutch's auntie. Dutch was by that time a notable chief within the Western Band, and dropping his name had the desired effect. The elders gave permission to settle on a parcel of land near the center of town. But it was not yet much of a town, with a population not much bigger than that of Uncle Dutch's ranch. It needed a store, though, and Ahyoka's would be the first one there. Johnny figured that this might work out well for them.

The other people in their wagon train were given living spaces as well. The group would collaborate to build four cabins. Tahlequah, being at the foot of the Ozarks, had access to plenty of timber. They set to work at once.

* * * * * * * * *

A week after settling in Tahlequah, Johnny asked Ahyoka to join him for a walk in the woods and meadows just outside this growing new town. She consented. When they were out of sight of the folks in town, Johnny took her hand, at which point he felt as if his feet would leave the ground; he was so elated. Ahyoka squeezed his hand tightly, lifting his spirits still higher. More shaking of his knees and heart pounding…

They walked in silence for several minutes, words unnecessary to convey what each of them was feeling.

At length, Johnny asked, "How did this come to pass?"

To his surprise, Ahyoka, who normally spoke Cherokee, answered in English. "After you left, life had no more meanin' for me. Not to say that I was very happy to begin with—I hadn't been that for a long time, but when you left, something inside me just died. And the feelin' didn't go away. I knew about your grandmother—you had told me all about her—and decided I wanted to meet her too. I hoped that somehow, through her, I would see you again. I prayed for it." She paused.

"So, how *did* you end up meetin' my grandmother?" he asked.

"Uncle Wohali could see that I was sad, that I'd lost my desire to go on livin'. He asked me if there was anything he could do to end my sadness. I told him that he could either kill me or take me to meet your grandmother. So, one day, before winter set in, he took me down the hill to Knoxville. He planned to buy some things at your grandmother's store. He looked forward to it because he had not seen her for years. So, we went down there, and he introduced me to her. He told her about your stay in our village. Of how you had hunted for us. And then he told her to let me tell the rest of it."

"Did you?" asked Johnny, wondering if he should be embarrassed.

"I put it pretty delicate, Johnny," she said with a smile. "Your grandmother's pretty smart, though. She figured it out...And she told me that it seemed I was a bit too old for you. I said I knew that, but that I loved you just the same. I told her I didn't expect nothin' like a marriage or anything like that. I told her I couldn't bear children. So, she asked me what I *did* want. I said I just wanted to be near you. That's all. And that I would serve her for the rest of her life in exchange for that privilege."

"That's a big promise, Ahyoka," declared Johnny. "That's not to say I ain't glad you made it...And by the way, you sure speak good English now. How did that happen?"

"Your grandmother and I made a deal to speak to each other in English. She was already good at it and thought it might be good for me to get good at it, too. Gettin' back to the story, though...

"Your grandmother thought about it for a while, as Uncle Wohali went through her store and picked out the things he needed. By the time we finished loadin' up the wagon, she invited me to stay with her. I'd brought some clothes and some women's things, you know, combs and things like that, in case she did invite me to stay. They were in Uncle Wohali's wagon.

"When I brought them out, your grandmother said, 'You're pretty confident of yourself, aren't you, Ahyoka?' And I said, 'That's because I have faith, Auntie.' I've called her 'Auntie' ever since."

"I noticed that right away," said Johnny. He smiled.

"So, Auntie asked me what I could do for her. I told her I could cook, clean, and do whatever chores she needed to have done in the store. Anything at all. And that's what I've done for the past year. When she decided to get out of Knoxville and come west, I helped her prepare. I helped her decide what to throw away and what to put in them wagons.

That wasn't easy. She was sentimental about a lot of the things she couldn't take with her," observed Ahyoka.

"I understand," commented Johnny.

Ahyoka changed the theme of her narrative at this point. She said, "Over those months, Auntie asked me lots of questions about my life. She wanted to know who I was, who I had been."

"I never even asked you that, Ahyoka. I was too busy thinking about just being with you," said Johnny. "As a matter of fact, it's all I can think of right now."

They were well out of sight of the little town and of its inhabitants. They were in the woods. They looked at each other with eyes glistening with desire. They embraced, and for the first time since they had reunited, they kissed.

Johnny had brought a bedroll and some blankets. He took them off Flower's saddle and asked, "Would it be all right if I laid these out on that soft grass over yonder, under that tree?" Ahyoka dropped her dress to the ground, as she had the first night they were together, revealing her luscious breasts.

"Don't do that yet!" Johnny exclaimed. "You'll catch cold!" He spread out the bedding, stripped down to his underwear, pulled her to the ground, and covered their bodies with his blanket. They embraced. And then Johnny's mind went into a dream…

An hour later, they lay side-by-side, their sensual appetites momentarily sated. Johnny asked, though it was more a comment than a question, "How did I live without you for this past year?"

Ahyoka turned her face to him and just smiled.

* * * * * * * * *

They arose. Johnny folded the bedding and the blanket and placed them back on Flower. They resumed their walk. "So," Johnny said, "My grandmother wanted to know all about you?"

"Yes, she did. And I told her," Ahyoka replied.

"Well, if you don't mind my askin', I'd like to know what you told her."

"It's time you knew, too, Johnny, so I'll tell you.

"When I was sixteen, I fell in love with a warrior who was about ten years older than me. His name was Pathkiller. His father named him after a famous Cherokee chief. You know how we give names. Parents who give names like that hope their young-uns will live into 'em, so to speak. Kind of like you did when you took the name 'Tenkiller'.

"Pathkiller had made a name for himself in the War of 1812, fighting the Red Sticks. Like my Uncle Wohali, who was much older than him at that time, he fought at the Battle of Horseshoe Bend. They helped Andrew Jackson win that battle."

"I know. That old sonofabitch...," said Johnny.

"Everyone admired Pathkiller. All the young girls wanted him. So, when he asked me to be his wife, I was excited. I said I would."

"Well, I can't say as I blame him for choosin' you," said Johnny.

"Anyway, a year later, I had a miscarriage. I was sick for a long time after. I never got pregnant again. Somethin' must have happened to my body."

She paused again. Then she added, "After a couple of years, Pathkiller, who desperately wanted children, left me for another woman."

Johnny, though still barely more than a youth, had suffered enough tragedy in his own life, enough loss to understand. He wasn't jealous that Ahyoka had loved someone else in her past. He felt sad for her.

After a moment's reflection, he asked, "Whatever happened to Pathkiller?"

"He moved into the Smokey Mountains with some other Cherokees. I heard he had three children: Two boys, the oldest one would be half-grown by now, and a little girl."

In a reverent tone of voice, Johnny asked, "Are you happy for him, Ahyoka?"

"Yes, I am. I understand why he had to find someone else. He was a good man. The best man I ever knew—next to you, Johnny."

Johnny didn't know what to say.

"But after Pathkiller left me, I was sad. I was lost. Because many men considered me pretty, I got a lot of attention. Not necessarily 'good' attention. I was so lonely. When I had a chance to have company with a man, I did not decline it. Pretty soon, all the women hated me. I understand why." Ahyoka paused again. Then she said, "And don't ever ask me again about that part of my life because it isn't somethin' I care to remember or to talk about. I don't even want to remember their names. Nothin' against them. I was just passin' the time. I didn't care about nothin', really. I didn't even know what I was livin' for."

After another moment of silence, Ahyoka continued: "I moved to Uncle Wohali's village two years before you showed up there. I wanted to get away from my past, but as luck would have it, there were a couple of people there who had heard this and that about me. That's why they were all over us when we had our relationship."

"Who gives a shit about what they think or what they thought at the time? My only concern with their opinions was that they might cause inconvenience for Uncle Wohali. Otherwise, fuck 'em!" declared Johnny.

Ahyoka winced at Johnny's profanity. She had never heard him speak that way before. Not once. Then, realizing he meant her no disrespect, she exclaimed, laughing, "Yeah, fuck 'em!"

Johnny, surprised at her expression of profanity, laughed, too. And then he kissed her.

"I'm happy you see it that way," said Ahyoka. "So, here is the rest of what I told Auntie: 'When I met your grandson, I found him beautiful, not just to look at, but something about him that shined through from the inside. I didn't just want him; there was something about him that I needed. I wanted whatever it was that he had, whatever it was that shined from him. It wasn't the sex—well, maybe it was that, too. But really, it was somethin' else."

Speaking directly to Johnny, Ahyoka concluded: "I can't put words to whatever that is. It doesn't matter that I can't say it. What's important is that I *feel* it."

"All that said, I don't know what the future holds. Who does? I'm just happy to be near you, Johnny Tenkiller. That's enough for me." And then she smiled.

Johnny felt as if he were floating up to the sky. And then he said, his chin slightly quivering, his eyes moistened by tears, "I love you, too."

* * * * * * * * *

By the end of November, the cabins were finished. Johnny and Beaver built a shed for his blacksmithing shop, and Johnny bought an anvil and other tools of the trade. He went up into the mountains to buy iron. He planned to spend the winter months making horseshoes, ax heads, and plowshares.

During this time, Johnny and Ahyoka had opportunities to take their furtive walks into the woods. One day, when they returned to his grandmother's cabin, she looked at them knowingly but said nothing. There was no suspicion, no recrimination in her glance, just warmth.

The next day, as Johnny worked on his plowshares and ax heads, his grandmother walked out to the shed where he had set up his smithy. He was building an inventory for the spring, as he had learned to do from Robert Franklin, back in Pittsburg. He planned to keep records of his sales from then on. Maybe, in time, he would be as successful as Mr. Franklin.

His grandmother silently watched him work.

He took a break from pounding a red-hot piece of iron and looked up at her, wanting to ask her something but without knowing how to choose the words.

He didn't need to.

She had already read his mind.

"I see that you two are in love. You don't need to conceal it or play it down anymore." She smiled, and a tear rolled down from one of her eyes. "It is so plain to see that you are happy. And I am happy for you, White Owl, or Tenkiller, or whoever you are nowadays. I believe you have been waiting for my approval."

Johnny just stood next to his anvil, wondering what his grandmother was about to say.

After a pregnant pause, she declared, "I approve."

Johnny put his tools down and walked to the elder Ahyoka. They hugged silently. Then she said, her eyes wet with tears of joy, "You might be too young to understand what I am about to say, but hear this anyway: In life, you will only have this once, maybe twice if you are fortunate, and live long enough. Rejoice in it. That is what I wish for you."

Swelling with gratitude, he said, "You will always be the pillar that holds up the sky for me." Then, from his heart, he said, "Thank you, Grandmother."

* * * * * * * * *

That evening, his Ahyoka prepared a meal. She, Johnny's grandmother, Beaver, and Johnny sat at the table—Grandmother had had one made by this time—but before they set it with the food, Johnny asked them to wait. He went into one of his bags and pulled out the pink tablecloth that Lizzie had given him on his departure from Pittsburgh. "I'd like to cover the table with this if y'all don't mind," he said. "I've been waitin' for a long time to use it."

The younger Ahyoka at once knew the significance of this tablecloth, but Johnny wanted to tell the backstory. Speaking English, he said, "When I was on the run after killin' the Stricklins, I wound up at a little hamlet up in the hills, northeast of Knoxville. There, I met Ahyoka. I stayed in a little one-room cabin about the size of my work shed. One day, I came home from the hunt and found it all cleaned up and decorated with beads and dried red and orange berries. It was so beautiful…And then, when we sat for dinner, she covered a rough wooden table with a pink cloth and lit an oil lamp. I'll never forget that pink tablecloth or how grand I felt that night, taking dinner in that humble little shed, decorated so nicely by Ahyoka. A dear friend who knew the story I just told you gave this to me when I left Pittsburgh last March. I would have carried it around in my saddle bag forever and never used it at all if I never saw Ahyoka again. But miracles happen. And I hope this tablecloth does for you what it did for me, back then."

The younger Ahyoka exclaimed, "I had no idea that you'd see that tablecloth that way! I was just lookin' to cover that raggedy wooden table with somethin' pretty."

Speaking English, for she was fluently bilingual, Grandmother Ahyoka said, "Well, let's be careful not to spill anything on it. It's clearly more than just a tablecloth to someone here. And I do feel elegant just sitting here with it."

She beamed a benign smile. "Shall we bless the food, now?"

* * * * * * * *

The next day, Johnny rose early. He didn't do any blacksmithing work. He had a promise to fulfill: Now that he had a place at which he could receive mail, he was obliged to let Isaac and Lizzie know so they could write to him, too. It was December, so he figured that Lizzie's child must have been born already. He wrote a letter and rode Flower to Fort Gibson so he could mail it to them. It read:

December 12, 1834

Dear Isaac and Lizzie,

I have been blessed. My two Ahyokas are now here with me in Indian Territory. I wish I could describe my overwhelming gratitude to the Great Spirit for making it so.

We have set up my grandmother's store, I have a blacksmith shop, and we all live together in a cabin we built this past fall. We will build another when Spring comes.

I never expected to see Ahyoka again, and yet, here she is. And my grandmother has given her blessing to us, even though she knows Ahyoka is older than I, and cannot bear children.

Last night, I took out that pink tablecloth that Lizzie gave me before I left Pittsburg. I saved it all this time for just such an occasion. I wish you two could have been here to share the moment.

Before they came, I was helping out at Uncle Dutch's new ranch on the Canadian River. We fought two battles with Comanche raiding parties.

We lost the first one but won the second. I found my "Number Ten" in the second engagement.

I guess that by now, your child must have been born. I pray that the child was born in good health and that you are both well. Is it a boy or a girl?

Now that you know how to find me, please write, and let me know. Send your correspondence to Fort Gibson, Indian Territory, and address it to "John Sullivan."

May the Great Spirit bless and keep you.

Your friend always,

Johnny

Part 5: The Far Side of the Trail of Tears

Chapter 16: Reunion

Johnny, Grandmother Ahyoka, and Beaver spent the next two years setting up their lives in Tahlequah. They built a second cabin. The younger Ahyoka cooked and cleaned and helped with other tasks when needed, as she had promised the elder Ahyoka, who ran the store. Johnny made ax blades, horseshoes, and plow shares for sale to other Cherokee and the garrison at Fort Gibson. The first year, with their income, they bought two sows and a boar hog.

In April 1835, Johnny received a letter from Isaac MacDermott. He and Lizzy had a baby girl. They named her "Ahyoka". Johnny was pleased to pass this information on to his two Ahyokas. And Isaac's furniture business was prospering. Johnny was happy for them.

Johnny's family and the other settlers learned a few hard lessons during those first two years. Summers in Tahlequah were very hot—significantly hotter than summers in Tennessee or Georgia. They had to plow deeper furrows to protect the roots of their crops during the summer. For this, Johnny learned to make longer shares for plows. Because of the deeper furrows, the plows would often need to be pulled by two horses, not just one. They learned not to plant too close to the streams flowing out of the Ozarks because these could become swollen with rainwater from time to time and wash some of their crops away.

During their second year in Tahlequah, they bought more sows. They fed them with wild acorns, plums, and corn. The hogs multiplied.

Grandmother Ahyoka created an herb garden behind the cabin. They were beginning to prosper.

* * * * * * * * *

Johnny had not seen Dutch for nearly two years when, one day in the fall of 1836, his uncle, accompanied by Enoli, showed up in Tahlequah, looking for Johnny and Dutch's auntie, Ahyoka. It was still a small town, and Dutch found their store, smithy, and cabins without difficulty. He walked into the store where the younger Ahyoka was busy straightening out the inventory. Grandmother Ahyoka, who had long since learned to count money and keep records, was doing this when Dutch walked in, wearing his turban, feathers, moccasins, and a fringed buckskin shirt. A well-dressed Cherokee. Not recognizing him, she greeted him as she would have greeted any other customer. In the Cherokee language, she said, "Good afternoon, sir."

Dutch, who had been informed by the Fort Gibson quartermaster, Sergeant Smith, knew whom he was looking at. But at this moment, the recognition was one-sided. She didn't know who *he* was. He smiled and said, "Hello, Auntie. I'm Tahchee."

She hadn't seen him since he was a boy, and he was now in his mid-forties. When he introduced himself, she brightened up with a warm smile. "Hello, my nephew! Are you hungry? I have some corn-and-bean bread, just baked. Come in and sit down at our table."

Dutch said, "Enoli and I would be pleased, Auntie. But where is White Owl? I haven't seen him for nearly two years, since he left our ranch to come up here and find you."

"He is outside in his shed, working," she replied. "I'll fetch him. I am certain he will be happy to see you." Ahyoka stepped outside and, in a moment, walked back in with Johnny.

"Uncle!" he exclaimed. He walked up to Dutch and took his hand, a gesture of respect for an elder or chief among the Cherokee. Then, he did the same with Uncle Enoli.

Dutch said, "I was wondering when I would see you again. It has been two years since last we spoke." He looked at Johnny's hair, which had grown long. It was gathered in a top knot, and the tail of it hung down almost to his shoulder blades. He said, "Well, White Owl, you probably won't pass for black Irish looking like that. If you shaved the sides, painted up, and added a couple of feathers, you would look like a wild Indian, like we used to." Everyone laughed.

"Let me wash my hands. I will be back in just a moment." While Johnny stepped outside to the well and drew some water, Dutch and Enoli were escorted into the cabin, where there was a dining table with six chairs. The younger Ahyoka prepared servings for everyone.

Johnny, who had been sweating in his smithy all day, washed his hands and scrubbed himself. Then he joined them. Grandmother sat at one end of the table, and Dutch sat at the other. Ahyoka sat next to Johnny along one of the sides. Enoli sat across from Johnny and Ahyoka, soon to be joined by Beaver.

Dutch wondered who this other Ahyoka was. He remembered Johnny's narrative about the niece of Wohali when he was on the run after fulfilling his vendetta against the Stricklins. Could it be the same woman? She looked a little old for Johnny, but one had to admit she was a very attractive woman. He figured he would find out in due course.

"Enoli has family in Georgia and Tennessee. He has some news about what has been happening back there," announced Dutch.

Enoli spoke. "Things have been getting very bad in our old land. Very bad. The government of Georgia has been giving away our lands to white people who win some kind of game of chance. A 'lottery'." He said this word in English, as there was no Cherokee equivalent for it. "They surveyed the land and put marks on it so that they can give it away or sell it—I am not sure which of these is the case—one piece at a time to white people. It is bad enough that they do this with land that is not settled by our people. Once that land is given to the whites, our people cannot hunt there or use it at all.

"But what is worse is that they also give land with farms and houses. Houses that our people built and live in. Once that land has been given, our people must leave. Sometimes, they will come back from a journey and find strangers dining at their tables, looking at them as if to say, 'Who the hell are you?' If the Cherokee resist, they will be arrested or beaten with whips until they leave, even in front of their children. It is a horrible thing. Many are wandering about that part of the country with no places to go and no homes. Living like dogs on the outer rim of a camp, hoping for scraps, or digging roots, or whatever else they can find to eat."

Johnny's forehead became wet with perspiration, not because of the weather, for it was a crisp spring day, but because of the torrent of indignation and rage building up within him. His eyes grew cold. He saw the opening of his dark tunnel.

Dutch, noting this, said, "White Owl, do not even think what you are thinking. You cannot kill every white man in the state of Georgia." He didn't laugh when he said this. Then, in English, he added, "Not even all of the sonofabitches that need killin'." Then he grinned.

Johnny took a deep breath to get hold of himself. He said, "Grandmother, I am so glad you came here after all. If you had been back there and suffered this kind of injustice, I would have gone back and killed more sonofabitches."

Dutch said, "But then, you would have to be on the run again, wouldn't you?"

Johnny, looking to make light of this unpleasant conversation, said, "Well, the last time I was on the run, I met her," looking kindly at Ahyoka.

Dutch said, "I had a feeling you were up to something besides hunting deer up there."

Enoli continued. "A group of wealthy Cherokees, including some chiefs, are said to have discussed 'Indian Removal' in Washington, D.C., where Andrew Jackson is now the great chief of the whites. The word is that they signed a treaty that sold all the Cherokee lands in the east and required everyone in the tribe to move out here. The Cherokee Nation will be paid a lot of money by the United States for that land, and a huge amount of land out here will be made available for them. People who have made improvements on the lands they have been using will be paid—so the white man says—a fair price for them. They can bring any movable property they have along with them. That includes their slaves if they have any. The costs of moving them out here will be paid by the white man's government. For the first year they are here, they will be fed and housed, paid for by the US government. They will also be given seed for planting, guns, blankets, and other things. It sounds like a reasonable deal."

"A very good one, considering the other choices they have right now," added Johnny's grandmother.

"What choices?" demanded Johnny, still cooling off from his outrage.

"That was my point, White Owl," said Johnny's grandmother, with a hint of impatience in her voice.

"One would think so," continued Enoli. "The problem is that the treaty has not been signed by people authorized to do so by our tribal laws. It was signed by some wealthy, educated Cherokees who have rank in our tribal councils. They were led by the Ridge family. In any case, it has not been made law yet. But it seems that 'removal' is inevitable, whether we like it or not. Consider: The Muskogee and the Choctaw are already here in Indian Territory. So are the Chickasaw and whatever Seminoles they could drag out of the Florida swamps. The Cherokee will be the last to go."

"What are the eastern Cherokees planning to do about this?" asked Johnny.

"Some of them—a few hundred—have already moved deeper into the mountains in North Carolina. But most of them, especially the full bloods, are hoping that Chief John Ross can get the white men to change their minds," replied Enoli.

"They will not," said Dutch in a matter-of-fact tone.

Johnny, whose blood was starting to boil again, asked, "Can there be anything worse than being conquered and ground down into dust? Because that is what is happening. How will those children who have watched their parents beaten and degraded see them after that? Will they still respect them? Will they grow up to respect themselves? Losing the land is a bad thing. Losing your self-respect is far worse. Is Chief Ross thinking about this?" asked Johnny. "Could Chief Ross persuade the full bloods to see how bad things will go for them if they try to stay there? Could he persuade them to make a choice that is better for them and for their children?"

"He probably could, but he is not inclined to do that. I do not know why. Maybe it is because he has a big plantation with a lot of slaves and prefers not to move," responded Enoli.

"Well," declared Johnny, still enraged by the news that Enoli had just shared, "Easy for him! He is wealthy. He can afford to buy another house if he is dispossessed, and he can take his slaves wherever he goes. He probably has a big bank account, too."

"Let us not rush to judgment," cautioned Grandmother Ahyoka. "Chief Ross probably has a plan."

* * * * * * * * *

After dinner, the two Ahyokas cleaned the table and the dishes. Meanwhile, the men went outside to sit and talk on the front porch.

Beaver said, "I have a lot of kin back east. I wish I could talk them into coming here. I understand that leaving will be painful, but they can build a good life if they come here. The land is rich and well-watered. And we who are already here would welcome them. I recall my life in Tennessee once in a while, but once I was out here, I grew to like it. I relish my childhood memories, but I do not long to be back in Tennessee." He looked at Johnny and smiled as he added in English, "…too many sonofabitches that need killin'."

Enoli said, "If Andrew Jackson has his way, and if the people do not accept the inevitable, removal will not be pretty. There will be much suffering."

* * * * * * * * *

At length, just before sundown, Dutch signaled to Johnny to come with him for a walk. Once they had gone far enough away to have a private conversation, Dutch asked, "Do you remember Sarah Studeville?"

"Yes," said Johnny.

Dutch said, "Did you know that she fell in love with you?"

"No. I thought she was too tough, too independent, to fall in love with me or anybody else." Johnny smiled as he said these words. "That does not mean that I do not find her attractive. Hers is the kind of beauty that grows on a man."

Dutch nodded thoughtfully. "I thought that the two of you would make a fine couple and, one day, raise a fine family. You could live on our ranch down on the Canadian. If I were looking for a wife, I would value one as pretty as she is…and who can shoot better than a man."

Johnny contemplated his uncle's words. But he suspected that his uncle did not fully understand how committed he was to Ahyoka. After a pause, he said, "I thought Sarah would be married by now."

Dutch said, "She does not want to marry anyone but you, White Owl."

"May I ask how you know that, Uncle?"

"She told me. After that second battle with the Comanche, things changed for her. She and you, side by side, fighting and killing enemies. She never forgot it. And—you already know this, I think—Enoli told her and others the story of your vendetta and the flight of Johnny Tenkiller. You are a hero to her. Like the great warriors of old. For her, no one else will do," concluded Dutch.

Johnny paused again to think. He revered his uncle beyond all other men. He owed him the life he had. And Dutch exemplified all those things young warriors admired: honesty, courage, loyalty, intelligence, and wisdom. Johnny would have, without hesitation, put his body in the way of an arrow or a bullet if aimed at Uncle Dutch. He looked for the right words to tell his uncle that he was, at this point in his life, committed to Ahyoka, even if she was not what others might regard as a perfect match for him. And he confessed to himself that he saw in Sarah what his uncle saw.

But then he recalled his grandmother's words, the day she gave her approval of his relationship with Ahyoka. She had said, "*You might be too young to understand what I am about to say but hear this anyway: In life, you will only have this once, maybe twice if you are fortunate, and live long enough. Rejoice in it.*" Was he to throw away this great gift, which many never find even the first time, because another choice was more "appropriate"? But what about Sarah? Would she become an "old maid"— she was already eighteen—if he let her love languish? Would it be his responsibility if she did become an old maid?

At length, Johnny said, "Uncle, I have heard your words. And I do admire Sarah. If I had never met Ahyoka, and if I were seeking a wife, I would have surely wanted Sarah. She is pretty, honest, and brave. And a good shot, too. She would be a good partner in life. It bothers me to think that she might go through life alone or with someone she would not have otherwise chosen, but for the choice I make now."

He paused, gathering the courage to say what he wanted to say to his uncle. "I love Ahyoka. And I feel her love every time I am in her presence. If I left Ahyoka to do the 'appropriate' thing, my soul would die."

Dutch, on hearing these words, was moved. He looked kindly at Johnny and said, "Tenkiller, I will respect your commitment. I did not understand the depth of your feelings until now. I will tell Sarah, who knows I have come to see you, that we had this talk." Then he closed by saying, "May you continue to find happiness with Ahyoka."

"Thank you, Uncle. Please send my deepest respects to Sarah." Wanting to change the subject, for he felt as if he had just swallowed a hot coal, Johnny asked, "So, have you seen any Comanches lately?"

They both laughed.

Then Johnny asked, "So, will I be 'Tenkiller' from now on?"

Dutch said, "Because I know you well, I do not need a proof of ten scalps. Your word is sufficient. From now on, 'Tenkiller' is what I shall call you."

"But only around other Cherokees, if you please," said Johnny.

Chapter 17: The Walking Dead

On a chilly, grey afternoon in early January 1839, as Johnny hammered a plow share into shape on his anvil, they came from the east.

Beaver stepped into Johnny's smithy. "Johnny," he said, "Come out here and look at this..."

Johnny did. He saw two processions. Coming from the east was a large group—it looked like hundreds—of bedraggled travelers, whom he quickly judged to be Cherokees. Some were in wagons, some were riding horses, but most of them were walking. Walking without spring in their steps.

Approaching them from the west side was a troop of US Army regulars from Fort Gibson. They were accompanied by many wagons that may have held provisions for those travelers. Johnny knew one of the mounted soldiers, the quartermaster, Sergeant Smith. He asked him, "Where are these folks gonna stop and rest? They look pretty worn out."

Smith replied, "They're Cherokees from the East. They're part of the 'Removal'. We're going to set up a temporary camp for them on the north side of town."

Johnny asked, "What happens next? Are they gonna stay here?"

"Some will," replied Smith. "The treaty states that they'll be given land to work. The problem is that they're also supposed to get subsistence money from our government, which hasn't come yet. That means the poorer ones won't even be able to buy a horse, or axes or plows or seeds for planting."

"That's a damned shame," observed Johnny.

The sergeant furrowed his brows and responded, "That's one way of looking at it."

Johnny stood by as the procession of dejected, physically ill, raggedly dressed, unwashed, often shoeless travelers with calloused, cracked, and bloody bare feet trudged into Tahlequah, the new capital of the Cherokee Nation. They had walked across a third of the continent during the fall and the onset of winter. For many, the clothes on their backs were about all they had. Many had died along the way from exposure and the sicknesses it brings. Old folks and small children especially. Some had lost their whole families. They had lost their lands, left the graves of their ancestors, and trudged westward, through the forests, prairies, and hills, through sleet and snow, sleeping on the ground, getting sick, suffering fevers and dysentery for more than three months, trudging westward, the direction that signified death in Cherokee cosmology.

The faces of these travelers were beyond stoic, beyond expressionless. They were the faces of the walking dead.

****

Johnny wanted to do something to help them. He spoke to his grandmother about it. He had been too busy to notice, but Ahyoka, his grandmother, had been building relationships with some of the other matrons in Tahlequah over the past couple of years. She now planned to use those relationships to help these newcomers.

She told Johnny, "These people have been eating nothing but salt pork and corn—most of it second rate, thanks to the greedy contractors who supplied it—for more than three months. I have been talking to some women—women of standing—about it. I have offered to contribute three of our hogs to feed these folks fresh meat. All these women have responded generously: Some have offered hogs, and others are supplying corn and beans."

"What can I do to help?" asked Johnny.

"When spring comes, they will probably need plow shares—the long ones you have been making," replied Ahyoka. "But I hope that they can get seed enough for a good crop."

"I was thinking I could do something right now," said Johnny. "I wonder if they have enough soap or enough pots to use to wash their clothes and blankets."

"I have two large pots and can give them away if needed," said Ahyoka.

"I'll ask the quartermaster if they'll be needing soap and more pots," said Johnny.

So, he approached Sergeant Smith and asked him, "Is there anything we can do that will help? Is the government supplying fresh blankets, soap, clothes, and the like?"

Sergeant Smith replied, "We've brought some tents and a few hundred fresh blankets. My guess is that their blankets are filthy and worn out. I hope we have enough to go around."

"If I were among them and got a fresh new blanket, I'd at least want to wash myself before foulin' it up," said Johnny. "Do y'all have soap?"

Sergeant Smith said, "I don't know if we have all that is needed. I also believe that they'll need some large pots to boil and clean whatever clothes they have that are worth keeping."

"When will you know whether you have enough soap and big metal pots?" Johnny asked.

"Tomorrow or the next day," Sergeant Smith responded.

"I'll wait and ask you again after a couple of days. I hope you don't mind if I do," said Johnny.

"Your offer to help is appreciated. I'll let you know," replied the sergeant.

* * * * * * * * *

Over the next two days, Johnny heard disturbing stories about the forced journey of this group from their homeland. Stories about old people, infants, and toddlers dying from exposure, measles, dysentery, and cholera. Sleeping on the ground with bitter winds blowing, keeping each other warm with their bodies and the meager coverings provided by their blankets. Stories about being stopped by whites who claimed, without substantiation, that the Cherokees owed them money for some debt and then said they would take horses instead. Worse, the Cherokee, who were accompanied by their own law enforcement—the "Light Horse Guard" as it was called—were not allowed to shoot these vermin. They could only use force to keep order among the Cherokee.

Before beginning their trek to the West, the Cherokee had been rounded up and placed into internment camps, where they were guarded by US Army troops, who were there to prevent desertions and to preserve order. For the most part, these troops were as polite and professional as they could be, but there were ugly exceptions. The worst story Johnny heard was relayed to him by Beaver, who had several kin among the group that had just arrived. Speaking in Cherokee, as he usually did, Beaver said, "Now, Johnny, when you hear this story, I want you to stay calm. I don't want you running over to the army camp and start killing people."

"It must be some hell of a story," said Johnny in English.

"It was hell for some of the people involved," said Beaver, who continued to speak in Cherokee. "Some soldiers grabbed a married woman, dragged her off to the edge of the camp site, forced her to drink whiskey, and then had their ways with her."

"What did her husband do?" Johnny asked.

"One of the soldiers drew a side arm, pointed it at him, and said, 'You just stay right where you are. We'll bring her back to you later.'"

"Where are these bastards?" demanded Johnny, speaking English.

"Do you think you can kill them here or at Fort Gibson, if that's where they are, and get away with it?" asked Beaver. "Besides, it happened in one of those forts back east where they kept the Cherokees they had rounded up. You would never find those scum."

Johnny became pensive. He paused and took a deep breath. "I know that killing them wouldn't solve anything, even if I could find them. The evil has already been done. But the truth is that I wish I could kill them. Do you know the victims?"

"I know the husband," Beaver answered. "He is my nephew."

"I am sorry to hear that," said Johnny. "Is he a warrior?"

"No. If he were, he would be dead right now, along with at least one of those soldiers."

Johnny wondered about the nephew's wife. "Did she come back after they were through with her?"

"She did. She walked herself back to my nephew. She said she understood why he was not able to protect her. And that she knew it was not his fault. She forgave him," answered Beaver.

"Do you think she did forgive him?" asked Johnny.

"I believe she meant what she said," replied Beaver. "But I doubt that he has forgiven himself."

"I hope he finds his way, Uncle." Johnny shook his head sadly. That was all he could say.

* * * * * * * * *

Two days after the arrival of the easterners, Johnny approached Sergeant Smith. "Did you find out about the needs of our eastern brothers for large pots and soap yet?"

Sergeant Smith replied, "We could use more soap—maybe two hundred bars—and five large metal pots. But we're still waiting for the government to send subsistence funds for these Cherokee. We would use those funds for getting things for the tribe. So, we won't be able to pay for these things for a while. We will reimburse you if you buy them, but I don't know exactly when the funds will arrive. How do you propose to pay for them?"

"I have enough money saved up to buy them. We have two large pots left in our store, and my grandmother wants to donate them. I think I can get three more and all that soap in Honey Creek. The Ridge family up there has a store that's much larger than ours. Maybe they have some pots and a couple hundred bars of soap they'd sell to me. I think I could buy all of it for around fifty dollars," said Johnny.

"That's a lot of money in these parts, Johnny," said Sergeant Smith. "What if the US government fails to give you a full reimbursement?"

"You're the quartermaster, Sergeant. You and I could write up a contract. I'll bring back written proof of what I spent and a list of the things I bought. You can bear witness that I have brought them and signed a document to that effect."

Sergeant Smith, normally aloof and reserved, smiled, and said, "Don't worry, Johnny, I know all about those documents. I'm impressed that you do. Few Indians are familiar with such matters. In fact, there aren't that many white people who are…" He continued, "I'll draw them up for us. We can sign the contract before you leave. We'll sign the other document when you return with the goods."

"Thank you, Sergeant," said Johnny. "I plan to leave tomorrow morning."

Johnny went back to the store and told his grandmother of his intent to go to Honey Creek and buy soap and metal pots.

Grandmother Ahyoka asked, "How much money will you need for this, White Owl?"

Johnny said, "I have about a hundred dollars saved. I think that fifty dollars will cover the costs. The government will pay us back, but I will take the risk and fund it myself."

Grandmother Ahyoka said, "No, you and I can split the cost. I will give you twenty-five dollars for the things you are going up there to buy, and I will donate the two big pots I have. It is best that you keep some of your savings. You never know when you might need the money." Then she added, "And do not worry about being repaid by the government. We will be repaid by the Great Spirit, in due course."

Chapter 18: Ridge

The next morning, Johnny set out for the Ridge estate in Honey Creek with a wagon drawn by two horses. The Ridges lived about two days north of Tahlequah.

On the afternoon of the second day, he descended into a shallow valley with two large, framed houses with pillars, both whitewashed. They looked more like Southern mansions than anything Johnny had ever lived in. Closer to the country road than those houses was a large general store. Johnny secured his horses and walked in. The storekeeper eyed him suspiciously, as he was carrying his rifle.

"Don't worry," Johnny said in English. "I'm not here to rob you." He smiled. "I just don't like leavin' my weapons unattended."

From his features and skin tone, Johnny could see that the storekeeper was of African descent, though of mixed race. Like Johnny, he had green eyes. Johnny said, "I've come here from Tahlequah. Hundreds of Cherokees from the east arrived this week. They're in terrible condition. I was hopin' to buy some soap and some large metal pots. Others in Tahlequah—those who have the means—are helpin' 'em too."

A deep, booming male voice behind him asked in Cherokee, "How many such pots, and how much soap do you need?"

Johnny turned around and beheld a large, imposing Cherokee man in his sixties. He looked like a full blood. He was taller than Johnny, big boned, and barrel-chested. He looked like he weighed at least two hundred forty pounds. He was dressed in dark cotton trousers and a white cotton shirt. His black hair was grizzled with grey, and he sported a white man's haircut. The only thing "Indian" in his attire were his fine moccasins. From his confident bearing, Johnny gathered that he was the one in charge, probably the owner of the store and everything else in sight. Johnny answered, in English, "I need about two hundred bars of soap and three big pots."

"May I ask you the purpose of these purchases?" asked the big man, who continued to speak Cherokee, though he obviously understood English.

Johnny replied to him in Cherokee: "Many eastern Cherokees have arrived in Tahlequah. Their condition is pitiful. The Army is going to bring them some fresh blankets. I wanted to give them some soap to clean the filth of that horrible journey from their bodies and whatever clothes they have that are worth keeping. Why soil those new blankets?"

"Isaiah," the big man said to the storekeeper, "Do we have what this young man wants? If so, will you figure out the price?"

"Yes, Major," replied Isaiah in Cherokee.

The big man said, "I am Ridge. People call me 'Major Ridge' because I was a major in Andrew Jackson's army. We fought the Red Sticks at the Battle of Horseshoe Bend."

"That old sonofabitch," muttered Johnny.

Major Ridge smiled restrainedly. Again, in Cherokee, he remarked, "That is one way of looking at it."

Johnny, who decided to speak Cherokee since that appeared to be Ridge's preference, replied, "I heard about that battle from an old warrior who was there," said Johnny.

"Do you remember his name?" asked Ridge.

"His name is 'Wohali'," replied Johnny.

"I knew him. Very tough warrior in his time" acknowledged Ridge. "He killed some Red Sticks but got a bad wound on his face. Where is he now?"

"I saw him up in the foothills of North Carolina about five years ago. His wound is just a long scar on the left side of his face now. He and the other people in his village were planning to go deeper into the mountains to avoid removal. I imagine that they have done this by now," said Johnny. "I hope they are safe."

Ridge merely nodded. He was studying this young man. He wondered what a member of the Western Cherokees was doing in the Carolina mountains. Meanwhile, Isaiah was busy verifying the inventory of soap and metal pots. After a short pause, Ridge asked, "What is your name?"

Johnny thought about how to answer that question. He recalled how swelled with pride he had been when Dutch had confirmed that he had earned the name "Tenkiller." In a flash, he replied, "My name is Johnny Tenkiller."

The major smiled broadly. "You must have king-sized balls to declare a name like that! Did you earn it?"

Before Johnny could reply, Isaiah, who had finished his errands, approached the major. "We have the soap, but we will need to order more in the next shipment of goods we get from the East. And we have the three large pots as well."

"How much do I owe you?" asked Johnny.

"Fifty dollars," said Isaiah.

Johnny had the money. "OK, good." He counted out the money and then asked, "Will you write up a receipt for me and list the items, their costs, and the total for me, please?"

Ridge was impressed. Here was someone who was already claiming to be a tenkiller at his tender age who could also read, write, and cipher. The "new" Cherokee that he, Ridge, had envisioned when he was about Johnny's age. Back then, he had read the writing on the wall—in a manner of speaking, since he was illiterate—after losing the Chickamauga Wars, the last of the Cherokee wars against the whites. Those wars ended in 1794 when Ridge was twenty-three. He concluded that the Cherokee would have to adapt or go extinct, or worse, survive physically but live with the humiliation of being second-class citizens in their own ancestral lands.

It appeared that Johnny Tenkiller was on a path like the one that Ridge had envisioned for himself when he was in his twenties. He wanted to know this young warrior better.

Ridge said, "It's a couple of days' journey back to Tahlequah. I have a lot of room in my house. Would you like to stay the night and leave in the morning? You can take dinner with me, too."

Johnny was pleasantly surprised, though the invitation seemed more like a requirement than a choice. After a few seconds of reflection, he said, "I would be honored, Major."

Isaiah wrote up the details of the transaction.

While Isaiah and Johnny were finishing up their business, Ridge stepped out and returned with a young woman servant. She was tall, willowy, and fair-skinned. She reminded Johnny of Lizzie. The major said, "This is Eleanor. She will show you to your quarters. It is almost dinner time, so you have time to clean up." This, too, sounded more like a requirement than an option.

Johnny grabbed a bag with his personal effects and followed Eleanor upstairs to his room. He took a clean cotton shirt out of his bag. Then she led him to a well in the back of the house and offered him soap and a washcloth, which he accepted. It was chilly, so Johnny made haste. When he finished, she came out and led him to the dining room.

Sitting at the head of a long table was the major. No one else was present. His wife, Susanna, was having dinner at the home of their son, John, who lived with his family in the other big house. When Johnny was seated, and dinner was served, the major said, "Since we lost the Chickamauga Wars, there are few young men these days who fancy themselves to be warriors—at least, not in the sense in which I and my generation were warriors. A lot of them seem to be overly fond of whiskey. The only fighting they do is in drunken brawls. Not the kind we used to do."

Johnny said, "I tried whiskey once. It was vile. I don't see what the white men see in it."

Ridge laughed. "That is no doubt a virtue." Changing the subject, Ridge asked, "So, Johnny, will you share with an old warrior how you became 'Johnny Tenkiller'? I assume 'Tenkiller' was not your birth name."

"Yes, Major." Then he told the story, beginning with his vendetta against the Stricklins and ending with the second engagement with the Comanches at the ranch on the Canadian River. When he told of his written confession, in which he declared that Johnny Tenkiller had been the killer of the Stricklins, Ridge laughed and exclaimed, "You *did* have king-sized balls, didn't you!"

It took a couple of hours to complete the narrative because Major Ridge, like Wohali, asked for details that would either trip Johnny up if he were lying or confirm that he was telling the truth.

"So, all that time, you went by more names than I can keep track of. Who gave you the right to use 'Tenkiller' as a name rather than as an aspiration?" asked the major.

"My uncle Tahchee," replied Johnny. "But for reasons of which you are now aware, I asked him to only use it around other Cherokees."

"Is he a chief of the western Cherokees?" asked Ridge.

"Yes," replied Johnny.

"I have heard of him," said Ridge, who then changed the topic: "What impresses me the most about you is not that you have been so good at killing people, though that used to be, for us, a great virtue. It is that you spent several years learning to read and write the white man's language and to work with numbers," said Ridge. "I never learned to read and write, but I made sure my son, John, and his cousin, Buck, did. They both have fine white man's educations. I had great hopes for my 'boys' and, through them, for the Cherokee people. But now I have reason to doubt that those hopes will ever be realized."

Johnny wanted to know why Ridge said that. He decided to take a more indirect approach. "If I may ask, how did you come to be the gentleman who is my gracious host this evening?" asked Johnny.

"That is a long story. It is already dark. Do you care to stay up to hear it?"

"I would be greatly honored," said Johnny. "If I fall asleep driving the wagon tomorrow, the horses know which way to go."

Ridge paused and cleared his throat. "Very well. In my youth," he began, "I went on raiding parties with a war chief named Doublehead. He was even bigger than I am. And he was cruel, ruthless. Had a hollow space in his chest where most of us have a heart. Killed men, women, and children without remorse. Once, when we were raiding in Kentucky, Doublehead complained that we were out of tobacco. So, we killed a white family along the way just to take their tobacco. For tobacco!" Ridge paused for a moment. Even after all the years that had passed, he still felt outrage and remorse about the murder of white settlers, just so Doublehead could have a smoke. He continued, "That was all we took from them, except that we scalped them as well. When we returned to our camp, I wept. Doublehead, who respected me otherwise, saw that as a weakness. Well, if it is a weakness, I am glad to be weak."

Johnny looked at Ridge. He was a formidable man. He looked anything but weak.

"Anyway," the major continued, "I didn't weep when I killed Doublehead twenty years later. But that is another story…

"Back then, Cherokee raiding parties ranged over that part of the country, raiding and killing whites and raiding and killing other Indians, too. Our thinking was that these people were intruders. Killing, scalping, and plundering them was just what we did when discouraging people from invading our lands.

"But there was another reason for doing these things: Raiding and plundering people of other tribes, taking scalps, loot, and even slaves from them was the way warriors gained honor and status in the olden days. Everyone else—the Choctaw, Chickasaw, Muskogee, Shawano, and Haudenosaunee—did the same. With us Indians, killing and raiding were usually thought of as acts of vengeance, though no one really knew when this unceasing series of vengeful killings and raids began. No one ever wondered when they would end. It had just always been, and as far as we knew, always would be. But through these acts of vengeance, *men attained standing* among their people.

"Of course, the whites were enraged by our actions. And much of what is happening to the tribes these days is probably revenge for the people that Indians killed, scalped, raped—the whites aren't the only ones who do that—and plundered. Knowing what I know now, I might hate us too."

He chuckled.

"Our actions justified terrible retaliations. You probably already heard about how Colonel Sevier burned several of our towns and crops. His last burning destroyed a whole fall harvest along with several of our towns. This caused great hardships for our people.

"We were outnumbered, outgunned, and more vulnerable than the whites were. They knew where we lived. They could burn our homes and our crops. On the other hand, they lived everywhere. Where would we begin if we wanted to pay them back?"

"We would have to burn the whole United States—a perfect impossibility," commented Johnny.

Ridge said, "That was my conclusion. When I saw that we could not win a war with the whites, I realized that we would have to learn from them if we were to survive. But I was not sure of where to start. That was the problem. But I was certain that life as I had known it in my youth was over." Ridge paused, probably for effect.

Then he continued: "Well, after I returned home from the wars, my wife Susanna and I moved to a place called Pine Log in Georgia. There was a lot of land there that belonged to the Cherokee, but it was unused. Our tribal rules made it permissible for us to make our own improvements to it if it was not already being used by someone else. We planted peach and apple trees—just a few the first year, but more and more as the years passed. By the time we left and came out here, we had over a thousand trees in our orchard.

"Now, there were two mixed-blood Cherokees who also moved to Pine Log, where Susanna and I were. One was James Vann, and the other was Charles Hicks. Both were prosperous, especially Vann, who had become a wealthy planter. But I was more interested in Hicks, who read English literature, and even more fascinated by the white man's books that he had. I wondered how these 'books' could store so much information and how, once written, they could communicate ideas to people who never met their writers. I began to imagine the next generation of Cherokee leaders. I hoped they would become educated, learn to read, write, and figure with numbers, and be able to deal with the whites on their terms. At the time, I saw this as the path for the Cherokees' survival as a people, as a sovereign nation within the United States. I believed that if we adopted the white man's 'civilization', if we no longer raided and killed white settlers, if we learned their methods of farming and learned to make and use their tools, we could still have our own nation and government, and deal with the whites on an equal basis."

"So, you did not see removal as certain at that time?" asked Johnny.

"No. We still had reason to believe that removal was not certain. Even Thomas Jefferson said good things about our progress. For consider: Many of our women were spinning cotton and weaving cloth. Many of us were raising our own livestock and farming cotton. We lived in log cabins, joined by iron nails. Some of our young learned to read and write English and went to missionary schools. Like you did. We had blacksmiths. Like you. A lot of our people became Christians and went to church. And some of us owned slaves."

Johnny knew that Ridge had slaves. But he had no intention of disrupting this conversation by sharing his hostility towards slavery. Instead, he asked, "How did you get your slaves, Major?"

"Before I answer that, Johnny, and just in case you ever meet my wife, Susanna, she prefers to call them 'servants', not 'slaves'. That said, I got them the old-fashioned Indian way: I stole them!" He laughed from his belly. "Over time, I accumulated more than twenty of them and began to raise cotton, like the white planters do."

"What made you want to do that?" asked Johnny.

"I wanted to provide as many advantages as I could to my children so that they could be leaders of our people. That usually means having money to pay for things like education," replied Ridge. "Now, most of the Cherokee doing these things were mixed bloods. Even I am a quarter Scottish, though most people think I look full-blooded. Vann and Hicks are both half-breeds. Most of the full bloods, on the other hand, were not ready to adopt white practices. They knew they could not win a war, but they did not know what to do after they were defeated. They held stubbornly to their past. They continued to believe in their shamans and witchcraft and all the rest of it. But they couldn't raid anymore, or at least not as much. They knew that if they raided white settlers, they would be hunted down and killed.

"As I mentioned before, in the days of old, raiding was a big part of what it was to be a warrior. It was how a man gained standing, a way of being somebody. Having that option taken away from them, they no longer knew who they were or who they should be. At a loss of what to do or who to be, many of them despaired, drifted without purpose through life, and drowned their despair in whiskey."

"I know," said Johnny. "I saw it as well. And I saw how the whites abused them. It was one of the things that made me want to kill white men. But since you are here in Indian Territory, did you change your mind about the Cherokee becoming part of white society?"

"Before I answer that question, let me tell you another story," said Major Ridge. "Doublehead, the ruthless warrior I told you about earlier, was very corrupt, very self-serving. He was the second-ranking chief of the Cherokee and used his status to sign away tracts of land to white speculators. He took bribes in return and became quite wealthy. He did not bother to take these matters to the tribal council. And he did not share his bribes with anyone.

"Now, it is one of our blood laws that no one can sign away lands without the approval of the tribal council. The penalty for breaking a blood law is death. So, I spoke about this at a council meeting. No one wanted to challenge Doublehead, who was, even in his sixties, a giant of a man who could still kill. So, I said *I* would enforce the blood law. The tribal council voted to let me do it. I could go into detail about the execution—it was a messy kill—but the point is that I killed Doublehead for signing away Cherokee land without the authorization of the tribal council. You will understand in a moment why I have told you of this…

"I sent my son John and his cousin Buck to the Foreign Mission School in Connecticut. This school was financed by wealthy Easterners of the Christian faith. Indians from several tribes went to study there. And there were young men from places on the other side of the world. Places I never heard of, like Hawaii, India, and New Zealand.

"While they were up there in school, Buck was sponsored by a rich white man named Elias Boudinot and adopted. Buck took the name of this white man, and now everyone calls him 'Elias'. Elias is working with a missionary to translate the New Testament into Cherokee, using the way of writing developed by Sequoiah. And my son John is now a lawyer.

"We saw what was happening to our people, especially the poor full bloods, who still believed in shamans and witchcraft and thought that they could just close their eyes and wish that the future would bring back the past. Meanwhile, the Georgia people were treating the Cherokees like dogs, even whipping them like dogs. It was sickening to see, sickening to even know about. Like you, there were moments when I just wished I could kill all those white men. But since that was not possible, the more important question was this one: Was it possible to end this misery by other means? That is where the treaty idea came from.

"In 1832, John, Elias, and other Cherokees of standing went to Washington and pleaded our case against Georgia to all three branches of the United States government. In the beginning, they just wanted to stop that ugly lottery system in Georgia. But although there was much sympathy for the Cherokees, there was not enough to get the support of the legislature. And even if the Supreme Court had ruled in favor of the Cherokee—which it had, at least once in the recent past—President Jackson had already said that he would not enforce the ruling. This left Georgia free to continue its policies against the Cherokees and other Indians. Even the missionaries, who had supported our cause for years, urged us to negotiate a treaty while we could still get favorable terms and to remove to the West. They told us—with great regret—that it was all over. Time to just give up and move.

"When John and Elias returned from Washington, they shared this knowledge with me. They believed we should make a treaty now, get the best possible terms, and move to the West. And even before John and Elias returned from their unsuccessful trip to DC, I had toured the Cherokee Nation and despaired over what I saw. As my boys and I saw it, the alternative was extermination, reduction to beggary without a land to call our own, or some combination of these and even worse things. I did not want my people to continue to suffer the awful indignities of conquest. I did not want the children to see their parents whipped and humiliated. Imagine how that would affect them…"

"I know how it affects them. Seeing such things turned me into a killer of white men," remarked Johnny.

"That is one outcome," said Ridge. "There are other, less worthy outcomes. How about quiet acceptance that you just are not as 'good' as white people? How about accepting contempt and abuse as something natural, something you deserve because you are a lesser being? How about having your kids see you being pushed around by bullying white men? How about seeing your mother stripped and whipped like a dog because she does not want to abandon her home to white lottery winners? I could go on…

"In the spring of 1835, we and other Cherokees of standing worked with a US agent appointed by Andrew Jackson to draft a treaty. It was signed by less than a hundred Cherokees at our capital, New Echota, Georgia, in December 1835. We planned to go to Washington in February 1836 to close on the terms of the treaty.

"Now, before we even went to Washington, we wanted to discuss the treaty with the tribal council. We had hoped that Chief Ross could use his relationship with the full bloods to convince them that their situation in Georgia, Tennessee, and Alabama was hopeless. But he made this impossible. He wouldn't even talk to us about removal, and he blocked our access to the tribal council. So, we never had a chance to gain more support for the treaty.

"When we got to Washington, Ross was there, still trying to change the unchangeable, and I still hoped to persuade him of the benefits of the treaty. But even then, he would have nothing to do with us. We went ahead and presented the treaty to the Senate. To our surprise, it quickly ratified the treaty and passed it on to Jackson, who signed it on May 23, 1836. One of the conditions of the treaty required that any Cherokees who had not already left by May 23, 1838, would be removed by force. That gave them exactly two years to prepare and leave.

"Did Jackson know that by ratifying that treaty, he made you and your supporters into outlaws, that you could be killed for signing it?" asked Johnny. "Did he even give a shit?"

"Oh, Jackson gave a shit all right," said Ridge. "He gave a shit about expanding his own real estate holdings. He also gave a shit about getting elected to two terms as President. Giving away our land for free or selling it cheaply to the hordes of white people coming from the eastern shores made him popular with voters. For Jackson, it was about politics and personal gain. For me, conceding to the Removal policy was about preventing our people from being ground down into dirt. That treaty was the only thing that Jackson and I agreed about.

"And you now see the results of John Ross's approach: Those pitiful people walking into your town from the east. This could have been avoided. They did not have to wait until the last moment and be driven from their homes with little, if anything, other than the clothes on their backs. They had two years to prepare, but their hopes were kept alive by John Ross's dreams. They did nothing to prepare...

"And now, by the old blood law, which I myself have enforced, we and some others who signed that treaty are the walking dead. We will be killed. I just do not know when. But when we signed that treaty, we also signed our death warrants. Some among those pitiful people you're helping may be our executioners."

"Do you regret signing that treaty?" asked Johnny.

"I regret that John Ross, whom I once supported to be Principal Chief, allowed his own wishful thinking to create so much misery and grief for all those full bloods, who loved and trusted him. I believe he could have persuaded them to prepare for their removal. They would not have been driven out of their homes with their dinners sitting on the table, never to be eaten...But to answer your question, no. I do not regret signing the treaty. I believed then, and believe even more firmly now, that it was the best solution for our people. If I suffer the penalty of the blood law, so be it."

By the time Johnny had heard Major Ridge's narrative, it was late, almost midnight. They were ready to retire for the evening when Johnny said, "Thank you for telling me your story, Major Ridge. I am quite inspired by it. When I was a boy and wanted to find that third road between being who I am—a Cherokee—and being able to walk with my head up and my shoulders back in the world of the whites, I must have imagined being someone like you..."

"Except that you can read and write, Tenkiller. I think you might have gone beyond me."

"Major, what you have accomplished is remarkable. I doubt that I can ever match it," said Johnny. "Thank you for this talk. I shall never forget it."

* * * * * * * * *

The next morning, Johnny arose before sunrise, dressed, and loaded his wagon. Before he could untie his horses and hitch them up, Ridge called out to him. "Want to have some coffee before you leave? I would not want you to fall asleep on your way home. Some wild Indians might jump you!" He laughed from his belly. For someone who had killed at least twice as many in his life as Johnny had, the major still had a pleasant, upbeat personality.

"Well," said Johnny, "How can I refuse an invitation like that?"

Eleanor brought two cups of freshly brewed coffee to the front porch of the store, where there were two chairs with a small table between them. They each took their first sip of the hot brew, its fragrance wafting seductively through the chilly January morning air.

Ridge spoke: "I feel sorry for those full bloods. Most of them did not—and probably still do not—understand what has happened to them. But out of respect for full bloods, let me relate a tale to you. Do you know who the Red Sticks were?"

"I heard about them. They were Creek Indians, weren't they?"

"Yes, that is what the white man calls them. They call themselves by other names. 'Muskogee' is the main one. Anyway, the Red Sticks heard and believed the message of Tecumseh. Their shamans told them to abandon all the things that the white men had brought and go back to being what they were before the white men came. Well, they gave up the cotton garments and metal pots. They still used traditional war clubs. They painted the ends of them red. That is where their name, 'Red Sticks', came from. But they had sense enough to keep their guns and steel knives. And they made havoc for a few years. Massacred white people every chance they got. Killed other Muskogee, too—especially mixed bloods who continued their 'white' practices. And I fought them at the Battle of Horseshoe Bend under Colonel Jackson."

"That old sonofabitch," Johnny muttered in English. He couldn't help himself.

Ignoring Johnny's commentary, Ridge continued: "One thousand Red Stick warriors, with about three hundred women and children, were holed up at a bend on the Tallapoosa River. Their camp was surrounded on three sides by the bend in the river—like a giant horseshoe—and the fourth side, which faced outward from the river, was fortified with breastworks. We fired several volleys at the breastworks but without effect, even with our two cannons. When it got dark, some of us Cherokee waded across the river and cut loose some of the Red Sticks' canoes. We used them to bring other Cherokee warriors across the river to harass the Red Sticks from behind their breastworks on the water-facing side. Now, they were caught in a crossfire between Jackson's men and us.

"Just so you will know how brave, how committed those Red Sticks were, know that there were over four hundred Cherokee warriors, more than two thousand white soldiers, and a couple of hundred Indians from other tribes fighting the Red Sticks that day. The Red Sticks were outnumbered by about three to one. We had two cannons as well, so they were quite outgunned.

"The battle went on all day and into the night. Their shamans, with their black-painted faces, red batons, and drums, chanted all through it. And no matter how many of them fell, the Red Sticks would not surrender. Jackson even sent some emissaries to offer peace. The Red Sticks shot them. Dead. In the end, we killed almost all of them—a thousand Red Stick warriors. Maybe twenty of them got away. The rest died. We took their women and children captive.

"Now, we can call these men savages. But were they any more savage than the white men who were scalping the dead warriors and skinning their corpses for strips they planned to make into belts? Savages or not, they were courageous warriors, preferring death to surrender. Take a few moments to consider this on your long drive home: A thousand warriors, knowing they were going to die unless they surrendered, chose to fight on, knowing that their death was certain. They did not have a chance of winning. They did not care. They were committed to their cause. They preferred death to life on the white man's terms. Can you imagine being one of them?

"To this day, over twenty years later, I feel ashamed of taking part in that slaughter. I killed six of them myself in hand-to-hand combat. If everyone knew how hopeless the Red Sticks' position was, how outnumbered, how outgunned they were, would Jackson have been considered a great war chief? One can wonder about that…After more than twenty years, I still remember their courage, how their commitment to a life that I myself had once lived was more powerful than their fear of death."

He paused and, seemingly choking back a sob, declared, "They were *great warriors!*" His eyes were misty. He said no more.

Johnny and Ridge rose at the same time. Johnny said, "Major, though we have known each other for less than a full day, I feel like I have known you for half of my life. I feel aggrieved that I must take my leave of you."

"Perhaps you feel this way because you and I are of the same spirit, Tenkiller."

In English, Johnny said, "You honor me too much, sir." He took Ridge's hand and gave a slight bow.

Major Ridge, whose eyes were still misty, looked at Johnny and said, in Cherokee, "Good hunting."

He stood on the front porch as Johnny drove his wagon away. Johnny turned around to wave one more goodbye. Major Ridge, the great Cherokee warrior and statesman, waved back.

As Johnny drove away, he found himself thinking about the Red Sticks and about how Major Ridge seemed to have choked back a sob when he exclaimed, "*Great warriors!*" The choked-back sob meant something. Was it a farewell to a part of him, something that he still treasured in some way, which was lost forever, like his youth? Was it an expression of sorrow over having killed six of these Stone Age warriors with his own hands, knowing that their situation was beyond hopeless? Was he reviewing his own life, contemplating his own transformation from a young warrior—one who had much in common with those Red Sticks—to the prosperous planter and man of affairs that he had become in his maturity? Knowing he would almost surely die soon, was he celebrating his own colorful, successful life and all the people in it, including those he had killed?

Johnny thought about the consequences Major Ridge would face and the stoic indifference he seemed to have about them. Did he do the right thing? Was he thinking about sparing Cherokee children the deep scars that must come from having a home one day, having none the next, and watching their fathers and mothers be beaten and humiliated? He surely realized that Removal was going to happen, no matter what. The Treaty's terms were reasonable. Better that Removal happen that way than the Cherokees being rounded up, placed in internment camps, and force-marched a thousand miles to the middle of nowhere, like the ones who had just arrived in Tahlequah.

The Red Sticks died serving what they believed to be a purpose more important than their lives. Had the major made the same sacrifice? Was he sacrificing his life for the sake of the children he hoped would not have to see their parents beaten like dogs, beaten by dogs with whips? Was he facing his doom with the same stoicism as have true warriors since the beginning of time? When he called them "great warriors", was he feeling, as he faced almost certain death himself, kinship with those fierce, resolute Red Sticks?

Johnny recalled his grandmother's words when he was eleven years old, seething with rage at the Stricklins, vowing revenge against them. She had told him that to exact vengeance, he would have to learn the way of the warrior. And she added at the time, "The warrior's way lies beyond the mere use of killing tools. It is a matter of the spirit." Johnny realized that Major Ridge, who had in his youth been skilled at the use of killing tools, had become, in his old age, a different kind of warrior. A warrior in spirit.

He thought, "Ridge broke the blood law because he cared for his people and, above all, for their children. He will die for that. A great warrior, indeed."

Chapter 19: 1839

When Johnny arrived back in Tahlequah in the late afternoon, the area was bustling with activity. There were many fires, and the aroma of the fresh meat being cooked over those fires filled the air. Before going to his cabin, Johnny sought out the quartermaster, Sergeant Smith. When he found him, he was talking with a clerk, who was still recording the names of the people who had arrived a week earlier.

He greeted the sergeant. "Good afternoon, sir. I have gotten the goods listed in our contract. When you have a chance, here's the receipt. Will you verify that the contents of my wagon fulfill the terms of our contract?"

The sergeant walked over to the wagon and quickly verified that the deal was complete. There really wasn't much to count. He signed the invoice and added the goods to his inventory records. He handed a copy to Johnny.

"Where shall I put this stuff?" asked Johnny.

"You can just leave it right here," said Sergeant Smith. "I'll have my men store it."

"Thank you, Sergeant," said Johnny as he unloaded his wagon.

He soon found his grandmother, who was directing the cooking and distribution of meat to the new arrivals. Having lived on salt pork and corn for three months, these people must have been grateful to dine on fresh meat and corn-and-bean cakes.

Neither Grandmother Ahyoka nor the other ladies of standing had bothered to secure their gifts with guarantees of reimbursement from the US government. They were still Cherokees, after all, and some things mattered more to them than money. Johnny, for his part, felt a bit ashamed that he had securitized his donations, especially when he recalled his grandmother's words:

"Do not worry about whether we are repaid by the government. We will be repaid by the Great Spirit, in due course."

* * * * * * * * *

Sickly, demoralized, bedraggled contingents of Cherokees continued to flow into Tahlequah and Fort Gibson through March 1839. More sad tales of leaving their homes and possessions behind and walking through rain, sleet, and winds, often barefoot. More reports of death along the trail. More narratives that inspired moral outrage.

Meanwhile, Grandmother Ahyoka continued to work with the leading matrons in Tahlequah to collect and distribute donations to the arriving contingents of Cherokees coming in from the East. Her reputation spread among the old settlers and the new arrivals. Women who had Ahyoka's kind of influence and used it for charitable ends were sometimes referred to as "beloved women" by the Cherokee. The noble Ahyoka was becoming a beloved woman, indeed.

* * * * * * * * *

Chief John Ross arrived in March 1839. Three months later, on June 22, 1839, Major Ridge, his son John, and his nephew Elias were assassinated for having signed the treaty. They had been "tried," though they weren't present at these trials, and convicted. The assassins also targeted Stand Watie, Elias's brother, who was also tried and convicted in his absence. But he had been warned and fled to safety.

Johnny heard about Major Ridge a few days after his murder. The major had been in Arkansas on that day. The assassins knew where he was staying and laid in wait for him. They ambushed him as he was riding from his host's home to visit a sick slave. Shot him off his horse.

John Ross professed not to have had anything to do with the assassinations. His son, Andrew, had supposedly kept him in the dark about them.

On hearing of the major's murder, Johnny was indignant but not moved to vengeance. The situation was too volatile, and he had too many vulnerabilities: His grandmother, Ahyoka, and the store, for starters. It was clear that the killings had been the work of embittered new arrivals from the East. If you added together the number of Old Settlers—at this point, Johnny was one of them—and the Treaty Party, led by the Ridges, the whole group would be outnumbered at least three to one by the easterners flooding into Indian Territory.

Johnny paid his final respects to Major Ridge in solitude. He remembered the end of his conversation with the major, when Ridge had choked back a sob as he honored the fallen Red Stick warriors. Johnny choked back a sob of his own when he spoke these words to himself: "Major Ridge was a *great warrior!*"

* * * * * * * * *

Johnny stayed out of the conflicts that followed, the back-and-forth vengeance wrought by those loyal to the Ridges and those loyal to John Ross. It seemed like there was a murder or two every week, sometimes every day. Murders became so common that people didn't even mention them much of the time. Because of Ahyoka's reputation as a benefactor to the Cherokees who had traveled the Trail of Tears, she, her familiars, and her store were not threatened. Considering this, Johnny was confident that if he took a trip to visit Dutch, whom he hadn't seen for three years, his two Ahyokas would be safe.

In September 1839, when the summer heat started to wane, he prepared for a trip to the ranch on the Canadian River. By this time, his horse, Flower, was about eight years old and still good for the journey. He borrowed a pack horse from his grandmother.

Before he left, the younger Ahyoka asked, "Why are you going to your uncle's ranch right now? And when will you return?"

Johnny found it strange that Ahyoka would ask these questions at this point. He replied, "I miss Uncle Dutch. I haven't seen him for three years. I owe him a visit. Remember where I got Flower? She was a gift from my uncle. And I heard he has a little boy now. I'd like to meet him, since he's my nephew."

"Can I come along with you?" asked Ahyoka.

Johnny was surprised by this question, too. Then he became more surprised—at himself: Why hadn't he even considered that Ahyoka might wish to go with him? He was suddenly embarrassed over not asking her in the first place. He asked, "Well, do you suppose my grandmother can do without you for a couple of weeks?"

"I believe so, but I'll ask her," replied Ahyoka.

"If she agrees that you should go, we'll take the wagon instead," said Johnny.

Grandmother Ahyoka was managing her store when Johnny and the younger Ahyoka walked in. Ahyoka said, "Auntie, Johnny is going to the ranch down on the Canadian. He plans to be gone for a couple of weeks. I was hoping to go as well." She stopped, knowing that Auntie would answer the unasked question.

Grandmother said, "We have been here for five years, and you have gone nowhere except to Fort Gibson a few times. Maybe the trip would help you feel better."

Johnny wondered if Ahyoka had not been feeling well. In English, he asked, "Have you been hidin' somethin' from me, Ahyoka?"

The two Ahyokas gave each other a quick, knowing look. The younger Ahyoka answered, "No, not really."

Johnny didn't believe her. He became alarmed. "What's wrong, Ahyoka? What haven't you told me?" he demanded.

Ahyoka cast her eyes downward. Grandmother spoke for her. "Johnny, she has not been feeling well lately. We are not sure why. I have tried some remedies, but they have not worked."

"What have you been feelin', Ahyoka?" Johnny asked.

"I have these pains inside my stomach and abdomen. They come, and they go. I don't whine about 'em," replied Ahyoka, who seemed to be forcing a smile as she spoke.

Johnny quickly changed his plans. "I'm not going to the Canadian River right now…We're going to Fort Gibson to see a doctor. Grandmother, I'd like to use the wagon, if you don't mind," said Johnny.

"I do not mind, White Owl," responded the elder Ahyoka.

"We won't be more than a couple of days," said Johnny. "Thank you, Grandmother."

Fort Gibson was a long day's trip by wagon from Tahlequah. "Let's decide what we need to take and plan to leave by sun-up tomorrow," said Johnny.

The next morning, Johnny and Ahyoka left for Fort Gibson. By this time, the road between Fort Gibson and Tahlequah had been well-traveled, and much of it had been conditioned by crews from the fort, so it was not as bumpy as it had been five years before. The ride was comparatively comfortable. They arrived at Fort Gibson just before sundown.

Johnny knew where the office of the quartermaster, Sergeant Smith, was. He took his rifle from the wagon, and he and Ahyoka entered the fort. At the gate, a guard looked menacingly at him and asked, "What d'you need that rifle for?"

Johnny replied, "Don't worry, sir, it's not loaded. I just didn't feel safe leavin' it unattended in our wagon. Would you like me to leave it here with you?" He handed the rifle to the guard.

The guard inspected the rifle and verified that it was not loaded. He said, "This is a fine piece of work, this rifle. It looks like you've taken good care of it because I can see that it's pretty old."

"It still shoots straight and true, sir," said Johnny.

The guard handed Johnny's rifle back to him. "Go ahead and keep it with you, young man," said the guard, who stepped aside and let them pass.

They found their way to Sergeant Smith's office. Johnny knocked, and the sergeant came to the door. "Hi, Johnny! What brings you here today?"

"Hi, sergeant. This is my wife, Ahyoka." The sergeant extended his hand, gave a courtly bow, and said, "I'm Sergeant Smith. Pleased to meet you, ma'am."

"Ahyoka needs to see a doctor, Sergeant. I believe we have one or two here at the fort, don't we?" asked Johnny.

"Yes, we do. Do you need my help to get one?" asked the sergeant.

"Well, if you show me where their office is, I can manage the rest myself," replied Johnny.

Sergeant Smith walked them to the doctor's office.

"Thank you, Sergeant," said Johnny. Then he knocked on the door.

Soon, the door opened. Standing before them was a sunburned, white-haired man in his fifties. "Good afternoon, son," he said. "Is there something I can help you with?"

Johnny said, "You should probably talk to her. It might be better if I stepped away and let y'all do it in private. She is a full-blooded Cherokee, so may I assume that your services are paid for by the US Government on behalf of the Nation?"

"You are correct," said the doctor. "I'm Dr. Winston. What are your names?"

"I'm Johnny Sullivan, and she is Ahyoka," replied Johnny.

"Well, pleased to meet you both," said Dr. Winston. "Ahyoka, will you step into my office? Johnny, you can wait here if you wish," said the doctor.

"Sergeant Smith is a friend of mine. I can go sit a spell in his office," said Johnny.

An hour later, a soldier showed up at the quartermaster's door. He said, "Dr. Winston is ready to see you."

"Thanks," said Johnny, who quickly walked to the doctor's office.

"Come in, Johnny," said the doctor. "Let's talk about your dear Ahyoka's condition." By this time, the doctor knew that Ahyoka had miscarried in her youth and had become barren afterwards. He knew that this information and the symptoms she had reported might indicate uterine cancer. But he was not certain. He provided some recommendations about changing her diet, as she had complained about constantly feeling bloated and having pains in her lower back and abdominal region. He closed by suggesting, "Come back here in a month after making the changes to Ahyoka's diet, and we'll see if it has helped. Do you have any questions?"

Neither Johnny nor Ahyoka dared to ask any. Johnny didn't even know what a "cancer" was. And he didn't want to know. Ahyoka, for her part, knew something about it but was afraid of knowing more.

Johnny said, "Thank you, Dr. Winston. We'll be back in a month. Hopefully, by then, Ahyoka will feel better."

They went back to the wagon. They drove it to a nearby well, where others who were visiting the fort had pitched their tents. They set up their tent, drew some water, and dined on smoked pork and corn cakes.

They didn't speak much that night. It was as if they feared tainting the future with depressing thoughts or words. When Ahyoka said she was having lower back pain, Johnny asked her to lie on her stomach. Then he rubbed her back until she fell asleep.

They left for home early the next morning.

* * * * * * * * *

For the next three weeks, Ahyoka prepared meals for herself according to Dr. Winston's advice. At first, they seemed to have a good effect, but beginning in the third week, Ahyoka's bouts with pain became more frequent and more severe.

Johnny was at a loss. He hadn't a clue as to what to do. Watching her suffer grieved him. He wasn't going to wait until a whole month had passed. He decided they should go back to Fort Gibson to see Dr. Winston right away. He packed the wagon for another trip.

On the way to Fort Gibson, Ahyoka broached a subject that he didn't even want to think about. In Cherokee, which was still her most comfortable idiom, she said, "Johnny, if I have the sickness that rots the insides of my body, I will surely die. It will just be a matter of when."

Johnny, out of control, exclaimed, "No, you won't die...Do not even say that!"

"Maybe I will not," she said, "but if I do, there are some things I wish to tell you…if you will hear me."

Johnny, feeling as if he were the one facing death, got hold of himself. He said, "I want you to live at least as long as me. I can't imagine life without you."

"Are you ready to listen to what I have to say?" asked Ahyoka.

"Not really," said Johnny. He took a deep breath and said, "But speak. I will try to listen."

"That is well," she said, continuing in her native tongue. "If I do not survive, here is what I want for you, my dear Johnny White Owl Tenkiller Sullivan. I want you to follow your path, whatever it turns out to be, wherever it leads you. Do not be angry with the Great Spirit if He does not answer your prayers about my well-being. While powerful faith can cause miracles—I believe this—the miracles do not always show up. The Great

Spirit may have a different plan. So, I have two promises that I ask you to make to me."

"I hope I can keep them," responded Johnny.

"The first one is, even if I do not survive, do not lose your faith. Your faith brought us together when it seemed we would never see each other again. Always remember that. Will you promise me that?"

Johnny paused to reflect. He took another deep breath. As he exhaled, a sudden, deep calm overtook him. "I give this to the Great Spirit. I promise, Ahyoka. What is the second promise?"

Ahyoka said, "That pink tablecloth...I suspect that should I die, you might consider burying it with me."

"I would have. What would you have me do with it?" asked Johnny.

"Please keep it with you as a remembrance of me and the love we have shared. And if your path should lead you to another person for whom you might feel a great love, I wish for you to use it when you dine with her."

"So, what is the second promise, Ahyoka?"

"Everything I just said," she replied.

"I keep the tablecloth. If I should ever fall in love again, you want me to use it with her," said Johnny.

"That is right," said Ahyoka.

"Well, beautiful one, you are still alive. But I promise to do as you have asked if that is the way things happen."

Johnny was moved. And he was a bit sick to his stomach. He desperately wanted his Ahyoka to be cured. As to how, he had no idea.

They arrived at Fort Gibson in the late afternoon. Johnny left Ahyoka and his rifle in the wagon and hurried to the doctor's office. Dr. Winston was there.

"Good afternoon, doctor," said Johnny. "Perhaps you remember me and my wife, Ahyoka, from a month ago?"

"Yes, I do. And your name is 'Johnny', right?"

"It must be hard to remember people's names when you have so many to see," commented Johnny.

"I make a point of trying to remember folks' names. I don't always succeed, but I try. How is Ahyoka?" asked the doctor.

"She followed your advice, and for a couple of weeks, she seemed to be better. Then it got worse. That's why I've brought her here today. Will you see her, doctor?"

"Yes, of course. Please bring her in," said Dr. Winston.

Johnny went to the wagon and brought Ayoka in. He brought his rifle this time. The gate was guarded by the same soldier as the last time they had come. He saw Johnny and the rifle. He remembered them. He waved them through.

When they returned to the doctor's office and sat down, Dr. Winston pulled out three brown glass bottles. They were unlabeled. "These," he announced, "are for pain. When you are suffering, take a teaspoon of it. It will make the pain go away, and you will probably feel good. Which is actually something to watch out for. This medicine is made of opium, which comes from poppies. It helps us deal with intense pain. But it can also make a person addicted."

"What does that mean?" asked Ahyoka.

"Have you ever known someone who drank too much whiskey, who said they wanted to stop but just couldn't? That is addiction," replied Dr. Winston. "Your body just craves something. You just have to have it. You get angry if you cannot get it." He paused for effect, then continued: "However bad you may think a whiskey addiction is, this is far worse. For this reason, I strongly suggest that you only use it when you're really in pain, but not otherwise. Don't just take it to make yourself feel good."

Dr. Winston knew well that it wouldn't work out that way. Ahyoka would almost surely become addicted because if his diagnosis of cancer was correct, she would spend the last few weeks of her life in agony. This "medicine" would minimize that and probably contribute to bringing her life to a merciful end.

"Thank you, Dr. Winston," said Johnny and Ahyoka in unison. They took the bottles. The next morning, they returned to Tahlequah.

* * * * * * * * *

A month later, on a cold, grey day in November, beautiful Ahyoka's spirit departed this earth. Grandmother had been her companion in her last moments. Though the younger Ahyoka was in a dreamlike state for most of the last few days of her life, she and "Auntie" had opportunities to talk. On one such day, Ahyoka said, "Auntie, have I ever told you how much I appreciate that you adopted me as your niece?"

"You have thanked me every day through your actions, Ahyoka," said the elder. "For these six years, you have helped me in all ways, and you have never complained about anything. Your work is always thorough and neat. When I was out finding people to help the Easterners, you were with me. When it was time to serve fresh meat to the people, you were there to help. When it was time to plant corn, you were out there, getting muddy in the fields. And then you washed yourself and helped me prepare a meal. I rarely go to church, but you went almost every week, and every week, you placed an offering when they passed the basket, didn't you?

"Whatever you may have been in the past, here there are many people, including people of high standing, who admire and respect you. You have made my dear grandson happy. And you have made me proud. I could not ask for more." She broke into tears as she added, "I wish you had been my daughter, for you have brought me more happiness than she ever did! And I do not know what I will do without you, my dear Ahyoka!"

"Do not cry, Auntie. Soon, I will be in the bosom of the Great Spirit. You, Johnny, Will, and I will join one another there and live on in eternal bliss."

"I hope so, I pray so," said the elder Ahyoka.

"I know so, Auntie."

"How do you know it, my dear?"

"I can already see it, like a rainbow over a valley, after it rains, and the sun comes out from behind the clouds."

* * * * * * * * *

Johnny, knowing that Ahyoka's time was near, had paid a Cherokee named Tsali ("Charlie") to make a pine box for her burial. It was already done when Ahyoka went to her rainbow. Another Cherokee knew how to make headstones. Grandmother, expecting the end, had paid him in advance for his work.

The day after Ahyoka passed away, a crowd gathered at her gravesite. It was a large crowd—over two hundred people. They knew her from the store, from the communal feasts, and from her presence wherever the Beloved Woman, the elder Ahyoka, went. They had been partners in soothing the suffering of their people since they had reached the far side of the Trail of Tears.

The pine coffin, with Ahyoka lying in state, sat at the side of the rectangular hole Johnny and Beaver had dug. On the headstone was inscribed:

Ahyoka Sullivan, beloved by her people and now by the angels.
Born: 1804 Died: November 15, 1839.

Her eulogy was given by the elder Ahyoka. Tall and erect as a queen, she spoke: "When this fine woman passed away from us, she went to a better place. But for those of us who loved her, she left a great hole in our hearts." She started to sob but managed to stop before being engulfed by a flood of tears. "Whatever she may have done in her youth, that has not mattered since I met her six years ago. Since she has been with me, she has been as close to a perfect being as I have ever known. May the Great Spirit open His arms in welcome to my sweet Ahyoka!"

There were dozens of Christians at this gathering. Upon hearing the words of the noble Ahyoka, they said, in almost perfect unison, "Amen!"

After the service, Johnny hugged his grandmother. "I'll be back later," he said. "I need to spend some time alone."

Ahyoka nodded her understanding.

Then he walked to the woods at the edge of town. He found the place where he and Ahyoka made love for the first time after she, Johnny's grandmother, and Beaver had arrived from Tennessee five years earlier. He sat cross-legged on the dry grass and spread the pink tablecloth before him. He just stared at it. He wanted to sing his death song but could not even get himself to begin.

All he could do was cry.

Part 6: The Path

Chapter 20: The Colt Paterson

For a week after Ahyoka's service, Johnny's grief prevented him from getting much of anything done. Now, he, too, was one of the walking dead.

His grandmother noticed his listlessness. One afternoon, she asked, "White Owl, why don't you take the trip you had planned in September? Why don't you go to your uncle's ranch on the Canadian River?"

"Will you be comfortable and feel safe if I go?" asked Johnny.

"I have friends here, both from the old settlers and the new arrivals from the East. Beaver has relatives here as well, and they will protect me if needed. Go see your uncle. Perhaps the trip will be healing for you," said Ahyoka.

"I don't know if I will ever heal from this misery, this dark emptiness I feel inside," said Johnny.

Johnny's grandmother looked at him kindly, with eyes full of wisdom. She said, "I know, son. But time heals. One day, you will remember with fondness those precious years you lived with your Ahyoka. And one day, you will find your rainbow. On the other side of it will be your Ahyoka, Tommy Smith, your grandfather Will, and me, too." She smiled. "Now, pack up and go down to the Canadian River."

Packing for a trip of a few weeks' duration was a welcome distraction for Johnny. He made a list of the things he needed to take with him. He started gathering them up. He would take two horses—Flower and a pack horse that he would pick from his grandmother's small herd.

The trip south to Dutch's ranch could be traveled, if one made haste, in two long days. But there was no need to hurry.

It was the middle of November. Winter had not yet arrived, and the remnants of Fall still colored the landscape with bits of orange, red, and yellow. It would be a lovely ride. Johnny decided to take three days for the journey.

* * * * * * * * *

As he rode southward, Johnny noticed that some farms were beginning to appear on the prairies. He recalled how, just a few years before, when the land was still ruled by the Osages, these were just open prairies. Now, the Osages no longer lived there. They were concentrated around Fort Gibson and the area to the north of it. Like the Cherokee and other eastern tribes, they were learning the white man's sciences of farming and metallurgy. At this point, it seemed to Johnny that the Cherokee, with all the murders and revenge killings going on between the factions, had more to fear from each other than from the Osages…or anyone else, for that matter. They were still locked into the same mentality—back-and-forth vengeance—as their Stone Age ancestors. Johnny wondered when it would ever stop.

Late in the afternoon of the second day, he noted a gathering of ominous, dark grey clouds. It looked like rain was on the way. He saw flashes of lightning off in the distance, followed by the rumbling of thunder. He decided to camp at the edge of a wooded area that butted up against a broad prairie. Finding wood suitable for a lean-to in these woods, which were mostly full of short, gnarly, twisted oak trees suitable mostly for firewood, would be time-consuming. But already knowing this, he had brought his tent. He pitched it and built a fire.

He thought about Ahyoka. A dark, sad spirit engulfed him. He sang his death song for a few minutes. It helped.

He hadn't wanted to eat since Ahyoka's passing. He only ate because he knew his body needed it, not because he was truly hungry. From one of his bags, he pulled out a corn cake and some smoked pork.

About the time he finished his dinner, it began to rain. He let the rain put out his fire as he sat cross-legged in his tent. He recalled a night like this, back when he was traveling from St. Louis to Fort Gibson. He remembered that he had longed for Ahyoka, who was still somewhere in the east, believing he would never see her again. It occurred to him at this moment that that powerful longing may have—must have—translated into a prayer to the Creator, the Great Spirit, God, or whatever other name humans have used to designate the Lord of the universe, the all-powerful, unknowable Mover of all that is. A prayer from the heart, which hoped, but not the mind, which "knew" better. Knowing that if this heartfelt longing had been a prayer, it had been answered, he realized that he had not even said "Thank You."

He wondered how he could have forgotten that. He mused to himself, "I hope God doesn't think I'm an asshole!" He laughed. And then he sent up a heartfelt prayer of thanks for bringing his Ahyoka to him when it seemed impossible. For the five happy years they had shared. For the memories that would live on in his mind and his heart.

After that, he slept well.

* * * * * * * * *

Late the next afternoon, he arrived at the ranch on the Canadian River. He rode straight to Dutch's cabin and dismounted just in time to see his uncle come out of his front door.

"Hello, Uncle Dutch!"

"Welcome home, Tenkiller," replied Dutch. "How is your family?"

Johnny's eyes cast downward, and he answered, "My grandmother is doing well." He paused and then added, "My Ahyoka died last week."

Dutch, not one to waste words or to speak without sincerity, just said solemnly, "I am sorry for your loss."

After a moment of respectful silence, Dutch introduced his wife. Speaking Cherokee, he said, "You have not met her yet, but this is Walela" (Cherokee for "Hummingbird").

Johnny, speaking Cherokee, replied, "Nice to meet you, Hummingbird." She smiled and nodded slightly. He noticed that she was about the same age as Ahyoka. She was still slender, and her movements were quick and graceful. Perhaps this had something to do with living into her name, Johnny thought. Or maybe it was the other way around: The name might have been given to her because of those quick and graceful movements.

Dutch and Hummingbird had a boy child who looked to be about four years old. Dutch grabbed his boy's hand and said, "Say hello to your Uncle Tenkiller."

The boy was bashful. He ducked behind Dutch's leg and peered out cautiously.

"Don't be afraid," said Johnny. Looking at Dutch, he said, "Maybe you scared him when you called me 'Uncle Tenkiller'. Might have been better to just call me 'Uncle Johnny'." They laughed.

"What is his name?" asked Johnny.

"When he grows up, he can earn a new name if he wishes to. But for now, his name is Tludatsi (Cherokee for 'Panther')," said Dutch.

"With a powerful name like that, he may not need a vision quest," said Johnny.

"Maybe not," said Dutch. "Now, Panther, greet your uncle," commanded Dutch.

The boy spoke only Cherokee. In that language, he said, "It is an honor to meet you, Uncle Tenkiller." He took Johnny's hand as a gesture of respect.

"He has fine manners," said Johnny. "Befitting a chief's son."

Changing the subject, Dutch observed, "It seems a lot of things—not all good—have happened up where you stay. Perhaps you can tell me about them after we have dinner."

"That is well," said Johnny.

* * * * * * * *

After dinner, Johnny and Dutch sat outside on the front porch and smoked Dutch's pipe, sitting in silence. Dutch took a swig from a bottle of whiskey and offered Johnny. Johnny reminded his uncle that he found whiskey to be the vilest thing he had ever tasted.

Dutch laughed and said, "That is just as well." He took another drink and said, "So, will you tell me what has happened in the three years since we last met?"

Johnny obliged. He told of the miserable, bedraggled contingents from the East that had straggled into Tahlequah and Fort Gibson. He told of the heroic efforts of his grandmother and other prominent Cherokees to help them get settled. He told his uncle that the elder Ahyoka's reputation had grown, and that people were starting to refer to her as "Beloved Woman". Dutch nodded approvingly when he heard this. Then Johnny told of his meeting with Major Ridge.

Dutch was familiar with the Treaty Party, as the Ridges and those who supported them were known. Though he had not met Major Ridge, he had heard of him, and his view was favorable. He also knew of the assassinations, which, while inevitable, he found regrettable. When Johnny brought up the topic of the assassinations, all Dutch said was, "The fires of Hell will follow this, probably for many years. Some of our people—the Old Settlers—have taken sides, mostly against the newcomers and especially against Chief John Ross. For my part, I try to stay neutral."

Johnny said, "I found Major Ridge to be one of the most impressive men I have ever met. I bet if you and he had met, you would have been friends."

"Could be," said Dutch, who quickly changed the subject. "And how are you dealing with the loss of Ahyoka?"

"There are days when I do not even wish to go on living, Uncle."

"I understand," said Uncle Dutch. "I lost a wife once." He paused thoughtfully and said, "Perhaps you should consider going far away on a new journey. That might heal your wounds."

"I have thought of that," said Johnny. "But as long as my grandmother lives, I will stay by her side."

Dutch knew that Grandmother Ahyoka was well into her sixties. He surmised that Johnny may not have to wait very long for his next journey. All Dutch said was, "That is worthy."

Then he changed the subject again. "I have something for you, Tenkiller. Wait a moment, and I will bring it out to you." He stepped inside the cabin and soon came out with a leather bag and a long-barreled pistol. "I got this from the United States Army. It was a reward for my service to them as a hunter and a scout over the last few years. It is a remarkable weapon. It can shoot four or five bullets before it needs to be reloaded. Tomorrow, I will show you how to use and load it. I plan to give it to you. The only problem with it is that it makes killing men far too easy. There is no honor in it!" He laughed. "First thing in the morning, we can ride out into the country, and I will show you how it works."

Johnny was excited. He said, "I can hardly wait to see how it works, Uncle!"

* * * * * * * * *

The next morning, Dutch showed Johnny how the new weapon worked. He said, "They call this gun the 'Colt Paterson Number 5' because there were earlier versions of it. The good thing about this one is that you don't have to take it apart to reload it like you did the older models. It's still time-consuming to load, and you must buy the caps that set off the powder." He presented the gun to Johnny. "There are five chambers in this cylinder, one for each bullet. If you are going to carry it in a holster, it is best to load only four of the five chambers and put the hammer on the empty chamber unless you want to accidentally shoot off your foot. But in battle, you should load all five chambers. It would be even better to have two of these guns. Now, let's go to the edge of our village and practice shooting it."

They went to the north side of the village where Sarah and the other girls used to practice with their rifles, back in the time when they were getting ready for the second Comanche raid. He wondered about Sarah but hesitated to ask about her at this moment. There was a target at the edge of a wooded area. Dutch aimed the gun and fired, hitting the target near its center. He passed the gun to Johnny, saying, "Now you try."

Johnny found the revolver to be awkward. He held it the same way as Dutch had, pointed it, and fired at the same target. The bullet missed the target altogether.

"Like anything else, you will have to practice with this weapon to master its use," commented Dutch. "But once you have, you will become a very dangerous warrior. The Texas Rangers, I am told, plan to issue this weapon to all their men. It's the only thing that is likely to give them an edge on the Comanches, who usually get the better of them in fights."

Johnny, confident that he would master the use of the Colt Paterson, said, "I can see why. The real problem would be in getting the caps and the lead balls. I would need a couple hundred of them to master this awesome weapon."

Dutch said, "You could probably buy a lot of caps and balls at Fort Gibson. The gun is expensive, but caps and balls are not. I have enough on hand right now to give you a chance to practice loading and shooting. It is important to become good at both. Not much good having a repeating weapon if it takes you all day to reload."

"Thanks, Uncle." Changing the subject somewhat, Johnny said, "I bet Sarah Studeville would be very dangerous with a weapon like this!"

Dutch replied, "Probably better not give her one. She might use it on you." He grinned.

Johnny looked at his uncle quizzically. "Really?"

Dutch replied, "She was very hurt when I told her about you and Ahyoka. She did not take it well."

"Did she ever marry?" asked Johnny.

"Yes. She married Billy Starr," said Dutch. "Two years ago."

"That is not what I would have expected. I thought he might carry a grudge about her getting credit for killing Ten Bears…Did they have children yet?" asked Johnny.

"They have a baby girl," Dutch replied.

Johnny was at a loss for words. All he could say was, "Well, I hope they find happiness."

"I hope so as well," said Dutch. He didn't want to say so at this point, but the marriage was not working out well. Billy drank whiskey. He was violent…

Johnny changed the topic back to the gun. "Well," he said, "Maybe you can teach me how to load this thing."

"Use up those last three bullets, and I will show you how," said Dutch.

* * * * * * * * *

Johnny spent the next week practicing shooting and loading the Paterson Colt for 1-2 hours per day. His ability as a rifleman soon translated into his skills with the revolver. He used up over a hundred caps and balls in the process. He told his uncle, "I'll replace the ammunition next time I go to Fort Gibson."

Dutch replied, "You won't need to do that on my account. Did you forget? I'm giving all of that to you, along with the gun. I am very pleased with your progress. Next time you can spare twenty-five dollars, I suggest you spend it on another Paterson. When you go on your next journey, I suspect it will serve you well to have two such weapons."

"Thanks, Uncle," said Johnny. "How will I ever repay you for all the things you have done for me?"

"Be considerate to everyone. Be honorable. Only kill sonofabitches that need killin'. I will not put any further requirements on you. If the opportunity arises, you can pay it forward, as you did when you helped your friend, Isaac, to repay Tommy Smith for saving your life. Tommy did not require any compensation from you. Nor will I."

* * * * * * * * *

Being at the ranch, learning to use the Paterson, and talking with his uncles was good for Johnny. Though the sick feeling in the pit of his stomach lingered, especially when he thought of Ahyoka, he was beginning to conceive of a life without her. He started to miss his grandmother. But he wasn't ready to go home yet. He feared returning to the cabin where he and Ahyoka had lived, only to find it empty. His heart sank at the very thought…

One day, while he was practicing with his new pistol, he heard a woman's voice behind him. "Good mornin', Tenkiller."

Johnny turned around and saw Sarah Studeville. She was carrying her one-year-old on her hip. She was a bit heavier than he remembered her to be but still well-proportioned and pretty. He smiled and said, "Good morning, Sarah. I'm so happy to see you. And I'm sure happy you're not totin' a gun."

"Why would you say that?" she responded.

"I told Uncle Dutch that you would be real dangerous with a weapon like this here pistol. And he said you'd probably use it on me if you had one." Johnny laughed. Sarah laughed, too. He added, "I know you wouldn't have missed with it, neither. Would've only needed one of these bullets, not the whole cylinder."

Sarah came closer. Johnny could see the remnants of what appeared to be a black eye. "How's married life?" he asked.

"I think you just saw and figured it out," said Sarah.

"So, your husband hits you?" Johnny felt his anger rising.

"He's not bad when he is sober," said Sarah. "But when he drinks…"

Johnny was angry. He thought about giving Billy Starr a beating. He had no doubts as to whether he could. But then he recalled something Brother McLaurin had told him about Marcus Aurelius, the last 'good' Roman emperor. In his reflections, Aurelius had given a warning to anyone who might read them: "Beware of becoming what you hate." Johnny had asked Brother McLaurin to explain what that meant. Among other things, Brother McLaurin said, it meant that one should not use his strength to oppress others. That is what evil men do, isn't it? He asked himself what good end would be served by beating up Billy Starr. It would make Billy bitter, perhaps make him want revenge, and it might not—probably would not—help Sarah. In his thoughts, Johnny concluded, "Just because I can doesn't mean I should."

Having concluded this, Johnny's heart softened. He said, "I feel sorry for you and for Billy as well. Has anyone talked to him about this?"

"Your uncle did. It didn't help," replied Sarah.

"Well, if Uncle Dutch couldn't change him, I doubt that I can. But I will try to talk with him anyway," said Johnny.

"I would be fine with that, as long as you don't kill 'im," said Sarah.

"Oh, I wouldn't do that!" protested Johnny. "I'd rather try to become his friend…maybe take that approach."

Sarah was silent for a moment, apparently thinking about what to say next. "Might you be interested in joining us for dinner tonight?" asked Sarah.

"Well, if it's fine with Billy, I'd be pleased to come."

* * * * * * * *

Billy had spent a couple of hours tending cattle that day. He came back home in the mid-afternoon. Sarah asked him if Johnny could come to dinner.

Billy, who had already consumed a bit of whiskey, asked, in a querulous tone of voice, "Why?"

Sarah, who was quick on her feet, responded, "We all fought the Comanches together. He just wanted to say hello."

Billy thought for a few moments. Then he said, "Sure, why not?"

It was Sarah, not Billy, who walked to Dutch's cabin to invite Johnny to dinner. When she had left, Dutch said, "Why are you doing this?"

Johnny said, "Maybe I can make Billy a friend. Maybe I can help him get his head out of his ass."

"Oh, that is a fine start," said Dutch, with a definite hint of sarcasm. He continued, "Go ahead and try."

An hour later, after he freshened up and put on a clean shirt, Johnny walked to Billy and Sarah's cabin. Billy greeted him at the door. In English, he said, "Well, come on in, Mr. Tenkiller!" His voice smelled of whiskey, but he seemed under control in that nether world between sobriety and drunkenness.

Johnny shook hands with Billy and said, "It's good to see you."

Sarah said, "Hey, Johnny! Come sit at the table, I'm fixin' to serve dinner."

Turning to Sarah, he said, "Well, if you can cook as good as you can shoot, this will be a heck of a good meal!"

"I'm not that great a cook, Johnny," she protested. "Maybe I cook half as good as I shoot."

"Well then, in that case, I'm sure it's gonna be good." He sat down at the side of the table, noting that often, Cherokees had the same kind of furniture as whites.

They dined on freshly cooked pork, beans, collard greens, and corn. The ingredients were all of decent quality. It may not have been a meal made by a virtuoso chef, but it was tasty and nourishing. During the meal, they didn't speak much, and such conversation as they had was casual, of little substance.

After dinner, Billy asked Johnny if he wanted to go out on the porch to have a smoke. Sarah said, "Y'all go out there and have a nice smoke. I'll clean up in here."

So, they did. Billy loaded up his long pipe—the Cherokees still used those—with some recently harvested tobacco. He lit it up, took a draw, and passed it to Johnny, who did the same. Johnny only smoked pipe occasionally. He coughed. And coughed. He felt like he was going to choke to death.

Billy laughed and said, "You're not used to this, are you?"

"No," said Johnny, laughing at himself, still coughing as he spoke. "I do it once in a while, and mostly, I'm careful not to take too big a draw." Finally, his coughing fit ended. Then he said, "Guess I liked the sweet smell of your tobacco and got carried away."

Billy had a jug of whiskey on his porch. He reached down, picked it up, and took a drink. He presented the jug to Johnny. "Why don't you take a little nip of this? Made it myself out of the corn."

"I'm impressed. At least you don't have to pay white men for it anymore. I like the smell of the stuff, Billy, but I can't drink it."

"Why not?" Billy asked, with a somewhat demanding tone of voice.

"I got so sick on that shit once upon a time that I can't even stand the idea of drinkin' whiskey. But thank you for the offer…I must respectfully decline your generosity."

"Suit yourself," said Billy as he took another sip.

"How has life been treatin' you?" asked Johnny.

Billy, still somewhat sober, paused a moment. He grew pensive and said, "The old folks say that life don't always turn out like you want it to. I'm not even thirty years old, Johnny, but I'm startin' to see the wisdom in them words."

Johnny did not expect to hear anything like this from a man like Billy, whom he expected to grow up to be an asshole. Maybe he was just part asshole—the part that gave Sarah that black eye. He wanted to get to the point at which they might talk about that but needed a way in. He asked, "How is married life treatin' ya, Billy?"

"That was one of the things I was thinkin' about when I spoke of the wisdom of the old folks," he said. He looked Johnny straight in the eye and said, "I know you saw what was left of Sarah's black eye. If you think I did it, you're right. I did. There ain't no honor to be had from hittin' a woman. I know that. Shame on my drunken ass!"

Johnny asked, "Well, can't you just be a happy drunk? When my uncle drinks, he's always happy. He don't get mad; he just goes to sleep. And then again, he don't do it too often."

"Your uncle has a lot to be happy about, Johnny. He's a chief. He's a legend. He's a big man in this world. What am I? Just a dirt farmer."

"Dirt farmers feed all the people in the world, Billy. It's not somethin' to be disrespected," said Johnny.

"Depends on what it's bein' compared to, Johnny, Mister *Tenkiller…*" he said in a voice with a noticeable hostile edge. "Everybody around here knows that you, Johnny Tenkiller, are a great warrior. The first year I tried to court Sarah, all she could talk about was you and the legend you left behind."

Johnny said, "I'd hate that too, Billy, if I'd been in your place." Wanting to change the subject, he asked, "Can I tell you a couple of things about my life?"

Billy said, "Sure, go ahead."

Johnny said, "The reason I'm a tenkiller has less to do with me than it does with the things and people that were thrown onto my path, or maybe that my path threw at me. I'm still thinkin' about that. Anyways, you probably know about how my cousin's girlfriend was gang-raped by those three hill-rods, don't ya?"

"I've heard that damned story about a dozen times." Billy smiled grudgingly.

"I hated them sonofabitches every day of my life until the day I killed 'em. And boy, did I enjoy that! I still enjoy just thinkin' about it, even after six years." Johnny became more animated; his breath became shallow. "I wish I could do it all over again, sometimes." He exhaled a long breath and grew calmer. "But think about this, Billy. If them mangy dogs had never been born, I'd probably stayed in school with them missionaries. I'd be a preacher or a teacher right now. I hope I woulda been a good one. And that's my point. If I'd been a preacher, or a teacher, or both, I would just try to be the best damned teacher around. And I'd be proud of that. Even if I never killed a single human being. So, what I'm sayin' is, if you had run into the things I'd run into in my life, you would be the one they called 'Tenkiller', not me."

"I don't know, Johnny. I mighta been knocked off 'fore I got to number three. Some folks are just born to do that kind of shit. Like you."

"Well, Billy. Here are some undeniable facts: You wounded Ten Bears. And you were there, fightin' Comanches—the scariest sonofabitches in this part of the world—right alongside the rest of us. You weren't scared. And if you remember, you wanted to go after 'em that night. I had to talk you out of it. You're fuckin' crazy, Billy...a true warrior." Johnny smiled.

Billy, who may have thirsted for the recognition he had just gotten, smiled, too, and his inner tension seemed to dissipate. His expression relaxed, and he stared into space for a minute or so. Johnny just sat there quietly.

It was Billy who broke the silence. "I shot Ten Bears, but it was my lovely future wife who finished him off."

Johnny recalled how he felt when he first saw Sarah shoot. He said, "You know, I still remember watching Sarah do target practice before our second battle with the Comanches. I'm gonna tell you a secret now: She scared the hell out of me! She's a better shot than I am. And I ain't bein' falsely modest here. I'm a damned good shot. She's better. Now, the only reason that would ever matter to me, if I was you, would be if she was aimin' that thing at me!" Both Billy and Johnny laughed. "Otherwise, I'd be proud."

There was another moment of silence. Then Billy mused, "I guess I should be." He smiled faintly, seemingly lost in thought.

Johnny added, "Imagine if you two ran a store. I would pity the sonofabitches that tried to rob you with the two of you there. The number of bullets y'all had would be the number of dead bodies after the fact. Unless y'all ran out of outlaws 'fore you ran out of bullets!"

Billy laughed. Again, they sat in silence for what seemed like several minutes.

At length, Billy spoke again. "You know, Johnny, you just gave me an idea. Maybe me 'n' Sarah *should* start a store. There's more people movin' into this part of the territory, and we ain't never had a real store at this here ranch." He paused for a minute. Then he added, "Why, the thought of it's enough to make a man wanna stop drinkin'."

Johnny took a moment to choose his next words very carefully. He felt an opportunity at hand and did not want to blow it. Then he asked, "Why, Billy, are you thinkin' about givin' up that drunken Indian shit?" Johnny smiled as if to make his last statement into a joke.

Billy cast his eyes downward and just said, "I know I should." Again, he was lost in thought.

About this time, Sarah came to the door and asked, "Ain't y'all comin' in for dessert? I made a plum pie!"

Johnny said, "I'm so full of that fine dinner you made that I don't have room for dessert; thank you. And besides, I'm gettin' ready to go back to Tahlequah. Gonna leave tomorrow. So, I'm gonna go back to Uncle's house to get some rest and start makin' plans. But I want to thank both of y'all for that dinner and a fine evenin'."

Johnny and Billy stood up and shook hands. Johnny, for his part, felt that this was the right time to leave. He didn't want to mess up what seemed to be a promising moment by staying longer and throwing more words at it.

As Johnny turned to leave, Billy said to Sarah, "Wait, honey, I want you to watch this. You too, Johnny!" He solemnly picked up the jug of whiskey and emptied the whole thing onto the ground. He smiled and said, "Honey, we're gonna have us a store one day. And if I ever hit you again, for any reason, please shoot me!" Then he, Sarah, and Johnny all laughed. Billy and Sarah hugged.

Johnny beamed a smile at them as he turned and walked back to Dutch's cabin.

* * * * * * * *

The next morning, Dutch asked Johnny, "How did your dinner go? Did you make that asshole Billy Starr into a friend?"

Johnny said, "I don't know if I did, Uncle. But when I left, he emptied his jug out in front of the porch and told Sarah that if he ever hits her again, to shoot him."

Dutch, who was smoking his pipe, looked Johnny straight in the eyes and declared, "That sounds like a miracle."

"Well, if it is, it wasn't my doing. To be honest, Uncle, I didn't know what I was doing. It all just happened without a plan," said Johnny.

Dutch merely nodded and continued to puff on his pipe. To himself, he thought that maybe Johnny had, in this instance, "shot from his center."

* * * * * * * *

By noon that day, Johnny was ready to leave. He thanked his Uncle Dutch and Hummingbird for their hospitality. He hugged Panther. To Dutch, he said, "And thanks, Uncle, for that gun and the ammunition. I promise to use it for good."

"Deciding what's good—and what isn't—can be a tricky business," observed Dutch.

Johnny mounted up and turned to ride away. "I look forward to seeing you again, Uncle."

Dutch just said, "Good hunting, Tenkiller."

Chapter 21: Baker's Dozen

Johnny returned to Tahlequah in December 1839. He continued to make plowshares, hoes, and horseshoes. In January 1840, he rode to Fort Gibson. While he was there, he found that Sergeant Smith had received funds from the US government as per the treaty. He hailed Johnny, who was shopping for lead balls, powder, and caps. "Hi, Johnny," said the sergeant. "I have your reimbursement."

Johnny remembered that he was owed $50. "That is good to hear, Sergeant. And I have some ideas about how I'd like to spend it," said Johnny. "Are you paying in cash or in some kind of scrip?"

"You can buy most anything here at the fort with scrip," replied Sergeant Smith. "What are you looking to buy?"

Johnny pulled out his Paterson and showed it to the sergeant.

"Where the hell did you get that?" asked Sergeant Smith.

"The Army gave it to my uncle. I'd like to buy another one and a lot of powder, shot, and caps," replied Johnny.

"I've heard of these pistols," said the sergeant. "I heard the Texas Navy bought some, but they didn't keep using them. Don't know why."

"Well," said Johnny, "However it was that it got into my uncle's hands, now it's mine. I hope to get another one, too." Meanwhile, I need some lead balls that will fit the barrel and the chambers in the cylinder. And some caps."

"I heard you can buy one of those Colt Patersons for about $25," said the sergeant.

"The question is, where can I get another one and plenty of ammunition," commented Johnny. "It's ammunition that I need most—if I can find some."

"Unless you're thinking of traveling down to Houston or some other place in Texas where the Texas Rangers are stationed, I don't know where you're gonna find any," said the sergeant.

"Shit," said the disappointed Johnny. "Well, at least I have another few dozen rounds. My uncle gave 'em to me along with the gun."

"So, have you learned to use it?" asked Sergeant Smith. "It looks like a pretty complicated contraption."

"I used up over half the ammunition he gave me learning to shoot and reload it," said Johnny. "It's pretty accurate, as long as your target is less than sixty feet away. That's not bad." Then he said, "I guess I'll take those fifty dollars in cash, Sergeant."

* * * * * * * * *

The violence in the Cherokee Nation continued. While it was mostly factional in the beginning, it had already begun to be hard to distinguish, by the early 1840s, between politics and common criminality. A mixed blood named James Foreman, who had helped organize the executions of the Ridges and Elias Boudinot was killed by Stand Watie—Elias's younger brother—in 1842. Watie killed him in hand-to-hand combat. Old school. Cherokee style. Johnny had heard that Foreman was one of the bushwhackers that shot Major Ridge. If so, the sonofabitch needed killing. He hoped to meet Stand Watie someday.

On the other hand, there were other acts of violence and theft that were hard to dress up in political terms. One spring day in 1843, a group of three Cherokees swaggered into Grandmother Ahyoka's store. Two of them appeared to be full bloods. The apparent ringleader looked half-white. They demanded whiskey. Ahyoka told them that she did not sell whiskey.

The leader said, "Well, then give us some lead. We need ammunition."

Meanwhile, Beaver, sensing ill intent, had gone out the back door to Johnny's smithy. He said, "There's some bad Indians in your grandmother's store. You better go in there and make sure things don't get out of hand."

Johnny grabbed his revolver and went into the store. He kept it concealed under his leather tunic until he stood next to a pile of merchandise. Then he let the pistol hang on his right-hand side, the pile of merchandise making it invisible to the three visitors. The Colt was loaded with four rounds.

He quickly sized them up. They all had on white man's boots, and the boots looked new. The mixed blood, who looked like the eldest of the bunch and was probably their leader, was wearing a relatively new, wide-brimmed hat, as was one of the two full bloods. The other full blood was wearing a derby and what looked like a Seminole tunic with yellow, blue, and orange horizontal stripes. It hung to his knees. Like his boots, it looked rather new. The combination of the derby and the traditional Seminole garment gave the young man an almost comical appearance. But beyond that, nothing about him seemed funny at all.

Johnny spoke in Cherokee to the three men: "What can we do for you today?"

He smiled.

They didn't.

The leader said, "We need some lead and powder. You have some?"

"Sure," Johnny said. "How much do you want?"

The leader said, "We haven't decided yet. We'll let you know."

"Good," said Johnny. He looked at the youth with the colorful tunic and asked him in English, "Are you Seminole?"

The youth, who spoke English, answered, "No." That was all.

"Where'd you get that fine tunic?" asked Johnny.

"A Seminole gave it to me," said the youngster.

Johnny responded, "Well, that was mighty nice of him, wasn't it?"

The youth replied, "How d'you know it was a 'him' that gave it to me? Maybe it was a 'her'."

"Arrogant little shit," thought Johnny. But he said nothing at this point.

The other two sniggered.

One of them started grabbing lead balls from a box near the counter where Grandmother conducted her transactions. He was brazenly putting them into his pockets. The leader was scooping gunpowder into what appeared to be an empty powder horn.

In a calm voice, Johnny said, "I didn't say to just help yourselves. Put that shit back where you got it right now. And leave."

The leader asked, "What are you going to do if we don't?" The other two grinned mischievously.

Johnny smiled. He said in English, "I'm about to give you all the lead you sonofabitches are ever gonna have. Get out of my grandmother's store. Now."

The mixed blood drew his pistol. Johnny quickly cocked his Paterson, raised it, and fired. In an instant, the mixed blood lay on the floor, oozing life on the wooden floor of Grandmother's store. The one without the Seminole tunic went for his pistol. Johnny shot him, too. The outlaw either didn't know about repeating firearms yet, or else he wasn't expecting to find one in Indian Territory. As the young outlaw with the Seminole tunic reached for his gun, Johnny looked him straight in the eye and said in Cherokee, "Please do not make me kill you."

Johnny judged this member of the gang to be about eighteen years old. He did not want to kill him. He was barely more than a boy. They looked at each other in silence. The young man's eyes were cold as stone. The eyes of a predator. Johnny surmised that he had killed before. The young man drew his pistol. Johnny shot him. Dead.

Ahyoka stood by in horror. "Johnny, why would you kill these men over some lead and powder? I would have given it to them—as long as they were not too greedy—and sent them along their ways." She had a soft spot in her heart for full bloods. After all, she was one herself. She felt sorry for them.

"What if they didn't stop at lead and powder, Grandmother? What if they just ransacked your store or demanded all your cash?" asked Johnny.

"If my cash was what they wanted, why would they bother with powder and shot?" asked Ahyoka.

"Maybe they were getting low on powder and shot and wanted to stock up before holding you up," said Johnny. "These were not nice men, Grandmother. Did you notice that they were wearing new boots and hats? Even that Seminole tunic looked new. Do you suppose that they were decent, hardworking men who saved their money up and bought those things? Maybe they were…or maybe they were what they seemed to be: Outlaws. Besides, Grandmother, I tried to let the last one walk away. He chose to die."

Ahyoka said, "I think you might have been able to talk him down if you had put more effort into that. He was just an ignorant boy." She shook her head.

Beaver and Johnny dragged the bodies out to the street. Johnny went to the local constable—a member of the Cherokee Light Horse Guard, which was essentially the Cherokee Nation's police—and explained what had happened. The constable came back to the store with Johnny. He noticed the Seminole tunic.

He said, "I'm pretty sure I have heard about these men. They have been roaming Indian Territory, stealing, robbing, and sometimes killing folks who have stores. They prey on their own people—the Cherokees—but they have also been making mischief among the Choctaw and the Seminole. They do a dirty deed and then run across the border into Arkansas. They hole up with some other Cherokee outlaws who stay there, so we can't arrest them and try them in our courts. Looks like they got a different kind of justice today." He paused and concluded, "Well, you killed them. You can bury them as well."

Johnny asked, "Since they were Cherokees, their clan brothers may come back for vengeance. What should we do?"

"Well, the eastern Cherokee changed the blood laws a few years ago. And thanks to Chief Ross, we're now living under their version of Cherokee law. It used to be that if someone killed a member of your clan—it didn't matter for what reason—you were obligated to kill him or someone from his clan. Nowadays, this blood law only takes effect if the killing was unjustified. If someone was trying to steal your horse, and you killed him, no vengeance is required from his kinsmen. If you killed someone in self-defense—in this case, you clearly did that—no vengeance is required. At least not by our laws.

"That said," concluded the constable, "You still might want to leave town for a while."

"I am worried about my grandmother," said Johnny. "What if his kin come after her?"

"I doubt that," said the constable. "Everyone respects and loves your grandmother. And I will look out for her."

Johnny and Beaver dug three graves. They didn't bother with pine boxes. They didn't mark the graves, either.

Ahyoka didn't speak to Johnny for the next two days.

* * * * * * * * *

On the third day, Ahyoka approached Johnny at his workplace. She said, "White Owl—or should I call you 'baker's-dozen-killer' now? I have been wanting to talk with you about those men you killed."

Johnny stopped what he was doing. "Baker's dozen?" he asked.

"A baker's dozen is thirteen—twelve for the dozen the baker plans to sell, and one he keeps for himself to eat," said Grandmother. "One for each life you have taken."

Johnny was relieved that she was talking to him again but fearful of what she might be about to say. He waited for her to begin.

Ahyoka said, "Two of them were full bloods. Many of the full bloods are still living in desperation. Can it be a surprise that some resort to predation? They were forced to leave the land of our ancestors. They were forced to march a thousand miles in fall and winter. Many of them died. Those who survived lost many loved ones. They are bitter. And as I said, many of them are desperately poor. And ignorant. So, some have found robbery to be a way of surviving. That does not make it right, but don't you think they deserve at least a little compassion?"

"Well, Grandmother, which one of them should I have *not* killed?" asked Johnny. It was an honest question. He didn't know.

"The boy—for he was little more than a boy—in the Seminole tunic," replied Ahyoka.

"Grandmother, did you see his eyes?" asked Johnny. "That 'boy,' as you call him, was a killer. He would have killed me, you, and Beaver if he had the means. And he would not have lost a wink of sleep over it."

Ahyoka pondered this for a moment. Then she said, "Can you be certain about that? And if you were not certain, did you need to kill him?"

"Are you suggesting that I could have disabled him, wounded him, instead?" asked Johnny.

"As I said before, maybe you could have talked him down and not had to kill him," she replied.

Johnny, for the first time in his life, felt remorse over killing someone. His first reaction had been to try to justify his decision. But he respected his grandmother's judgement. He said, "Maybe I should have. At the time, I felt our lives were in danger. But let me think about this for a while, Grandmother. Maybe I was wrong."

"While you're thinking about this, White Owl, you should realize that if you were wrong, there is nothing you can do to change what you have done. You ended a young man's life. He is no more…and will never be again."

His grandmother's criticism cut him to his soul. He said, "I will ponder this lesson, Grandmother." Then he said, "And I think I will move to Uncle Dutch's ranch for a while…in case the kin of these outlaws come looking for revenge."

"That is well," said Ahyoka.

As she walked away, a tear rolled down her face. She loved Johnny. She was convinced that he needed the guidance—however painful it might have been—that she had just given. Brother McLaurin, whom the thirteen-year-old Johnny had visited before leaving for Arkansas, had quoted Marcus Aurelius for his benefit: "Beware of becoming what you hate." Was the noble Ahyoka helping him to be aware of what he might become?

Johnny closed his smithy. He washed up. He took the pink tablecloth and went to the special place in the woods. His and Ahyoka's special place. There, he sat and spread the pink cloth on the grass. He thought about the young man. Was he really a killer, or was he just good at acting tough? Had Johnny taken a life needlessly? But the worst of all his thoughts was this one: For the first time in his life, his grandmother had disapproved of him.

He felt his heart breaking.

He looked down at the pink tablecloth.

And for the first time in the three years since the death of the younger Ahyoka, he cried.

* * * * * * * *

As Johnny packed for his move to the ranch on the Canadian River, his thoughts were troubled. Had he just been looking for an excuse to use his advanced weapon? Were those three outlaws just an excuse for him to explore its killing power? Were all three of them really sonofabitches that needed killing? He fell into a deep depression.

He would need a wagon to take his blacksmith tools down to Uncle Dutch's ranch. He said to Ahyoka, "Grandmother, I need a wagon and two horses to take my smithy and tools down to Uncle Dutch's ranch. I'll turn right around and bring them back to you. May I?"

"Yes, White Owl," replied Ahyoka. That was all she said. Johnny's heart was still breaking. He felt like his grandmother was throwing him out.

He loaded the wagon and left the next day. He left Flower in Tahlequah. He would come for her when he returned Ahyoka's wagon and horses.

As he drove southward towards the Canadian River, Johnny reflected. In the hands of the Texas Rangers, this repeating pistol would be the beginning of the end of the Comanche empire on the southern plains. Killing with it was, as Uncle Dutch had said, so easy that there was no honor in it.

He thought about his grandmother's words. A baker's dozen is thirteen. Should he have just stopped at the first two—an even dozen—and found a way to let the kid in the Seminole tunic live? If he had spoken in a less provocative manner, would it have made a difference? Could he have talked the boy down?

His mind went around in circles over these questions all the way to Dutch's ranch on the Canadian River.

Chapter 22: Beloved Woman

Johnny arrived at Dutch's ranch three days later. He set up his smithy but didn't resume working right away.

He visited Billy and Sarah. He found that they were doing better now. So far, Billy had fulfilled his promise to stop drinking whiskey. He took a "nip" once in a while—when Sarah wasn't around—but avoided becoming intoxicated. There had been no more violence in the marriage to date. That was why Billy was still walking around among the living, Johnny mused, grinning to himself. And they had a store where they sold cotton cloth, axes, needles, metal pots, gunpowder, guns, and lead, among other things.

Johnny asked Billy, "How did you get the store started?"

Billy said, "I increased the amount of land I was workin' so I could sell some of my harvest for cash. I worked my ass off. And I borrowed some money from your Uncle Dutch. I paid him back from the money the store made. It took most of the last couple of years, but we did it."

"That's good to hear," said Johnny. "How do you keep track of what you're sellin' and how much you're makin' on it?"

"I do it in my head," replied Billy.

"That's a lot of stuff to keep in your head, seems to me," observed Johnny. "I used to keep track of my grandmother's store on paper. It's useful and not too hard once you know how. If you want me to, I'll teach you and Sarah some tricks of the trade one of these days. Do you know how to cipher?"

"I know how to count, add and subtract," said Billy.

"That's a good start," said Johnny, who began to wonder how he might teach Billy and Sarah how to do division. Division was necessary to calculate averages. They would need to know how to do that if they were going to plan how much of each item to buy when they re-stocked their shelves. Johnny still had the primer he had studied when in missionary school. It taught basic math. He had kept it for nearly twenty years since he had stopped attending school. He didn't know why he had. It was, for a reason unknown even to him, a precious object. But now, it would serve a purpose. "I have a book, Billy, that you, Sarah, and I can study together. When you learn what's in it, you'll probably become rich." Johnny grinned.

"Well, Johnny, you got my attention now! I never was much for book learnin', but if there's money involved, I think I might be right interested," said Billy with visible enthusiasm.

Johnny, encouraged by Billy's response, said, "I don't wanna seem too pushy, but when should we start?"

The spring planting was done, and for the next few months, farm work would be less demanding while the crops grew. Billy said, "We can start whenever you're ready. I'm ready now."

"All right," said Johnny. "Let me have a couple of days to put together a plan. I had a feelin' that you might want to do this, so I brought us some paper and pencils from Tahlequah. "Oh, and one more thing," continued Johnny. "Do you know how to read and write Cherokee using Sequoia's system?"

"A lot of us in the West learned it. My parents made me learn it. Sarah can read it, too."

"Good," said Johnny. "One of the things we'll do is start writin' down how many of this, that, and the other thing you sell every day. We'll keep your records in our language. You'll be surprised to find how useful that information is once you learn how to cipher real good."

* * * * * * * * *

For the next four months, Johnny divided his time between his blacksmithing work and teaching Billy and Sarah how to cipher. He helped them set up a ledger and accounts for each item they sold. Sarah spent about two hours a day keeping these records up to date. Because Billy and Sarah were motivated, mature, and pretty smart to begin with, they were able to do long division by the fall of that year, 1843. Then Johnny taught them how to calculate average sales and use this information to decide how much of each item to buy when the steamers brought goods up the Arkansas River to Fort Gibson every month or two.

By spring 1844, their little store was prospering. Sarah and Billy were starting to make money. Meanwhile, Sarah had another child. Johnny started to spend less time in his smithy and more time helping Billy and Sarah run their store.

* * * * * * * * *

Johnny had been on the Canadian River for a year when, late one afternoon in April 1844, a horseman rode into the town that had grown up at Dutch's ranch. The horseman was Beaver. He was looking for Johnny.

When Beaver rode up to the smithy near Dutch's cabin, Johnny noticed that his horse was lathered with perspiration. He judged that Beaver and the horse had probably left in the middle of the previous day, camped for the night, and made haste to go the rest of the way to Dutch's ranch.

Johnny yelled out, "Hi, Beaver! You must have been in a hurry. You about ran that poor horse into the ground."

Beaver said, "Johnny, I have come here to tell you about your grandmother."

Johnny's heart jumped into his throat. "Is something wrong?" he asked.

"She is still alive, Johnny. But she hasn't been feeling well. She gets dizzy a lot, and she has just been lying in bed for a couple of days now. She desperately wants to see you," said Beaver.

The next morning, they left for Tahlequah. All the way there, Johnny prayed that his grandmother would be alive when he arrived. When they arrived at noon two days later, Ahyoka, though bedridden, was still alive.

* * * * * * * * *

Two women from the community were attending to Ahyoka. When Johnny arrived at her cabin, one of them answered the door.

Speaking Cherokee, he said, "I'm Johnny, her grandson."

"I know who you are. Your grandmother is eager to see you. Please come in."

There was a chair next to the bed where Ahyoka reposed. Johnny approached her and gave her a hug. Then he sat down on the chair.

Ayoka spoke. "It has been over a year since I saw you. I expected you might come back sooner."

"I was busy helping some folks start a store down on the Canadian River by Uncle Dutch's ranch," he said. "I thought it would be a good idea to stay away for a while so things could cool off. Did you have any trouble from the kin of those outlaws?"

Ahyoka replied, "A couple of men came to the store about a week after you brought my wagon back. They asked where you had gone. I told them you went down to Texas. They asked me what had happened, and I described it. One of them said it looked like self-defense. But they wondered how you were able to kill three armed men all by yourself, with a pistol. I told them about the repeater you had."

"Did that explanation satisfy them, Grandmother?" asked Johnny.

"I do not know. But if, after all this time, you have not heard from them or any others who might seek vengeance, it is possible that they just decided to let it go. I guess they knew that those men were outlaws and would eventually meet the same end, somewhere else and at someone else's hands," concluded Ahyoka. Changing the subject, she asked, "Have you thought about our last talk?"

"I did not just think about it, Grandmother. I suffered over it. In my whole life up to that point, you had never disapproved of me so strongly," said Johnny. "I was heartbroken."

Ahyoka said, "After you left, I thought about it as well. I realized that I might have been too hard on you."

"That depends on what you were trying to achieve, Grandmother. If your aim was to cause me to think carefully about what it means to kill someone, to end a life, you certainly did that. I remember your words clearly. You said of that young man in the Seminole tunic, '*He is no more, and will never be again.*' For a while, I wept every time I thought about that young man, who was barely more than a boy.

"I thought about those outlaws many times and asked myself if I was just looking for an opportunity to test my new weapon. And if so, was that a good reason to end someone's life? I decided it could not be. At the time, it looked like I had to kill or be killed and maybe get you and Beaver killed, too. I finally decided that I could not have done things differently without putting all of us at risk of being killed.

"But once I concluded this, I kept thinking about your words. Thinking about them and wondering how I could ever be pleasing to you again caused me to reconsider the value of human life. I decided that unless they draw a weapon on me, I will think twice before killing someone again. Unless I know for sure that they need killing." Johnny smiled. "Like the Stricklin boys."

Ahyoka, who seemed to be lost in thought, didn't comment. Johnny waited for her to speak again.

At length, she said, "I do not know how much longer it will be before I go to sleep and never wake up again. It could be tonight, or it could be in a week or two. But I believe I am about to find my rainbow, as our sweet Ahyoka called it. So, 'baker's-dozen-killer'"—she laughed as she said these words—"I have a few things I want to speak to you about." She paused again as if gathering her thoughts.

"There is so much I want to say. Years ago, I sent you to your Uncle Dutch so he could teach you the warrior's way, so you could take revenge on the Stricklins. As you know, I wanted them to pay for what they did as much as you did. Did I expect that by the time you were twenty, you would have already killed ten men? I did not think that far ahead. However, the Cherokee in me is proud of you and what you have become.

"I regret causing you so much grief this past year. I was too hard on you. But I am happy to know that you are not just a killer. You are a sensitive, reflective man. You are a credit to all of us who raised you up. If you live as long as I have, I expect you will share your wisdom and give guidance to many, young and old. I will not be here to bear witness to that, but that is what I see in your future." She repeated, "*If* you live as long as I have..." Ahyoka did not laugh when she said this. It wasn't meant to be funny.

Johnny took Ahyoka's hand in his and said, "Grandmother, thank you for setting my spirit free."

Ahyoka said, "I love you, Johnny Tenkiller."

Johnny just kissed his grandmother's hand. A tear of gratitude rolled down his cheek.

* * * * * * * * *

The next day, Johnny visited his grandmother again. She had more to say. "I want to tell you some other things while I am still here with you," she began. "Take two horses from our string with you. Your pick. And whatever is in the store that you need, take it as well. Also, I have saved some money and want you to have it. It is hidden over there..." She motioned to a chifforobe in the corner of the room where she lay. "Take it all. And don't worry about Beaver. I am giving him the rest of the horses, the other livestock, and whatever you do not take from the store. He has been helping me for more than ten years now, and he is not getting any younger. He will continue to use the land we have been using. His nephew has been helping us and will continue to do so. And Beaver has saved his own money."

"I think that is fair, Grandmother. Uncle Beaver deserves it," commented Johnny. "And when you find your rainbow, please watch for me. I hope to join you, and Grandpa, and Ahyoka, and Tommy in due course."

"Do not hurry, my son," said Ahyoka. "And now, you are free to continue on your path, wherever it might lead you. I told you over ten years ago that you would not be bound by your promise to stay by my side. But you kept the promise anyway. As it turned out, I am happy that you did.

"I do not know where your path will lead you. You probably do not know either. Whenever you are confused about which way to go or what to do, consult the Great Spirit—or the Creator, or God, or whatever else you call Him. It seems that He has as many names as you do." She smiled benignly. "Whatever His name is, He has always been with you. I pray He always will be."

* * * * * * * * *

That night, the noble Ahyoka, the Beloved Woman, found her rainbow. She was seventy years old, passing away like King David, who, having lived his threescore and ten, died full of days.

It had been expected by those who knew her. A few days later, a service was held for her in the center of Tahlequah, the capital of the Cherokee Nation. Nearly a thousand people came from all around to attend.

The day after Johnny had left the ranch, Dutch hastened to Tahlequah. Though he barely knew her, Ahyoka was his blood. Above all, he loved Johnny like his own son and wanted to be there for him.

The day after Dutch arrived, the service was held, officiated by a Baptist minister who gave a sermon about Christian charity and how Ahyoka had exemplified it. When he finished, a couple of hundred Christianized Cherokee said "Amen" in unison. Then he asked if someone from Ahyoka's family would speak for her. He knew that Dutch had been elected to represent the Canadian River District in the Cherokee tribal council. He was something like a senator. So, the minister asked Dutch to speak for his auntie, Ahyoka. Dutch, however, deferred to Johnny, who was, at this point, standing right next to him.

Johnny took Dutch's hand and acknowledged him. Then he walked to the center of the town, where the minister had stood behind a pulpit, which he now offered to Johnny. He straightened his back, slowly scanned the multitude with his eyes, and spoke these words in the Cherokee language:

"As you know as well as I, my grandmother was one of the finest human beings who ever walked this earth."

The full bloods, in unison, all grunted their approval.

"I was blessed when the Great Spirit caused me to be born to her daughter, to be her grandson, and I have been blessed ever since. I hope her spirit soars over us right now so that she can see the reward for the good she did in this life. For her reward is here." He paused and waved his hand expansively across the crowd and added solemnly, "It is all of you."

Again, the full bloods grunted their approval. The Christians, in unison, said, "Amen."

"There is nothing more I can say that you all do not already know. I thank all of you for honoring my dear grandmother with your presence. May the Great Spirit, God, the Creator, the Mover of all things, bless all of you richly. And may the sun shine forever on the Cherokee people!" He bowed his head reverently. The Christians, in unison, repeated, "Amen." And then they began to sing a hymn.

At the same time, the shamans, pounding their skin drums, began to chant an ancient funeral dirge. Hundreds of full bloods chanted along with them, echoing the ancient verses from the mists of time, in this new land, far from their original homes, for the Beloved Woman, Ahyoka. She who brought happiness.

Johnny thought about how Ahyoka's funeral rites mirrored the life she had led, with one foot in the Stone Age and the other in the world that would sweep it away. They mirrored his own life, too. The Christian hymn, sung in three-part harmony, accompanied by the tom-toms and ancient chants called by the shamans and echoed by the rest, all going on at the same time, seemingly oriented to one another, converging to the same musical key, touched him in the seat of his soul. At this moment, those two worlds, which could hardly have been more different, seemed united in a vast, cosmic harmony, a harmony he felt in his heart, his mind, and his soul.

Chapter 23: The Path

The remains of the beloved woman, Ahyoka Sullivan, were put to eternal rest that afternoon. Dutch and Johnny stood in the front row of the multitude as the minister pronounced the verses of the last rite. The headstone on her grave read:

Ahyoka Sullivan, Beloved Woman of the Cherokee People
Born: 1774. Died: April 12, 1844

* * * * * * * * *

The next day, Johnny asked Beaver for some time to talk about Ahyoka's last wishes for her estate. They sat on the front porch of the store. Johnny shared the details. Beaver, for his part, did not expect anything, least of all anything like the generosity of Ahyoka's last will and testament.

Beaver asked, "Are you sure you want me to have all of those things?"

Johnny said, "My grandmother was wise, Uncle Beaver. Aside from the fact that you have surely earned what she left to you, she wanted to lighten my load. She knew that there was little left of my life here in Tahlequah. Indeed, here in Indian Territory."

"What do you mean?" asked Beaver.

"On the eve of the day I killed the Stricklins," Johnny began, "I begged my grandmother to move to Indian Territory. And I told her I would stay by her side until the end of her life.

"She argued against that. She told me that she would not hold me to that promise, that if I needed to continue on my path, wherever it led, and perhaps never see her again, she would understand. She thought it more important that I do that than keep a promise made when I was, at nineteen years of age, little more than a boy."

"But you kept your promise," said Beaver.

"I did. I have no regrets at all about that. But now I am ready to respond to the longing, which comes from deep within me, to follow that path again…even though I do not know where it leads or what I'm supposed to do whenever I get there," said Johnny.

Beaver, in his fifties at this point and not lacking in wisdom, said, "Johnny, a big part of the warrior's path is to see things in just that way. The warrior must be ready to die at any moment and greet the possibility of death with indifference. Making big plans, for this reason, is not compatible with a warrior's path. If you have too many reasons to live, you will fear death. If you fear death, you might lose courage. In some circumstances, that could cause you to be even more likely to die. It is a strange thing, this warrior's path."

Then Beaver changed the subject. He said, "You did not have to honor your grandmother's wishes and leave all this to me. I would have accepted anything you gave to me with gratitude."

"I know that, Uncle," said Johnny. "But by relieving me of having to deal with all those things—the store, the hogs, and so on—you and my grandmother have done me a favor. I am unburdened. Free. And that is what my grandmother wanted for me."

"Ahyoka had a higher understanding of things than we do," said Beaver. "She wanted you to follow the trail of Johnny Tenkiller, wherever it might lead. In her last will and testament, it may be that the greatest gift she left was to unburden you so you could follow that trail."

Johnny and Beaver stood up and went into the store. Johnny helped himself to some blankets, a couple of pots, lead balls for his rifle, gunpowder, soap, two pairs of trousers, two cotton shirts, and two pairs of moccasins. He also took a new pack saddle for his second horse. Then he loaded up.

They stood silently in front of the store. Johnny looked around one more time at the place he never expected to see again: The store where his two Ahyokas had worked together. He smiled at the memory of their conversations while they worked. They used to remind him of the chirping of a couple of songbirds. Then he said to Beaver, "I want to walk around our whole place one more time."

They walked behind the store, where the two cabins and the smithy stood. He remembered the grey day in January 1839 when Beaver told him to look to the east, the direction from which hundreds of Cherokee survivors of the Removal straggled into Tahlequah. Off in the distance, he saw the wooded area where he and Ahyoka had had their passionate reunion. After that, they had always considered it their special place. And he remembered sitting there, with that pink tablecloth spread before him, on another grey day five years ago, in November 1839, when he mourned the passing of the younger Ahyoka, the love of his life.

At the end of this brief tour through the world of his memories, he viewed the cabin where they used to live. Nobody was there. It was just an empty shell of a happy life that no longer was.

Having gotten his fill of memories, he looked at Beaver and said, "Uncle, from the time before I knew you until now, you have been a blessing to my family and me. I do not know how to thank you."

Beaver said, "You already know how, and you have done so." He paused, probably for effect. Then he added, "Go your way, Tenkiller. Protect good people and kill sonofabitches that need killing. One day, when you have tired of this—assuming you are still alive to think about it—you may find another way to be Johnny Tenkiller…whoever that is. In the meantime, may your journey, wherever it leads, be a fruitful one."

* * * * * * * *

Two days later, he was back at Dutch's ranch. He gave Hummingbird one of the pots he had taken from the store. He gave the other one to Billy and Sarah, along with a couple of blankets. He kept the rifle balls, powder, clothes, moccasins, another blanket, and soap for his personal use.

In the afternoon of that day, Dutch invited Johnny to join him for a smoke. They sat down on the front porch of his cabin. Dutch loaded his pipe, took a draw, and passed it to Johnny, who showed restraint when he took his draw so he wouldn't choke half to death. They sat for half an hour in quiet contemplation. It was Johnny who broke the silence.

"I am lost right now," said Johnny. "I have no life left in Tahlequah. Do not misunderstand—I am very fond of Uncle Beaver and grateful to him for all the help he gave my grandmother and me. But he has his own family, even a couple of grandchildren. Grandmother left him most of our possessions, and I am happy for him." He paused.

Dutch asked, "What did she leave to you?"

Johnny responded, "She gave me a couple of fine horses and her cache of money. It's a considerable sum. Four hundred dollars. I'm not sure where to put it, and I don't know at this time what to do with it. She also told me I could take anything I wanted from the store. I didn't take very much. Just the pots I gave to Hummingbird and to Billy and Sarah and some things for my personal use."

Dutch asked, "What do you plan to do now?"

Johnny replied, "I no longer know what I care about. I mean, I care about you, your family, Uncle Enoli, and Billy and Sarah Starr. And Uncle Beaver in Tahlequah, of course." He paused, searching vainly for the words he felt in his heart. He said, "But there is something I wish for, something drawing me away from this life. I don't know what it is. But it is very, very powerful."

Dutch said, "Tenkiller, I wish to tell you a story about something I did in my youth. It might be of use to you…

"Once upon a time, when I was young, I decided to go on an adventure. This was more than thirty years ago. It was still quite 'wild' in these parts. I took a canoe and three dogs up the Neosho River."

"What was your aim?" asked Johnny.

"Well," continued Dutch, "I had two aims. I planned to hunt beavers and bring back their skins to sell. I did not know how much money they would bring. In those days, when it came to money, I only distinguished 'a little' from 'a lot'. I thought I would make 'a lot'."

"Why the three dogs?" asked Johnny.

"Three things," replied Dutch. "I learned from the Osage how to use dogs to pull burdens. Before they had horses, they used dogs. They took two long poles, attached them to a harness, and connected them behind the dog's body with a panel of leather. You can put things on this leather panel—it is like a bed—and the dogs will pull the burden for you. The white men call this thing a travois. The Indians on the Plains use horses for this nowadays. But once upon a time, they used dogs and still do if the burdens are not so heavy that they need horses to pull them. The other thing is that the dogs would sound the alarm if, while I was sleeping, danger approached. And there was a third thing: They kept me company.

"When I traveled up the Neosho, the river became more and more shallow. When it became impassable by canoe, I hid it in some bushes and traveled on foot. I went north to the Missouri River and got all the way to the western mountains. I had to sneak through the lands of some wild Indians to get there. That was a challenge. It was dangerous, but at the same time, I found it very exciting. Anyway, I eventually found a land in the western mountains that was rich in beaver. I trapped some and cured their hides. Then I made two of those travois, harnessed them to two of my dogs, loaded the skins, and returned to the east."

"Did you ever find that canoe you left up the Neosho River?" asked Johnny. "It seems unlikely."

"Tenkiller, the trouble with some of you 'civilized' Indians is that you do not realize how our ancestors could read Nature and everything in it the way you read books." Dutch shook his head in mock exasperation and took another draw from his pipe. "To answer your question, yes, I found my canoe. I threw in the beaver skins, and then my three dogs and I had an easy voyage downstream to the Arkansas River, where Fort Gibson is today. It did not exist yet, back then."

"So, did you sell the skins?" asked Johnny.

"Yes, I did. And here is what I did with the money: I bought a lot of gunpowder and a bottle of whiskey." Dutch laughed. "You probably wish you could have been there…"

Johnny laughed, too. There was no need for him to repeat his narrative about wishing for his death, the one time he had ever indulged in whiskey. "How long were you gone, Uncle?"

"Three seasons," said Dutch.

"And you were alone all that time?" asked Johnny.

"Yes. Except for my three dogs. Now, at the beginning of this story," Dutch continued, "I said I had two aims. One was to get beaver pelts. I have just told you about that. So, you might be wondering about my other aim," said Dutch.

Johnny said, "Yes, I want to hear about that."

"The truth is, I did not know what the other aim was, but, like the one that seems to be pulling you, it was powerful. I was alone for three seasons.

I traveled through regions that were dangerous, not just because of the big brown bears you find in the west—they are awesome beasts—but because of the people who are native to those lands. Like we once were, and as the Comanches still are, they were fierce warriors. I tried to be invisible to them. Fortunately, on the few occasions I did meet up with them, they were not hostile to me. It was as if they could see that, though I was not a member of their tribes and could not speak their languages, I was somehow one of them. Maybe they saw that I was another 'Indian'. Perhaps it was because I was by myself and no threat to them. Whatever their reasons may have been, they let me pass through.

"When I returned to my home in Arkansas, I was astonished that I had made it back alive. But I did not think about the end of my journey while I was on it. I lived one day at a time. I hunted for my food, made moccasins out of the hides of deer and buffalo, and ate roots and wild berries. I wasn't in a hurry to get anywhere. I just took my time. When I saw dark clouds, I used my hatchet to cut branches and make a lean-to, as you did on your journey. I made soap from tallow and ashes, warmed water in a pot when I wished to bathe myself, and then jumped into streams—and froze my ass off.

"When you are living on the edge like that, every day is an adventure. Every time you kill game, roast the meat, fill your belly, and wake up to a new day, you don't just feel grateful. You feel something much heavier—I cannot think of another word in English or Cherokee to describe it—that makes you feel more alive than you ever felt before. And you feel as if you have enormous power."

He paused to find the words he hoped to say to Johnny. "Whatever that power was, my life has been blessed ever since. It was as if every day, I had a talk with the Great Spirit. And every day since, I have felt His presence, His protection." Then Dutch said, "This is what I wished to tell you." He paused again, then declared, "I have finished."

Johnny's mind spun in circles. Unable to connect Uncle Dutch's story to his own life, he asked, "Can you guide me, Uncle, as to how this applies to me and my current sense of being lost?"

Dutch replied, "A person can only be lost if he knows where he is going and then finds himself in a situation in which he does not know where he is. If he does not know where he is going, on the other hand, he cannot be lost."

"That was helpful, Uncle," said Johnny, with utterly no conviction in his voice.

Dutch, sensing Johnny's confusion, said, "If you do not have an end in sight, what are you 'lost' from? If taking the journey is itself your 'end', if the journey itself is your destination, you will never be lost," said Dutch. "In that case, you will be present to the journey itself, as I was when I took that long hunting trip to the western mountains." He added, "As for what this all means to you, you will find out when you leave this land for a while. Possibly for a long while. Go somewhere you have never been, somewhere you never thought of before. *Be* there, wherever 'there' is. Then you will know..."

Johnny thought about the best times of his life. The flight from eastern Tennessee to Pittsburgh, down the Ohio River, and from St. Louis to Indian Territory was one of his fondest memories. Now thirty years old, even after ten years, the events and people of that year were firmly enshrined in his memory.

He shared his thoughts with his uncle. "I had an experience like that when I left the bodies of the Stricklin boys back in Tennessee," he said. "I had never felt so alive. And I haven't felt that way since. I am not saying that my life has not been good. It has. And when I was with Ahyoka, I just did not think about it much, if at all. One doesn't think about such matters when one is happy."

Johnny thought for a moment and then said, "I wonder where I should go..."

"Have you ever heard of California?" asked Dutch.

"Yes," admitted Johnny.

Dutch said, "People are starting to go west, some to California, some to Oregon. If you got another Paterson and plenty of shot, caps, and powder, you could probably get paid to protect a wagon train. You could go to California for free. And you might also want to replace your

Tennessee carbine. It is more than fifteen years old, and as you know, it's been well-used."

Johnny began to grow excited. He said, "Now I believe I am starting to understand. I'm going to follow your suggestion about the guns. And next year, if possible, I'm going to find a wagon train that is bound for California."

* * * * * * * * *

Over the next few months, Johnny spent most of his time working in Billy and Sarah's store. As days, weeks, and months passed, the sadness he had felt when he left Tahlequah was gradually displaced by the sense of excitement he felt about his path and where it might lead him. He would cross parts of the continent he had never seen. He would see California. He might even see the great western sea. He had heard about both, but to him, they were mere abstractions. If he took this journey, they would become real. And he expected to encounter people and experience places he could not, at this point, even imagine.

Part 7: On the Trail of Johnny Tenkiller

Chapter 24: The California Trail

In 1845, the US government began to catch up on the payments promised to the Cherokees in the Treaty of New Echota, ratified by Congress in 1836. Billy and Sarah's store prospered as more Cherokee farms were established.

In the spring of 1845, Johnny went to Houston and bought another Colt Paterson revolver, a new rifle, and plenty of shot and caps. By the time he returned, it was too late to go to Independence and try to find a wagon train headed west. So, he stayed another year, making plowshares and other tools needed by the Cherokees, who now had funds to pay for them. He continued to help Billy and Sarah with their record-keeping and inventory planning, which became a bit more complicated now that the demand for several of the goods they sold was increasing, thanks to the increasing availability of funds flowing to the Cherokee people.

Johnny became fond of the Starrs' little girl, who was almost seven years old. Her name was Annabelle Adsila Starr. Adsila ("Blossom" in Cherokee) was the name of Sarah's childhood friend—the one who swung the wooden target for her when she was learning to shoot, preparing for the second Comanche raid. They named her Annabelle in memory of Tommy Smith's wife-to-be, but they usually called her by her middle name, except when scolding her, in which case they used all three of her names. Like her father, she had black hair and slate gray eyes. Like her mother, her skin was the color of coffee with two teaspoons of cream.

From time to time, Adsila would come out to Johnny's work shed and ask him what he was doing. His first reaction was to tell her to stay away so as not to get burned. She would say things like, "Don't worry, Uncle Johnny, I ain't stupid!" Johnny would always laugh when she said things like that. He would respond with comments like, "You think you're pretty clever, don't you?" And she would reply, "I *am* clever, Uncle Johnny."

In the summer of 1845, the Starrs had a baby boy. They named him William Onacona Starr. The boy's middle name ("White Owl" in Cherokee) was given in honor of Johnny. The first name was for his father, Billy, whose given name was "William". His parents called him "Billy

Junior", but as he moved beyond the toddler stage, they just called him "Junior".

Johnny hadn't planned it, but he now had a family of sorts, and he was becoming quite attached to them. He began to wonder how easy it was going to be to pursue his path, to go to California and either never come back or come back years later. He wondered what he might miss…

He was also concerned about his uncle. He noticed that Dutch was sleeping longer these days, sometimes not getting up until after the sun began to peek over the eastern horizon rather than at first light, as he had done all his life.

For the rest of the year, Johnny avoided thinking about his path and disappeared into his routine. As he did so, he found that his grieving came less often and was less intense when it showed up. His grandmother, the Beloved Woman Ahyoka, had been right about the healing power of time.

* * * * * * * * *

In February 1846, Johnny made his decision to go to Independence and sign on as a guard for a wagon train. He knew that there was a risk. It was almost 300 miles from the ranch on the Canadian River to Independence, Missouri. There was a chance that, after all that traveling, he would not get hired on. He didn't care. He would pay the fee—whatever that was—and go to California anyway. He didn't need his own wagon. His horses would do fine, and he had a tent in which to sleep if the weather got too rough to sleep in the open, as many on these treks did. He knew that the Starrs would do well without him, though he would miss them. Billy had become like a brother to him. His relationship with Billy had led him to regard Sarah as a sister-in-law rather than someone who might have been, at one time, a romantic interest.

His main concern was with his uncle Dutch. He was fearful that if he left, he might never see Dutch again. He brooded over these unhappy thoughts for a couple of days.

One day, as they took dinner, Dutch noticed. He said, "Tenkiller, after dinner, how about us having a smoke? We haven't talked for a while."

Johnny, never one to decline an invitation like this, said, "Sure, Uncle."

After dinner, they went out onto the front porch. Hummingbird and Panther stayed inside. Dutch loaded up his pipe, took a draw, and passed it to Johnny. As he did so, he said, "It seems that something is afflicting your spirit. Does your path still beckon you?"

Johnny said, "It does. It's powerful. And I will miss all of you. But my deepest fear is that you might not be here when I return, whenever that may be." He held his composure, but his voice quivered when he declared, "Uncle, though I haven't lived very long—thirty-one years so far—I've lost almost everyone I've ever loved in this world. I feel alone, and if you were gone as well, I would feel as if the world had nothing left for me. Well, except for Billy, Sarah, and their kids. But they have each other…I'll have no one."

Dutch thought for a moment. What words could he choose to liberate Johnny to pursue his path? Then he said, "I have never been one to complain about my health, about my ailments, other than my rheumatism." Dutch, who was now in his mid-fifties, laughed as he added, "If you live long enough, you'll find out about that."

Then, he addressed Johnny's unspoken question. "Sometimes, my heart skips a beat, and this happens a couple of times a day nowadays. Some days, I do not feel like jumping out of bed and getting busy working, or hunting, or waging war, as I did for most of my life. I have a wife and a son. I am a chief. I am responsible for many people. Sometimes, it all weighs heavily on me. My life has been fulfilling, and I have no regrets. None. But there are times when I just feel very, very tired."

Johnny said, "Uncle, I can stay here and help you. You do not have to carry all this weight alone."

Dutch looked at the young man whom he had long regarded as his own son. His intense, black eyes seemed to mist up a bit when he said, "Tenkiller, you have already done everything you can do to make me proud, to make me happy. If you stayed here any longer, if you did not follow your path, I would be less happy. Do you understand what I am telling you?"

Johnny said, "I don't want to understand you, Uncle."

Dutch said, "If I die while you're gone, remember me for all the things we have done and the things I have tried to teach you. Not just things that involve killing people." He laughed. Then, resuming his serious demeanor, he added, "You were the son I never had until Panther came along in my old age. I won't live to see how he ends up. But I have watched you attain the summit of Cherokee manhood. When it's my time, I will rest in peace, knowing that as your uncle, I fulfilled my clan obligations. Do not worry if you are not here when I take my last journey."

Johnny started to shed tears, though silently. His chin began to quiver.

Dutch, recalling the last breath of Tommy Smith, shook his head admonishingly: "Do not forget, Tenkiller—*we're warriors!*" As he said this, Johnny could see that Dutch's eyes, too, had become misty.

Johnny choked back a sob, wiped his eyes, and straightened his back.

Dutch, regaining his stoic composure, concluded, "Now, my son, do not hesitate. Go on your journey. I will be with you always, if not here, then in spirit."

* * * * * * * *

Two weeks later, Johnny set out on his journey to Independence, Missouri, which was about three hundred miles away. He arrived in Independence during the first week of April 1846.

Independence had the look of a boom town. Its main industry seemed to be outfitting wagons, selling supplies, and providing lodging for those waiting for their wagon trains to embark on the long, arduous journey west. There were several hotels there. He went into one and asked the man behind the counter how to get hired to work on a wagon train. The clerk told him to just walk over to where all the wagons were, ask for a wagon master, and talk to him about it.

Johnny paid for his room.

Afterwards, he walked over to an area on the west end of town where dozens of wagons had assembled. He looked around—what did a wagon master even look like?

Then he heard a voice behind him. "Johnny, is that you?"

He turned around and saw a man who appeared to be about thirty years old. He was six feet tall, lean, with long brown hair and a beard, both well-groomed. He looked at the man's blue eyes. There was something familiar about them, but he couldn't place the man's face.

The man said, "I'm Josiah Jones. Remember me?"

The recognition struck Johnny like a thunderbolt. He exclaimed, "Cave-in-Rock! Sorry, Josiah, you didn't have much of a beard the last time we saw each other. How did you recognize me after all these years?" The two men enthusiastically shook hands.

"Well, your hair is a lot longer than it was back then, and you still *don't* have a beard," said Josiah.

"I probably won't ever have one, or much of one," said Johnny. "Indians usually don't."

"I always thought you might be an Indian," declared Josiah. "I recognized you because of those light eyes and because your face ain't covered with a beard."

"Well, I'm glad you did," said Johnny. "How is your family?"

Josiah said, "They're fine. The farm's doing well. My uncle is making good money selling feed to these travelers. A lot of people are heading west these days, and all the main trails to the West start in Saint Joe or else here in Independence. Our farm is close by. We got lucky, I guess. So, what brings you here, Johnny?"

"I was hoping to go west myself," replied Johnny. "To California. I was thinking that I could pay for my trip by working as a guard on a wagon train."

Josiah said, "This will be my second trip doing just that."

"So, you're a guard, Josiah?" Johnny asked.

"Yes. I started last year," Josiah replied. "It's a pretty hard journey, but I love the freedom of being in the wild west: the plains, the mountains, even the deserts."

"You have to go through deserts on these wagon trains? Other than going to the edge of a desert in west Texas, I haven't had much to do with deserts," said Johnny. "The one I saw in Texas was damned ugly."

Josiah said, "The main thing is to load up on water and not to overwork your oxen and horses while you're in the desert. There are about forty miles of desert on the California Trail. That's what I heard, anyway. Both the Oregon and California Trails are the same until you get to a place called Fort Hall. Then they split. One goes north to Oregon, and the other goes southwest to California. The one that goes to California has a stretch called the 'Forty-Mile Desert'. Since I take the Oregon Trail, I've not yet experienced that forty-mile stretch. But there are some pretty dry areas even on the Oregon part."

"Do you know who I can talk to in order to join one of these wagon trains?" asked Johnny.

"Yes, I do," said Josiah. "Maybe you can get on with the one I'll be traveling with. We'll travel as far as Fort Hall before our trails part ways. Anyway, I've seen what you can do. I know it's been a long time—how long has it been?—but I doubt you've lost any of your skills."

"It's been twelve years," said Johnny. "And I would be real grateful to you if you could put in a good word for me."

"That won't be hard," said Josiah, who then changed the subject. He asked, "Remember when we were shooting those scoundrels on that keelboat? There was a moment when, after shooting one of them—he surely died—you said, 'Number nine'. I asked you what you meant, and you said it was a private joke between you and your best friend in Texas. Was that the truth?"

The days when Johnny worried about being found out as the killer of the Stricklins and the slavecatchers had long passed. He was no longer worried about being hunted down and arrested. So, he said, matter-of-factly, "The truth is that that man was my ninth kill."

"I had a funny feeling about that," said Josiah.

"Well, now you know the truth," said Johnny.

"If you don't mind my asking, how many have you killed so far?" asked Josiah.

"Thirteen," responded Johnny. "So far."

"Do you plan to kill more?" asked Josiah.

"Only if I run into more sonofabitches that need killin'," said Johnny with a smile. "The world seems to have a pretty good supply of 'em. Not just white men, either."

Josiah said, "I remember when you said that about them pirates on the Ohio."

"What'd I say?" asked Johnny.

"My uncle said you squinted your eyes at 'em as they came towards us in that keelboat and said something like, 'Them sonofabitches need killing,'" replied Josiah.

"Now I remember," said Johnny. "How about you, Josiah? I saw you make your first kill. Have you had any since Cave-in-Rock?"

"Not yet," replied Josiah. "The Indians on the trail haven't been a problem. And no white men gone wild have shown up, at least not where I've been." Then he turned towards a group of covered wagons and said, "Come with me."

Johnny walked with him to one of the wagons in that group. On their way, Josiah said, "The wagon master I've been working for is an old ex-mountain man. His name is Sam Morgan. I'll tell him about you. If he asks, I'll introduce you."

"Much obliged," said Johnny.

* * * * * * * * *

Johnny waited by a tree, away from Josiah and Sam. Josiah was apparently telling Sam what he knew about Johnny. After a quarter of an hour, Josiah motioned to Johnny to join them.

Josiah introduced Johnny to Sam and left them alone to talk.

Sam was in his fifties. He had made many trips from St. Louis to the Rockies and back, beginning when he was only twenty in 1809. That was in the early years after the Louisiana Purchase and the Lewis and Clarke expedition, during the height of the fur trade. Just surviving into his fifties must have been a miracle, given all the dangers that lurked on the great, partly charted but largely unknown frontier. He was not a big man—maybe five feet, nine inches tall, and weighing about one hundred seventy pounds—but he exuded strength. His beard was white, but one could see that his mostly white hair had been red in his youth. Born with the fair skin of most redheaded white men, he was covered with freckles and other blemishes that come with age and excessive exposure to the sun. His sleeves were rolled up, revealing his deeply creased, sinewy forearms.

In a deep and raspy voice, he asked Johnny, "What kind of experience have you had as a guard?"

Johnny replied, "I have no experience as a guard, at least not on a wagon train. I've fought in several engagements against Comanches and Osages and shot some brigands who tried to rob my grandmother's store. And maybe Josiah told you about our experience at Cave-in-Rock. Did he?"

Sam said, "Yes, he did. He said his family still talks about it." Sam looked at the small arsenal Johnny carried on his belt and on his back. "You're pretty damned well-armed. Where did you get those Colts?" he asked.

"My uncle gave me one of them. I had to go down to Houston to get the other one. While I was at it, I bought this rifle as well. Up to that point, I used my old Tennessee carbine," said Johnny.

"You got plenty of powder and shot?" asked Sam.

"Yes, I brought my own," said Johnny. "Lots of it."

"Do you have other skills we might need"? asked Sam.

"I can do blacksmith work. I understand that there'll be times when the metal treads on the wagon wheels need to be repaired or replaced. I can do that kind of work, too. I've shod more horses than I can count. And I can hunt, too," said Johnny. "Is there a wagon with blacksmithing tools on this train?"

"Yes," responded Sam. He added, "We have a blacksmith already, but it never hurts to have a backup." Then he asked, "Do you have a place to stay this evening? You can set up a tent here if you want."

"I've already got a room at one of the hotels," replied Johnny. "And since it's gonna be a while before I get another real bath, I'm going to a bathhouse tonight."

Sam said, "Good. I'll do the same before we leave. Let's talk again tomorrow morning and work out the rest of the details."

They shook hands. Johnny went back to his hotel. He went to a bathhouse nearby. Then he and Josiah met for a steak dinner. Johnny treated.

Once their dinner was served, Johnny asked Josiah, "Can you tell me a little about what you've been doing for these past twelve years? I don't mean to be nosy…"

Josiah quickly responded, "You're not being nosy at all, Johnny. I just didn't take to farm work. And to be honest, there weren't a lot of people out there yet, and I didn't care for any of the young girls who were available. So, I started looking for reasons to leave."

"If you don't like farm work, is there some other kind of work you'd rather do?" asked Johnny.

"I don't know yet. I like being a guard on a wagon train. Get to see the frontier, the mountains, the western pine forests, and the rivers flowing out of the Rockies with their fresh, cold, pure water. I've done some hunting, too. Elk and deer. I haven't messed with those grizzlies, though. They're real scary beasts."

"I've never seen one yet," said Johnny, "but I've heard about 'em. Heard they're hard to kill."

Josiah said, "I heard that, too. And I've seen a couple. Last year, one of 'em took a steer from the rear of our train. Sam told me not to bother trying to shoot him. It would just piss him off, and then he would make mayhem for us. Said to let him have the steer. He'd have something to eat for a few days, and we'd be long gone. I guess that's the best way to handle a grizzly," concluded Josiah.

Johnny changed the subject. "Where does the Oregon Trail go—I know it goes to Oregon—but where in Oregon, and to what kind of place?" asked Johnny.

"It goes to a big, long valley around a river called the Willamette," said Josiah. "The Willamette Valley. There are two or three towns spread out along that valley. Now, if someone wanted to farm, it would be a fine place. The weather is milder than anything you've ever seen. The soil is rich, and you can grow all kinds of crops there. It rains a lot. The grass grows two or three feet high after the rains. And it's a great place for livestock."

"It sounds like you still have some 'farmer' left in you, Josiah," Johnny said with a chuckle.

Josiah, wanting to change the subject, asked Johnny, "What are *you* looking for? I mean, what kind of life do you want?"

Johnny, having thought about this at length, groped for words. He said, "I don't know, Josiah, to be truthful with you. Right now, I'd like to see the great western sea. The Pacific." He paused.

"That's it?" asked Josiah, who seemed surprised by Johnny's answer.

"For now, that's it," declared Johnny. "And I don't know why. I just have this powerful 'something' pulling me away from my homeland, where I have little left to hold me anyway. I have enough money to afford to be a drifter for a couple of years if I want. But if I could work as a guard on a wagon train, I'd spend less money getting to California than I would if I was one of these pilgrims and had to buy a covered wagon and some oxen. My uncle suggested it, and I thought about it. Decided it was a good idea. Want to go in half on a wagon?"

"We won't have to do that, Johnny. Since we're going to be guards—and to be honest, we're gonna be taking care of a lot of animals, too—we'll be earning our keep. We can dine with the wagon master every day. We'll take our meals from his supply wagons. And we'll get paid on top of that…$25 a month. That said, our horses will do just fine."

"Considering we're being fed and that we won't have much opportunity to spend what we make, that could turn out pretty good," said Johnny.

Johnny motioned the server to come to the table. She presented the bill. He paid. Then he and Josiah arose, shook hands, and went to their respective hotels.

* * * * * * * * *

The next morning, he met with Sam again to discuss the terms of his contract. Sam said, "For your guard work and such blacksmithing as you might do, I can pay you $25 a month plus meals, which are served to all the people who work for the wagon train. Breakfast and dinner. If you want a wagon, you can buy one for about $100."

"I won't need a wagon, Mr. Morgan," said Johnny. "I have two horses, and among my other supplies, I have my own tent if I need one."

"So, you accept the terms of this deal?" asked Sam.

"Yes, sir," affirmed Johnny.

"What are your plans after getting to the Sierra Nevada?" asked Sam.

"Is that where you part company with this wagon train?" asked Johnny.

"Yes," replied Sam.

"I want to go to Sutter's Fort and then to the Pacific Ocean," replied Johnny. "How are we supposed to get the rest of the way there?"

Sam said, "There is a town on the Truckee River at the base of the Sierras where there are some people who know how to get over those mountains and into the valleys of California. You might be happy to know that you just have to deal with your horses at that point. People often have to leave their wagons behind or take 'em apart and scale those mountains, using their oxen as pack animals. Once over the peaks, they put the wagons together again and go mostly downhill the rest of the way. But it takes a lot of time, and it's pretty dangerous."

"Who pays those people to guide the rest of the journey?" asked Johnny.

"I do. I take some of the fees they paid for the whole trip and give it to the next wagon master. We have a contract," said Sam. "And you'll still be paid to be a guard. I'll pay you for the work you've already done and pay you in advance for the rest of the journey to Sutter's Fort. That will take about another month."

"Thanks," said Johnny. "I'll do my best."

"I figured that," said Sam.

"When will we be leaving?" he asked.

"In three days," said Sam. "You're welcome to set up camp over here if you want to get around paying for your hotel."

"Thanks," said Johnny. "I'll just stay in the hotel for the next two days. And thank you, sir, for this opportunity."

* * * * * * * *

Johnny stayed the next two nights in the hotel. On the morning of the third day, at first light, he showed up at the point of departure for the wagon train. Josiah was there, too. Everyone who had signed up for the trip had completed their preparations the previous day. The only thing left to do was to take the first steps westward.

Sam's wagon, which would head up the train, pulled forward. Johnny and Josiah directed the next two wagons to follow, then the next two, then the next two, and so on. There were nearly 80 wagons and almost two hundred domestic animals that would follow them. Among the animals were horses, beef cattle, milk cows, mules, and some extra oxen. Johnny, Josiah, and three other guards would rotate jobs between animal herding duties at the rear and riding guard at the front of the wagon train.

It was expected that the group would cover 12-15 miles a day on good days. On not-so-good days, it would cover about 8 miles. The whole trip to the base of the Sierras would take a little over five months. The plan was to leave after the bulk of the spring thaw and to arrive at the Sierra Nevada before the first snowfall, which typically occurred in October. It was now the end of the second week of April. That gave them about a month of slack to deal with unexpected events and bad weather.

* * * * * * * *

The wagon train followed the Missouri River upstream, towards its confluence with the Platte River. Then, they would follow the Platte towards its source in the great western mountains, the Rockies. The river was lined with trees, but otherwise, the terrain seemed like a vast, flat sea of grass that was slowly turning from bright green to gold as spring gave way to summer.

They saw herds of buffalo but did not hunt them. Sam discouraged it, saying that the local tribes treated the buffalo the same way the white men treated their livestock. They might take offense, he said. He pointed out that it would be even more hazardous if the Pawnee were still as numerous as they had been in his youth before smallpox had wiped out more than half the tribe.

* * * * * * * * *

After they had been on the trail for a month, a party of Indians approached the wagon train on horseback. They wore scalp locks like the Eastern tribes and were covered in red paint, with black paint around their eyes, stretching back to their ears. They looked quite fierce.

Sam, appraising them, said, "Well, I didn't say the Pawnee had perished altogether. Them comin' are Pawnee for sure. I think they're about to charge us a toll for passin' through their land. Josiah, why don't you ride to the back and get a couple of steers? That's one of the reasons we brought them with us. Johnny, you stay here with me in case they get hostile."

Josiah obediently rode to the back of the train. The steers that were brought for toll passage had red ribbons tied to one of their horns. He lassoed one of them and asked another one of the guards to lasso another. As they were bringing them to the front of the train, Sam spoke to the leader of the Pawnee group. Having encountered Pawnee many times over the past thirty years, as he traveled back and forth through their lands between the Rockies and Saint Louis, he spoke limited but passable Pawnee.

In their language, he said, "We thank you for granting us passage through your homeland. As a token of our gratitude, we have two steers for you."

The Pawnee leader, replying in his native tongue, said, "The white men have been killing our buffalo. Now, there are not as many as before. We want three of your cattle." His demeanor was not friendly.

Johnny fingered one of his pistols nervously. He hoped he wouldn't have to kill any of these Indians.

Sam, noticing this, said, "Don't get trigger-happy, Johnny. He just feels obliged to bargain for more. That's how they deal with outsiders." Turning to the Pawnee chief, he said, "We can only afford two. There are other tribes along our journey who will want gifts. But look!" he said as he motioned to the two steers being led from the back of the wagon train. "Those are fine, healthy cattle. They have much meat."

The chief, expressionless, sat astride his horse and waited patiently. When Josiah and the other guard brought them to the front of the train, he assessed them and spoke to the others in his party. After a couple of brief exchanges, he turned back to Sam and said, "We accept your gift." Josiah and the other guard led the steers to the Pawnees and removed their lariats. Two of the Pawnees dismounted and placed their own ropes around the necks of the steers. Then the chief said in English, "Go in peace," as they turned and rode away with the steers.

Johnny asked Sam, "Have you ever had to fight the Indians out in these parts?"

Sam said, "I've had skirmishes with the Blackfeet and the Arapaho in Montana and Colorado, but so far, none with the Pawnee. That doesn't mean I take them lightly. Once upon a time, they were feared out here. But they had a big disadvantage. Their enemies, who surrounded them on all sides, had direct contact with the whites before they did. So, their enemies got guns and iron weapons before they did. It was a terrible thing for them. They used to get raided and lost many of their people to the slave trade. So many of 'em were taken to Canada that up there they referred to all Indian slaves as 'Pawnees'. Even if they weren't really Pawnee." He added, "They have guns now, though."

Johnny recalled meeting Joe Black Wolf on one of the earthen pyramids at Cahokia. "Have you ever seen those ruins east of Saint Louis?" he asked.

Sam said, "Yes, I've seen them. Some folks say that the Ten Lost Tribes of Israel built 'em."

"With respect, sir, I think that's probably bullshit," said Johnny. "I met a Pawnee shaman when I was there. He said his ancestors had built 'em hundreds of years ago."

"Well, how did they wind up in their present state, then?" asked Sam.

"There was some kind of pestilence," replied Johnny. "It must have been a pretty big pestilence because it seems to have affected a lot of the peoples east of the Mississippi. My people built those kinds of pyramids a long, long time ago. And they have some in Indian Territory, too."

Josiah, who was listening to the conversation, interrupted Johnny. He asked, "So, is that why you rode with us up the Mississippi to Saint Louis back when we first met? You wanted to go and see that place?"

"Yes," replied Johnny. "And while I was there, I met Joe Black Wolf, the Pawnee holy man who told me that his ancestors were the builders."

After a moment of silence, Sam, with a sly smile, asked, "Did you smoke pipe with this holy man?"

Johnny, noting Sam's sly look, said, "Well, as a matter of fact, I did."

Sam said, "I've smoked pipe with the Pawnee myself. By any chance, was what he put into that pipe made from mushrooms that grow out on the prairie, underneath buffalo shit?"

"That's the stuff," said Johnny.

"If I didn't have to run this here wagon train, I'd go out there and get some of them mushrooms," said Sam, with another of his sly smiles.

"I'd smoke it again, too," said Johnny. He added, "…if had a day or two to burn and get nothin' else done." They both laughed from their bellies.

Josiah, confused, asked, "What are you fellas talking about?"

Sam looked down and did his best to suppress further laughter.

Johnny said, "I'll tell you about it tonight, after chuck."

Johnny never had a chance to have that conversation. As he would eventually discover, Josiah was interested in something besides mushrooms growing out on the prairie under buffalo shit.

* * * * * * * * *

As the wagon train continued, following the Platte River in a northwesterly direction, all they saw was a nondescript sea of level grassland expanding endlessly on either side of the river and the trees that grew around it. After forty days of their journey, they saw Chimney Rock. It jutted three hundred feet up from the plains, like a centerpiece on a flat dining table. They looked at it in wonder as their oxen-drawn wagons plodded by.

Two days after passing this landmark, they encountered another, even more imposing, formation called Scott's Bluff. It was about twice as high as Chimney Rock, another sudden rise of stone above the otherwise flat, nearly featureless plains. Around sunset that day, Johnny noticed a different kind of landscape rising ever so slightly, far off on the western horizon: Shimmering purple mountains' majesty. Though he couldn't see any details yet, other than that they looked purple from a distance, they boded something that was tantalizingly refreshing. It was getting very hot on the plains, and he longed for what he hoped would be cool mountain air and fresh mountain spring water. He asked Sam if those were the Rockies. Sam said they were.

The trail began to incline slightly as they continued towards them. More days passed. The boring grasslands that never seemed to end were gradually replaced by foothills with short pine trees, aspens, and sagebrush. The climb was gradual, so they made good progress. Five days later, they arrived at Fort John (which would be known one day as "Fort Laramie"). They paused there for two days, resting their animals, and replenishing their supplies.

A month after that, the wagon train arrived at South Pass, which led them to the far side of the continental divide. Though the pass was high (over 7,000 feet above sea level), getting to it and then getting over it, given the gradual ascent and descent, was not particularly difficult. It was a wide gap shaped like a saddle. There were few trees at the bottom of it, but there were plenty of trees on the mountains that rimmed it.

One morning, on the western side of the pass, they saw an adult grizzly bear with two smaller ones—Sam said they were cubs. They were sauntering along a lightly wooded mountain side. "Hopefully, they'll be too busy with whatever they're eatin' to bother our animals," Sam remarked.

Fortunately, they were.

Day after day, the wagon train plodded northwestward, heading towards a place called Fort Hall, at which point the Oregon and California trails would diverge. Two and a half months after leaving Independence, plodding along at about fifteen miles a day, they had crossed over South

Pass. Sam said it would take between three and four more weeks to get to Fort Hall from there.

* * * * * * * * *

During the first few days after leaving Independence, Johnny and Josiah had spent an hour every once in a while, sharing information about their lives since the last time they had seen each other in the spring of 1834. After that, it was mostly silence—other than the lowing of the cattle and oxen, the hoof beats of the animals pulling the wagons, and of those trailing behind the wagon train. And the creaking of wagon wheels. And the crunching sounds they made as they rolled over the dirt and sand that formed the road on which they travelled. And the buzzing of insects.

There was small talk at breakfast and dinner, accompanied by the singing of birds as they did their morning and evening foraging. Sometimes, the wind howled. Otherwise, it was silence, silence, and more silence.

Johnny had experienced a month of solitude when he made the journey from St. Louis to Indian Territory twelve years before. Now, though he was in the company of hundreds of people, he had experienced virtual silence for nearly three months. Hour after hour, day after day, week after week. At first, he spent much time remembering the events of his past, how he had felt while living through them, and what he was thinking at those times. But one can only do so much of that. For the past month, he was simply present, putting one foot in front of the other when he walked alongside his mounts or letting his horse put one hoof before the other when he rode. Other than watching for signs of danger, which rarely showed up, he didn't think much at all. He just existed. Occasionally, he thought about California, which was still, to him, an abstract idea.

Not long after reaching Chimney Rock, Johnny had noticed that Josiah was beginning to spend time with the Puckett family, which had two wagons. The elder Pucketts were farmers from Illinois. They had four children, two of them grown and two that were still children. The young ones, both boys, looked to be eight and ten years old. The older ones included a boy of about fourteen years of age and a pretty girl of about seventeen.

Her name was Ann. She was slender and had long blond hair, which she usually tied up under her bonnet, and blue eyes. Her skin was tanned from exposure to the sun and made a startling contrast with those blue eyes, which shined like a pair of sapphires from under the shade cast by the visor of her bonnet. Johnny was certain that Josiah had noticed them, too. Though Josiah was more than ten years her senior, it began to look as if he had become infatuated. Johnny didn't ask questions. But in his private thoughts, he suspected that something might come of it.

* * * * * * * * *

The wagon train arrived at Fort Hall on July 18, 1846. This was the point at which the Oregon and California trails diverged. Josiah would be going on to Oregon. Johnny would be headed to California.

Johnny asked Sam, the wagon master, "How much farther is California?"

Sam replied, "From here to the base of the Sierra Nevada is about six hundred miles. But the worst part of your trip will be getting over the Sierras. There is nothing like a South Pass to use to get over them. It's dangerous. Distance-wise, we're well over half-way there. Timewise, a bit over half-way."

"This is one hell of a long trip," observed Johnny.

"Well, going back by horse takes a lot less time. I do it every year," said Sam.

"That's good to know," said Johnny.

Just before dusk, Johnny walked to the edge of a wooded area, not for any particular reason other than to stretch his legs, as on this day he had ridden horseback. He paused to take in the view. As he scanned the horizon, he saw two figures standing behind some dwarf pines. Not wanting to be rude, he looked at them out of the corner of his eyes. He saw them embrace and kiss passionately. He turned his back on them and slowly walked away, looking at the ground. He smiled to himself as he did so. One of the two was Josiah Jones. The other was Ann Puckett. He guessed that this might be the first time Josiah had ever been in love. He recalled how first love felt and was happy for Josiah, whose feet must have left the ground with that kiss. He surmised that soon, the girl might become "Ann Jones".

The wagon train replenished its supplies. Repairs and maintenance on the wagons and harnesses were made. The train was reorganized into two smaller units. About forty of the wagons would head to Oregon. The remaining thirty-five would take the other trail to California.

Two days after arriving at Fort Hall, the California train was ready to move out. Because of the treacherous weather and terrain of the Sierra Nevada range, it was imperative that the wagon train arrive at its base in September, as heavy snows could begin to fall as early as October, and September snowfalls were not unknown. The party going to Oregon would leave the day after.

On the morning before the day Johnny's group was to leave, he approached Josiah. He said, "Old friend, we might never see each other again after this. I wanted to thank you for introducing me to Mr. Morgan. And to wish you a happy life in Oregon."

"What makes you think I'm going to settle in Oregon?" asked Josiah.

"I guess I was just assuming," replied Johnny with a knowing smile.

Josiah blushed.

"It's none of my business, really," said Johnny, wondering if he had overstepped.

"Have you been spying on us?" asked Josiah with a jovial attitude.

"No," said Johnny. "But the other night, when I took a walk to stretch my legs, I saw a couple kissin' in the woods over yonder. I tried not to look, but I took a glance and saw that it was you and that girl, Ann."

Josiah took a breath and exhaled slowly. "You're right, Johnny, that was us."

"She's a beauty," said Johnny. "Are you in love?"

"We are," said Josiah, smiling faintly with a distant look in his eyes. "And her parents and brothers like me, too. We've had a lot of time to get to know each other. They know I'm basically a farmer just like them."

"So, it looks like you've changed your thinking about farming, Josiah," observed Johnny.

"I'm actually pretty good at it," said Josiah. "Maybe the problem was that I just wanted to find the right girl. She sure wasn't there anywhere near our farm out in western Missouri. Who would've thought I'd have to travel half-way across a continent to find her?"

Johnny asked, "Do you expect to get married?"

"I'm thinking about it," replied Josiah.

"Well, don't think about it too hard," suggested Johnny. "Thinking too hard about most things can get you in trouble."

"What do you mean?" asked Josiah.

"When I was learning to shoot bow and arrow, my uncle told me that I was thinkin' too hard about hittin' my target. He told me to just shoot from my center," said Johnny.

"What the hell does that mean?" asked Josiah.

Johnny said, "He told me to imagine that my mind was in between my chest and my navel, to relax my eyes while still focusing on the target, and to let the arrow fly. He said the arrow would know just where to go. And you know, he was right. My accuracy got better, right away."

"Well, I'm afraid I still don't get it," commented Josiah.

"I'm not sayin' it's bad to think things through when you're makin' plans," continued Johnny. "But sometimes, it's best to listen to what your heart wants. Sometimes, our plans are just full of shit." Johnny and Josiah both laughed.

"When I rode out of Saint Louis to Indian Territory," Johnny continued, "back in the year we met, a thought kept comin' up in my mind. It went somethin' like this: God hears the prayers of our hearts, but He doesn't pay much attention to the prattle of our minds. It kept comin' back to me, over and over again. And over the years, I've concluded that He speaks to us through our hearts. I'm wondering if He's speaking to you right now, as a matter of fact."

Josiah was silent. He seemed lost deep in thought.

"What's your heart sayin' right now, Josiah?" asked Johnny.

"It's kinda obvious," replied Josiah. "If I said what my heart wants, I'd tell you that I want to marry that girl, work a farm, and raise the children we'd have," said Josiah.

Johnny said, "A plan that's backed up by the heart is likely to be successful…in my experience, at least."

Josiah was silent for a long moment. He looked at Johnny intensely and asked, "How do you know all this shit?"

"I don't know it," said Johnny. "Sometimes, the words just come through me. Like they're not even mine. Like the ones I just spoke. I think maybe I was 'shootin' from my center, so to speak. They just felt right to me. I guess the real question is, what feels right to you?"

"I always thought I'd wind up going back to my family in Missouri," said Josiah.

"Does that feel right to you, now?" asked Johnny.

"I love my family. But the thought of losing Annie…it would be like cutting out a piece of my heart," said Josiah.

"I know that has to be a hard decision," said Johnny. "I don't suppose that you would want to take her back to Missouri with you, would you?"

"I would rather not separate her from her parents and brothers. If someone must bear that, I'd rather it be me," replied Josiah.

Johnny surmised that Josiah, who put Ann's happiness above his, must have truly loved her. And maybe he really didn't like living on that farm in western Missouri, for whatever his reasons might have been, and now he had an attractive option. A very attractive one…

Johnny said, "You can always write letters. If you write one as soon as you get to Oregon and give it to the wagon master, he could take it back to Independence for you and drop it at whatever feed store your uncle sells his grain to."

Josiah, suddenly resolute, declared, "I'm not gonna wait 'til I get to Oregon. I'll ask for her parents' blessing tonight. If they approve, I'll write a letter to my family and give it to Sam. I know I can trust him to deliver it. And he might get back to Independence sooner than our Oregon-bound wagon master."

* * * * * * * * *

The next morning, as the California-bound wagon train was rolling out, Josiah trotted up to Johnny, who was taking care of the rear of the train, where the animals were. "Johnny, since we're not likely to see one another again, I had to tell you something before we part company."

"What's that?" asked Johnny, with one eye on Josiah and the other on the livestock.

"I asked Mr. and Mrs. Puckett for Ann's hand in marriage last night."

"And…?"

"They asked what took me so long. Then they said they would be happy to have me as a son-in-law!" Josiah was exuberant.

"Well, I'm sure happy for you," said Johnny.

"I wrote that letter to my family, too," said Josiah. "I gave it to Sam this morning."

"Good," said Johnny.

"I have to admit, though," said Josiah, "that I had trouble sleeping last night, even though I was very happy about Ann's and my engagement."

"Why?" asked Johnny.

"Well," Josiah began, "Well before we talked about it yesterday, I'd thought I'd turn around and go back to Independence after we got to Oregon. And tell my folks about my plans to stay in Oregon. But when I thought about spending a whole year before I saw Ann again, I got a big knot in my stomach."

"Sounds like your heart and your mind disagreed," said Johnny.

"That's one way of looking at it," said Josiah. "When I thought about it, I realized that the decisions I made yesterday were the right decisions, even though I made 'em in haste. As I tossed and turned in my bedroll, I realized that I'd made the only decision I could have made. And then, all the rest of the doubt left me. It felt like a burr inside me just broke up into tiny pieces and disappeared. And then I was able to sleep."

"Sometimes it's good to just tell your mind to shut the hell up," said Johnny. After a short, thoughtful pause, he said, "I wish you and Ann and your families well." With a broad smile, as he jumped down from his horse, shook Josiah's hand, and gave him a ritual hug, he added, "And may you learn to love farm work!"

"I claim all those good wishes," said Josiah.

Johnny, who hated farewells, stood there for a moment, reliving Cave-in-Rock and this long trek on the California Trail—his history with Josiah Jones: Josiah's first battle, and twelve years later, finding the love of his life. Then he looked at Josiah with the kindest of eyes and said, "Goodbye, my friend."

"Goodbye," said Josiah, who stood there for a moment, not wanting to turn away but not knowing what else to say, as Johnny mounted up and rode off.

Many thoughts raced through his mind as he stood there. Thoughts about this strange man, this warrior, Johnny Tenkiller. It seemed as if every time Johnny showed up in his life, something of significance had happened to him. He recalled how he had felt he owed Johnny after Cave-in-Rock. And although he couldn't quite define it, he felt he owed Johnny in some way for the momentous decision he had just made to marry Ann and settle in Oregon, half a continent away from the place he had hitherto regarded as home. He believed he would probably have made this decision anyway, but his conversation with Johnny had left him in a state of inner peace. He no longer had mixed feelings about following his heart—a gift in its own right. At length, he turned around and walked towards the Oregon-bound wagon train. As he did so, he sent up a silent prayer that Johnny would have a happy journey…to wherever it was that he was going. Not just in space, but in life.

Chapter 25: The Great Western Sea

After what seemed like an endless journey through the sagebrush-covered, shadeless, and hot expanses of the northern Nevada desert, the wagon train arrived at a small town at the base of the Sierras. They managed to get over the summit, followed by a long downhill journey to Sutter's Fort. Aside from the arduous work of disassembling wagons, hoisting them over parts of the trail that were too steep and too dangerous to be pulled by the oxen, using the oxen as pack animals and as engines to pull the wagon parts over the nearly impassable parts of the trail, the journey was uneventful. No one was injured or killed by falling wagons or by slipping from the precipices into the gully cut by the clear, cold waters of the Truckee River.

Johnny spent the winter at Sutter's Fort. John Sutter was quite generous. He provided lodging and food for the travelers, hoping to encourage more people to settle on a large land grant he had received from the Mexican government. But by January 1847, the land had been annexed by way of conquest by the United States. However, Sutter retained his title to a large chunk of what would one day be called California's Central Valley.

While Johnny was there, he joined a group of men who tried to rescue the ill-fated Donner Party. The Donner Party had taken an alternate route, leaving the Oregon Trail before Fort Hall. It was supposed to be a shortcut. It wasn't. They arrived at the foot of the Sierras in October. A few miles before the summit, they were hit by heavy snow. Then, more snow. They were stranded. Some men from the party traveled by horseback to Sutter's Fort to inform people about the desperation faced by the Donners and those who had traveled with them. A rescue party was organized. But the snowfall was unusually heavy that year, and they couldn't get through until after the beginning of the spring melt. Johnny, for his part, had never seen so much snow. Tragically, nearly half the Donner Party would perish.

In the spring of 1847, another rescue party was formed. But Johnny did not join them. He had already set out on his journey to the Pacific Ocean.

* * * * * * * *

In March, when Johnny turned thirty-three, he and his horses traveled southward along the Sacramento River from Sutter's Fort to a marshland, fed by this river and runoff from the local winter and spring rains. Several miles southwest of this marshland, Johnny encountered a gigantic body of water that would one day be known as the San Francisco Bay. He cut southward, moving along the eastern edge of the bay, and arrived at a ferry service. A few miles across this body of water lay the recently renamed town of San Francisco.§ As the ferry approached the town, he caught a glimpse of the great western sea, which lay beyond a gap between two ranges of mountains off to his right.

He disembarked with his two horses and sought a hotel. There were several of them in this town of about five hundred residents, the streets of which were still muddy from the late winter rains. He found a hotel and paid for a room. He unpacked his bags and stabled his two horses. He asked the hotel proprietor for advice on the best place from which to view the Pacific Ocean. The proprietor pointed to the top of one of the wintergreen-covered hills that rimmed the town.

Johnny walked to the top of that hill. When he got there, he gasped. To the west, north, and south of him was a seemingly endless expanse of dark blue water, stretching as far as the eye could see. He looked for a place to sit. It wasn't hard to find one. The hills were covered with soft green winter rye grass. It seemed as if one could walk barefoot here and not step on anything that would cut one's feet. Bright yellow buttercups, purple lupines, and an incipient growth of orange poppies made a striking, almost other-worldly contrast with the wintergreen glow of the grassy hillsides. A cool wind, still carrying the bite of winter, blew from the north, leaving a refreshing sting on the skin of his face.

He found a place that felt like just the right place to be and sat down cross-legged, facing the ocean. He looked over his shoulder at the bay he had just crossed. It was big, all right, but he could see the green mountains on its far sides—north, east, and south. When he looked back at the ocean,

---

§ Before the annexation of California by the United States, it was known as Yerba Buena.

all he saw was blue water, which seemed to go on forever. No mountains to the west were visible.

For a reason he could not fathom, he found this great body of water intimidating. It filled him with indescribable awe. He wondered how big it was. He looked over his shoulder again, focusing on the harbor beside the town. There were over a dozen wooden ships there. He realized that those ships had sailed on that great ocean from other places in the world. He wondered how they did it. He shuddered at the thought.

He sat still for over an hour, letting his mind drift into a deep silence. The stinging wind made him conscious of where his individual physical being left off and the rest of the universe began. Faintly, off in the distance, he could hear the crashing of waves against the shore. Sitting by this huge, endless sea, he saw himself as a tiny speck on the surface of a world of unimaginable vastness. He wondered how he fit into it. He wondered why that even mattered… Then he stopped wondering. He just sat there for another hour and dozed into a state of semi-sleep, still sitting upright.

* * * * * * * * *

He was roused from his trance by rustling footsteps in the deep green grass behind him. He turned around and saw a group of five men. At first, he thought they were Indians. He acknowledged them with a friendly glance. They were wearing white men's clothes. He wondered what tribe they came from. They didn't look like the Indians of California, though, or any other Indians that he knew of. They were brown-skinned men with wavy, thick black hair. They were taller and much heavier boned than the California Indians he had met since crossing the Sierras. One of them had enough hair for about five people, tied up in a topknot. His thick hair hung down to his shoulder blades. He stood about six and a half feet tall, with broad shoulders and a body mass comparable to that of a small grizzly bear. He looked like he was in his forties but was still quite fit. He had a mustache and a thin, neatly trimmed black beard. Johnny could see from his calm, confident demeanor that whatever he was and wherever he had come from, he was a warrior. For a moment, he remembered what his uncle Enoli had said about projectile weapons…

One of the men in the group approached Johnny, who stood up to meet him. The stranger extended his hand, and Johnny did likewise. They shook hands white man style. He appeared to be in his late forties. The stranger said, "My name is Thomas Kaupu [**]. I am from Hawaii."

Thomas was about Johnny's height, with short curly hair. He had broad shoulders and probably weighed well over two hundred pounds. Even so, he was dwarfed by the giant warrior with enough hair to cover five ordinary human heads.

Johnny said, "My name is Johnny Tenkiller. I am from a lot of places, but I'm originally from Tennessee, way back east. Where is Hawaii?"

Thomas turned his head and looked southwest over the deep blue ocean. "Far off, in that direction."

"What kind of place is it?" asked Johnny.

"It is a group of islands in the middle of that ocean."

"Did you come here on one of those ships?" asked Johnny, looking down at the harbor.

"Yes," answered Thomas.

"How far away is Hawaii?" asked Johnny.

"About as far as it is from here to Tennessee," replied Thomas.

Johnny wondered how Thomas knew so much about the geography of the North American continent but decided he would find out in due course. Meanwhile, his mind was boggled at the thought. He asked, "So, there's nothin' but all that water between here and where you came from?"

"Nothing but the ocean," Thomas responded.

Johnny was terrified at the thought of traveling in a wooden boat that far over such an immense body of water. He changed the subject. "So, you came here on one of those white man boats?"

"Yes," said Thomas.

"When did the white man come to your islands?" asked Johnny.

[**] Pronounced kah-oo'-poo

"The first ones came in 1776. Englishmen, led by a man named Captain Cook. He was arrogant. We killed him." He grinned and added, "Then we cooked him. Seems like his name was aspirational."

Johnny laughed. "That's one way of lookin' at it. Did you eat him, too?"

"No one talks much about that," said Thomas, seeming to withhold a sly smile, though only partially. "But they sent his bones to the other islands to show that he was just a man like us and not a god."

"It looks like more white men came after that," said Johnny.

"Yes," Thomas agreed. "Whale hunters came after that and settled in a town on one of our islands. Then, missionaries from New England came. If you are wondering why I seem to know so much about your country, it is because I went to the Foreign Mission School in Connecticut," said Thomas.

"Some of my people went there as well," said Johnny. "Did you know any Cherokees there?"

"I knew several. I became good friends with a very smart young man named Elias. The other Cherokees called him 'Buck'," said Thomas.

"I knew his uncle, who was a noted Cherokee chief," said Johnny. "You may not know this, but they were assassinated several years ago. Tribal politics stuff," said Johnny. "I can tell you more sometime if you're interested. But may I ask you where you and your friends are going from here?"

"We are going to a place called Sutter's Fort," responded Thomas.

"I just came from there. If you don't mind, I'll travel with you," said Johnny.

"That will be good," said Thomas. "I was wondering what brought *you* here," he added.

"I wanted to see this great ocean. The Pacific," Johnny replied as he turned his head to the west to view it again. "I've never seen anything like it." After pausing briefly, he asked, "When were you planning to leave?"

"Tomorrow, I plan to buy some horses, saddles, and packs to carry our things," said Thomas. "We'll leave the day after."

"I'm sure we'll have plenty of time to learn from each other along the way," said Johnny. "But I have another question that I want to ask…If those islands of yours are in the middle of that big ocean, and if the white men got there less than a hundred years ago, how did *your* people get there? And where did they come from?"

Thomas, knowing that he was about to tax Johnny's credulity, laughed. He said, "We came from islands far to the south of Hawaii. We traveled there in double-canoes with sails. Made of wood…with no metal parts," he added.

"You traveled hundreds of miles on that vast ocean in wooden canoes?" asked Johnny, incredulously.

"Yes," said Thomas. "Actually, it was a couple of thousand miles. I believe we will have plenty of time to discuss this, too, on our way to Sutter's Fort if you're interested."

"That *would* be interesting," said Johnny as he turned to walk down the green hill. "I'm stayin' the night in a hotel down there. Where are you stayin'?"

"We haven't gotten our rooms yet," answered Thomas.

"Maybe they have some rooms left where I'm stayin'. Want to walk there with me?" asked Johnny.

Thomas spoke to the other Hawaiians in their language. Then, they all walked down the hill together towards the hotel where Johnny stayed.

* * * * * * * * *

They were approaching the hotel on a boardwalk that lined the muddy street when they saw a group of six white men walking towards them. They walked three abreast, spanning the width of the boardwalk. Johnny and his new acquaintances thinned out into single file, politely leaving room for the white men to pass. The white men did not reciprocate. When Johnny, who walked at the head of his group, was about six feet away from them, one of them said, "Get off the walk."

Both groups of men stopped walking.

Johnny said, "Are you telling us to walk on that muddy street?" gesturing to his left, where the street was.

"That's what I'm sayin'," said the white man, a tall European with a strange accent that reminded Johnny of the Irish accent of his grandfather. He had light brown hair and a beard. Broad-shouldered, with brawny forearms and thick wrists, he had the look of a bad ass, confident of his ability to push his weight, all two hundred twenty pounds of it, on other men.

Thomas said, "Let's just let them pass." He began to step off the boardwalk.

Johnny said, "Please don't step in the mud, Thomas." Then, looking at the big white man who had told them to get off the walk, he said, "I don't think we want to do that."

The big white man, who had been doing the talking to this point, lunged at Johnny, who punched him in the face with a left jab, crushing the bridge of his nose, which gushed blood as he momentarily fell to his knees, probably seeing stars circling around his head. The other white men simultaneously jumped on Johnny, who landed a body blow on one of them with his fist. The man collapsed on his knees, trying to catch his breath. But as it happened, that was all Johnny had to do.

At that moment, the big Hawaiian charged into the group of white men and somehow—and very quickly—threw three of them into the muddy street. One moaned about a broken forearm. The other two, dazed, pulled themselves out of the street mud. That left three of the six white men, including the only one unharmed at this point, on the boardwalk. Johnny pulled out one of his Colts and cocked it. "That's enough, assholes," he declared.

One of the white men on the street went for the pistol in his holster. Johnny pointed his Colt at him and said, "Don't. Or you'll surely die today." His green eyes were as cold as those of a rattlesnake. They seemed to have a hypnotic effect on the man, who didn't move.

"Don't," said the one uninjured white man still standing on the walk, addressing the man who had been about to pull his pistol. He had sense enough to know they were outmatched. Meanwhile, the one with the smashed nose, still kneeling on the boardwalk and having recovered from the stunning blow he had taken from Johnny, started to get up. It appeared he had fight left in him. As he stood up, the big Hawaiian warrior landed a roundhouse kick on his left shoulder and sent him and his bloody nose into the muddy street. The one Johnny had hit with a body blow quietly stood up and leaned against the side of a building next to the walkway. He had caught his breath but still seemed disoriented. Johnny judged that he did not pose a threat.

The lone uninjured white man on the boardwalk asked, "What tribe are you people from?"

Thomas said, with a smile, "The Hawaiian tribe."

"I didn't know there was one," said the man. "So, you're from Owyhee?" he asked.

Thomas replied, "Hawaii," pronouncing the "w" like a soft "v."

Johnny added, "And I'm Cherokee."

Meanwhile, a small crowd of people had begun to gather on the opposite side of the street, watching this dramatic incident unfold.

Johnny, with his pistol still cocked, decided to educate these white men. He said, "As you should have seen, we were willin' to meet you men halfway. We could've shared this walkway. There was room. We could've behaved in a civilized way. We might've been friends, like a good Quaker man I once knew said we all should be. But y'all chose a different path." He paused for a moment, then continued: "It's a good thing this happened here in town 'cause if it happened out in the wild, someone coulda got killed. Maybe all six of you."

The man with the broken nose asked, "Where did you learn to box like that? You're an Indian, aren't you?"

Johnny smiled and replied, "From my Irish grandfather."

The man with the broken nose declared, "I'm Irish, too! What's your name?" He wiped his bloody nose with his shirt sleeve. Strangely, it seemed like the man might want to be friends.

"Well, I have a Cherokee name, too, but when I was in school, I used my grandfather's name. I'm Johnny Sullivan."

"I'm Jimmy Mehan," declared the Irishman.

Johnny uncocked his pistol, put it back in his holster, and extended his right hand. Jimmy extended his, and they shook.

Meanwhile, Thomas was translating the conversation into Hawaiian. The big Hawaiian warrior raised his right hand, palm outward, in what appeared to be a universal gesture of peace, looking at the men he had just tossed into the street. He stepped down from the walk, extending his hand to the man whose arm he had just broken, with a friendly look in his eyes. He beckoned him to come near. The man responded by reaching out with his good arm to grasp the Hawaiian's hand. The big Hawaiian looked at Thomas and asked him to explain what was about to happen.

Thomas said, "My brother knows how to heal broken bones with his bare hands by laying them on in a certain way. It's going to be painful, but he can help you. He can set your arm."

The man with the broken arm just nodded and allowed the warrior to put his huge hands on his injured arm. With an intense look of concentration on his face, and after taking a long, deep breath, the warrior did something with his hands that made a crunching sound. As he did this, he exhaled powerfully, exclaiming, "Ha!" as he did so. It all happened in a matter of seconds. As this occurred, the man let out a scream but then was silent. He looked at his forearm and saw that it was straight again. It would have to heal over time, but the bones were set. The big warrior just patted him on the back and stepped back up to the boardwalk.

The people watching from across the street applauded. Such a strange thing…

Johnny, watching closely, was deeply impressed.

Thomas said, "Now, you need to find a doctor. You will likely wear a sling for a while."

The white man, whose arm had just been set, said in what Johnny now recognized as an Irish accent, "Well, this is the first time I ever wanted to say, 'thank you' to someone who just broke me fockin' arm, but…" looking up at the giant who had just healed him, he said, "Thank you, whatever your name is."

Thomas said, "His name is Nalua[††]."

"Well, thank you, Nalua," said the Irishman. "I'd say it's been nice to meet you, but…" his friends laughed. Johnny and Thomas laughed, too.

Nalua beckoned Jimmy, the one with the broken nose, to come near. He did so. Nalua pinched the bridge of his nose and put it back in place as best he could.

Jimmy didn't make a sound, though it must have been quite painful. He thanked him and then asked the Hawaiians and Johnny if they cared to join him and his friends for a drink of ale. He was Irish, all right.

Thomas said, "Thank you, sir, but we don't drink. I'm a Christian missionary."

"Oh, I see," said Jimmy, who looked down sheepishly.

Johnny said, "I don't drink either." He grinned. "I was afraid I might turn into a drunken Indian." The other Irishmen didn't know whether to laugh or not, but Jimmy laughed, apparently getting the humor. He added to Johnny's wit: "Or a drunken *Irishman*!" The Irishmen all laughed from their bellies. So did Johnny.

Johnny said, "But thanks for the invite."

So, the men from both groups shook hands with each other and went their separate ways.

The onlookers applauded again. They weren't used to seeing such civility from participants in a street fight.

As he and his new friends walked onward to the hotel to see if there were any rooms for the Hawaiians, Johnny thought about the words spoken by the Quaker gentleman, William Johnson, thirteen years before when he was leaving Pittsburg. He had said, "*If everyone treated everyone they met as if they were an old friend, there would be no more wars. And most of the world's problems would go away. Remember that. And if you can, imagine it to be so.*"

Johnny thought, "Well, once in a while, there's an opportunity to do that." He remembered how he and Billy Starr had become friends when they could easily have become enemies, and the good that had come from

---

[††] Pronounced nah-loo'-ah.

Johnny's overture of friendship back in 1839. Today, another such opportunity came up. It could have easily resulted in carnage and death. Reflecting on it, he felt a warm sense of calm, of serenity. In the privacy of his thoughts, he added, "…and I'll take advantage of it when it comes up." Then he mused, "But I'll still kill sonofabitches that need killin'." Silently, he laughed at himself.

Chapter 26: Cump

The next day, Thomas bought eight horses for his group—five to ride, three to serve as pack animals. Aside from some money given by his church, Thomas, who was a son of an ali'i,‡‡ had money of his own to use for such purposes. The day after, Johnny and his new friends left for Sutter's Fort. They ferried across the bay and set out northeastward towards the Sacramento River.

Along the way, Johnny reflected on how Nalua had set the Irishman's broken forearm. He had never seen anything like it. While the arm required a sling, it looked perfect when Nalua had finished. He asked Thomas, "How did Nalua do that? Was it some kind of magic?"

Thomas said, "Before I explain this to you, I need to let you know that I avoid even talking about this subject. I am a Christian. Nalua is not." He smiled. "He's a heathen. He believes in guardian spirits, demons, and ghosts. He learned the ancient ways while he was growing up, and the lore behind them."

"Well," Johnny said, "If it don't bother you too much to talk about such things, I'm pretty curious."

"I'm not saying I believe in those things, but I, too, learned of them while I was growing up. So, I will tell you what I heard. Again, I do not believe in, nor do I support the belief in, these pagan matters." He added, "At least, not since I was baptized."

Johnny said, "Well, I was educated by Christian missionaries in my homeland, or what used to be my homeland before the whites forced my people to leave, but I wasn't baptized. I'm open-minded about matters of the spirit."

Thomas beckoned Nalua to ride his horse up next to him. He said to Johnny, "If I just translate what my brother says, I won't be advocating his heathen beliefs." Then he spoke Hawaiian to Nalua, apparently passing Johnny's question on to him.

---

‡‡ "Ali'i" is the Hawaiian term for "noble." It is pronounced ah-lee'-ee. Hawaii already had a well-developed system of social classes when the first Europeans arrived.

Nalua directed his gaze to Johnny and demanded, in broken English, "Why you like know?"

Johnny, looking Nalua straight in the eye, said, "Because I was impressed by your knowledge."

Thomas translated this into Hawaiian, to assure that Nalua understood that Johnny's intentions were pure.

Nalua began to speak in Hawaiian. He spoke at some length, leaving it to Thomas to translate his words into English.

Thomas turned to Johnny and said, "The kahunas—Hawaiian holy people—believe that our bodies have a spiritual 'double'. You have bones, and those bones have a spiritual essence. May I assume that you know what an 'essence' is?"

Johnny said, "Yes. It means somethin' boiled down to its very basic elements." He paused, then added, "Well, that's how I understand it, anyway. It sounds like Nalua believes that our bodies are not all there is to us. There is somethin' more basic. A spiritual essence. Am I on the right track?"

"That is close enough," replied Thomas, who continued: "So, when Nalua laid his hands on that Irishman, he focused powerfully, not on the broken bone, but on the *spiritual essence* of the bone. He prayed, breathed in and out as he concentrated, built up a strong emotion, visualized the spiritual element of the bone being healed, took a final deep breath, and as he let it out all at once with that 'Ha!', and sent his own spiritual power into the spiritual part of the bone. His faith and goodwill rode his breath into the spiritual double of the bone and made it straight again, with some help from his hands. That is what set the physical part of the bone." Thomas looked at Johnny for a moment and then added, "I realize this may seem a bit strange to you. I may have lost some of what Nalua said because it doesn't translate easily into English, but that, regrettably, is the best I can do."

Johnny reflected on his experience in Cahokia and the ghost, Oya Tse. He said, "I got no problem believing that. I've come to believe that we're all both physical and spiritual beings. I never thought of using that to fix broken bones, and I'm not sayin' that I could do it, but it makes sense to me. Your people seem to be pretty advanced in such matters."

"Well, we will become more advanced when we let go of our paganism," said Thomas, the Christian missionary.

Johnny replied, "With all due respect, sir, I'm not so sure that's true. I learned a long time ago that those of us who have been invaded by the whites, who have big advantages in their tools, weapons and methods of making things, are better off to learn what we can from them, without forgetting who we are, who our ancestors were, and what we have been…the better to become what we must become in order to survive in this new world…without losin' ourselves—who we are—in the process." Then he asked Thomas, "How do you say, 'Thank you' in your language?"

Thomas replied, "Mahalo."

Johnny looked again at Nalua, smiled, and said "Mahalo."

Nalua merely gave a stoic nod.

* * * * * * * *

On the third morning of their journey, as they neared Sutter's Fort, Johnny asked Thomas, "So, why have you come all the way over here?"

Thomas replied, "I'm a missionary. I want to teach the gospel of Jesus Christ to the natives who live here."

"I see," said Johnny. "While you're at it, maybe you can teach it to the white men as well. Seems they could benefit from it at least as much as the natives." His sarcasm was unmistakable.

A faint, benign smile crossed Thomas's face, but he didn't comment.

Johnny asked, "And what about the others who came with you?"

Thomas replied, "All of them but Nalua came here because they didn't want to farm sugar cane."

"Why not?" asked Johnny.

Thomas began by saying, "This is going to require a bit of explanation. The daughters of some of our *ali'i nui nui*[§§] married Americans. Mostly businessmen. We Hawaiians brought sugar cane with us when we came

---

[§§] The highest level of Hawaiian nobility was called ali'i nui nui.

from Bora Bora and Tahiti hundreds of years ago, and we grew what we needed. We did not grow it for sale or for profit.

"Now, the white men really like sugar. So, these businessmen saw promise in growing sugar cane in Hawaii because the climate is favorable and there is a big market for it in the United States. We only grew sugar cane to meet our needs. The white men want to grow it to sell. That means they want to grow far more than we ever did. That means they needed a lot more labor—more people—involved in growing it than we did in the past.

"One reason why it is so profitable to grow in Hawaii is because the ali'i already control the land, which they own by right of past conquests. They don't have to buy it. On the other hand, the common people are used to growing their crops on land that is possessed in common by each village. They produce or barter for the things they need. So, when they grew their own food for the most part, they could work for cheap. At least, they could in the beginning. This last fact made the labor inexpensive, and since the ones in charge didn't have to pay for the land, they could make large profits by selling sugar to people elsewhere—mostly in the United States."

"I see," said Johnny. "But why are they here instead of working on the sugar farms?"

"They were fine with the way things were before growing things was made into a business by the *haoles*," continued Thomas. "As more land was brought under sugar cultivation, more labor was needed. This took time away from working on their own farms, or harvesting fruit, or fishing. They didn't want to be forced to work in the cane fields. So, they took their chances by leaving their homes and coming to this new land."

"What are *haoles*?" asked Johnny.

"That is what we call white people," said Thomas.

"Oh," said Johnny, who figured he could follow up on this matter later.

Changing the subject back to his original point of curiosity, he asked, "What do these Hawaiians hope to find here? I don't mean Nalua—I'll ask about his reasons later."

Thomas replied, "They don't really care, as long as they don't have to work in the cane fields, making other people wealthy. It's just an adventure for them."

"What about Nalua?" asked Johnny. "He don't seem like a farmer or fisherman to me."

"He is ali'i," said Thomas. "He doesn't have to do menial labor. He's a warrior. He left the islands because he is on the run. He committed murder."

"I see," mused Johnny. "Who did he kill and why?"

"Nalua was a retainer to a high ali'i family. 'Ali'i nui nui', as we call them. Both he and I come from the next level down—the class that provides warriors and people of knowledge. We're still ali'i, just not high ali'i. That is not to say that the high ali'i aren't also people with warrior skills and knowledge. They are. Some are bigger than Nalua, and just as skilled at the fighting arts."

Johnny thought about that for a moment. He surmised that those ali'i nui nui must be fearsome warriors, especially if they were even bigger than Nalua.

Thomas continued, "Their kahunas are very powerful and can even kill people with death prayers—witchcraft. But they don't work in the fields, and neither do we. The common people work the fields, harvest fruit from the forests, and catch fish. Ali'i don't. We might fish for sport, but only rarely because we need to. The common people provide us with our food and other things we need."

"We had people like your ali'i in my tribe, long ago," said Johnny. "They were members of a privileged clan, called the Ani Kutani. This was long before I was born."

"What happened to them?" asked Thomas.

Johnny replied, "Well, they helped themselves to whatever they wanted, including the wives of commoners. At one point, probably hundreds of years ago, the people rose up and killed them all. Men, women, and children. All of them."

"Oh," said Thomas. "Well, without going into the details, it was something like that that led Nalua to kill an ali'i nui nui. The penalty for his action is death. Nalua could either stay and face execution or he could leave. That is why he is here."

"I see," said Johnny, who decided at this point to drop his line of questioning. He figured that Nalua's victim probably needed killing, but out of respect, and not knowing the whole story, kept these thoughts to himself.

They rode on in silence until Johnny, full of curiosity, followed up on a question that had occurred to him during Thomas's narrative.

"What does 'haole' mean in your language?" asked Johnny. "I mean, other than 'white person'?"

"The closest thing I can think of to answer that question is 'without breath'," replied Thomas. "Do you remember how Nalua let out a 'Ha!' when he fixed that Irishman's broken arm? When Hawaiians pray, they put a lot of emotion into it and accompany it with methodical breathing. The breath is more important than the words. Their prayers come from the heart, more than from the mind. Haoles throw a lot of words into their prayers. Hawaiians throw powerful breath and a lot of feeling into theirs. They create an image in their minds—without burying it in a lot of words—and it rides the breath to the *aumakua* ***. But if the heart doesn't propel this image, the aumakua won't receive the prayer and it won't be fulfilled. That is what our kahunas—traditional Hawaiian holy people—say."

"I hope you don't lose patience with me," continued Johnny, "but now I'm wondering what an 'aumakua' is."

Thomas replied, "Johnny, since I'm a Christian, I have to say that I don't believe in what I'm about to say, but since you have asked, here is the answer: It means something like 'guardian spirit'. The Hawaiians believe that there is a higher power that rules the universe but that this higher power is beyond our capacity to understand. We cannot reach it directly. And as in our society, you must go through levels to reach this higher power. The closest level to Man is the aumakua. It's a very personal

---

*** Pronounced ow-mah-koo'-ah.

thing…each of us has one. Get a prayer through to it, and it passes it on to higher powers, which will respond to the prayer."

"What do you have to do to get the prayer through to the aumakua, then?" asked Johnny.

"In this respect, it's a lot like the teaching of our Savior, Jesus Christ. The person sending the prayer must be free of all guilt and grudge. If the person is burdened by guilt, or afflicted with a grudge, the prayer is blocked," said Thomas.

Johnny surmised that this depended on the nature of the grudge. But he wanted to know more. He said, "I want to tell you a story." Then he told of the Stricklin brothers' evil deed, and how, eight years afterwards, he fulfilled his promise to kill all three of them, "Indian style". While he spoke, Nalua, who could apparently feel Johnny's murderous spirit, listened intently, picking up such fragments of English as he understood, as Johnny told his story.

Johnny concluded, "So, I had held a grudge against the Stricklins for eight years. And yet, all the powers of Heaven seemed to favor my execution of that grudge. How can that be so?"

Thomas, with a twinkle in his eye, responded, "Let me confer with a *real* heathen about this. He may have an answer."

He turned to Nalua, who had picked up enough information from Johnny's telling to be curious. Thomas filled in the details.

Nalua paused thoughtfully for several minutes.

Meanwhile, Thomas said to Johnny, "Nalua needs some time to think about this matter."

At length, Nalua spoke in measured tones in his native language. He paused and asked Thomas to ask Johnny a question.

Thomas turned to Johnny and asked, "How do your people regard vendettas?"

Johnny answered without a pause: "Among my people, *not* executin' a vendetta was a sin. Once upon a time, you could be punished, even killed, for not doin' so. And a real Cherokee would feel guilty for *not* executing a vendetta, even if he wasn't punished by tribal law."

Thomas translated this for Nalua, who again paused to gather his thoughts.

When he spoke again, Thomas translated: "The person making the prayer must be completely free of doubt as to whether he deserves what he is asking for. Otherwise, the aumakua won't receive it and pass it on to the higher power. Clearly, you felt fully justified in your actions against those haoles. You had no guilt, no unwarranted grudges. That is why your aumakua supported you."

When Thomas had finished his translation, Nalua, with a wry smile, said in broken English, "I weesh I was deah fo' see when you wen makeh dose bah-gahs!" Johnny caught only part of this effort to communicate directly to him. He looked at Thomas, wordlessly asking for a translation.

Thomas looked upwards before translating, as if to ask God for forgiveness for the words he was about to say. Then he gave a loose translation: "Nalua said he wished he could have been there to see you kill those 'sonofabitches'."

Johnny looked at Nalua, nodded, and exclaimed, "Me too!" He laughed, as did Nalua. It was the first time he had ever witnessed laughter from Nalua.

* * * * * * * * *

Johnny and his Hawaiian friends stayed through the fall at Sutter's Fort. Johnny worked in the smithy.

During that time—the fall of 1847—another group of Hawaiians, brought to California by John Sutter, went up the American River to build a grist mill. Their efforts would be guided by a carpenter and sawmill operator named James Marshall. Sutter had big plans for an agricultural empire. A water-powered mill would be part of those plans. But history was about to crash his dreams.

The site of the mill was near a native village in a valley they called "Cullumah", which meant "beautiful". As it happened, this was also the place where Thomas Kaupu sought to establish his ministry. The other Hawaiians busied themselves, building cabins and preparing the ground for spring planting. Even the aristocratic Nalua worked alongside them.

And then, on January 24, 1848, James Marshall found a gold nugget by the mill that had just been completed. He was encouraged to keep this a secret by John Sutter, who knew what was likely to happen if the word got out. But the word did get out later that year, partly because the military governor of California, which the US had just annexed from Mexico, and one William Tecumseh Sherman, a young lieutenant in the US Army, inspected the area near Sutter's Fort and wrote up a report to the government. The news got out. California would soon be overrun by gold seekers from all over the world.

Johnny, for his part, was disgusted by the conditions of the Indians at Sutter's Fort, who were treated worse than the African slaves of the American south. He tried to ignore this, since he was in no position to do anything about it. He figured he had better leave before going into his dark tunnel, possibly getting himself killed this time. Sutter, no man's fool, had plenty of bodyguards. So, Johnny was happy to move to the boomtown of Coloma—as Cullumah was now named—where his new Hawaiian friends had gone.

* * * * * * * *

The Hawaiians, who had by that time begun to grow produce on farms they had established in the area, brought their harvests to sell to the miners and other residents of Coloma. They prospered from this, but many of them took to panning for gold rather than farming. Meanwhile, Thomas Kaupu was having some success in converting native Indians to Christianity. Things were looking pretty well for them.

Early in 1848, Lieutenant Sherman, who had apparently learned civil engineering at West Point, was engaged by Sutter to lay out a street grid for the new city of Sacramento, which would quickly grow around Sutter's Fort. In the latter part of 1848, Sherman, who by that time received a brevet promotion to captain, decided to open a general store in Coloma. The store was quickly built. Sherman bought an inventory of mining tools and other things needed by the miners and other residents of Coloma.

Johnny, who was tired of doing blacksmith work, decided to approach Captain Sherman for a job. He walked into the store and found the captain auditing his inventory, planning the store's organization, and merchandising. He knew Sherman's surname and rank but did not yet know what the initials "W.T." stood for. He had heard Sherman addressed by one of his associates as "Cump".

He opened the conversation by introducing himself. Speaking his best English, though still with a Tennessee drawl, he said, "Excuse me, Captain Sherman, my name is Johnny Sullivan. I was wondering if you needed some help running this store. I have experience."

Sherman, who looked about thirty years old, was a lean, wiry redhead with a short, neatly trimmed beard. His demeanor was serious, almost too stern for someone his age. Johnny surmised that if he smiled, his face would break into pieces and fall on the floor.

He looked up from what he was doing and surveilled Johnny. He said, in a matter of fact but not hostile manner, "You look like an Indian."

Smiling faintly, Johnny said, "Yes. But I'm a civilized Indian."

Sherman asked, "So, what tribe are you from?"

Johnny replied, "Cherokee."

Something about Johnny's calm, confident demeanor fascinated Sherman. He said, "My father named me after a great Indian chief. The 'T' in my middle name stands for 'Tecumseh'."

"Well," said Johnny, "Then you and I are quite connected. My father fell with the great Tecumseh at the Battle of the Thames River a few months before I was born."

"But Tecumseh was Shawnee," countered Sherman.

"As you probably know, the Shawanos weren't the only tribe that stood by Tecumseh," Johnny pointed out. "Those who still had fight left in 'em supported his cause down to the very end. There were warriors from a lot of tribes involved, including some from mine, including the father I never knew."

Of course, Sherman knew this. It was one of the reasons his father had named him "Tecumseh". Like Johnny's grandfather, Will Sullivan, Sherman's father believed that Tecumseh was one of the greatest men who had ever lived.

Changing the subject, he asked, "What qualifications have you?" As an afterthought, he added, "Besides that arsenal you're carrying on your belt," eying Johnny's two Patterson Colts.

Johnny replied, "I learned to read, write, and cipher from some Presbyterian missionaries who started a school for Indian children where I lived. My grandparents, who raised me, had a general store east of Knoxville. After my grandfather passed away, I helped my grandmother run the store. Keeping track of receipts was kind of tricky because we often accepted goods in barter, rather than in money.

"Later on, I learned to forecast inventory from a blacksmith I worked for in Pittsburg. Years later, I helped some Cherokees set up a general store in a settlement on the Canadian River, in Indian Territory. I worked with them for about four years."

Sherman, impressed, asked, "What do you mean by the term, 'forecast'?"

Johnny replied, "You have to keep records of what sells, how much of it sells, and when it sells. When planning, you calculate averages, throw in a little extra, and then get that number of goods to make sure you have them on hand when the customers want them."

"Where did you learn to calculate averages?" asked Sherman.

"From the missionaries," replied Johnny.

"Do you make allowances in your forecasts for whether the goods are perishable or not?" asked Sherman.

Johnny replied, "If they're perishable, I'm more conservative about that 'little extra' part. But with metal goods, for example, I don't worry. If the extra parts don't sell, they won't spoil. They just become part of the inventory. Might mean we need to order less of them the next time around."

Sherman, apparently impressed at the sophistication of this "civilized" Indian, nodded approvingly.

Changing the subject, Johnny remarked, "I noticed that one of your associates calls you 'Cump'. Sounds like a nickname. May I ask if it comes from 'Tecumseh'?"

"Cump" broke into a smile. To Johnny's surprise, his face didn't break into pieces and fall on the floor. He said, "Yes, that's where the nickname came from." Then, getting back to the main topic, he said, "I plan to open the store this coming Monday. I would like to think about your application. Why don't you come back tomorrow after I've slept on the matter, and we'll decide then."

"That sounds fine," said Johnny.

* * * * * * * * *

The next day, Johnny showed up at the new Coloma General Store. Sherman was there, continuing to record the inventories. He had already begun to move things around for display purposes. As Johnny walked in, the captain greeted him, "Good morning, Mr. Sullivan."

"Good morning, Captain," responded Johnny.

Sherman didn't waste any time getting down to business. He said, "I would like to offer you a job here. You will be the assistant manager. I have another person who will be the store manager. The two of you should be sufficient to run the store. I would prefer you to keep those guns of yours out of sight unless you really need to use them, though. And, while you are well-dressed enough for the job, it wouldn't hurt for you to cut your hair a bit." By this time, Johnny's hair hung to the middle of his shoulder blades. Though he no longer shaved the sides of his head, he still wore his long hair in a topknot.

Johnny, happy to receive the offer, said, "Thank you, sir. I once had a white man's haircut, like Andrew Jackson. Is there a barber around here? I'll get it done today."

Sherman said, "Yes, there is one right down the street."

"I'll go as soon as we're finished here. Is there a contract for me to sign?"

The captain said, "Our words and a handshake will do. You can come tomorrow morning. You'll meet James, the store manager, and we can get this place organized and ready to open. I'm a bit surprised that you didn't ask about the pay."

Johnny said, "I could see from the way you carry yourself that you would be fair when it came to that."

Sherman asked, "Will you find a salary of $30 a month to be adequate?"

"Yes. And thank you for the opportunity. I'll do my best," promised Johnny, who extended his right hand. Captain Sherman extended his and they shook on it.

Chapter 27: Gold

Johnny worked at the general store in Coloma for almost a year. On his days off—typically Sundays—he visited Thomas, who oversaw a small congregation of Hawaiians and half a dozen Nisenan, as the original inhabitants of this area called themselves. They lived in a colony a few miles from Coloma, up a stream that flowed into the American River. Most of the natives were women or girls. One of the girls had begun to learn to read from the Hawaiian bible. Johnny was impressed. He saw in this girl hope for her people, not because of what she was learning to read, but because she was learning to read at all.

That is not to say that Johnny had a lot of time off. The store manager, James, was on the lazy side and left much of the record-keeping and planning, which took a few hours every day, to Johnny, who also tended the counter and handled transactions with customers. But the store was closed on Sundays, so Johnny would visit his Hawaiian friends on that day.

* * * * * * * *

One day in late July 1849, Johnny woke up before dawn, as was his custom. His thoughts were troubled. He didn't know why. Perhaps it came from a dream—a dream he could not remember—but suddenly, he felt pulled to leave this land. On awakening from this dream, Johnny wondered where he would go from here.

He reflected on his journey since leaving Indian Territory in the spring of 1846. At this point, he had been out west for over three years. It seemed longer than that to him. He had seen the Pacific Ocean. He had met new friends from a place he never knew existed, who could traverse the vast ocean in wooden boats and heal broken bones with their bare hands. But now his lust for travel, for novelty and adventure was sated—temporarily, at least. He longed to be in a place where he felt he truly belonged. He knew that it was not in California.

And then it hit him. He was ready to return home. To him, that meant Indian Territory.

He made his decision.

He knew he had to get over the Sierras by early September in time for the wagon trains to arrive. He hoped he could find Sam Morgan and travel back to Independence with him. That journey would take two months by horse. With another three weeks of travel after that, he could be back at the ranch on the Canadian River.

He hoped his Uncle Dutch would still be alive. He looked forward to seeing Billy, Sarah, and their kids again. Uncle Enoli, too…

The thought of it made his chest swell with happy anticipation. Another journey. Weeks of putting one step ahead of the next in the sacred silence of the mountains and the plains. The path that would lead him home.

When Sherman came in to visit the store that day, Johnny approached him. "Captain, do you have a moment?"

"Yes," said the captain. "What can I do for you?"

"Well, sir, you can accept my thanks for the opportunity to work in this fine store and for the fair way you've treated me since the day we met," Johnny began. "However, my heart yearns for my homeland and my people. I've decided to return to Indian Territory."

The captain paused thoughtfully. At length he said, "I understand. When were you planning on leaving?"

"Part of that depends on your needs, sir. That is the least I can do. But would two weeks be sufficient notice?" asked Johnny.

The captain really didn't want Johnny to go. Johnny was a valuable asset to the store, and he would have preferred to keep Johnny in his employ. The profits of the store over the past year were more than twice his captain's salary during that same period. But somehow, he was able to feel Johnny's powerful intent, even though Johnny didn't express his feelings in words. His intuition told him that trying to change Johnny's mind would be a waste of effort. After a moment's consideration, Sherman said, with a bit of sadness in his demeanor, "That will be fine, Mr. Sullivan."

Johnny asked, "Will it be possible for me to exchange my bank notes for gold? I don't know whether the bank notes would be honored where I'm headed, but I'm sure gold will be honored just about anywhere."

"Indeed," said Sherman. "I can arrange that. Aren't you worried that some outlaws might attack you and take away your gold?"

"Well, if they do, that'll be the last thing they ever try," said Johnny with a grin as he fingered his Colts. "There had better be at least nine of 'em because eight will die."

The captain and Johnny both had a good laugh. Then the captain said, "As you doubtless have come to know, I don't laugh easily. And I'm not known to be sentimental. But I must say that I am saddened by your impending departure. I will miss your presence in my store and in this town."

Two weeks later, Johnny met Captain Sherman to settle their accounts. Sherman had a leather bag containing some gold bars: Johnny's last paycheck and the gold equivalent of the banknotes he had asked Sherman to exchange. "Let's weigh this out," Sherman suggested.

In the store, Sherman weighed out the gold bars. Johnny had, by this time, learned the difference between various qualities of gold dust and bullion. It was high-grade gold. Johnny had given Sherman $500 in banknotes and was owed $30 for his last month of work. But when he did his calculations, he concluded that there was $600 in gold in that leather bag. "I should have only $530 here, sir."

"I knew you would notice, Johnny," replied Sherman. "The rest of it is a farewell gift. You have earned it."

Johnny protested, "I didn't earn it."

Sherman said, "Yes, you have, Johnny." He paused, looked Johnny straight in the eyes, and continued: "You are an inspiration to me. If you can help your people to learn how to navigate both of our worlds as gracefully as you have, you will be contributing, not just to them, but to America—the way it is *supposed* to be: *A great country built on the confluence of many different cultures and peoples.*"

Johnny knew better than to argue about the money. He just said, "Well, sir, thank you for those generous words. Now *I* feel inspired." He paused thoughtfully. "Your pa did well to name you after the great Tecumseh. What you just said is somethin' *he* might have said, had he been born under other circumstances."

"You can just call me 'Cump' if you wish."

"If I'm ever graced to see you again, sir, I will do so, but only in private. Wouldn't want to seem overly familiar to a general," said Johnny.

"I'm just a captain," said Cump.

"For now," said Johnny knowingly. "And if you ever see me again, you can call me by my Cherokee name, 'Tenkiller'."

Cump looked a little surprised. He asked, "Was the name given to you, or was it earned?"

"Well, the truth is, I claimed it before it was earned," said Johnny. "After I had killed five men, I took it as an aspiration. But I earned it with my tenth kill, and then my uncle, a Cherokee chief, granted it to me. If we ever meet again, you can call me 'Tenkiller' in private—the same circumstances under which I'll accept the honor of callin' you 'Cump'. I have reasons for not wantin' to use it in public, outside of Indian Territory."

He gave Cump a knowing look, which Cump returned.

After a brief, pregnant pause, Cump said, "Farewell, Tenkiller."

"Farewell, Cump," responded Johnny as the two men shook hands. Johnny took his bag of gold, packed up his things, and rode away, wondering if one day, he might meet Cump again.

* * * * * * * *

Johnny and his two horses took off northeastwards, following the American River towards the Sierras.

He wanted to see his Hawaiian friends before he left this part of the world. There was a tributary stream a few miles from Coloma. A couple of miles up that stream was the colony that his Hawaiian friends had built. He had been there many times. It was where he had gone on Sundays during the time he worked at the general store.

When he arrived, he was greeted by Thomas, who was regarded as the chief of this settlement. "Hello, Johnny. I don't think we have ever had a visit from you on a day other than Sunday. But it's good to see you, nonetheless."

"Hello, Thomas. I stopped here to say 'goodbye'. I am goin' back to my homeland," explained Johnny.

"You're welcome to stay here for a while if you wish," said Thomas. "It's Saturday, and we always have a fine dinner on Saturdays. And you can come to our church services in the morning if you like."

"I'd be much obliged," said Johnny. "I won't be able to stay long, though. I need to be on the other side of the mountains by early September when the wagon train from the east arrives." He looked around and saw that the village looked rather deserted. "Where is everyone?" he asked.

Thomas said, "The crops are in the ground and doing well, and it isn't yet time for harvest. So, the men are out looking for gold."

"How has that been working out?" asked Johnny.

"It depends on whom you ask," replied Thomas. "There is one Hawaiian here—the haoles call him 'Kanaka Jack'—who has found a vein somewhere up in the hills. Only he knows where it is. But he brings down more gold than anyone else."

"That sounds like a dangerous position to be in," commented Johnny.

"It may be," said Thomas. "Some haoles on horseback have already come through here looking for him. Nalua wanted to kill them."

"If they come back while I'm still here, *I'll* be pleased to meet 'em," said Johnny, with a slight smirk on his face.

Thomas, as a Christian missionary, could not support Johnny's probable intention. Instead, he said, "Last time they came, Jack was not here, and we all denied that we knew anything about his mine or about his doings."

"Did they buy that?" asked Johnny.

"I do not know," said Thomas. "But they went away."

"Is Jack taking his gold into Coloma and using it to buy things or sellin' it for banknotes?" asked Johnny.

"Yes," replied Thomas. "He has a bank account. He is literate and knows how to calculate with numbers."

"Is he an ali'i like you and Nalua?" asked Johnny.

"Yes, but he's not a missionary. He is more like a haole businessman."

"I see. "Well, you folks need to watch your backs," said Johnny. "The haoles will likely be back."

That evening, they had dinner. It was a splendid meal, with fresh fish topped with blackberries, among other delicacies. Johnny sat next to Thomas, on whose other side sat the warrior, Nalua. Johnny asked Thomas, "Does Nalua have an English name, like some of the others among you?"

"No," replied Thomas. "He never wanted one."

"What does his Hawaiian name mean?" asked Johnny.

"The name, 'Nalua', has at least two layers of meaning. On the surface, it refers to someone who practices Lua, which is a Hawaiian form of hand-to-hand fighting. A loose translation of the name into English might be 'breaker of bones'."

Johnny smiled and quipped, "He looks like he'd be pretty good at that."

"On another level, it means 'two'—not the number two, but a unity of two opposing forces. Good and evil, love and death, and so on," replied Thomas.

"That sounds philosophical," commented Johnny.

"It is and was meant to be."

"I'll have to reflect on that," said Johnny. "And what about you, Thomas? May I ask what your Hawaiian name is?"

"Ahi Wela," replied Thomas, pronouncing the "W" like a soft "V."

"What does it mean?" asked Johnny.

"It doesn't translate easily into English," said Thomas. The closest thing I can come up with is 'hot fire'."

Johnny thought about it for a moment. Everything about Thomas was calm, thoughtful, and moderated. Anything but a hot fire. He never seemed to lose control of himself. He wondered if deep down inside, behind that calm exterior, was an explosion waiting to erupt.

Thomas continued, "As a boy, I was easy to goad into fights. I had a short temper."

"Kind of livin' into your name, huh?" commented Johnny.

"You could say that. But when I found the Lord, the fiery energy of my youth was diverted…into the passion that drives me now."

Johnny, who had just taken a bite of trout, followed by some blackberry compote, nodded thoughtfully. Then he said, looking around expansively at the settlement the Hawaiians had built, "Your efforts seem to have resulted in somethin' worthy."

"If it is, it is only because of God's grace," said the ever-modest Christian missionary. Johnny's thoughts, ever so briefly, alighted on his memories of the Quaker gentleman, William Johnson. He wished that the world had more men like William and Thomas. And that more people would believe in—and practice—their teachings…

Before turning in for the night, Thomas asked Johnny if he had a mailing address. Johnny gave him the one he used at Fort Gibson in the Indian Territory.

The next morning, Thomas held a service. Everyone attended. Even the fortune-seeking miners. Thomas's sermon was based on scriptures from the book of Matthew, from words attributed to Jesus himself. It was from his Sermon on the Mount: a message of universal love and charity towards one's fellow man…even those whose actions should not, in Johnny's estimation, merit such generosity.

The pagan Nalua sat through the sermon politely, though with an air of detachment. But when it was time to sing, his baritone voice joined enthusiastically in a series of hymns, which the Hawaiians delivered in powerful three-part harmonies with their vibrato-rich, melodious voices. Johnny was impressed that such a fearsome warrior could sing so beautifully. His hair stood on end just to hear those Hawaiians sing. He fell into a trance.

The third song, along with Johnny's trance, was interrupted by the hoofbeats of half a dozen horses. A group of armed white men rode into the center of the settlement. Thomas got up from his chair and aggressively encouraged the singing to continue.

Johnny furtively slipped out of his chair and went to the house where Thomas lived. Sensing that trouble had just arrived, he grabbed both his Colts.

As Johnny arose from his seat at the dinner table, Nalua gave him a knowing look and arose as well. Both disappeared as Thomas continued to direct the choir.

When the last hymn was completed, Thomas led the congregation in a closing prayer. Then, he dismissed them and confronted the mounted visitors. Surprisingly, they had waited patiently for the service to end. "What can we do for you gentlemen today?" he asked.

The man who rode in the front of the group spoke. He said, "We're wondering where Kanaka Jack is."

At that moment, Johnny demanded, "Who's askin'?"

The man who had just spoken said, "Who are you?

Johnny replied, "Just a friend to these folks. By the way, you realize that it's Sunday and that this is a religious service, don't you?"

At this moment, a tall Hawaiian stood up and declared, "I'm Kanaka Jack. What you like?" His words may have been accommodating, but his demeanor was something else again.

The white man said, "We just want to know where you're gettin' all that gold."

Jack said, "I work hard for it. Why you like know?"

The white man said, with a note of derision, "I think you know why."

Johnny, knowing that things were about to deteriorate, said, "I think I know why, too. But this is Sunday, after all, and y'all should be sittin' quietly somewhere and contemplatin' the Lord, shouldn't you?"

The white man, who seemed incredulous, asked, "Who the fuck are you, Indian?"

As this exchange was occurring, Johnny saw Nalua, carrying a wooden staff about eight feet long, slipping up behind the horsemen, who were, at this point, focused on Johnny. Two more Hawaiians were with him, crouching in the bushes that rimmed the settlement.

"I'm an Indian, all right," said Johnny. "And proud to be one. And who the fuck are you?" He had not yet drawn either of his guns. But his mind and spirit had already entered his dark tunnel. He knew that today, there would be death. He just wasn't sure who would die. Then he continued. "Can't you see that these are good, hardworking folks? Why are you here, tryin' to take what ain't yours?"

"I reckon what's ours or not is yet to be decided," said the white man leading the group of horsemen.

Johnny, knowing that Nalua was ready to unleash his awesome fury, said, "It looks like you've made your choice, asshole." He pulled his Colt and shot the man off his horse. Then he shot the one right behind him. All of this in less than two seconds. As this was occurring, Nalua, wielding his staff with a frightful combination of power and grace, bashed the ribs of two of the other four horsemen, knocking them to the ground and then crushing their skulls with his blunt weapon. The other two horsemen, confused, had engaged their single-shot rifles, but were unsure of where to shoot. In their moment of indecision, the two Hawaiians with Nalua had grabbed one of them and pulled him down from his mount and were beating him with their fists. Meanwhile, Nalua charged the remaining gunman, who must have been terrified, having seen the results of Nalua's attack on his two comrades. He shot Nalua in the chest. Johnny shot this man off his horse. He fell to the ground with a bullet in his head. The other two Hawaiians finished off the last man less than a minute later.

The whole incident lasted less than two minutes.

Johnny ran to Nalua, who lay on his back with a bullet in his chest, bleeding out but still conscious. Thomas came, too. He began to pray for the salvation of Nalua's soul. But Nalua's attention was on Johnny, who clasped his right hand in his. They looked at one another, two warriors from different parts of the world, yet from a world, an epoch, that both understood well. A world where duty and honor mattered more than material wealth. A world in which warriors faced death with indifference. A world that was fading away.

Johnny solemnly looked him in the eye and said, "I'm glad that our paths crossed, Nalua. My life is richer for it."

Nalua looked questioningly at Thomas, who translated Johnny's words into Hawaiian, to assure that Nalua understood.

As his life ebbed from his body, Nalua smiled faintly as he exhaled his last breath and said, as the light went out of his eyes, "Good you wen makeh dose bah-gahs."[†††]

The two men that Nalua had knocked from their horses with his staff were lying dead on the ground. A third member of this group had been beaten to death by the other two Hawaiians. The other three had been killed by Johnny's bullets.

Thomas was horrified by the scene. He didn't know what to say. He called the congregation back together and led a prayer in the Hawaiian language. The Lord's Prayer. He repeated it several times.

Johnny continued to sit next to Nalua's lifeless body, silently mourning his death. Though they barely knew one another, he felt that at some deep level, they were connected, and that with Nalua's death, a part of him was dying as well.

Later, Thomas approached Johnny. He said, "I think it would be fitting for you to leave us now."

Johnny said, "I can help bury the dead."

Thomas said, "That won't be necessary."

Johnny said, "You need to unsaddle those horses, burn any papers that might identify these men, bury the saddles in random places, and then scatter the horses farther up in the hills. If anyone ever comes lookin' for 'em, say you know nothing. Or, if you want, you can blame it all on me. I'll be long gone by the time anyone even notices that those men are missin'. Just make sure that the local Indians don't catch any of the blame."

Thomas just said, "I do not approve of what you have done today, but I know you did it out of love for us. I hope that one day, you will extend your love to all. Even to 'sonofabitches' that need killing." He didn't laugh.

"Thomas," said Johnny, "I believe that you're grieving for at least two souls right now…and that mine is one of them, isn't it?"

Thomas nodded.

[†††] Loose translation: "Good you killed those sonofabitches!"

"Will you pray for my salvation, then?" asked Johnny.

"Yes, I will," said Thomas.

Johnny said, "I feel no remorse for what I've just done. But I do feel remorse for the way *you* feel about what I've just done. You are a truly good man who has made the world a better place wherever you've set foot. And I would welcome your prayers."

* * * * * * * * *

Johnny packed his things and saddled his horses. As he was mounting up, Kanaka Jack approached him. He was carrying a leather bag. He handed the bag to Johnny. It was surprisingly heavy. It weighed, as near as Johnny could figure, about five pounds. He asked, "What's in this bag, Jack?"

Jack said, "A reward for you, for what you wen do fo' us today."

Johnny looked in the bag. It was gold. High-grade gold bullion. Johnny said, "That is far more than I deserved. I would have done what I did for nothin' except, maybe, a little gratitude."

"Well," said Jack, "Dees my gratitude. Ge' plenty moah where dees wen come from."[‡‡‡] He grinned.

"Keep your secret well, Jack," said Johnny. He added, "And for what it's worth, I'll use this gold for a good cause when I get back home. I'm gonna use it to build a school for the children of my people."

The words just tumbled out of Johnny's mouth. He hadn't really thought about opening a school before. Now, suddenly, the resources for such a project had appeared. And along with those resources, a new mission for Johnny Tenkiller was born. Silently, he thanked the Great Spirit...

They shook hands. Jack said, "Aloha, Johnny!"

"Aloha, Jack!" responded Johnny, who mounted up and began his long journey home.

[‡‡‡] Translation: "This is my gratitude. There's plenty more where this came from."

Chapter 28: The Truckee River

In the early afternoon of that day, Johnny and his horses began the gradual climb up the foothills of the majestic Sierras. It was a hot, sweaty summer day, and since it was mid-summer, the days were long.

A couple of hours before sunset, he stopped and set up camp. The night would be warm, so there was no need to pitch his tent. He had prepared for the journey by packing some salted pork, but he had also developed a taste for trout, even though he had to watch for bones when he ate it. He remembered his trip down from St. Louis to Fort Gibson fifteen years before when he had shot a brook trout with his bow. He no longer carried it with him. And he had no fishing pole. So much for fresh fish.

He found a bush with blackberries and picked two handfuls. He washed them in a stream nearby. He had also brought a bag of pine nuts. The berries and the nuts added welcome variety to the salted pork. He thanked the Great Spirit.

After his dinner, as the sun went down, he reflected on his day. He had now killed sixteen men. But he didn't feel very good about it, even though he couldn't think of a single one of them that didn't need killing. Thomas Kaupu's disapproval of his actions earlier that day was eating away at him. He did not fall asleep easily. He tossed and turned all night long in his bedroll.

* * * * * * * * *

Two days later, as the trail grew steeper and steeper, he could see the gray, moss-covered granite walls that marked the point at which the broad-leafed trees gave way to the pine forest.

He arose at first light, packed up his things, and resumed his journey.

It was mid-morning when Johnny heard gunshots down in the river gorge below. He tethered his horses to a pine tree and clambered down on foot to see what was happening. He carried his rifle and his pistols with him out of habit. He trod silently on the dry pine needles on the forest floor. Then, he saw three men with rifles aiming at something down at the bottom of the gorge. That something turned out to be local Indians, probably Maidu. When Johnny got close enough to see them, they were no longer firing their guns. At the bottom of the gorge was a prone body, apparently that of an older woman, naked to the waist. A bit upstream from her body was what looked like ground acorn meal, which these people blanched on the sand next to streams. She had apparently been working at this when she was shot.

A white man at the bottom of the gorge was busy cutting off one of her breasts. Johnny had heard that men like him used the breasts of native women as tobacco pouches. "Bastards!" he thought.

The other two, young men in their twenties, were sitting on a boulder above the stream, watching. Johnny, hidden behind a pine tree, aimed his rifle at the man carving up the woman and fired. The man, hit in the back by Johnny's bullet, fell to the ground. "One less sonofabitch in need of killin'," he thought to himself. He didn't seem to be dead yet, though. Johnny figured he would deal with him in due course. He wondered what to do about the other two. Had they shot anyone yet? Or were they just along for the ride, as it were, watching someone shoot human beings as if they were ducks or turkeys? Doing this shit for fun. His rage boiled.

When the man at the bottom of the gorge fell, the other two looked around nervously, but not knowing exactly where the bullet came from, they weren't sure how and where to take cover.

Johnny yelled out to them: "Drop your weapons, assholes! Or you will wind up where your friend is. Dead."

One of them pointed his rifle in the direction of Johnny's voice but could not possibly have known exactly whence it had come. Johnny let out a war cry and slid downhill on the pine needles. The one pointing at Johnny fired but missed widely. Close enough to use one of his side-arms, Johnny drew it and fired at the shooter, grazing his calf. He bent over in pain, and a few seconds later, Johnny, with both pistols drawn, emerged from the brush. "Don't even think of tryin' anything right now, and I might let you pieces of shit live to see the light of another day."

One of the two men pleaded, "Please don't shoot us! We were just watchin'." Perhaps he had judged Johnny to be an Indian and feared vengeance.

"Toss your fuckin' guns over there," said Johnny, pointing to a flat piece of ground about ten feet away from where the men sat. They complied. Johnny quickly judged that, while they were accomplices, they weren't killers. "Now," he said, "Let's sit and talk for a while." He reholstered one of his pistols, sat down on a boulder a few feet away from these two men, and placed his other pistol on a flat rock to his right.

Johnny began, "I know that a lot of you white men think that these folks are fair game, free for the shootin'. I know that the bastard, John Sutter, encourages this kind of thing. But hear this! That little old lady down there was somebody's grandmother. Somebody's auntie. Probably somebody's wife." His nostrils flared, "She had a name! She was a human being, like you and me, like *your* grandmothers, you fuckin' assholes! She could make baskets, beautiful baskets that were so tightly woven that you could carry water in 'em. And that acorn meal down there...They don't just eat acorns when they fall off the oak trees. They shell 'em, grind 'em up into meal, and wash the poisons out of 'em with water from the stream. It's a sort of complicated process. And it's not fittin' to call these folks 'Diggers' just because they eat roots. Even for that they've got a process. Do you two jerks eat potatoes? What the hell do you think *potatoes* are?"

Then he paused, took a deep breath, and regained control of himself, and added calmly, "Did you ever think of any of that?"

One of them, who looked like he was in his early twenties, responded, "No, sir. To us, they aren't really people."

"Well, I was about to ask what you thought they were, if not human, but I didn't really want to hear your answer. Thanks for bein' honest...I guess." He turned to the other, who was also in his twenties. "What about you? What kind of shit were you thinking when you went on this venture?"

He replied, "I just went along with it because of him," pointing to the prone body of their associate, lying next to his victim in the gorge.

"I believe you," said Johnny, who instinctively knew the difference between a wolf and a jackal. "There was a time," he continued, "when I would have been happy to kill you two, along with the sonofabitch lying down there, who I intend to finish off anyways if he ain't already dead. But I'm tired of killin'. And I really don't wanna kill you. I want you to remember this moment when you could well have died. I chose to let you continue breathin' air, walkin' the surface of this earth. But I want you to admit, to yourselves at least, that you just stood by and let that shit ball down there kill somebody's grandmother. Somebody who had a name, a reputation, a purpose for livin'. Somebody who loved and was probably loved. A human being. Somebody like you!"

There was a brief silence. "Well," Johnny demanded impatiently, "Do you want to admit that it wasn't right for you to just stand by and let that pile of hog excrement down there shoot and butcher somebody's grandmother?"

One of the young men knit his brows and asked, "Hog...what?"

"Hog excrement, Dipshit!" retorted Johnny. "'Excrement' is just a polite word for 'shit'."

"Oh," said the young man, with a blank look in his eyes.

Giving up his line of questioning, Johnny declared, "So, here's the deal, which you can choose to honor or not: Don't stand by and let this kind of shameful thing happen again. When you're able to prevent it, do somethin'. Or, at least, don't be part of it. And if you don't honor this deal, know this: I'll be lurking in these woods for a good while. And I'll kill every sonofabitch I catch doing these things. I hope it ain't either one of you."

"Oh, it won't be me, sir!" exclaimed the first of the two men that Johnny had addressed.

"Me neither!" assured the other—the one Johnny had just addressed as "Dipshit."

"I hope not," said Johnny. "And by the way, if you tell other people about this, let them know that the Indian who lectured you was not one of these local folks, though I speak for them now. I am from the Indian Territory back east. My Cherokee name is 'Tenkiller'—closer to 'twenty-killer' now...And still countin'." He grinned.

Pointing at the bleeding calf of the one he had called "Dipshit", he said, "Put somethin' on that before you bleed to death." Fortunately, it was just a surface wound, as Johnny had intended it to be.

Johnny stood up, walked over to their rifles, and hurled them, one after the other, to the sand by the stream, where the man he had shot still lay, moaning as he bled from the bullet hole in his back. "I'll leave 'em there for you to pick up when I'm gone. And don't try to follow me, or I will do to you as I'm about to do to him," pointing at the prone body of the man at the bottom of the gorge. "I'd rather not, though. I think you boys have the potential to be better human beings than him. I sure hope so."

Johnny climbed down to the stream bed and turned over the body of the man who had shot and butchered someone's grandmother. He was still breathing. Johnny pulled his knife out of its sheath. He reached down, grabbed the man by the hair, and scalped him. The man, who was still alive, screamed as Johnny lifted his scalp, brandished it above his head, and looked across the stream, where he believed the woman's relatives might be. He let out a triumphant war cry. Several whoops in response came from the bushes on the far side of the ravine.

Johnny would never know the family of this woman, but he hoped he had served justice on their behalf.

Indian justice.

Inwardly, he laughed at himself. "Today," he thought, "I'm a real goddam heathern. Wish Uncle Dutch and Uncle Enoli could see me now!" He dropped the man's scalp next to his body, reached down again, cut his throat, and left him to bleed out. More whoops came from the bushes across the stream. Then, he picked up the two rifles he had thrown into the gorge. He tossed them into the shallow water downstream from the grandmother's acorn meal. With their powder wet, they wouldn't be of any use to the two young white men he had just spared, in case they had a change of heart. He turned around and trotted up the bank. As he passed them, he said, "You better hurry up and pick up those rifles. Otherwise, you might wind up dead or bald…You never know who's lurkin' in the bushes on the other side o' that stream."

The two young men at once ran down to the stream and recovered their rifles.

When Johnny got back to the trail, he untethered his horses and rode on.

That night, he pitched his tent, as it was much cooler up in the pines than it had been in the foothills. He slept with one eye open, not yet confident that he could trust the two men he had just spared. As he faded into and out of sleep, he hoped that his mercy would have a benign impact on these two young white men. He prayed, as he drifted into sleep, that at least one of them would be affected by what he had said, and maybe even spread the word. Probably not the one he called "Dipshit," though.

* * * * * * * *

The next morning, Johnny continued his journey up the Sierras. The scenery became more and more magnificent as he ascended the western-facing slopes, imposing walls of gray granite hundreds of feet high with tall pine trees and junipers growing right out of the rocks, which were covered on their north-facing sides by bright-green moss. There was a certain time in the late afternoon when the angle of the sun's rays gave the impression that it was shining right through the leaves of the trees and shrubs and reflecting off the moss, causing a pale green aura to glow above the plants and fade into the deep blue, cloudless mountain sky. The air was crisp but not cold, and it was filled with the smell of the pines. Johnny was overwhelmed by the majesty of those great stone mountains, the endless sky, and the green things with their afternoon auras. He felt as if something wonderful was about to happen, as if a great destiny were about to unfold, as if something of vast significance was about to be revealed to him.

A few days later, he passed through the place where the Donner Party had met its tragic end. There was no snow on the ground now, it being late summer. As he continued his trek, the mountains began to slope downward toward the east. He would follow the Truckee River gorge all the way to the bottom. But the bottom was still a few days away.

From time to time, he would stop and lay on his belly on a flat rock to have a drink of water. It was icy cold, fed by the summer melt of the glaciers above Lake Tahoe, and fast-moving enough to be inhospitable to algae, amoebas, and mosquitoes. One afternoon, as he lay on his stomach, alternately inhaling the pine-scented air and gulping the frigid, crystal-clear water, he looked at the polished grains of granite sand on the bottom, which was about eighteen inches deep where he was. The water was so clear he could see every grain. He looked upstream and saw the late afternoon sun gleaming on the calmer parts of the stream, the white foam at its center flashing as it swept its way down the gorge. Every so often, the stream's turbulence caressed his face with a cool, misty spray.

He got up from the rock and sat cross-legged on a soft bed of dry pine needles, watching the river flow by, his thirst fully sated and his spirit at peace. His memories of Sutter's Fort and Coloma were starting to fade, as he was riveted to the present moment by the chill water, by the singing of the river as it plummeted down the granite skeleton of California's brutal backside, and by the howling of the mountain sky.

* * * * * * * * *

A few days later, he was at the bottom of the Sierras in a meadowed area watered by the Truckee, which flowed out into the desert of northern Nevada. A few days after that, the wagon train arrived. Sam Morgan was still the wagon master.

Johnny approached him. "Hi, Sam, do you remember me?" he asked.

Sam immediately noticed Johnny's two Colts. He remembered his long, black hair and green eyes. He put these things together and then recalled Johnny from the wagon train he had led three years before.

"Why, I sure do," responded Sam. "Not many people come back once they've crossed those mountains into California. Aren't you interested in mining for gold, like the rest of the mob flowing in from the east?"

"Not really, Sam," said Johnny. "I wasn't looking for gold anyway."

"Well, I won't pry into your business, but did you find what you were looking for?" Sam asked.

Johnny, not wanting to disclose details, simply said, "Yes, I did. And then, I found that I wanted to go back to my homeland. That's why I'm here. Do I have to pay to return with you to Independence?"

"No," said Sam. "We only charge for the trip west. In fact, if you had stayed on as a guard, you would have traveled back with us—meals included—as part of your deal. Didn't Josiah tell you that part?"

"Maybe he did, and I just don't remember. Or I wasn't listening because I didn't know if I was ever gonna go back," said Johnny. "Anyway, that sounds good. When are we leavin'?"

"Day after tomorrow," said Sam. "We'll reach Independence by the middle of November."

And so, on September 4, 1849, Johnny began his journey back home: Eighteen hundred miles of the scent of the sage and the pines, the howling winds of the Great Plains, and two months of the sounds of sacred silence.

Chapter 29: Home

About a week before Sam Morgan's party left for Independence, two young men wandered into Thomas Kaupu's colony. They were looking for a place to pan for gold. But when they heard the ethereal voices of the Hawaiian singers during a Thursday afternoon service, they forgot about gold for the moment and approached the church, a modest white clapboard affair from which the singing seemed to be coming. They halted at the door. Some of the singers stopped, but the Reverend Kaupu urged them to continue singing. When the hymn was over, Thomas welcomed them in: "Welcome, friends. You can join us if you wish."

They walked into the church, found some open seats, and sat down.

When the service was over, Thomas approached them. "May I ask what brought you here today, gentlemen?"

One of the men said, "We wandered into this valley looking for a place to pan for gold. Then we heard your people singing. It was beautiful."

The other one said, "Yes, it was."

The first man then said, "Something happened, or almost happened to us the other day. A miracle. We were with a man out shooting at Digger Indians..."

"But *we* didn't shoot any!" protested the other.

"Let me finish, Wilbur," said the first one. "Then along came this big, scary Indian who called himself 'Tenkiller'. He shot the man we were with who had shot and killed an old Digger woman..."

"And he scalped him, too!" interjected Wilbur. "And he shot me in the leg."

"As I was saying..." continued Jacob, the first of the young men to speak, "He could have easily killed us. He might have been more likely to kill us after Wilbur shot at him and missed. But he didn't. He said he'd let us live if we just listened to him. He told us that that old woman had a name, that she was somebody's grandmother, that she was a human being, that there were people who loved her, and people she loved, that we should think about that. He warned us that he'd be lurking in the woods for a good while, and that he would kill anyone he saw trying to hurt the Indians. He said that we shouldn't be involved in anything like that again. And he was good to his word. That's why we're still here, talking about it."

"What is your name?" asked Thomas.

"Jacob," answered the young man.

"So, Jacob and Wilbur, did Tenkiller's words move you in some way?" asked Thomas.

"Yeah, they scared the shit out of us!" declared Wilbur. "Especially when he finished killing and scalpin' the man who killed that little old lady."

"It wasn't about being scared," protested Jacob. "It made me feel terrible that we were even there, even part of it." He paused and, clearing his throat, declared, "Sir, I wish to be baptized. I want to start my life over again."

"And what about you?" asked Thomas, looking at Wilbur.

Wilbur hesitated. Then he said, "It would probably do me good."

Thomas suppressed his impulse to show disdain and asked, "Have either of you men ever been to church? Before you are baptized, you need to know what being immersed in the water is all about. If you're willing to learn that, I will be honored to wash your sins away in the name of our Savior, Lord Jesus Christ."

"I went to Sunday school, but I'm still willing to be taught," said Jacob.

"Me too," agreed Wilbur.

"You can set up camp here," said Thomas. "And you are welcome to join us for dinner this evening."

"Thank you!" said Jacob and Wilbur in unison.

Thomas walked away, his mind spinning around the complexity of this whole affair. A man who had just killed four men that he knew of and scalped the last one had brought him two possible converts. "Well," he mused to himself, "*One*, anyway. And haoles at that…"

Had Johnny been moved in some way by the prayers Thomas had sent up to the Lord on behalf of his salvation? He wanted to think so. And he was glad that Johnny had left him his mailing address before he left. There was a post office in Coloma. Thomas would at some point mail a letter from there to Johnny, letting him know that his act of charity had been acknowledged, and that he would continue to pray for him.

* * * * * * * * *

Two months after they had left the Truckee meadows, Sam Morgan's crew arrived in Independence. Sam told Johnny that the town had a bank. Johnny exchanged his gold for U.S. dollars and opened an account. He asked for a letter of credit, for his intention was to transfer his funds to a bank in St. Louis, where he planned to buy books and school supplies.

The dollar value of Johnny's gold was worth several years' income. He would have enough money to buy many books—enough for a small library—and writing paper, blackboards, chalk, and pencils. When he left Indian Territory almost four years earlier, he was aware that Chief John Ross had been preparing to open a college—a men's seminary—in Tahlequah. Ross had been in the process of securing federal funds for this project. Johnny's plans were more modest. He wanted to invest in elementary education. A community had grown up around Uncle Dutch's ranch on the Canadian River. Johnny hoped to get children who lived there started on their education as early in life as possible.

He did not plan to just teach them to read, write and cipher. He would find and retain an elementary school teacher for that purpose. He understood that it was one thing to be able to write and cipher, and another thing altogether to *teach* those things to children who knew next to nothing that one could build upon. He knew he could teach math, but more importantly, he wanted to teach them how to "be" in this world into which they had, without a choice, been born: How to assess the situations in which they find themselves with clear eyes and informed minds, to adapt to them, to master them, to proudly accept who they were, to walk through life with their heads up and their backs straight. Their education, as Johnny visualized it, would include letters and science, along with learning martial skills, not so they could beat up others for fun, but so that they could hold their ground, when necessary. So that they could make it costly for others to try to bully them. With such skills in place, they could better concentrate on learning to read, calculate with numbers, and make their ways in the world.

He hoped to inspire the first few cohorts of students to become teachers themselves. The first step would be to find and buy books and student supplies. With this vision in mind, Johnny left Independence for Uncle Dutch's ranch. He planned to stop there and contact his loved ones before taking a steamer to St. Louis, where he hoped to find places to buy the books and school supplies.

* * * * * * * * *

Three weeks later, Johnny arrived at his destination on the Canadian River. He went to Uncle Dutch's house, which at this point really was a house, not a log cabin. When he showed up at the door, Panther, who was now fourteen, greeted him: "Uncle Tenkiller! Welcome back!" He spoke these words, to Johnny's surprise and delight, in English. They hugged.

Johnny said, "I'm happy that you remember me, Panther. Where is your father?"

Panther looked down in silence, not knowing what to say.

Hummingbird, Panther's mother, showed up at this time. She said, speaking Cherokee, "Your uncle passed away last year."

Now it was Johnny's turn to look at the floor in a moment of silence. He felt as if a piece of his heart had been cut out.

Hummingbird said, "Come with me, I wish to show you something." She led him upstairs to a room and opened the door. The room had a bed but was otherwise empty, except for one corner. In that corner were whatever possessions Johnny had left behind when he went on his journey: The old Osage orangewood bow and quiver, which still had almost twenty arrows left in it; a pair of new moccasins; a bag that held the $200 he had left behind, and the precious pink tablecloth. He had left it behind because he feared losing or destroying it by carrying it in a saddle bag across several thousand miles of wilderness. In any case, he hadn't been expecting—or even wanting—to find the next love of his life on that journey. Among the arrows were a few that Uncle Dutch had helped him make when he was new to the west, over twenty years before.

Hummingbird said, "My husband used to climb the stairs every so often and come to this room, just to look at those things. He never said anything. He just looked at them in silence. He always said, 'Make sure that when Tenkiller returns, he knows he has a home here.' And it is your home. It always will be," said Hummingbird. "He loved you, Tenkiller. You were like a son to him."

"And he was the only father I ever knew," said Johnny, his eyes beginning to moisten with tears. "How did he pass?"

"Like all good men," said Hummingbird. "His death came quietly. He passed away with peace on his face. He reminded me, the last day he was alive, to welcome you if you ever came back here. And I do," she said, with a most benign expression on her pretty face. "Welcome home!"

Johnny took her hand, in the same manner as if she were a chief, and said, "Thank you, Auntie. It is good to be home."

The weather was tolerable for December. The sky was gray, but there was only a breeze, not a winter gale, and it didn't look like rain was imminent. Johnny said, "I'm going for a ride. I'll be back in a while."

Hummingbird said, "I am preparing a meal. When you get back, dinner will be waiting. I am going to invite Enoli for dinner as well. I know he would like to see you."

"I look forward to seeing Uncle Enoli, too!" said Johnny. "And tomorrow I plan to visit the Starrs."

As Johnny went outside to unload his pack horse, Hummingbird wondered if she should tell him…

Johnny unpacked his second horse and left his luggage behind the house. He tethered the unburdened pack horse to a nearby hitching post. Then he rode to the back of the settlement—the northside—where Sarah and the other women and girls had practiced with their rifles before the second engagement with the Comanches, fifteen years before. He kept riding until he was at the edge of the woods, by the tree from which Adsila, Sarah's childhood friend, had swung the target that Sarah never missed. He smiled at the remembrance of that.

As he rode, he remembered fearing that Dutch wouldn't be here when he returned. Now that he had returned, the news of Dutch's death was as new to him as if it had happened yesterday, not two years ago. His heart was heavy.

He sat cross-legged on the soft, golden grass, looking across the meadow that separated the village from the woods. The battlements, old and weather-beaten now, were still in place. He remembered the second engagement the best: the one in which Sarah had shot Ten Bears right between the eyes as the fearsome warrior made the last charge he would ever make. Then he remembered the time when Dutch, observing his archery practice, told him to stop thinking so hard about his aim. "Shoot from your center!" he had insisted.

Johnny, whose temples were just beginning to turn grey, reflected, with the wisdom that only age can confer: "As in archery, so in life." He looked skyward and exclaimed under his breath, "Thank you, Uncle Dutch!" And at that moment, his chin quivered, and his tears began to flow.

He considered singing his death song, but he just couldn't. Uncle Dutch had given him that, too. So, all alone, in the silence of a chilly winter afternoon, heartbroken, he mourned the loss of the finest man he had ever known.

* * * * * * * *

A few minutes later, he heard a soothing woman's voice behind him. "What's the matter, Johnny?"

He quickly and furtively wiped away his tears and stood up. He turned around. He smiled broadly, trying to hide his sorrow. He exclaimed, "Hi Sarah! I was just thinkin' about you!" They hugged.

"Why didn't you come see us as soon as you got back? You're makin' me feel kind of unimportant," complained Sarah, though the complaint was just a ritual one. "You probably just found out about your uncle, I reckon."

Solemnly, Johnny said, "Yes, Hummingbird told me."

"You men have a pretty hard time dealin' with your emotions, don't you? But there's nothin' wrong with sheddin' tears when they mean somethin'—like yours do, right now. And I know they must mean a lot…A lot," she said, looking straight into his eyes and repeating herself for emphasis.

Until Sarah showed up, Johnny had felt a great, dark void in his heart. He had felt it when he left Ahyoka at Wohali's hamlet. He had felt it when his Ahyoka had passed away in Tahlequah ten years ago. He had felt it when his grandmother passed away a few years after that. But when Sarah arrived, the void in his heart was, for the moment, filled. Her presence warmed him. At this moment she was the only person he could think of who could comfort him, who might pull him from the abyss of grief into which he had fallen.

Wanting to change the subject, he said "I was gonna come to your place and visit as soon as I got settled in here. But right now, I was wishin' I'd been here for my uncle in his last days." Then he asked, "How's Billy?"

Sarah replied, "You're not the only one who's suffered loss in the last couple o' years, Johnny. He got scarlet fever two years after you left, the same year as your Uncle Dutch died. It killed him."

"Oh, Sarah, I'm so sorry," said Johnny. He meant it. He and Billy had become close friends.

"He was always grateful for the help you gave us while we were learnin' that business. Remember how you taught us to do division so we could figure averages? From that schoolbook you'd been carryin' around for God knows how long?"

"I do," said Johnny, with a hint of enthusiasm.

"Well, you might also be happy to know that our daughter, Adsila, went through that whole book while you were gone and now, she knows how to do division and everything else in it." Beaming pridefully, Sarah added, "And she's been a real help in the store."

Johnny said, "I remember how when she was about seven, when she used to come by the smithy and bother me, I used to tell her things like 'You think you're pretty clever, don't you?' And do you know what she always said to me after I said that? She said, 'I *am* clever, Uncle Johnny!'" Both Sarah and Johnny laughed. "I reckon she's proved that. Did she go through that whole book by herself?"

"I helped her some," said Sarah. "But she's got a knack for numbers. She did most of it herself. She is real smart…but she's still learnin' to be modest."

Johnny laughed. "The important thing is that she learned to do math. Life will teach her to be modest. I just hope the lessons ain't too hard on her. Where did she learn to read?"

"In Sunday school," replied Sarah. Changing the subject, she asked, "How'd you like to join us for dinner tomorrow night?"

Johnny, replying quickly, said, "I'd love to. Can you cook as good as you can shoot yet?"

"Well, last time you asked me that question, I said I could cook about half as good as I can shoot. Now, maybe I'm three quarters as good."

"Then I really can't wait to come over for dinner," said Johnny.

He didn't know it yet, but the big white house next to Dutch's big white house belonged to Sarah and Billy. They had it built the year after Johnny left on his journey. So, when Johnny arrived at Uncle Dutch's house, Sarah saw right away that he had come home. She had watched him unload his pack horse and ride to the northside. Then, she saddled up her own horse and rode out there to greet him. It was a special place for her for the same reason as it had been special for him. She remembered the swinging target and suspected that Johnny had remembered it as well.

It wasn't until they had ridden back to Dutch's house, and he saw her ride to the big house next door that he realized that she no longer lived in a cabin. "Hey Sarah!" he shouted as he saw her dismount by the front door, "I didn't know we were gonna be next-door neighbors."

"There's a whole lot o' things you don't know yet, Tenkiller." She beamed a big smile and shouted, "See you tomorrow at dinnertime!"

* * * * * * * * *

That evening, after he had bathed, Johnny sat at the dinner table with Hummingbird, her son Panther, and Enoli, whom she had invited to welcome Johnny home. They were curious about Johnny's doings for the past four years. Johnny, for his part, didn't know where to begin, or how much he should tell. He decided to tell them about the Pacific Ocean, the Hawaiians he had met while overlooking its vastness, and the brawl they had had with the Irishmen.

Panther was curious about the giant Hawaiian warrior, Nalua, and how he had set the broken forearm of one of the casualties of that fight. He also wanted to know about their style of fighting. Johnny shared what he knew about it.

Panther asked, "What happened to Nalua after that?"

Johnny replied, "We had a fight with some claim jumpers. He was killed. But he killed two of them with a staff before a third one shot him in the chest."

"That's kinda sad, Uncle," said Panther. "How many did you kill?"

Hummingbird, who understood English but was not fluent when it came to speaking it, protested, "Don't ask your uncle that while we eating dinner."

Johnny, grateful that Hummingbird had intervened, said, "Your mother's right, Panther, we shouldn't speak of this over dinner. But I'll answer your question without the details: I killed three of them with my pistols. But like your father once said, there's no honor in killin' with revolvers."

Panther, whose admiration was obvious, did not comment.

Johnny, wanting to change the subject said, "Panther, your English is real good."

Panther replied, "My father made me speak it as much as possible. He felt I needed to know both languages: Cherokee and English."

"Your father was wise, Panther. Can you read yet?"

"I can read and write Cherokee, using our system. I learned to read the English Bible from my Sunday school teacher," he said. "It don't come easy, though."

"That's a good start. I'm gonna take a trip pretty soon and bring back a lot of books for you and any other young ones who want to learn to read, write, and cipher. I'm gonna open up a school here."

Panther was silent. Johnny was concerned. He didn't seem too excited about the prospect of going to school. Momentarily taken aback by what he perceived as disinterest, Johnny wondered if his school would have any students at all.

Enoli, whose hair was now as white as snow, had apparently read Johnny's mind and noticed the shadow that had passed over his countenance and darkened his mood. He said in Cherokee, "I'm sure there will be children and young people who will be interested in learning to 'read, write, and cipher'." He said the last three words in English.

"I sure hope so," said Johnny.

Enoli continued to speak. "When you're settled in, Johnny, your Uncle Dutch wanted me to tell you about his last will and testament."

Johnny nodded. "How about tomorrow morning?"

* * * * * * * * *

The next morning, Enoli came to the house that Johnny now called home. Johnny boiled some water and made them coffee. They sat out on the front porch. They dressed warmly, as it was almost winter, and sat in silence as they took their first sips.

Enoli, speaking in Cherokee, began, "Dutch wanted you to take over this household, run the ranch, and take care of Hummingbird and Panther until Panther was grown into manhood. Even then, you would still have the responsibility and the right to oversee things here. At some point—perhaps when it is your turn to go to the Great Spirit—Panther would take over completely. But as long as you are alive, this place belongs to you. Dutch believed that you would be fair to his widow and son."

Johnny replied, "I will do as my uncle has asked. Do I need to be involved in politics, as he was?"

Enoli said, "When Dutch died, the people here elected me to be his replacement on the tribal council. So, you will not need to involve yourself in politics until such time as you feel pulled to do so. Or until I die," said Enoli.

"Well, Uncle, I hope that is not for a long, long time," said Johnny. "Since the assassination of the Ridges, I have not wished to be involved in tribal politics at all."

"I cannot blame you for that, Tenkiller," affirmed Enoli. "But we do not know what the future holds. There may come a time…"

Johnny, interrupting Enoli, repeated, "I hope that it is a long time away."

Enoli had hoped that Johnny would be more receptive to the idea that he would represent the Canadian River section of the Cherokee Nation in the tribal council. Because of his reputation as a leader, an accomplished warrior, and a businessman, Johnny had earned a great deal of respect in the tribe—at least among those who had known him. But Enoli could see that Johnny was uneasy about the prospect of inheriting his uncle's responsibility as chief.

He asked Johnny outright, "Do you not wish to follow in the footsteps of your uncle?"

Johnny, always forthright, said, "It's not that I do not want to. It's that I have another calling that beckons me, right now. I am thinking about the next generations of our people. I want to help educate them."

Enoli, believing that this goal would eventually lead Johnny into politics regardless of his own wishes, let the matter drop. The Great Spirit, he postulated, would take care of it, in due course.

"How do you plan to do that?" asked Enoli.

"I have some money. Enough to buy textbooks for a couple dozen students in all the main classes: History, literature, and mathematics. I can also pay for the building of a schoolhouse and for chalkboards, chalk, pencils, and paper. And to hire an elementary school teacher. I plan to go to St. Louis this coming March to look for these things. I will travel by steamer and bring them back here. I'll get the schoolhouse started before I leave. I'm not sure yet how or where I will find a teacher, though."

Enoli wondered how Johnny could afford to do these things. He knit his brows for a moment and then asked, "Did you find gold in California?"

"In a manner of speaking," said Johnny. "But I didn't pan or dig for it. I got it through other means."

Enoli smiled faintly. "Did those 'other means' involve killing anyone?"

Johnny was not offended by the intrusive questioning. After all, Enoli had taught Johnny the use of hand-to-hand combat weapons in his youth. He was the one who had made Johnny's sling club when he was still finding his way on the warrior's path. He had the right to ask.

So, he answered directly and honestly. "Yes, Uncle, it did." Then he told of his Hawaiian friends and the claim-jumpers, providing the backstory of the three kills he had admitted to during dinner, the night before.

"So how many did that make?" asked Enoli.

"Those three made sixteen. But a couple of days after, I killed again." Johnny narrated that episode as well. He grinned as he concluded, "And I scalped the sonofabitch, too! He needed it."

Enoli, on hearing about the scalping, laughed. "I thought you were too civilized to do that, especially after all these years. So, by my count, you've killed seventeen and scalped three. Those would have been good credentials, back when we were 'wild' Indians. Enough to make you a chief!"

"I guess," said Johnny. "But to tell you the truth, Uncle, if I never killed another man, I would feel fine about it."

Enoli knew that it was likely that Johnny would kill again. He knew that a serious conflict, in which slavery was the key issue, was brewing in the United States. There were pro- and anti-slavery factions among the Cherokee and the other civilized tribes in Indian Territory. He feared that, if an American civil war broke out, it would involve them, and that their internal tribal politics would somehow get mixed up in it. Beyond robberies and assassinations, tribes might be divided from within by taking sides with the belligerents. There would be battles with large groups on each side. There would be death. And if it turned out this way, he believed that Johnny would most likely be involved.

Rather than sharing these dark thoughts, Enoli just said, "Well, let us hope you never need to kill anyone else." Changing the subject to Johnny's planned trip to St. Louis, he asked, "When do you think you will be back?"

"If I leave in March and find all the things I want in St. Louis, I should be back in May," replied Johnny.

Enoli, unwilling to let the matter of Johnny's participation in tribal leadership drop, said, "There will come a time, Tenkiller, when you will have to get involved with politics. But for now, I support your plan.

Educating our children should be a priority. And do not forget to teach the boys the warrior's way," admonished Enoli.

"I surely will not forget that, Uncle," said Johnny.

They sat in silence for several minutes after this exchange, finishing their coffees.

They both stood up.

Johnny said, as he took Enoli's hand in a gesture of respect, "Thank you, Uncle Enoli, for letting me know my uncle's will. I promise to take care of his widow, his son, and his legacy."

As he walked back to his own house, Enoli thought, "This man does not know it yet, but he is a chief."

* * * * * * * *

That evening, Johnny bathed, dressed in clean clothes, and walked to the house next door, the house that Billy and Sarah built with the money they had saved from running the store. He was greeted at the door by Adsila, who was now going on twelve years of age. She was well-groomed, poised, and graceful in her movements. Her facial features resembled those of her mother, but she had black hair and slate grey eyes, like her father. She was striking…sure to become a beautiful woman, he thought.

"Welcome home, Uncle Johnny!" she said, standing back from the door she had just opened, giving him room to enter. She led him to the dining room. There he was greeted by Sarah, who was wearing a black dress. Her hair, no longer the sandy brown it had been in her youth, had darkened with age. It was long, hung to her waist, and was immaculately coiffured. It glistened in the light of the oil lamps that lit the dining room. Her sandy brown eyes hadn't changed. They looked almost golden, making a dazzling contrast with her long, shiny, very dark brown hair. They reminded him of the golden sagebrush-covered foothills of the eastern Sierras. Sarah, the woman warrior, had become beautiful and elegant in her maturity.

"Thank you for inviting me to your home, ladies," said Johnny. Though he kept his composure, something about Sarah made his heart jump into his throat. He struggled not to stare at her.

Meanwhile, Billy Jr., who was now four years old, walked into the dining room. "Welcome, Uncle Johnny!"

Johnny smiled, "Well, look who's all grown up!"

Junior's chest swelled with pride.

"Let's all sit down and have dinner now," directed Sarah. She called out to her maids in Cherokee, "Ruth and Esther, can you bring in our dinner now, please?" The tone of her voice was gentle and kind.

Johnny approved of the way she treated her helpers. Noting that they had English names, he figured they probably went to church. They looked like full bloods in their teens and probably could have done much worse than having Sarah Starr for a boss.

"The girls helped me make the dinner," said Sarah, "but I was the head cook, Johnny." She smiled broadly, hoping that she had made the point that she really *could* cook.

Johnny said, "Well, I am hungry enough to eat a horse. And I'm lookin' forward to tastin' your cookin'."

So, he dined with the Starr family. Silently, he grieved over Billy. Silently, he felt uncomfortable about his inner reactions to Sarah, whom he had placed, up until a few moments ago, in an "untouchable" category, since he regarded Billy as a brother.

Sarah and her children were full of curiosity about Johnny's trip across the continent, about the Pacific Ocean, and about his experiences in California. He shared as much as he could without talking about the violence he had encountered and the kills he had added to his list.

As he walked back to his house, he reflected on Sarah's beauty that night. It was all he could think about, other than that she had become an excellent cook.

It had been ten years since his Ahyoka had passed away. He remembered the promise that Ahyoka had secured from him a month before she died. It involved that pink tablecloth. She had said,

"Please keep it with you as a remembrance of me and the love we have shared. And if your path should lead you to another person for whom you might feel a great love, I wish for you to use it when you dine with her."

At the time, Johnny could not even conceive of loving another woman as he had loved Ahyoka. Now, despite his inner conflicts, he wondered…could Sarah be the one?

* * * * * * * * *

For the next three months, Johnny planned the construction of the schoolhouse he planned to build. He drew blueprints. He found a carpenter, and together, they developed the blueprints further and made a list of building materials. Some would require timber from local sources, and some could be purchased. Regarding those that could be bought, he worked with Sarah. He was happy that Sarah was interested and that, as the seasoned owner of a general store, she knew where to get things and how to haggle over prices.

More than this, he was happy that his project gave him reasons to talk with Sarah several times a week. The thought of seeing her on those occasions made him jump out of bed to get his day started. When he visited her store to discuss getting the things needed for the schoolhouse, his breathing became shallow at the very sight of her. He could hardly think, it seemed, when he was near her.

Years before, his love for Ahyoka had made him forget his attraction to Sarah, which had arisen before he expected Ahyoka to reappear in his life. And then, when he and Billy became friends, he placed Sarah on his "untouchable" list. Because he loved Billy like a brother, Sarah became, in effect, his sister-in-law. And now he was falling in love with her. It just didn't feel right to him.

In early March, when Johnny was about to leave for St. Louis, he visited the store in the middle of the afternoon. Sarah was updating her records when he showed up.

"Hi, Johnny, what brings you here?" asked Sarah.

Johnny replied, "Nothin', really, except wantin' to visit with you. And I plan to leave tomorrow for the Arkansas River. Thought I'd spend a little time with you before I left. I was wonderin' if you might want to go to the northside and sit a spell. It's a nice day."

Sarah needed no persuasion. She said, "Sure, Johnny. I'm almost finished workin'. When I'm done, let me grab a few things to eat, and maybe we can just have a picnic. What d'you think of that?" She smiled and looked Johnny straight in the eye with those bright, sandy brown eyes of hers. Johnny felt a tickling sensation in his solar plexus. His knees were beginning to shake again.

He said, "That sounds real good, Sarah. Let me go back to the house and grab a couple of things, too."

So, Johnny went back to Uncle Dutch's house and asked Hummingbird if she had some corn-and-bean cakes he could take for a picnic.

Hummingbird looked at him and smiled. "Are you having this picnic by yourself, or will you be taking company?" Of course, she knew…

Johnny said, "Sarah will be joining me."

Hummingbird said, "It is about time. Why have you taken so long?"

Johnny replied, "What do you mean?"

"Your feelings for her are obvious. But it seems that something is holding you back," responded Hummingbird. "I think I know what it is, but may I ask *you* what it is?"

"Billy was like a brother to me, Auntie," said Johnny. "That meant that I had to see Sarah as a sister-in-law, not as someone to…you know."

As she wrapped some corn-and-bean cakes into a cloth napkin, Hummingbird paused thoughtfully. Then she said, "Tenkiller, hear me. In the days of old, when a warrior fell in battle, leaving his wife and children behind, one of his brothers would take his widow for a wife. Even if he already had a wife." She looked Johnny in the eye and smiled. "The good thing is that you do not have to deal with *two* wives. That has probably not been easy since the beginning of time."

Johnny said, "So, are you suggesting that it would be proper for me to take Sarah as my wife? If she was willing, of course."

Hummingbird almost laughed. "Tenkiller, though no one talks about it—it would be rude to do so—everyone here knows that Sarah was in love with you since back in the days when we fought the Comanches. Everyone knows that when Billy was drinking, he beat her because he knew she loved you. When you chose to become Billy's friend, and he chose to quit drinking, everyone here noticed and admired both of you for that. Now Billy is with the Great Spirit. I doubt that he would want Sarah and the children to be alone in this world." She concluded, "Do you really think he would object to you protecting his family, now that he is gone?"

"Given the way she can shoot, I doubt that Sarah needs anyone's protection but her own." He grinned.

"That was not my point," said Hummingbird, with a note of exasperation.

Johnny thought about it. He said, "Auntie, I meant no disrespect. The truth is that I have not heard such wisdom since my grandmother passed away." With gratitude in his heart, he said, "Thank you."

Immediately, he ran upstairs and pulled out the ancient pink tablecloth he had carried with him since leaving Pittsburg. It was still in good shape, with no holes or loose threads. He shook it out and folded it neatly. As he did so, he remembered with fondness Ahyoka's wish that he would keep it and use it one day, should he ever find someone else to love. She feared that he would bury it with her and lose it forever.

Back then, as now, he was overwhelmed by Ahyoka's generosity of spirit. The face of sweet Ahyoka came into his mind as he remembered the moment back in 1839, as they rode from Tahlequah to Fort Gibson to see Dr. Winston, when she asked him to make that promise. Now, there was someone about to take her place in his life, but he felt that Ahyoka would always be with him, too. He resolved to share the story of that tablecloth with Sarah, one day. He was certain that she would understand.

When he went downstairs, Hummingbird had a basket ready for him, with corn-and-bean cakes, berries, and some venison from a deer that Panther, who was a skilled hunter, had killed, cleaned, and smoked a few days before.

"My goodness, Auntie, there are only the two of us," declared Johnny.

"What you don't eat, you can bring home," said Hummingbird.

So, Johnny took the basket and the tablecloth, saddled up, and rode next door.

Sarah had already saddled up and had a basket of her own. They rode to the outskirts of the settlement—the northside—to their special place in the woods. Though the breeze still carried the sting of winter, the grass was thick, green, and lush. Purple and yellow flowers were beginning to explode into their spring bloom, and the bluebirds were singing a spring serenade. Because it was still rather cold, there were no mosquitoes to be seen. A perfect early spring day, if ever there was one.

Johnny and Sarah dismounted at the same time in a clearing near the edge of the woods. He tethered his horse to a birch, took the pink tablecloth from his saddle bag, walked to the center of the clearing, and spread it out. Then he fetched his basket. Sarah brought hers, too. They placed them on the tablecloth and sat down, cross-legged in the thick, soft grass, but hesitated to begin dining. Sarah wondered about that pink tablecloth but didn't ask about it. She figured there was a narrative behind it and would hear it in due course.

Meanwhile Johnny, not usually one to have trouble finding words, couldn't bring himself to speak about the feelings that were in his heart.

Sarah, noticing that he was tongue-tied, said, "Let me help you out a little bit, Tenkiller." They looked at each other, their eyes glazed with passion. "I know what's eatin' you."

"I think you *do* know," said Johnny.

"If Billy was floatin' around here in the spirit, lookin' at us, do you really think he would disapprove?"

Johnny said, "I hope not."

Sarah shook her head. Then she said, "Come closer, Johnny."

Johnny obliged. Then he took the initiative. He held her hand, stood up, and she followed suit. Then they hugged, looked into one another's eyes, and engaged in a lingering, passionate kiss. It was a kiss that Johnny wished would last forever. His heart pounded so hard and so fast he feared it might burst out of his chest. His knees shook. He felt as if his feet had left the ground.

When they finished their kiss, Sarah said, with misty eyes, "I've been waitin' for that moment for half of my life, Johnny Tenkiller. I love you. I have always loved you."

"But didn't you love Billy, too?" he asked.

Sarah said, "I came to love him, especially when he changed. I tried not to think about you or the feelings I had for you. Billy and me made a good team. We built a life. And I did grieve for him when he died. I got over it by concentratin' on runnin' our store. I tried not to think about anything else 'cept takin' care of Adsila and Billy Junior.

"I had no idea as to when you might ever come back, or even if you *would* come back, but I resolved to wait for you. You probably have no idea how excited I was when I saw you get here last December."

"I think I do have an idea about that," said Johnny. "Every time I see you, every time I hear your voice, I feel…" He decided not to finish the sentence. Instead, he went straight to the point: "Sarah, I love you, too. And I always will."

As he said these words, he realized that Ahyoka would be happy for him. That was why she had secured his promise to keep the pink tablecloth. For just this moment, should it ever come to pass…

After another long, lingering kiss, they sat down again, though now they were holding hands. Johnny said, "I can't believe this is happening. I've never felt happier in my life."

Sarah just looked at Johnny and smiled.

He continued, "Will you marry me?"

Sarah said, "Of course I will."

They kissed again. Then, Johnny said, "I can't wait 'til the first time…"

Sarah, with an inviting smile, asked, "What are you waitin' for then?"

Johnny stood up and went to his horse. He took the bedroll off his saddle and a blanket out of his saddle bag. He looked at Sarah and said, "I hope you don't think I was bein' too presumptuous."

* * * * * * * *

About an hour later, Sarah and Johnny got around to dining on the food they had brought for their picnic. Then, they rode their horses back to their homes, their eyes glazed with the bliss of deep, fully requited love. They rode side by side until they reached the middle ground between their houses. When they parted company, their gazes lingered on one another.

Looking back at Johnny as they rode away from each other, Sarah gave him a little finger wave and said, "I'll be over tomorrow mornin' to see you off."

* * * * * * * * *

Back at Dutch's house, as he unsaddled his horse, Johnny recalled the words his grandmother had said to him on the day she gave her approval to his relationship with Ahyoka:

"You might be too young to understand what I am about to say, but hear this anyway: In life, you will only have this once, maybe twice if you are fortunate and live long enough. Rejoice in it. That is what I wish for you."

Feeling as if his heart was connected to Sarah's and already missing her, he wondered, "Is this that second time?"

It was a rhetorical question.

His heart knew.

Chapter 30: Tenkiller's Truth

Johnny went to St. Louis. He stayed for a month, and with some difficulties, he found the books and supplies he was looking for.

In one of these bookstores, as he shopped for elementary school primers in reading, he saw a darkhaired woman browsing in the same section as he. She appeared to be in her thirties. She had a pleasant aura about her. In fact, in his judgment, she looked like she might be a schoolteacher. His curiosity aroused, he decided to approach her.

"Excuse me, ma'am," he began. "I hope I'm not bein' too presumptuous, but I was wonderin' if you might be a schoolteacher."

The woman replied, "Yes, sir. I am."

Johnny, gratified that he had made an accurate guess, continued. "I'm openin' a school for Cherokee children in Indian Territory. That's why I'm here in St. Louis. I'm buyin' books and supplies for the school. Though I have a bit of education myself, I'm aware that it's one thing to know the kind of things I hope our children will learn, and another thing to *teach* those things. I'm sure there are folks who would be better at that than I am. Anyways, I might be able to benefit from your knowledge of these matters." Then he showed her an armload of books he had picked off the shelves. "Do you think these will do for teachin' young kids the basics of readin' and writin'?"

Thoughtfully, she looked over the books he had chosen for this purpose. There were seven of them. She took several minutes to do so. She opened each of them, viewed the tables of contents, and then randomly thumbed through their pages. At length, she said, "I like all of them except for these two beginners' books." She took two potential replacements off the shelves and said, "These would be better."

Without asking why, Johnny thumbed through the pages of her recommended textbooks. He saw that they were clearer and moved more slowly than did his first choices; proof that there were, indeed, people in the world whose wisdom in such matters exceeded his.

He introduced himself. "My name is Johnny Sullivan."

"Pleased to meet you," she responded. "My name is Molly. Molly Johnson."

The fact that her name was "Molly" moved Johnny. He said, "I knew a 'Molly' once upon a time. She went to the same missionary school as I did. She could walk across a room balancing a book on her head without it fallin' off."

"I learned to do that, too!" said Molly Johnson. "I guess it's part of how Christians train young ladies to be ladies. Especially young *Indian* ladies." She smiled. She wondered who this other "Molly" was to Johnny. But she made no further comment about it.

"I'm Cherokee," said Johnny. "Are you Indian?"

"I am," said Molly. "My people are the Haudenosaunee[§§§]. But like you, I am of mixed blood."

"How do you know I am of mixed blood?" asked Johnny.

"Your Irish surname and those green eyes kind of gave it away," said Molly, who almost laughed.

"So, you're sayin' I could get away with claimin' to be 'black Irish'?" quipped Johnny.

Molly laughed. "Other than those eyes, you pretty much look like an Indian," replied Molly. "Did you ever try to get by as 'black Irish'?"

"Well, when I got my first 'white man' haircut, a Quaker gentleman said to me, 'Why Johnny, you're starting to look like one of us!'"

They both laughed.

Johnny said, "The black Irish thing has kinda been a joke since my uncle brought it up the day we met. He noticed my green eyes, too. But I've never thought I would, or even that I could, pass for black Irish. Truth is, I've always been proud to be what I am. A Cherokee Indian…May I ask to which of the Six Nations you belong?"

"One of the ones your people used to fight with," said Molly with a smile. "The Mohawks."

[§§§] "Haudenosaunee" is what they call themselves. The Americans know them as the "Six Nations"; also as the Iroquois. The Six Nations include the Cayuga, Mohawk, Onondaga, Oneida, Seneca, and Tuscarora.

"But we're friends now, aren't we?" asked Johnny, with an unmistakable air of joviality.

"Actually, we have no choice at this point, do we?" Molly expressed this more as a comment than as a question.

Johnny, hoping he might have found the teacher he was looking for, asked "Do you plan to go back to New York or wherever your people live these days? Or do you have a different destination in mind?"

Molly paused, as if to gather her thoughts, before answering. Then she said, "Two months ago, my husband passed away. He was much older than I, and we had no children. He was a schoolteacher like me. A good, generous man. He was wealthy—for an Indian—and like me, a mixed-blood. He was descended from Sir William Johnson[****], the great British Indian agent.

"One morning, about a month ago and a month after he passed, I woke up and realized that my life had lost its meaning. I mean, I love to teach, but there are enough teachers where I lived. I wanted to do something of significance, something that would really make a difference. I've read about the forced removal of your people and the other civilized tribes from the Southeast. I know they have suffered terribly. So, I am on my way to the Indian Territory."

Johnny's interest in Molly intensified. Perhaps she was the teacher he was looking for. He asked, "Have you plans as to where to go, once you're in Indian Territory?"

Molly said, "I plan to go first to Fort Gibson."

Johnny said, "Our ranch is about two days south of Fort Gibson. I'm buildin' a school there. There are Seneca in Indian Territory. Have you made any commitments to them?" The Seneca were Haudenosaunee, so it was a reasonable question for Johnny to ask.

"I haven't made any commitments at all, at this point, except to myself. I want to teach wherever it will do the most good," replied Molly.

[****] Sir William Johnson was a real historical personage from the 18th century, not to be confused with the fictional Quaker gentleman, William Johnson, encountered earlier in this book.

"Would you like to teach Cherokee children?" asked Johnny. "I can pay you well and can offer you a place to stay until we build you a house." The words just came pouring forth. Johnny did not really think before he spoke, but his intuition compelled him to make the offer.

Molly said, "Thank you, Johnny, for your gracious offer, but I'll need to think about this for a while."

"That's fine, Molly. I'll pay your fare on the steamers we'll take to get from here to Indian Territory. We'll have plenty of time to discuss things. And if you choose otherwise, I will still be grateful to you for helpin' me pick the right books for the children."

Molly replied, "I am grateful for your charitable offer, Johnny. But I have my own means. I'll pay my own way."

"Suit yourself," said Johnny. "We can still be traveling companions, if you wish."

"I don't see why not," said Molly.

* * * * * * * * *

As they rode the steamer from St. Louis to the confluence of the Arkansas River and the Mississippi, Molly and Johnny had time to discuss what each of them hoped to do with their lives. Like Johnny, Molly hoped to teach Indian children to navigate two worlds: The one that would confront them as they grew up and the one Johnny and Molly hoped wouldn't be altogether swept away. The one in which they would still maintain their identities as Cherokee, or Seneca, or Mohawk, or Chickasaw, or whatever other nation they came from.

Molly must have been moved by Johnny's narrative, because by the time they reached the confluence of the Arkansas and the Mississippi, she had accepted his offer. Johnny was sure he could offer her lodging in Uncle Dutch's house while a small house was built for her next to the school, which, in turn, was near the complex where the homes of the Starrs and Uncle Dutch stood. Molly said she could pay for the house. She had resources. So, Johnny, who had considered offering her $35 a month plus lodging for her services, raised the offer to $45 a month plus meals. Molly said she could provide her own meals, though she would be pleased to show up as a dinner guest at Johnny's residence. They shook hands to close the deal. Johnny's dream of opening a school was about to become real.

* * * * * * * * *

Three years later, in 1853, the school had fifteen students—four girls and eleven boys. The oldest three boys, who were between eleven and twelve years of age, were ready to begin their warrior training.

Johnny reminded them, as he had many times before: "To receive this training, first you need to do your homework. No homework, no teaching you to fight. Understood?"

"Yes, Mr. Sullivan!" the boys said in unison.

One of these boys, David Shackleford, was especially bright. He inherited his English surname from one of his grandfathers. Otherwise, like Johnny, he was three quarters Cherokee. He was twelve years old and a tall boy for his age, with long black hair and eyes that were almost as black as those of Uncle Dutch. He had been attending school for four years. Though he had a late start, he was diligent. He studied at home after school. And he was especially talented when it came to numbers.

While Johnny loved all the students, he had taken a special interest in David, who soaked up mathematics like a dry rag soaks up water. The problem was that he was less interested in reading.

Johnny, who had high hopes for this boy, told the boys about "shooting from one's center" when instructing them in archery. When the other boys dispersed after practice, David lingered. He asked, "What does that mean, Mr. Sullivan? I still don't understand."

Johnny took a moment to gather his thoughts. He took the notion of "shooting from one's center" for granted. It was obvious to him. Not so, he realized, to a bunch of half-grown boys.

He said, "My uncle taught me about it when I was about your age, when teaching me the use of the bow and arrow. He said, 'As you shoot, stop thinking, imagine that your mind is not in your head, but instead is somewhere between your heart and your belly. Relax your eyes—don't squint—look at the target, draw the arrow and let it fly. It will go right where it needs to go. Like it has a mind of its own.'"

"With respect, Mr. Sullivan, I heard you say that the first time. But I still don't really understand," admitted David.

Once again, Johnny had to search for words. At length, he said, "Before you can shoot from your center, you must *have* a center. That means that you have to learn the basics of something first, and then you need to practice—over and over again. In between practices, you think about it, looking for ways to improve, looking for the 'art' in it.

"Once you master the moves, the 'how-to' part of what you're doin', you might notice, after a while, that something inside you seems to know what *it* wants to do. And if you try to force it to do otherwise, it'll fight you. Try lettin' it have its way. If the results are good, you have likely found your 'center' for that activity. If not, don't run away from it. Struggle with it. Eventually, it will come into being, like a newborn child, and take on a life of its own." Johnny paused for effect, then added, "And as in archery," concluded Johnny, "so in life."

He paused again, beginning to doubt his ability to make the point about shooting from one's center. He added, "David, in math, you're already shootin' from your center. You already have a math 'center'. Now you just have to develop a 'readin' center'."

David said, "I like to work with numbers. Readin' don't come so easy to me."

"If you struggle with it for a while, it'll come easier to you. Just because somethin' is hard at first don't mean you don't have a gift for it. And even if you don't have a gift for it, you can still become *good* at it. Don't fear it. *Overcome it*. That is the warrior's way."

After a brief pause, Johnny added, "And by the way, David, bein' a warrior don't necessarily mean killin' folks. Remember that, too."

* * * * * * * * *

That same year, in August, Johnny and Sarah had a baby boy. They named him "Johnny". Johnny hadn't wanted to choose this name, but Sarah insisted. They didn't bother with a Cherokee middle name. If he were to have one, he would have to earn it himself.

One evening, when the baby was a few weeks old, they sat out on the front porch of the house Billy and Sarah had built years before, enjoying the cool evening air of summer turning to fall. Johnny had kept his own room in Uncle Dutch's house. He just couldn't bring himself to move into the other house and sleep in the same room as Billy had.

Sarah held their baby boy, swaddled in a blanket. They sat in silence, as they often did, communicating their love without the aid or artifice of the spoken word.

Johnny calculated the time since the Stricklin vendetta had been completed. Twenty years. It seemed more like two hundred years. During that time, he had done pretty much as he pleased. His path seemed broad, and the options it presented seemed boundless. Now, with little Johnny, Adsila, Billy Jr., Sarah, and the school, he realized that his path had narrowed considerably. There were boundaries now. But with those boundaries came the clearest purpose he had had since fulfilling the vendetta against the Stricklins. Along with that clear purpose and those boundaries, strangely, had come a sense of freedom. But more importantly, with that clear purpose came something he had always secretly craved: A sense that, at last, he had found a home, a place from which his path did not beckon him to go forth—in search of what, he never quite knew. Until now.

"Sarah, I've been thinking," he began. "I realize that I've found somethin' that I always wanted, but never thought I'd have."

"What would that be?" asked Sarah.

Johnny continued: "Ever since I was about ten years old, I had a vision about us and all the other Indians. I believed we could find a third path that straddled the options of physical extermination, on the one hand, and bein' absorbed as second-class citizens, if even that, into the world of the whites. It would be a path where the Indian could survive, walk with his back straight and head up, and preserve the worthiest elements of his tribal heritage, whether it be Cherokee or whatever other nation he belonged to. At first, I thought it would involve killin' sonofabitches that needed killin'—especially white sonofabitches. Then I kept runnin' into white people that I liked and admired. And all that time I spent on the trail gave me a chance to reflect on things. I came to see that we're all really the same when you think about it.

"Buildin' this school and havin' students who wanted to learn—I wish there were more of 'em but I'm happy with the ones we have—was my way of tryin' to make that vision I had as a ten-year-old come to life. I feel it's the worthiest thing I could do in this world. Better than killin' folks that in my view needed killin'. I know it's small, when you put it into the grand scheme of things, but to me, it's worth doin'." He paused, seemingly in search of words to complete his thoughts.

Breaking into the pause, Sarah said, "Looks to me like you've set a fine example in the way you've lived your own life, Johnny Tenkiller." She looked him in the eye as she said these words, momentarily breaking his concentration, as was usually the case when she looked him in the eye.

Recovering his focus, he said, "I guess what I was tryin' to say is that I had always secretly hoped for a home. A real home. Permanence. A worthy purpose. The school. You and the kids. I just didn't know it. But it must have been buried in my heart, in a secret place, somewhere inside me."

Sarah did not comment. She sensed that Johnny had more to say.

"I now realize that my heart had a destination all along. It wasn't clear to me at all, but it was there. I remember the insight I had when I traveled from Cahokia to Fort Gibson, twenty years ago. A voice within me said, *'God hears the prayers of our hearts, but doesn't pay much attention to the prattling of our minds.'* And now, I realize that He has answered my prayers. The ones that came from my heart, even though I spent hardly any time thinkin' about 'em. I don't think *I* even knew what they were. But they were there."

Johnny stopped speaking. He looked upwards and sent up a silent prayer of gratitude. Then he added, "And now I'm here."

Sarah leaned over and kissed Johnny on the cheek. She said, "And I'm sure glad."

Then it came to him. "Did I ever tell you about the day I left the Quaker house in Pittsburgh, how that gentleman, William Johnson prayed for me?"

Sarah said, "I don't recall."

Johnny said, "Well, I haven't thought about it much since then, but when it happened, I felt this strange energy running from the top of my head to the soles of my feet. And when Mr. Johnson was done, I asked him what he had prayed for. He said something like, 'I prayed that one day you would find your truth.' I didn't know what he meant. What the hell did I know? I was only twenty at the time. But I suspected that my friend, Isaac MacDermott—the man who worked in wood—had found his. I didn't think it would take me twenty more years to find it, or to recognize it if I ever did find it. But now, I think maybe I have."

"Well, that makes me feel comfortable," said Sarah. "I hope that means you won't go skippin' off to the four corners of the world, followin' that 'path' of yours."

Johnny reached over and grabbed Sarah's hand. "Don't worry about that. My path led me *here*. Here is where my truth is."

* * * * * * * *

One morning, a few days later, Sarah and Johnny sat on the front porch of Sarah's residence, sipping their morning coffee. Panther showed up and greeted them. Now, going on eighteen, he was practically grown. Tall, broad-shouldered, and handsome, he was truly the son of Uncle Dutch.

Panther had recently acquired a Colt Paterson. He said, "Uncle Tenkiller, I've been practicing shooting this thing. Want to join me for some target practice?"

Something about Panther's demeanor—was it a smirk? —caught Johnny's attention. Was he just asking his uncle to join him in a friendly activity? Or was he challenging him?

Johnny said, "Sure, let's go to the northside. I'll get my pistols. Haven't practiced for a while, but I'm sure it'll come back to me."

Panther said, "I just went to Fort Gibson and bought a load of caps and balls. I'll provide if you need some." He grinned slyly.

Johnny, looking at Sarah and grinning slyly himself, asked her, "Would you like to come along? It'll be good to remember the old days." Looking back at Panther, he said, "Our pistols are already loaded. Thanks for the offer, but we won't be needing any powder, caps, and balls."

Sarah called out to her daughter, Adsila, who was in the house making breakfast with Ruth and Esther. "Will you keep an eye on little Johnny for a while? We're gonna take a ride to the northside."

Johnny went inside and grabbed three pistols. Two of them were his, and one was Sarah's. Johnny always kept them loaded. They saddled up and rode to the site where it had become a tradition to practice shooting.

When they arrived, Panther could barely wait to show off his prowess. An old wooden target still hung by a rope from the branch of a tree at the edge of a clearing. It was about fifty feet away. Panther unholstered his gun and fired all five shots at the target, hitting it in a pattern less than four inches wide around the center. Impressive.

Johnny picked up another slat of wood that lay nearby with no marks on it. He hung it from the same rope, walked back to the firing line, and fired five shots. The bullet holes formed a pattern around the center of the target, but when they compared it to Panther's, they found that Johnny's were not quite as closely grouped. Johnny looked at Panther and acknowledged, "Well, boy, it looks as if you have bested me." Then he grinned and said, "Why don't we give Sarah a chance to play?"

Panther, who had heard of Sarah's prowess with a rifle, seemed confident. "Sure," he said. "Auntie should get a shot."

Sarah took her Colt out of its holster, which hung on her saddle. It had only four bullets in it, so she took a moment to load the fifth chamber with powder, cap, and ball. Then she said, "Let's make this a little challengin'. Panther, will you go over there and swing that target for me?"

Panther, incredulous, asked, "Are you saying you want to shoot at a swinging target? Me and Uncle just shot while it was hangin' still."

"That's all right, boys. I think y'all need a little bit of an advantage. Now, please swing that target," demanded Sarah.

Panther obliged and then quickly retreated to the firing line as the target swung back and forth.

Sarah took aim and fired, hitting the target dead center, pausing for a moment while its swing, perturbed by her first bullet, stabilized. Then she shot two more times. Her second bullet made a hole an inch from the first shot. But the third bullet appeared to have missed the target altogether.

Panther's chagrin from being shown up by Sarah's first shot disappeared and he declared, triumphantly, "Well, Auntie, you did good with the first two, but it looks like you was a little overconfident."

"Overconfident, my ass," replied Sarah, with a big smile. "We'll see about that. Anyways, I ain't done yet. Will you swing the target one more time for me?"

Once again, Panther obliged.

Sarah fired two more rounds. "Now, let's have a closer look," she said as she ritually blew the lingering smoke from the barrel of her pistol.

The three of them walked over to the target. There were four holes, spread over a circle with a diameter of about three inches, like the pattern Panther had made with his stationary target. Any reasonable person would have declared Sarah the victor of this contest, since her target was moving and the pattern of bullet holes had the smallest radius, but Panther, not wishing to admit defeat, asserted, "Well, at least all five of my bullets hit the target."

Johnny, laughing, said, "Not so fast, young man, as he pulled his knife from its sheath. He had noticed that one of the holes in the target—the one made by Sarah's first shot—was a little larger than the rest. He stuck the point of his knife blade into it and dug out the ball. Underneath it was another ball from Sarah's pistol. "Looka here," he said. "My lovely wife just piled two bullets, one on top of the other. Dead center. On a swingin' target! How about that?"

Panther, seeming completely overwhelmed, exhaling with an air of resignation, just said, "Shit."

Johnny and Sarah both laughed. Johnny, trying to soothe Panther's wounded pride, said, "It's a real comfort to know that, besides havin' a lovely wife, I got a bodyguard if I need one."

Sarah said, "Panther, thanks for inviting us out for some shootin'. But now, I have to get back to the house to tend to Little Johnny. See you fellas later." Then, she mounted her horse and rode away.

Panther, still stinging from his defeat, said, "Uncle, I shot from my center. How did I lose?"

Johnny gathered his thoughts. After a significant pause, he said, "Well, your father didn't tell me that part. I had to figure it out myself. But here's what I came up with...When you shoot from your center—after you've developed one—you do the best that *you* can do, which is a good thing. But that don't mean you'll do it *the best that it can be done.*"

Johnny paused again, this time for effect. Then he continued. "Not everybody has the same gifts or the same level of whatever gifts they have in common. When folks find—or maybe 'stumble upon' would be a better way of puttin' it—one of their gifts and build on it, they'll do better than those who weren't as gifted to start with. And part of what makes it a gift is that they'll enjoy doing whatever that gift is for. They'll think about it even when they're not doin' it, and think about how to improve, even when they're not doin' it. And for them, it'll be fun. Like the fun you had practicin' with that Colt. Like the fun I had wrestlin' and boxin' with Tommy Smith. Sure, we got black eyes and bruises sometimes, but warriors find that kind of stuff to be fun."

Johnny paused. Even after more than twenty years, he had moments of grief, followed by a sense of gratitude, whenever Tommy Smith, who had been his best friend in his youth and saved his life in his first battle, came to mind. A faint smile, accompanied by a distant gaze into space, came over him for a few seconds.

Then he continued, "...or like the fun you have when you go huntin', kill a deer, and clean, butcher, and cook the venison. And I've been meanin' to tell you that from what I can see, you've made every one of those things into an art. Not just findin' and killin' a deer, but all the rest of it. For example, I've never been very good at butcherin'. It's not that I can't do it—I've done it many times. But I really don't *like* doin' it. And that's why, compared to you, I'm kinda sloppy. For you, it really seems to be an art. You have a gift. A gift I don't have. And I'm always happy to eat your venison. Because of the way you cut it up, it looks almost as good as it tastes. And my world is a better place for it."

"Thank you, Uncle. I haven't thought about that at all. I just do it," said Panther.

"That's the way of gifts," commented Johnny. "They come easy to us. We take 'em for granted. But to other people, what we take for granted can be quite a mystery. When you do somethin' that's so easy that you don't even think about it, and somebody asks, 'How did you do that?' and you say, 'Do what?' you've probably uncovered a gift." Then he repeated, "That's the way of gifts."

Panther, still seeming a bit downhearted, asked, "So does that mean Auntie is more gifted than I am?"

Johnny replied, "I don't know about that. Maybe, maybe not. When I first watched your auntie learnin' to shoot twenty years ago, when we were gettin' ready for the Comanches, I realized that she was a better shot than me. Don't get me wrong. I was real good, too. But I saw that she had a gift…a greater gift for that than I had. It was humblin'. But I comforted myself by bein' glad she was on our side. That's the way I looked at it. And I feel the same way about the way you hunt, clean, butcher, and cook venison."

Panther was silent, lost in thought.

Johnny wanted to say more, but again, he had to search for the right words. After pausing again to think about it, he continued: "Panther, it's never a bad thing to admire the skills of other people. And it's a good thing to acknowledge their mastery, especially if they're better at something than you are. Now, that might be a temporary situation, somethin' you can overcome if that's what you really want to do, or they might just be better than you, no matter how hard you try.

"Either way, don't let it eat up your insides. The comparison that should matter most to you—or to anyone else—is this one: Who do *I* want to be tomorrow, compared to who I am today? *That* is somethin' you can control. And that's a challenge you can almost always overcome with discipline, humility, and the heart of a warrior. You don't have to be 'the best that ever was' to be the best that *you* can be, at whatever it is that you're doin'. Just strive to be the best that you can be. Who can ask more of you than that?"

Johnny grew pensive as he looked at Panther, the son of his beloved Uncle Dutch, and now his ward, who had just learned a lesson in humility.

Hoping to cheer him up, Johnny said, with a smile on his face, "And look on the bright side, son…at least you beat me."

* * * * * * * * *

THE END